Archaic Greece

Archaic Greece

Greece

The City-States
C. *700-500* B.C.

L. H. JEFFERY

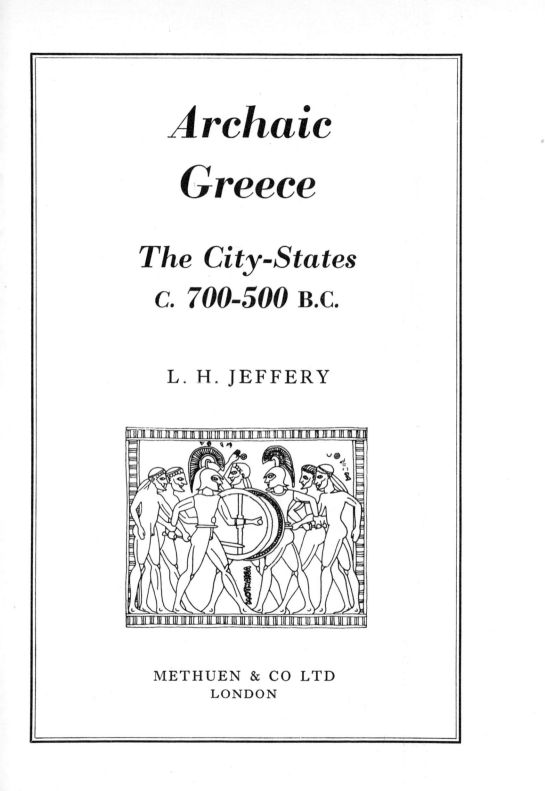

METHUEN & CO LTD
LONDON

First published in 1976
by Ernest Benn Limited
25 New Street Square, Fleet Street, London EC4A 3JA
and Sovereign Way, Tonbridge, Kent TN9 1RW

First published as a University Paperback in 1978
by Methuen & Co Ltd
11 New Fetter Lane, London EC4P 4EE

© 1976 L. H. Jeffery

Book designed by Kenneth Day
Maps by E. A. Chambers

Printed in Great Britain at the
University Press, Cambridge

ISBN 0 416 71630 X

Contents

I INTRODUCTION

II CENTRAL AND NORTHERN GREECE

CONTENTS

List of Illustrations

(*All are placed between pages 144 and 145*)

9

Arkadia
21   Bronze statuette of a countryman. *c.* 500 B.C.

Corinth
22   Miniature polychrome oil-flask from Corinth in the Protocorinthian style. *c.* 650 B.C.
23   Corinthian jug in Transitional to Early Corinthian style. *c.* 650–625 B.C.

Sikyon
24   Delphi: limestone metope almost certainly from the early Treasury of Sikyon. *c.* 560 B.C.

Aegean Islands
25   Polychrome votive plate from Thasos. *c.* 650 B.C.
26   Two 'Daedalic' korai (casts), one from ?Crete (*c.* 625–600 B.C.), the other dedicated on Delos (*c.* 650–625 B.C.).
27   Amphora perhaps from Paros. *c.* 650 B.C.
28   Delphi: part of the marble north frieze of the Treasury of Siphnos. *c.* 530–525 B.C.
29(a) Large storage-jar, perhaps made in Tenos, showing the sack of Troy. *c.* 675 B.C.
29(b) Detail of the Wooden Horse.
30   Upper face of a flat gravestone from the main cemetery of Thera. *c.* 600 B.C.
31   Clay vase, almost certainly from Crete. Early sixth-century B.C.
32   'Fikellura' amphorae from Kameiros, Rhodes. *c.* 550–540 B.C. and *c.* 525 B.C.
33   Part of a small Subgeometric cup from Rhodes. *c.* 700 B.C.
34   Polychrome votive plate from Kameiros, Rhodes. *c.* 600 B.C.

Ionia
35   Lifesize marble statue, from the Sacred Way to Apollo's temple at Didyma. *c.* 560–550 B.C.
36   High relief from the sculptured base of a column from Didyma. *c.* 540–530 B.C.
37   Marble lion from Miletos. *c.* 525 B.C.
38   Head of a colossal marble kouros, identified as Samian work, with east Greek traits. *c.* 550 B.C.
39   Ivory kneeling boy, from the Heraion at Samos. *c.* 625 B.C.
40   Ephesian electrum coin found in Halikarnassos. *c.* 600 B.C.
41   Sherd used for a deft graffito sketch, from Smyrna. *c.* 600–575 B.C.
42   Marble flying Victory, dedicated to Apollo at Delos. *c.* 550–540 B.C.
43   Two fragments from a Klazomenian BF neck-amphora, found in Egypt. *c.* 550–540 B.C.
44   Chian chalice from a tomb at Marion (Cyprus). *c.* 600–575 B.C.
45   Small marble statue of a recumbent feaster holding a tankard, dedicated at Myous. *c.* 550–525? B.C.
46   Polychrome jug from Rhodes. *c.* 600 B.C.

Maps

Acknowledgements

Acknowledgement for kind permission to reproduce photographic illustrations
is made to the following:

J. Boardman: 26
The Trustees of the British Museum: 4, 9, 15, 20, 22, 23, 32a, 34, 35, 40, 46
J. M. Cook: 41
Council of the Society for the Promotion of Hellenic Studies: 44
Department of Antiquities, Ashmolean Museum, Oxford: 2, 10, 31, 32b, 43
Department of Bronzes, National Archaeological Museum, Athens: 6, 17
Department of Oriental and Classical Art, National Museum, Copenhagen: 33
Deutsches Archäologisches Institut, Athens: 11, 12, 13, 14, 29, 38, 39, 42
Ecole française d'archéologie, Athens: 18, 24, 25, 28
Glyptothek, Munich: 19
Metropolitan Museum of Art, New York: 3 (from the Cesnola Collection,
purchased by subscriptions, 1874–76); 8 (Fletcher Fund, 1932)
Museum Antiker Kleinkunst, Munich: 5
Museum of Art, Rhode Island School of Design: gift of Mrs Gustav Radeke:
21
Museum of Fine Arts, Boston, Mass.: 7
Nationalmuseum, Stockholm: 27
Soprintendenza Antichità, Firenze (Florence, Museo Archeologico): 1
Staatliche Museen Preussischer Kulturbesitz (Antikenabteilung; West Berlin,
Dahlem): 36
Staatliche Museen zu Berlin (Antiken-Sammlung; East Berlin): 16, 37, 45
Plate 30 is from the author's own collection.
Acknowledgement for text figures is:
Fig. 1: from *Archaeological Reports, 1970–71* (article by Giorgio Buchner),
       published by the Council of the Society for the promotion of Hellenic
       Studies and the Managing Committee of the British School at Athens
Fig. 2: from E. Kunze, *Olympische Forschungen II* (1950), Beilage 13, 1,
       published by the Deutsches Archäologisches Institut, Athens
Fig. 3: from Herbert Hoffmann, *Early Cretan Armorers* (1972). Drawing by
       Suzanne Chapman

Abbreviations

AA   Archäologischer Anzeiger (Beiblatt zum Jahrbuch des deutschen archäologischen Instituts)

AAA   'Αρχαιολογικὰ 'Ανάλεκτα ἐξ 'Αθηνῶν/Athens Annals of Archaeology

ADelt   'Αρχαιολογικὸν Δελτίον

AE   'Αρχαιολογικὴ 'Εφημερίς

Aesch., PV   Aeschylus, Prometheus Vinctus

Aeschin.   Aeschines, Orations

AJP   American Journal of Philology

AM   Mitteilungen des deutschen archäologischen Instituts: Athenische Abteilung

Anat. Studies   Anatolian Studies: Journal of the British Institute of Archaeology at Ankara

Anc. Soc. and Inst.   Ancient Societies and Institutions: Studies presented to Victor Ehrenberg on his 75th Birthday (1966)

Ann.   Annuario della Scuola archeologica di Atene e delle Missioni italiane in Oriente

Ant. Class.   L'Antiquité classique

AntJ   Antiquaries' Journal

Ant. Kunst   Antike Kunst

Arch. Class.   Archeologica classica: Rivista dell' Istituto di Archeologia della Università di Roma

Arch. Reports   Archaeological Reports (joint publication, JHS and BSA)

Arias-Hirmer-Shefton   A History of Greek Vase Painting: photographs by Max Hirmer, text and notes by P. E. Arias, translated and revised by B. B. Shefton (1962)

Arist., Pol.   Aristotle, Πολιτικά

Athen.   Athenaeus, Δειπνοσοφισταί

Ath. Pol.   Aristotle, 'Αθηναίων Πολιτεία

BCH   Bulletin de Correspondance hellénique (École française d'Athènes)

BICS   Bulletin of the Institute of Classical Studies of the University of London

BMQ   British Museum Quarterly

Boardman   John Boardman, The Greeks Overseas² (1973)

Bowra, GLP²   C. M. Bowra, Greek Lyric Poetry from Alcman to Simonides² (1961)

BSA   Annual of the British School at Athens

Buck   C. D. Buck, The Greek Dialects (1955)

Burn, Lyric Age   A. R. Burn, The Lyric Age of Greece (1960, revised imp. 1967)

CAH   The Cambridge Ancient History

Charites   Charites: Studien zur Altertumswissenschaft (Festschrift Ernst Langlotz, 1957)

CIG A. Boeckh *et al.*, *Corpus Inscriptionum Graecarum* (1825–77)

Coldstream, *GGP* J. N. Coldstream, *Greek Geometric Pottery: A survey of ten local styles and their chronology* (1968)

CP *Classical Philology*

CQ *Classical Quarterly*

DAA A. E. Raubitschek, *Dedications from the Athenian Akropolis: a catalogue of the inscriptions of the sixth and fifth centuries* B.C., edited with the collaboration of Lilian H. Jeffery (1949)

Davies, *APF* J. K. Davies, *Athenian Propertied Families* 600–300 B.C. (1971)

Dem. Demosthenes, *Orations*

DGE *Dialectorum Graecarum exempla epigraphica potiora*, ed. E. Schwyzer (1923)

DM *Mitteilungen des deutschen archäologischen Instituts* 1–6 (1948–53)

Entretiens Hardt *Fondation Hardt: Entretiens sur l'Antiquité classique*

Epigraphica *Epigraphica: Rivista italiana di epigrafia*

''Εργον Τὸ ἔργον τῆς 'Αρχαιολογικῆς 'Εταιρείας

FD *Fouilles de Delphes* (École française d'Athènes)

FGH F. Jacoby, *Die Fragmente der griechischen Historiker*, I–III

Forrest, *Emergence* W. G. Forrest, *The Emergence of Greek Democracy: the character of Greek politics*, 800–400 B.C. (1966)

Front., *Strat.* Frontinus, *Strategemata*

Graham, *Colony and Mother-city* A. J. Graham, *Colony and Mother-city in Ancient Greece* (1964)

GRBS *Greek, Roman and Byzantine Studies*

Harv. Afr. Studies *Harvard African Studies*

HCT A. W. Gomme, *A Historical Commentary on Thucydides* (1945–): A. W. Gomme, vols. i–iii (Bks. 1–5.23); A. Andrewes (Bk. 5.24–end) and K. J. Dover (Bks. 6–7), vol. iv

Hdt. Herodotos, *Histories*

Hesiod, *WD* = Works and Days; *Th.* = Theogony

Hesperia *Hesperia: Journal of the American School of Classical Studies at Athens*

Hignett, *Hist. Ath. Const.* C. Hignett, *A History of the Athenian Constitution to the End of the Fifth Century* B.C. (1952)

H. Hymn *The Homeric Hymns*, ed. T. W. Allen, W. R. Halliday, and E. E. Sikes (1936)

IC *Inscriptiones Creticae, opera et consilio Friderici Halbherr collectae* I–IV, ed. Margarita Guarducci (1939–50)

IG i² *Inscriptiones Graecae: Inscriptiones Atticae Euclidis anno anteriores*², ed. F. Hiller von Gaertringen (1924)

IGRom *Inscriptiones Graecae ad res Romanas pertinentes*, ed. R. Cagnat *et al.* (1906–)

Il. Homer, *Iliad*

Istanb. Mitt. *Istanbuler Mitteilungen* (*Deutsches archäologisches Institut, Abteilung Istanbul*)

JdI *Jahrbuch des deutschen archäologischen Instituts*

JHS *Journal of Hellenic Studies*

Journ. Egypt. Arch. *Journal of Egyptian Archaeology*

JRS *Journal of Roman Studies*
Justin, *Epit.* *Justin, Epitome of Pompeius Trogus, Historiae Philippicae*
LSAG L. H. Jeffery, *The Local Scripts of Archaic Greece* (1961)
Marm. Par. *Marmor Parium* (Jacoby, *FGH* 239)
Meiggs and Lewis *A Selection of Greek Historical Inscriptions to the End of the Fifth Century* B.C., edd. Russell Meiggs and David Lewis (1969)
Num. Chron. *Numismatic Chronicle*
Od. Homer, *Odyssey*
ÖJh *Jahreshefte des österreichischen archäologischen Instituts in Wien*
Ol. Forsch. *Olympische Forschungen*
Overbeck, *SQ* J. Overbeck, *Die antiken Schriftquellen zur Geschichte der bildenden Künste bei den Griechen* (1868)
Ox. Pap. *Oxyrhynchus Papyri*, edd. B. P. Grenfell and A. S. Hunt
Pap. Rylands *Catalogue of the Greek and Latin Papyri in the John Rylands Library, Manchester*, edd. A. S. Hunt et al.
Paus. Pausanias, ῾Ελλάδος Περιήγησις
PdelP *La Parola del Passato; Rivista di Studi classici*
Phoenix *Phoenix: the Journal of the Ontario Classical Association*
Pind., *Isthm.* (*Ol.*, *Pyth.*) Pindar, *Isthmian* (*Olympian*, *Pythian*) *Odes*
Pliny, *HN* Pliny, *Historia Naturalis*
Plut., *Mor.* Plutarch, *Moralia* (*QG* = *Quaestiones Graecae, Mor.* 291d–304f)
Polyaen., *Strat.* Polyaenus, *Strategemata*
Polyb. Polybius, *Universal History*
REA *Revue des Études anciennes*
REG *Revue des Études grecques*
Rend. Linc. *Rendiconti dell'Accademia dei Lincei*
Rev. Arch. *Revue archéologique*
Richter, *AGA* G. M. Richter, *Archaic Greek Art against its Historical Background* (1949)
Riv. Fil. *Rivista di Filologia e di Istruzione classica*
Sb. Akad. Wien *Sitzungsberichte der Akademie der Wissenschaften zu Wien*
SEG *Supplementum Epigraphicum Graecum*, ed. A. G. Woodhead
SGDI *Sammlung der griechischen Dialekt-Inschriften*, i–iv (1884–1915), edd. H. Collitz et F. Bechtel
SIG[3] *Sylloge Inscriptionum Graecarum*[3], ed. G. Dittenberger (1915–24)
Solon Solon, *Poems* (*Iambi et Elegi Graeci ante Alexandrum cantati*, ed. M. L. West, 1972)
Str. Strabo, *Geographica*
Stuart Jones *Select Passages from Ancient Writers illustrative of the history of Greek sculpture*, ed. H. Stuart Jones (1895)
TAPA *Transactions of the American Philological Association*
Travlos, *Pict. Dict. Anc. Ath.* J. Travlos, *Pictorial Dictionary of Ancient Athens* (English edition, 1971)
Wade-Gery, *Essays* H. T. Wade-Gery, *Essays in Greek History* (selected articles, 1931–58)
Xen., *Hell.* Xenophon, *Hellenica*

Preface

This book is based on lectures given over the past 25 years to undergraduates in their first term of Ancient History; and, as the footnotes show, it has profited throughout from the contributions to Archaic Greek studies made by other scholars, particularly by many now, or once, in Oxford. My first apprenticeship in the history of Ancient Greece came *via* its local dialects and scripts, thanks to the teaching of two great experts in these fields, S. G. Campbell in Cambridge and M. N. Tod in Oxford; and in Greek art my first attachment was to the local rather than the Panhellenic types. Hence this book does not claim to make a general survey of Archaic Greece as a unit, but rather to consider the variety which made up the whole. Even so, little is said on the western and northern colonies, and even less on the 'half-Greek' areas of Macedon and Aitolia, Akarnania and Epeiros. Similarly, something is said on Greek achievements in politics, social life, literature, and art, but nothing on philosophy, a field wholly outside my competence. The omission of a separate bibliography is also deliberate. To create one for a historical work of this general type would have meant much repetition of material already in the footnotes, which are themselves intended as the quarry for a reader in search of general as well as detailed background. In the perennial problem of Greek names, my intention has been to spell them as in Attic Greek, except for such Latinized or Anglicized forms as seem now a part of our own language (Athens, Corinth, Mycenae, Thucydides); in other words, inconsistency is rife, as the reader will find. Except in cases where it seemed essential to retain the original Greek, single Greek words have been transliterated, and quotations from Greek authors given in translation; the blame is mine for all inadequacies in the latter.

My warm thanks go to Ernest Benn Limited for the invitation to write this part of their monograph-series on early Greece—and my lasting gratitude to their editor John Collis for the learning, skill, and heroic patience with which he has checked and improved, indeed rescued, the text, footnotes, and index at innumerable points. The many specialists from whose knowledge and advice I have profited appear in the footnotes, notably A. Andrewes, J. Boardman, A. R. Burn, W. G. Forrest, G. L. Huxley, C. M. Kraay, D. M. Lewis, R. Meiggs, B. D. Meritt, G. E. M. de Ste. Croix, among many others. Particularly I would record my gratitude to all the Greek archaeologists whose expert knowledge and generosity saved me continually from errors: notably Mme Semni Karouzou, MM. Andronikos, Dontas, Kallipolitis, Kontoleon (deceased), Mastrokostas, Mitsos, Platon, Verdelis (deceased), Yalouris, M. and Mme Zapheiropoulos, and, lastly, the three especial names of a longstanding friendship, Mlle Barbara Philippaki, Mme Dina Peppas-Delmousou, and, above all, Mme Athena

Kalogeropoulou. Her wide archaeological learning and unrivalled knowledge of excavations, sites, and museums throughout Greece have constantly illuminated for me the past history of her country, just as the generosity of all Greek friends, but especially of her and her family, has exemplified the two age-old and ineradicable Greek traditions of *philoxenia* and *eleutheria*—hospitality to the stranger, and freedom for all.

Oxford   L. H. JEFFERY
September 1975

I

Introduction

1 The Background

Geography

The mythology of a country constantly reflects its landscape. Greece is the country where Earth bred the two Titans Koios and Enkelados who, to raise a siege-mound against Mount Olympos in their war with the gods, heaved the long range of Pelion right on to the conical peak of Ossa. Among the central islands of the Aegean Delos bobbed round unanchored until the goddess Leto found sanctuary there to bear her twins Apollo and Artemis, when four pillars shot up from the seabed to stabilize Delos then and thereafter. Some of the rivers – Styx in Arkadia, Acheron in the far north-west – carried the power of Hades in their waters, for their course was believed to have somewhere threaded the Underworld, just as the springs of Alpheios, for example, did in fact sink into holes and then emerge far on.

Tumbled rocks in Thessaly, new islets breaking surface from the submarine depths round volcanic Thera, pot-holing rivers, and other geological phenomena, all had their places in a landscape which by its continual variety affected not merely the mythology but also, naturally, the distribution of the population. The inhabitants tended to cluster in the many highland or lowland plains, in river valleys, along the coastal strips backed by mountains, and on the scattered islands. Thus they formed a network of settlements of varied size and wealth, mostly separated by hills or sea from easy contact with each other. Throughout their history the Greeks have crossed these barriers continually; but the geography fostered, though it did not alone create, an incandescent individualism which made it hard for any Greek city-states to combine for long together. The record of Archaic Greece is basically a set of separate parts, fusing most easily at those times when (to borrow a modern comment on some historic Cretan reactions to foreign dominance) a city produced more history than could be consumed locally. Each state developed politically at its own speed, worshipped its own concept of the Olympian gods, spoke its own dialect of the common language, and wrote its own version of the common alphabet. By the end of the sixth century Athens had laid the foundations of the first truly egalitarian system of government while her Boiotian neighbour Thebes was still ruled by a close aristocracy. The Demeter worshipped at Eleusis is described in the old Homeric Hymn as radiant in beauty – it breathes round her, her dress is scented, light shines from her skin, her yellow hair falls about her shoulders; but at Phigaleia in Arkadia a new statue dedicated in the fifth century still showed her as the local cult there interpreted her: a Medusa-type with a horse's head and snaky hair, who held a dove and a dolphin, perhaps to symbolize her power over air and water.

23

The common language formed roughly four groups: (1) West Greek, which itself divided into (a) North-west, the basic dialect of Epeiros, Akarnania, Aitolia, Phokis, and Lokris, which then crossed the narrow straits at the west end of the Gulf of Corinth and extended over Achaia and Elis; and (b) Doric, spoken in Megara, Sikyon, and Corinth, Argos and most of the Argolid, Lakedaimon and Messenia, and the south Aegean islands Melos, Thera, and Crete, together with the Doric Hexapolis (Kos, Knidos, Halikarnassos (an Ionic-speaking, lapsed member) and the three cities of Rhodes); (2) Aiolic, spoken in Thessaly and Boiotia, which crossed the north Aegean to Lesbos and the tract of Asia Minor called Aiolis; (3) Ionic, spoken – in variant forms – in Attica, Euboia, the north and central Aegean islands, and the Ionic Dodekapolis; and (4) Arcado-Cyprian, the old dialect which is recognized by philologists as nearest in structure to the Mycenaean Greek now extracted from the Linear B script, and which survived in mountainous Arkadia and far-off Cyprus because these places were physically isolated from the influences which either created or modified the other three groups. Varieties of dialect also arose within these groups alike through isolation (as in the Doric spoken in the closed valley of Lakedaimon) and association (as in Thessaly, where both North-west and Aiolic met). The Greeks recognized their language as a unity; this fact shows at its simplest in their use of the onomatopoeic word *barbaros* only for non-Greeks. None the less, the dialects must have been a real obstacle to ready comprehension. The differences will have gone deeper than we can grasp today by merely reading ancient authors and inscriptions. For the pronunciation we see only what is spelt out for us: as, that in Sparta they drawled the medial *s* into an aspirate, and in Elis they swallowed the final *s* into an *r*; but of all the minor idioms which are abundant in all local speech we can know only what survives in letters, graffiti, or the more formal phraseology of literature and public inscriptions. There must have been innumerable quirks of pronunciation and idiom which were not shown by the written word, and indeed one doubts if the average Athenian could have understood a real Megarian or Boiotian or Spartan half as well as he understood their stage-types in the plays of Aristophanes. As for the variants on the common alphabet, nearly every city had its own versions of certain letters, thus producing a local script of its own. This must have made things awkward for any learned outsider seeking local data; but in the Archaic period the spoken still outran the written word, and there is little in early Greek history to suggest that even the well-educated traveller of those days wanted to spend much time in reading the public decrees, records, dedications, or epitaphs of another city. If he were interested in such of them as were available to a non-citizen, probably a local friend would read them aloud to him. In the great common sanctuaries such as Delphi or Olympia, where each city generally used its own script in the dedication on its offering, guides could assist him.[1]

The Start of the Archaic Period

Modern convention sets the start of the Archaic period of Greek history in 776 B.C., the year when the Games were said to have been officially founded at Olympia in Elis. This precise date is due to the research of the learned sophist

Hippias, himself an Elean (fl. *c.* 400 B.C.). He was the first to use the data in the sanctuary to reconstruct a complete list down to his own time of all the victors in the sprint (*stadion*), the original and most important of the athletic contests held there. Apparently he made the total about 94 names, for 776 B.C. in our usage (400 + (4 × 94), the Games being quadrennial) became thereafter the accepted date for Olympiad I. Plutarch observed that Hippias had based his list on very shaky evidence; but by Plutarch's time the Greeks had long accepted the Olympic list as a general chronological system to date events in the history of all or any of the states: the Argives won the battle of Hysiai 'in the fourth year of Olympiad 27, when Eurybotos of Athens won the stadion'.

For the ancient Greeks this was natural; but why should any modern students of Greek history retain as an era for the whole Archaic period the start of one set of games which in fact only attracted local competitors during its first fifty years? The period around 776 B.C. ranks as an epoch for a different reason. Four great civilizing events are held, on internal evidence, to have happened at about this date. Firstly, after centuries of illiteracy when the Linear B script had gone with the rest of the Mycenean civilization, the country got a script once more: the simple, practical, easily-taught alphabet, from which all our Western scripts descend. Secondly, the Greeks, already familiar with the coast of Asia Minor, now opened out the much longer and more difficult journey westward to the rich areas of Sicily and southern Italy. Thirdly, Greek skill in metal-working, the basic craft essential for war and peace alike, took an enormous stride forward. Fourthly, the two great Homeric epics began to take the shape in which we have them now, with momentous results not only for the literature of the world but for the Greeks' own religion thereafter.

Any one of these achievements is remarkable enough. Why did they all happen at about this time? To put the answer in its simplest (and so, unavoidably, its most exaggerated) form: because now was coming the feed-back to mainland Greece of Eastern inventions and skills absorbed by those Greeks who (following in many areas their own Mycenean predecessors) from the Protogeometric period onwards had been settling in Ionia and in the south and south-east of the Aegean (Crete, Rhodes, and Cyprus) and in northern Syria, at Al Mina and other ports further south. They were in contact with Eastern nations, great and small, already long possessed of certain advanced technical skills. The Greeks absorbed these in their characteristic way, transforming not so much the tools as the idea.

Let us look at these four achievements in a little more detail. First, the alphabet. The full Greek alphabet had 27 letters. No city used the lot; they picked and chose, depending on their dialect, on the chances of transmission, and doubtless on other factors unknown to us. Of the full alphabet, 22 letters have been taken (sign, name, and sound) from the north Semitic alphabet (αβγδεϝζη (=*h*)θικλμνξοπM(=*san*)φρστ). The consonants were taken fairly closely from their Semitic models, except that the names+sounds of the four Semitic sibilants (*zayin*, *shin*, *tsade*, and *samekh*) seem to have been jumbled, the sign I (*zayin*) being given the name+sound of *tsade* (*zeta*) and so on. The Semitic models for α, ε, ι, ο, each had a certain vocalic value, but were strengthened to pure vowels by the Greek tongue. Five letters are non-Semitic extras: the two vowels υ(Υ) and ω(Ω) appear to be 'doublet' letters formed by the Greeks from their F (*vau* (=w), used by most Greek dialects though not the Ionic) and o respectively; while the origins of ϕ, χ, ψ have still to be satisfactorily explained. In the recited alphabet these follow the doublet υ (which all the Greek scripts used), and so, presumably, were added later than it; but they precede the doublet ω, a letter which originated among the eastern Ionic states and spread only gradually to reach mainland Greece during the fifth century, or in some country areas even later (Pl. 1).

The Greek alphabet must have been born either in some Greek settlement on the Semitic coast, like Al Mina (below, p. 62), or in a Greek area where Semites had settled; both Crete and Rhodes, for example, show many north Syrian and Phoenician imports of the ninth and eighth centuries, and it now seems likely that there were Semitic settlements at that time in Crete, and possibly in Rhodes also. Actual settlement would seem necessary, for to transfer a script between two speech-systems so different as the Greek and the Semitic implies a society where at least some members speak both languages. If the male settlers marry into the local families, as happened in many of the Greek colonies (below, p. 57), sooner or later some bilingual speakers will think of using the existing script of one familiar language to express the other also. Such a transference seems unlikely to have happened merely from trading contacts of the kind described by Homer or Herodotos, when the foreign ships were beached on the local shore for a short time only, while goods were bartered and local maidens swept off willy-nilly, to luxury or toil, but in either case not in a situation to promote the interests of literacy.

Adapted to the Greek tongue, the ex-Semitic alphabet spread rapidly. Its reasonably small number of signs could be readily mastered by any intelligent adult or child who had someone to teach him; this was not a complicated ideographic or syllabic script, an arcane professional skill like the scripts of the Egyptians, Hittites, and Assyrians. The earliest surviving Greek inscriptions range round (roughly) the middle of the eighth century. They are mostly personal, scratched on pots or sherds: a name, or a possessive phrase, or some other brief comment, pensive or rude. A little later, perhaps still in the eighth century, certainly by the early seventh, examples occur of a wider and more practical application. We find stone markers on graves – plain pillars (stelai) or flat slabs, bearing the name of the dead – and also objects offered to deities, bearing a dedication or marked, e.g., 'I am Hera's', and, on painted vases, occasionally the maker's signature (Fig. 1, p. 64; Pl. 33).

Secondly, the Greek exploration and settlement of Sicily and southern Italy. The Greeks living on the coasts of the east and south-east Aegean must have known of the highly skilled Semitic shipbuilders from north Syria down to Palestine who, using the renowned timber of Lebanon, had exported it also to the shipyards of Egypt. Greeks from Euboia were the chief settlers in Al Mina *c.* 800 B.C. (below, p. 63) and it is stated by the ancient authors and confirmed by archaeology that Euboians also made the first Greek settlements in the West, in the area of Naples. Much of this voyage to the west side of Italy was done by coasting; but even so, it was very long, and involved threading the dangerous straits between Italy and Sicily, exemplified by the story of Skylla and Charybdis.

All in all, the journey must have involved a much greater strain on ships than did the island-hopping runs across the Aegean, and this suggests that the Euboians at least had learnt from foreign mariners how to improve their shipbuilding.

The natural question 'Why did the Euboians sail so far into the West to found their first colonies there?' introduces the third phenomenon of that period, the great advance in Greek metalwork. This the Greeks were certainly learning from the skilled metal-workers of the Near East: how to hammer sheet-bronze into reliefs over wooden cores, instead of the primitive, wasteful solid-casting; even, in time, how to weld iron. The islands offshore from the Naples area were metalliferous like Campania itself, with iron in Elba and gold in Pithekoussai (modern Ischia). Land-hunger has been at all times the strongest single motive for emigration, but the Euboians in the early eighth century could have satisfied this by going no further than Sicily. It seems that they were prepared to push so far because they wanted the metals.

The early history of Corinth too shows the same East-West link. She lay better placed than Euboia, on an isthmus which made a natural East-West junction, and the influence of the Near East showed in many of her cults. She produced a notable shipwright named Ameinokles, possibly in the eighth century, and her colonies Kerkyra and Syracuse were among the earliest and most famous in the West.

As for the fourth great achievement, the Homeric epic, the complexity of the problems involved must be left to the experts. The view is here accepted that the *Iliad* at least was formed among those Greeks who, settled amid the rich but alien corn of Asia Minor, nostalgically preserved and expanded the unwritten records of old family traditions and glories, real or imagined, with which their ancestors had emigrated from the Greek mainland in the hard times following the fall of the Mycenean civilization. In the eighth century these were fused and developed by a Chian master-singer named Homer (according to the Greeks' own tradition, with variations on his exact birthplace) to the scale and unity, basically, in which we have them now; and their spreading to mainland ears caused not only a great literary awakening but also the first definition for the Greek nation of the pantheon of Olympic deities, and also, more parochially, the start of some new local cults – namely, the worship of the great Homeric heroes in their traditional mainland seats of rule. A cult-precinct of Agamemnon has been excavated at Mycenae and of Menelaos at Therapne outside Sparta, both of which appear to have started in the last years of the eighth century; and offerings of late eighth-century date have been found poked into the dromos of several Mycenean tombs in Attica and the Argolid.

Many modern scholars hold that there is a causal connection between the invention of Greek alphabetic writing and the appearance of the epics. Others do not see the two events as necessarily thus connected, believing that neither the composition nor the recitation of early epic needed the mnemonic aid of writing, and that the epics were only written down much later, in the sixth century, for political and cultural reasons – for example, by an ambitious tyrant such as Peisistratos at Athens or Polykrates of Samos. Be that as it may, it is not for us to venture here into the battlefield which might decide whether the *Iliad* and *Odyssey* are contemporary in their development, or whether the *Odyssey* is substantially later (or earlier); but many scholars have agreed in feeling that the *Odyssey* reflects the outlook of this Western colonial period, that it takes part at least of its colour from the background of high seas and travellers' tales about the wide western Mediterranean, when the Euboians and others were opening up the two sea-routes past Sicily, the northern through the straits to Kyme, the great successor of Pithekoussai, and the southern, later, along the strange coast of Libya. Odysseus himself can be seen as a reflection of these sea-captains, not an *Iliad*-type of hero, splendid and soon-dying, but a hardy explorer, a real portrait though expanded to an outline of epic size and endurance. Travellers' lies, of course, abound in the *Odyssey* – the self-steering Phaiakian ships, the evil magic of Circe, and so on; but there are realities too, such as the wind and current from the east Peloponnesian coast southward, which took Odysseus' ships down to the Libyan coast. Some readers go further and find historical reality in the brilliant description of the monstrous seas which hurled poor Odysseus against the first, inhospitable stretch of the Phaiakian coast. These echoes, they suggest, are not from the tideless Mediterranean, fierce though its storms can be, but from the thundering tidal Atlantic, of which some Greek sailors may have had information well before the late seventh century, when the Samian trader Kolaios (below, pp. 212–13) actually sailed through the Straits of Gibraltar and tapped the silver supplies of Spain.[2]

The Background of Archaic Art

By the second half of the eighth century the new skills from the East were showing their effect on Greek art. Bronzework was to be transformed; but the change wrought in draughtsmanship was no less profound.

The pot-painting style of the ninth and eighth centuries is called Geometric by modern scholars because of the linear designs which cover the pot in symmetrical, close-laid patterns, among which the human figure has sometimes a part, indeed by the mid-eighth century sometimes the chief part, but is still confined within a limited concept which shaped a black silhouette out of arcs and triangles and set him sometimes singleton, sometimes in a row of repeated manikins. The basis of the Geometric style is a layered and recurrent pattern formed by brushwork which follows the slowed circling of the potter's wheel. In the fine red clay of Attica, where the Geometric style perhaps had its origin and certainly reached its greatest splendour, the potters of the mid-eighth century made funeral amphorae of monumental size – some over 5 feet high – which stood as markers on graves. The Corinthian potters made similar types of vases, smaller but no less finely assured in technique. The Attic ware was exported as far as Asia Minor, Cyprus, Italy, and Sicily. But by the end of the century the fashion had changed; the pot-painters had moved out of repeated geometric patterns into a new free-dom of outline-drawing. New ideas had jolted them out of their traditional style. The contact with north Syria and other vassal states of the Assyrian Empire had brought in portable decorated objects such as Phoenician ivories, Assyrian and north Syrian bronzes, patterned textiles. Instead of the black geometric silhouette these bore a variety of outline-figures, incised on the ivories or with incision out-line round the raised relief on the metal – gods, humans, plants, lions, goats, deer, horses, monsters; and so, as well as other new techniques – in making bronzes, in casting clay figures in moulds, also an Oriental skill – Greek craftsmen developed from this outline-drawing a new ability in art (Pls. 2, 3, 22, 27, 31, 46).

Something will be said briefly in later chapters on the different local styles of pottery and sculpture which were evolved in different Greek states. Meanwhile, this change in Greek art from a rigid to a freer style may perhaps be compared with that in British art between the start of the eighth and the early ninth centuries A.D., for there too a strongly geometric, inbred style of native decoration was fertilized afresh by the advent of a new style of figure-drawing brought in on objects from an older civilization farther east. The comparison is interesting because in both cases the historical background seems to have been roughly similar. In western Europe before the eighth century the intricate style of decoration which in Britain we know best in Irish and Northumbrian art, the filigree-style of strap, tendril, and curlicue, proliferating and returning upon itself, exquisite and endless, has been recognized as the typical art-form of a still-unsettled community. Its field being necessarily the portable and therefore smallish object – brooch, bracelet, knife-handle, and so on – it favoured a perpetual elaboration of the same pattern as ornament, rather than any expanding, naturalistic development, or any large-scale metalwork. But as the spread of Christianity by the seventh century was bringing Britain into contact with the Byzantine church in the eastern Mediterranean, so the inhabitants of Britain built more of their churches in stone, and began to set the figures of the Evangelists into their Gospel-paintings and to essay the narrative style of drawing; and the abstract fantasies of their 'metalwork' painting-style gave way to copies, naïve at first, of Byzantine miniature-painting, which developed into the fine draughtsmanship exemplified in the local schools of illumination at Canterbury, York, and elsewhere.

So in Greece too the tap-roots of the Geometric style may perhaps go back in time through Protogeometric to the unsettled period after the fall of the Mycenean kingdoms. With these kingdoms disappeared the monumental stone buildings, the large frescoes, the prodigal diversity of pottery shapes and decorations, the stone reliefs and terracotta sculpture, the fine metal-chasing by smiths, and the miniature-work of jewellers: in short, the secure ornaments of a settled people. Ambitious developments in art need rich, assured patronage. From the eleventh to the eighth centuries in Greece there was intermittent shifting among the population; and the Geometric style, abstract and repetitive, may owe much to an original concentration on the decoration of portable objects. It reached its best in the pottery; but there is also the work of goldsmiths in simple, flat sheet-metal hairbands or wristbands stamped with a recurring design and of bronze-workers in small sticklike figures, solid-cast, mostly of men and horses. The biggest objects made in bronze during these centuries were the tripod-cauldrons, utensils needed by short-term settlements no less than by permanent ones. They were often used as gifts to a god and as prizes at funeral games (below, pp. 79–80). The cauldron (*lebes*) still appeared as a unit of barter (though probably as a standard of reckoning, not literally) in Crete at a surprisingly late date (below, p. 191).

Some of the finest works of Greek art were produced in the Archaic period, during the seventh and sixth centuries. Here again comparison with later Europe is instructive, for there the existence of patronage was usually at the back of any great advance in art. As the patronage of the monasteries produced a new style in British art by the eighth century A.D., so we may suspect that some such element was there to spur on the competitive skill of the Greek artists in the early seventh century B.C. The wider horizons of farther travel were producing greater wealth in many of the Greek states, and cult-centres like the precincts of Hera at Samos, Apollo and Artemis at Delos, and on the mainland Zeus at Olympia, Hera outside Argos, Apollo at Delphi, all must surely have been influential in the promotion of more and more ambitious work. True, they had no professional, dedicated priesthood, as Christianity had; but royal or aristocratic administrators of a cult could be equally zealous in seeing that some of the wealth brought back from the wider horizons was diverted into tithes in the form of fine pottery and bronzes, jewellery, and large statues of stone instead of wood. The individual families in whose hands lay the control of most of the cults in each state will have started the work of patronage in art and poetry which the tyrants were to carry on in a still more spacious manner in the late seventh and sixth centuries.

It is probable that the concept of really big stone sculpture, in the round or in relief, came to Greece about the middle of the seventh century, when the new Pharaoh Psamtik I (c. 663–609), who had seized power by the aid of Greek and other mercenaries, settled his Greek veterans on retirement in a permanent camp on the Pelusiac (eastern) branch of the Delta. This gave other Greeks a chance to see, if not settle in, the country, and, though a permanent Greek *emporion* at Naukratis was not founded until the sixth century (below, pp. 53–4), visiting Greek craftsmen had evidently profited earlier from this new experience of huge stone buildings and statues. The Greek kouros (youth) is directly copied from the Egyptian in shape, stance, and proportions, except that the Greek statue is naked and – a bold move – freestanding, whereas the Egyptian figure has some kind of supporting strut (Pls. 8, 18).

The earliest school of Greek monumental sculpture will presumably have been in some area which was open to Egyptian influence and had itself a suitable quarry of marble or other carvable stone. In fact, the earliest kouroi and korai (maidens) found as yet come from the Aegean islands – dedicatory or funerary works from Delos, Naxos, Thera, and Samos. Since Samos was among the leading states of the twelve which maintained the *emporion* at Naukratis, and has good marble, and did build a large and very early colonnaded temple (see below), it is possible that she was the first intermediary. But all that we can safely say at present is that the first Greeks who learnt this skill from Egypt probably lived in the central or south-east parts of the Aegean or on the Asian coast.

Late in the seventh century the Greeks started to build temples in stone. Earlier temples usually had walls of plastered mud-brick, with only the footings of stone; the roofs were of clay tiles or thatch, supported by an internal row of wooden posts if the span was wide. At Samos the excavators found the remains of such a temple, over a hundred feet long, with traces of colonnading all round the cella itself, which was wide enough to need internal posts to carry its roof. The first stone temple (p. 215) was a huge building of the second quarter of the sixth century, roughly contemporary with the Artemision at Ephesos on the Asian mainland. At Smyrna a stone temple was started before the end of the seventh century; it was never finished, but unfluted white stone column-drums prepared for it have been found rebuilt into a fourth-century stretch of terrace-wall. The old Heraion at Olympia is an early mainland example (*c.* 600?) of a peripteral stone temple, and even here the differing profiles of the capitals of the limestone Doric columns show that these were not parts of the original plan, but were added later one by one to replace wooden originals.

Thus the wealth and piety of the great families in the seventh and sixth centuries stimulated the development of architecture, sculpture, and pottery. It was not only for the glory of the patron deity and other gods of their city. The rites of family burial also required the best works that could be afforded, fine pottery and personal belongings to be put in the graves, stone sculpture to stand as monuments above them. The same types of sculpture in the round could serve alike for dedications or funeral monuments. A kouros, a kore, or a seated statue of a man in chiton and himation might be commissioned either for tombs (the seated figure for a death in ripe old age, the other two for untimely deaths) or for a precinct, the seated figure to flank the Sacred Way to the temple (Pl. 35) after the Egyptian fashion, the standing figures perhaps to do likewise, but more often to be set as separate showpieces wherever space could be found. The rocky platform of the Athenian Acropolis, for example, with several lesser precincts crowded on to it as well as the great Athena's, cannot have afforded space for an approach as long or straight as did those on flat levels, like the Heraion at Samos or the Apollonion at Didyma near Miletos.

The relief-stele, its figures shown in profile, was used almost invariably for graves, not in sanctuaries, in the Archaic period. It developed from the primitive stone marker. Its seventh-century prototypes, with the figure incised, occur in Crete – limestone stelai bearing, for example, a man in armour, a woman with her spindle. The fine Attic marble relief-stelai surviving from the sixth century show various types: the kouros, the man in armour, the official(?) bearing a staff (the last an early stele in limestone). No sixth-century relief-stele of a standing kore has yet been found, but some inscribed Attic bases which commemorate women show by the long narrow cutting on top that the lost stele was unusually wide, and thus almost certainly showed the woman seated in profile (perhaps with her baby, if she died in childbirth) and a standing girl facing her. These were evidently early examples of a sculptural type dominant in the Classical period, of which the stele of Hegeso (*c.* 410–400) is the most famous example.

In the modern European tradition the artist and the poet have long moved before the public eye in the same kind of aura. The true artist, like the true poet, is the man with the creative fire who can teach the craftsman: that is, he formulates ideas and creates shapes which the craftsman adopts. He is inspired, or, as the Greeks said of a poet, breathed on by the Muses. Concerning the poet indeed there is no real difference between the ancient and modern views. As we might describe it crudely, a person had initially a cast of mind which was capable of withdrawal inside itself, and sometimes external circumstances, by enforcing the withdrawal, virtually created the poet; the child was blind, or a herdboy perhaps, whose work placed him in strange scenery and weather, sometimes in the high, thin air of mountain-tops, and always in solitude. Such a background was traditionally behind Hesiod on Helikon, even Archilochos on Paros (below, pp. 181–3), and many another in other times and countries. They heard the voice, met the Muses, and became either poets or, if their minds broke down, *nympholeptoi*, 'seized by the nymphs'. We are conditioned to think of the artist as 'inspired' no less than the poet. But here the ancient Greek attitude differed sharply. No Greek artist seems to have begun his career by meeting his Muse in lonely places, for there was no Muse to meet; even when the Nine became canonical, sculpture and painting were left unrepresented. Instead, the traditions about early Greek artists usually concern technical points: Boutades of Sikyon invented the relief by filling in with clay the outline of a shadow on a wall, and so on. Instead of a Muse they had patron deities or heroes, Hephaistos for the bronze- and ironsmiths, Prometheus for the potters, Athena Ergane (Worker; possibly an attribute added rather late to Athena's older aspects) for the sculptors. The dividing-line was firm. Some poets indeed might be commissioned to produce their verses, as epic poets were and many lyric poets later, such as Simonides and Pindar; but the inspiration was still a thing apart. The artist was a technician, his achievements produced by a trained manual skill; he made his wares, or oversaw their making, specifically to sell them. Mostly the buyer was not buying merely for his own aesthetic pleasure, but ordering a special object to be offered in a sanctuary, or set above or inside a grave. As far as we know, no freestanding marble statue, or even small bronze, stood in an Archaic Greek house; only the pottery and jewellery were produced for personal as well as for religious use and pleasure. As a member of the community the artist was not held in the same respect as the poet. 'No gently-born youth, looking at the great Zeus at Olympia, or the Hera at Argos, wants to *be* Pheidias or Polykleitos; it does not follow that, if the work delights you, its creator need be of any importance' (Plut., *Pericles* 2; cf. Pl. 13). Few, probably, of the Archaic artists and craftsmen had the citizenship of the place where they worked (except in tyrannies), because, as technical experts, they were apt to travel and finally to settle their skill in the state which would best employ it, as respected aliens. Nor were their surrounds enviable, unless to a young bystander whose fingers itched to draw or shape things too. The marble-sculptors worked in stonedust and flying chips, the statuaries sweated by their charcoal furnaces, the potters sat stained with clay in open sheds or stoas with wet lumps of unworked clay all round them, and those painting the pots were probably only a few degrees more comfortable. But some of them at least made fame and fortune, and lived well. We recall with pleasure that it cost the state of Sikyon a lot of wealth and pleading to get back the services of the offended sculptors Dipoinos and Skyllis (below, pp. 164, 166); and a dedication made *c.* 500 B.C. on the Athenian Acropolis carries a wise couplet:[3]

> If you have wisdom, invest it in a skill;
> for he who has a skill has got the better life.

NOTES

1 Comment on Crete: *The Short Stories of Saki* (Bodley Head, 1930), 158. Demeter: *H. Hymn.* 2. 275–80; Paus. 8. 42 (Phigaleia). Local dialects in general: C. D. Buck, *The Greek Dialects* (1955). Scripts: L. H. Jeffery, *The Local Scripts of Archaic Greece* (1961); M. Guarducci, *Epigrafia greca* I (1967).

2 Hippias: *FGH* 6 F2 (= Plut., *Num.* 1). On early Greek exploration see in general T. J. Dunbabin, *The Western Greeks* (1948) and *The Greeks and their Eastern Neighbours* (1957, ed. J. Boardman); N. Coldstream, *Greek Geometric Pottery* (1968); J. Boardman, *The Greeks Overseas*² (1973). Semitic settlements in Crete: see especially Boardman in *Dädalische Kunst auf Kreta im 7 Jh. v. Chr.* (Exhibition Catalogue of the Museum für Kunst u. Gewerbe, Hamburg, 1970), 14 ff.; H. Hoffmann and A. E. Raubitschek, *Early Cretan Armorers* (1972), esp. ch. 6; in Rhodes, N. Coldstream, *BICS* 16 (1969), 1 ff. (I owe this reference to Mr Boardman.) The case for the bilingual factor was first made by Rhys Carpenter in *AJA* 37 (1933), 8 ff., a basic work for all later studies of the earliest Greek alphabet. Homeric studies: see the useful commentary by J. B. Hainsworth, *Homer* (*Greece and Rome*: New Surveys in the Classics no. 3, 1969). Later cults of Homeric heroes: J. M. Cook, *BSA* 48 (1953), 30 ff. (Agamemnon at Mycenae) and in *Geras A. Keramopoullou* (1953), 112 ff.; cf. also T. Kelly, *AJA* 70 (1966), 117, on a possible parallel in cult. On the *Odyssey* and the western Mediterranean see esp. R. Carpenter, *The Greeks in Spain* (1933) and *Folktale, Fiction and Saga in the Homeric Epics* (1946), ch. 5.

3 Among the many excellent works on Archaic Greek art may be noted those of G. M. Richter, *Archaic Greek Art* (1949), E. Homann-Wedeking, *Archaic Greece* (1968; first published in German, 1966), and J. Boardman, *Preclassical* (1967). The impact of the Christian art of the Mediterranean area upon the northern 'portable' style was brilliantly discussed by E. Kitzinger in *Early Medieval Art in the British Museum* (1940), ch. 2; cf. in general M. Rickert, *Painting in Britain: the Middle Ages* (1954), ch. 1. For the development of early Greek *narrative* art see J. Carter, *BSA* 67 (1972), 25 ff. Psamtik I's Greek mercenaries: Hdt. 2. 152–4. Stone temples: Samos, J. M. Cook, *The Greeks in Ionia and the East* (1962), 75 ff.; Homann-Wedeking, op. cit., 29 ff.; Smyrna, Cook, *The Greeks in Ionia*, 81 f.; Olympia (Heraion), W. Dinsmoor, *The Architecture of Ancient Greece*² (1950), 53 f. and n.2. Relief-stelai: Cretan, K. F. Johansen, *The Attic Grave-reliefs* (1951), 80 ff. (their funereal character is doubted in Kurtz and Boardman, *Greek Burial Customs* (1971), 220); Attic, G. M. Richter, *The Archaic Gravestones of Attica* (1961); stelai for women, Jeffery, *BSA* 57 (1962), 149 f. On the Greek tradition of the poet's encounter with the Muses cf. most recently M. L. West, *Hesiod: Theogony* (1966), 158 ff. Boutades: Pliny, *HN* 35. 151. The Acropolis verse: A. E. Raubitschek, *Dedications from the Athenian Akropolis* (1949) no. 224 (the Greek restored by Hiller, *IG* I² 678).

2 Ancient Sources for Greek History

It seems certain that no chronicle of events was kept in any Greek state before the fifth century B.C. The absence of any systematic, let alone annual, records of early Greek history was stressed by the Jewish historian Josephus in the first century A.D. Understandably irritated by the extravagant claims of some (not all) Greek writers, he maintained that the Greeks had only become literate long after the Egyptians, Assyrians, and north Semitic peoples: that some Greeks themselves held that even Homer had been illiterate: that the genealogists and logographers, who were the first near-historians, barely preceded the fifth century: and that the non-existence of early chronicles was proved indirectly by the disputes and contradictions among Greek writers themselves over the details of their own early history.

All this is roughly true. The lack of chronicles in literate Archaic Greece is not surprising. The monarch of an Oriental kingdom was concerned to have his deeds recorded in order to impress his sublime powers in peace and war upon his far-flung subjects and posterity. But a Greek polis was too small for any monarchy, whether of king or tyrant (let alone for an annually elected magistrate), to nourish a concept natural to theocratic rulership with its hubristic core.

Though not concerned to chronicle the past, the Archaic Greeks, like most peoples, cherished those aspects of it which were distant enough to loom the larger for being misty. Hence they revered the epics of the Trojan War, the Theban expeditions, and many other sagas now fragmentary or wholly lost to us. This is an understandable interest for any aristocratic society, the feats of whose ancestors are enshrined in this way. It had its own concept, limited but not ignoble, of history not as an inquiry into the past but as a song for later ages to remember about men who fought always in the forefront of the battle. Hence too the old myth in Hesiod (perhaps recast from some earlier source in Near Eastern saga) was long accepted, the tale that the past began with a Golden Age and worsened by stages through silver, bronze, and ashwood to the chill iron of the present.[1]

The two kinds of prose work which founded the methods of historical research and record came only at the end of the sixth century. Over in Ionia, where older literate nations bordered the Greek settlers, Hekataios of Miletos (fl. *c.* 520–490) compiled genealogies and more particularly accounts (*logoi*) of peoples: their secular and religious customs, their towns and countryside, and any historical events worth noting. His sceptical reaction against myth-cherishers inspired his famous opening sentence: 'I write the following as the truth appears to me; for in my view the Greeks' own accounts are numerous and laughable'. On the Greek mainland the learned Pherekydes of Athens (fl. *c.* 500–460) began to correct, record, and expand the genealogies of famous local families, as for example the family of Miltiades: '... his son was Hippokleides, in whose archonship the Panathenaic Festival was established [566 B.C.]; [his son was Kypselos]; and his son was Miltiades, who colonized the Chersonese'. In the collecting of *logoi* lay the basis of historical inquiry, and in the establishment of family trees lay the germ of annalistic recording, since they could provide a systematic chronological framework for past events. The backwoods of Sparta, as might be expected, yielded the best timber for this purpose, since the generations in their two royal families went back to Herakles.

Obviously, in order to use family trees for making a chronological framework and fixing individual dates, one must first decide the average number of years in a single generation. Three generations per century, i.e., 30–33 years each, a reckoning still valid in fairly recent times, was certainly used in early Greece; on average a man was thought to marry when about thirty and to die of old age at about seventy, when his grandchildren were still small. But another traditional way of reckoning made a generation last 40 years, which produced some remarkable claims to longevity: a man's floruit was at forty, he died at eighty, but if like old Nestor in the *Iliad* he lived until his grandchildren were begetting *their* first children, then he must have died at about 140. Most of the examples of this longevity quoted by the Greeks were non-Greeks – Iberian, Persian, Ethiopian; but it is thought (though not fully established) that the Spartans reckoned at least their royal generations thus. Hence if an ancient historian uses a round number, as 'it is 60 (80, etc.) years since x happened', we infer that this comes from a reckoning by generations; if it suggests multiples of 40 rather than 30–33, we take the number of generations to be correct but the total of years to be wrong, and scale it down accordingly.[2]

Herodotos, the father of history, was sensibly chary of trying to reconstruct either individual dates or any overall chronological system into which he could fit all the events which he describes. He seems to have accepted what was offered to him by his many informants, whether it was the actual length of kings' reigns, or round numbers reckoned now by 30- and now by 40-year generations, or simply the number of the generations. It was his immediate successors, trained in the professional scholarship of the Sophists, who made the study of the past into a science. First, they rejected the concept of a past Golden Age, and formed instead a picture of primitive man slowly ascending from articulacy to technical inventions. Secondly, they were concerned to publish not only the reconstructed pedigrees of private families but also their public equivalents, the lists of state office-holders, or of winners at festivals, especially the well-known lists which were, or might be, used by the city concerned as its own dating-system. The list of Athenian archons, probably those from 682 onwards, was set up in stone in the Agora c. 425, and fragments of it still survive. The Spartan list of annual ephors may have been published too at about the same time. Hippias of Elis listed the victors in the *stadion* (sprint) at Olympia (below, p. 167). Antiochos of Syracuse published a foundation date for his city and, by comparing their traditions, for some of her neighbours too. Doubtless many such lists had been kept in some fashion by many states, and the systems had been used to date their own local events. Two surviving inscriptions of the sixth century, for example, tell us in passing that a certain law was passed in Eretria 'when Golos was archon', and that in Aigina the precinct of the goddess Aphaia was embellished 'when (X) was priest'. But the first scholar to publish such a list as a chronological framework for a History of all Greece was Hellanikos of Lesbos (c. 490–405?), who used the list of priestesses at the great Heraion near Argos. It professed to give the name of each holder of this life-office, and the year of her tenure, from before the Trojan War until at least 429 B.C. He constructed the first general history of Greece, past to present, entitling it 'The Argive Priestesses of Hera', and dating each event 'when Chrysis [for example] was in her 48th year of office', and so on.

How far back such lists truly went we cannot tell. Before public inscriptions became common practice the names will have been kept in the memory of each successive official whose business it was to memorize them in the normal way of duty – officials with titles like Remembrancer (*mnemones, anamnemones,* or priestly *hieromnemones*). The date when it was finally decided to write up such a list in public, and maintain it annually thereafter, presumably varied from city to city. Some may never have done this until a researcher like Hippias prodded them into the duty; others may have been able to show such researchers a written list already of some antiquity. The early stretches of all these lists were presumably patched and padded where necessary by the researchers. Later authors suspected Hippias' efforts; and the list used by Hellanikos cannot have gone back to the Bronze Age, although, if the Argives copied the idea of such a list from Egypt, it may have gone back as far as the seventh century, when Psamtik I allowed some Greeks to settle in the Delta after mercenary service in his army. It is profitless to speculate on how Hellanikos selected the particular year in his framework to which he fitted each event of early history which he had collected; the resulting chronicle, though monumental, was evidently so dull that very little has survived, though some of his dates may lie behind the round numbers which Thucydides offers tersely in his brilliant but condensed account of early Greece.[3]

After Hellanikos the great *History of Greece* by Ephoros of Kyme (c. 405–330) began at the Return of the Herakleidai, which occurred traditionally two generations after the Trojan War. It was not annalistic, but arranged by topic, the events of each topic in chronological order. The compiling of local histories (*hōroi*) had also been undertaken by Hellanikos, who wrote the first *Atthis* (History of Attica); other writers may have been slightly earlier in this field. From the fourth century onwards scholars carried on the process of recording the immediate past and copying or improving on earlier versions of older history. Of all the local dating systems that of the Olympiads prevailed, with the Athenian archon-list a close second. Several ancient chronographies (tables of events) survive at least in part, the best known being among the latest – the *Chronicles* and *Canon* of the bishop Eusebius (c. A.D. 260–340), a compilation derived in its pre-Christian parts from Hellenistic scholarship.

Thus the ancient Greek historians writing of their country's early history could get various degrees of help from the following: facts recorded by their predecessors; events and approximate dates from family trees aided by family recollections; lists of annual officials ('if *A* was polemarch in 550, then the war against Aigina was in that year'); victor-lists ('if *A* won in 580, then the colony which he led to Sicily was settled at least 15 years later, since an *oikistes* would be over 30 years of age'); and victory dedications offered in local or Panhellenic sanctuaries (often unhelpfully brief, but the local guide might preserve a tradition basically true, and some dedications did give details). Pausanias at Olympia records an archaic Attic epigram:

> To Olympian Zeus men from the Chersonese offered me.
> They took the fort at Aratos; Miltiades led them.

Since the verse does not say if this was Miltiades I or his famous nephew Miltiades, the victor later at Marathon, a modern epigraphist would hope to date the campaign by the script; but Pausanias must have had to rely on the guide. The offering itself (a pleasing token to Zeus from his childhood, 'Amaltheia's horn', she being the goat which had suckled him, according to the old Cretan tradition) may well have been an aurochs-horn drinking-cup, for the Thracian Chersonese came within the ancient territory of the aurochs, whose horns could measure over 3 feet in length.

Ancient Greek historians could also extract details of Archaic history, roughly datable at least, from allusions in early Greek poetry; Herodotos' brief references to the Cimmerian invasions of Asia Minor, and to the brave resistance of some Ionic cities to the Lydian attacks (below, pp. 213, 223), are probably derived from lost poems by Kallinos, Mimnermos, and others who lived during those crises. For modern historians also the surviving fragments of early poetry continue to be valuable sources of social, political, and military material, though they have become aware that not all the persons or events mentioned in apparently personal poems need be historical: for there were certain conventions, formulae implying personal experience, used traditionally by early poets like Archilochos in Greece no less than by other song-makers in other times and places – especially in the repertoire of love-poetry – which the unwary reader in a later age might take to be literal truth. And lastly, ancient historians no less than modern ones, using interpreters if necessary, might get dates from barbarian annalistic records (Egyptian and Persian certainly, Lydian too if they existed) about events in which Greeks had been involved.[4]

Basically therefore our dates for early Greek history rest on the compilations gathered in such ways by generations of later Greek and other writers. Each new generation of scholars doubts some dates but confirms others, and even adds more from new finds and interpretations of papyri and inscriptions. The resulting system is at least workable, and the main structure continues to hold.

NOTES

1 Josephus, *In Apionem* I. 2–5; cf. Jeffery in *Europa* (Festschrift ... Ernst Grumach, 1967), 158 ff. Golden Age: Hesiod, *WD*, 109–201; cf. P. Walcot, *Hesiod and the Near East* (1966), 85 f. M. West (*Early Greek Philosophy and the Orient* (1971), 205) holds that such 'eastern' material is more likely to be lingering traces from the Mycenean tradition than the result of Oriental contacts in Hesiod's own time.

2 Hekataios, *FGH* 1 F 1; Pherekydes, *FGH* 3 F 2. (The text is corrupt in places, but there seems no valid reason to doubt that the historical comments were Pherekydes' work.) Cf. in general Jacoby, *Mnemosyne* 13 (1947), 25 ff.; J. K. Davies, *Athenian Propertied Families* (1971), 294 f. The 30-year generation: Hesiod, *WD* 695–7; Solon F 19; Hdt. 2. 142,2. 30-year treaties: Hdt. 7. 148,4; Thuc. 1. 115,1. 40-year generation: Hdt. 3. 22,4 (Persian); 1. 163,2 (Iberian); 3. 23,1 (Ethiopian) – the last two are allegedly lifetimes of 120 years. On chronological reckoning by generations see in general W. van den Boer, *Laconian Studies* (1954), Pt. I; F. Mitchel, *Phoenix* 10 (1956), 48 ff. On scaling down numbers which appear to have been reckoned on the 40-year basis see the sensible observations of A. R. Burn, chief pioneer in this work, in *The Lyric Age of Greece* (1960), 403 ff.

3 The ascent of primitive man: cf. (e.g.) the speeches of Prometheus in Aeschylus, *PV* 436–506, and in general E. A. Havelock, *The Liberal Temper in Greek Politics* (1957), ch. 3. On the early public lists and their use for dating cf. Jeffery, *LSAG*, 59 ff. The Athenian archon-list: Meiggs and Lewis no. 6 and (for an exemplary general study) T. J. Cadoux, *JHS* 68 (1948), 70 ff. Spartan ephor-list: Buck, 268 ff. no. 71 and Jeffery, *LSAG*, 60, 196. Antiochos and his foundation dates: see K. J. Dover in *HCT* iv. 198 ff., a thorough discussion which accepts the view of R. van Compernolle that Antiochos' calculations were based on a 35-year generation. Eretrian law: *IG* xii. 9. 1273–4 (most recently, E. Vanderpool and M. Wallace, *Hesperia* 33 (1964), 381 ff.). Aiginetan record: *IG* iv. 1580 (most recently M. Guarducci, *Epigraphica* 31 (1969), 47 ff.). Hellanikos' 'Priestesses of Hera': *FGH* 4 F 79b and 83. The old Argive Heraion was begun in the first half of the seventh century (P. Amandry, *Hesperia* 21 (1952), 223 ff.), so it is conceivable that the real list also dated from that time. Round numbers in Thucydides' 'Archaiologia', 1. 12,3; 13,3–5; 18,1.

4. Pausanias at Olympia, 6. 19; the name Aratos(?) is corrupt in the text. The aurochs, native to eastern Europe, died out finally in the 16th c. A.D. See Athen. 468d and 476c–d on the huge horns of Molossian cattle and, more particularly, the vast drinking-horns in Macedon and Thrace (= Theopompos, *FGH* 115 F38 and F284). The pair of aurochs' drinking-horns in the Sutton Hoo burial (7th c. A.D.?) were wrongly restored at first and will be republished; cf. R. Bruce-Mitford, *The Sutton Hoo Ship Burial*[2] (1972), 33, 35. On the use of the personal factor in early poetry see esp. K. J. Dover in *Entretiens Hardt* 10 (1963), 181 ff. Lydian annalistic records: their existence has been postulated from a late author's statement that a certain brief reign was not recorded in the king-lists, and Hdt. 1. 6,4, where twenty-two royal names occupy a total of 505 years. Various modern attempts have been made to explain these numerals, mostly maintaining that one or other is corrupt; see H. Kaletsch, *Historia* 7 (1958), 1 ff.

3 The Archaic City-state and its Government

The Polis

A Greek polis (city-state) was a unit of people who (a) occupied a territory containing as its central rallying-point a town which held the seat of government and was itself usually clustered round a walled citadel (acropolis) which had originally contained the whole settlement; and (b) had autonomy in that their government was provided by and from their own ranks, not from outside. In some states that government might be a form of hereditary kingship, but not in the early pattern of a theocratic monarch, supreme in his functions, whose decisions could annul the advice of his Council of Elders. Only once, in the *Odyssey*, is a ruler described in terms of a god-given monarch, embodiment of divine power on earth, through whose judgements and leadership the people flourish, the black earth bears wheat and barley, the trees bend under their fruit, the flocks bear unblemished young, and the sea provides countless fish. Moral precepts to rulers about justice were the stock-in-trade of Egyptian and Near Eastern monarchies, where the theocratic concept of kingship was still accepted; so this picture in the *Odyssey* could be some echo of these didactic works, such as may be found also in Hesiod. By Oriental standards the Archaic Greek kingship was very modest. Thucydides briefly defines it as hereditary and conditional upon certain stated privileges; Aristotle adds that it depended on the people's will and that the triple function of the *basileus* was to lead the people in war, to preside over such sacrifices as were not the traditional right of certain families, and to judge. Both definitions are based on the *Odyssey*'s pictures of Alkinoos in Phaiakia and Telemachos in Ithaca. Alkinoos has certain fixed dues: a royal estate (*temenos*, as the kings of Kyrene had in the sixth century); first choice of spoils in a foray; the right to convene the other twelve *basileis* in Phaiakia and propound a line of action for their comment; and direct control of the city's manpower for, for example, manning a ship. But all this rested ultimately on the citizens' goodwill. 'May Areté and Alkinoos', says Odysseus, 'be able to hand on in peace to their children the goods and the dues which the people has given them'. And Telemachos in Ithaca reminded the suitors that if Odysseus were indeed dead, the hereditary succession was not inevitable: one of the other *basileis* in the island might succeed to the chief power. Classical Greece had no word for a crown prince until 'diadochos', properly the word for one succeeding to a duty usually military or naval, developed to this meaning.

Why do we find the evidence for hereditary kingship clear in some places (as in Sparta, Argos, Corinth), but remote and shadowy in others (as in Athens, Boiotia, Thessaly)? It is better to phrase the question thus, I think, than in the usual way, which asks 'Why did the kingship disappear earlier in some places than in others?' The point is that not all kingships were necessarily the same in origin. The 'clear' cases seem to come mainly from the Peloponnese where, after the Mycenean power had broken down and the population dwindled, bands mostly of north-westerners filtered in and settled in different areas under their tribal leaders; the areas were not large, the leaders were powerful, and so they perpetuated their authority in royal lines which lasted as long as they kept to their stated privileges. Sparta's dual kingship lasted into the second century B.C. The Argive line of Temenidai lasted to the end of the seventh century and a limited, military 'basileia' at least into the fifth. The Corinthian king-list may well be bogus in its earliest stretches, but at the turn of the ninth and eighth centuries we get king Bacchis, who was succeeded by five or seven successors, all with normal-sounding names. Sikyon too had a long king-list, bogus at the start but with normal names in the late stretches; and Messenia was under a king when she was attacked by Sparta late in the eighth century. But in the three big, non-Doric areas of central and northern Greece the tradition of hereditary kingship seems fainter. We have no proudly quoted Thessalian or Boiotian king-lists, bogus or otherwise. Thessaly was too vast an area for any one dynasty to hope to perpetuate a hereditary rule over the whole in the Archaic period. The *basileis* of Boiotia, another big agricultural area, in Hesiod's descriptions resemble the twelve petty rulers under king Alkinoos, the local lords in the towns or villages, each keeping the hereditary authority within his own family. The same was probably true of Attica, a large area in which the different districts, the demes, gradually accepted the city of Athens as head of the whole lot, and agreed to form one common Council, that of the Areiopagos, whose members should be confined to the current heads of the ex-ruling family in each deme. For it can scarcely be doubted that each Attic deme did originally have a *basileia* of some kind, presumably hereditary. Athens herself preserved not only the *basileus* as a religious official with his wife the *basilinna*, but also four *basileis* who were the heads of the four old Attic tribes. But again these sound like the Hesiodic rather than the 'Doric' type. The lengthy Attic king-list is thought to have been worked up by the learned Hellanikos in the late fifth century for his *History of Attica*, all gaps being caulked with the names of famous ancestors in these high families ('Eupatridai'), whom each family claimed had been a *basileus* in the remote past.

Kingship ceased when those collaterals nearest to the throne insisted that its privileges be extended outside the single direct line: in other words, when dissension within the royal clan itself came to a head. The three basic powers – military, priestly, judicial – were distributed at first within the royal family itself, then further among other families closely connected with it, so that by the start of the seventh century most Greek states which had had kingship had lost it, and were being governed exclusively by the leaders of certain families which alone had this right by heredity, a situation well paralleled in the famous *Libro d'Oro* of Venice. The government in Corinth was monopolized by the Bacchiadai, the families which claimed royal descent from king Bacchis and kept the lineage pure by endogamy (below, pp. 145–6). In Athens were the Eupatridai, in Mytilene the Penthilidai, in Erythrai the Basilidai, and so on. Among the colonies, those which had gone forth from a metropolis under kingly rule often maintained some kind of monarchy, as at Taras in Italy and Kyrene in Libya, colonized respectively from Sparta and Thera (below, pp. 115, 185–7). Others, sent out from a metropolis governed by an oligarchy, followed that pattern, the closed ring in their case being the descendants of the original founding families (as in Thera, colonized traditionally from Sparta but not by a member of the Spartan royal blood, and in Illyrian Apollonia). But always the original shift away from the monopoly of ruling power, once made, went on increasing, for peers in an aristocracy were apt to quarrel, and in these breaches rich and ambitious men whose families were outside the closed ring of government might make their resentment heard, and so the widening process continued. The concept of justice (*dike*) in the sense of laws to which all ranks alike are subject was known to Hesiod at the end of the eighth century, although the *basileis*, he claimed, could still get away with unjust decisions in their courts. Gradually through the seventh century the oligarchies became less exclusive, and below the heights of the high office-holders the ordinary citizens too could look for increased rights: as, that the aristocratic council should send on more schemes to a Citizens' Assembly for approval before adoption; that neither the definition of a crime nor the size of the penalty should depend on the judge's personal interpretation of precedent; and that, since battles in boundary wars between states were now fiercer and more sustained affairs than simple tailing behind chiefs, the new method of fighting in massed ranks of hoplites – the adoption of the phalanx formation – should have its privileges no less than its dangers. The adoption of this style of fighting c. 675–650 gave the middle class of citizens, who formed the majority in the ranks, more contact with the upper class, perhaps promoting new friendships and lessening social antipathies, but strengthening overall the claim of the middle class to a greater share in the conduct of the city's affairs (below, p. 67). During the seventh century at least one aristocratic council (the Spartan) gave to its citizens the final decision in certain matters, perhaps in all (below, pp. 117–18); and slowly in the cities the magistrates accepted the idea that the laws should be written up in public.

Thus in the developed Archaic polis the triple function of the old *basileus* was transformed. The chief deity was no longer in the care of the royal household, but housed in a precinct outside, with a priesthood which would indeed be confined to a family in the cream of aristocracy, but not necessarily to the ex-royal family in perpetuity. War meant not simply following one ruler in raiding or staving off raids, but that the mustered ranks were now led by a nobleman elected by his peers and approved by the assembly as their war-leader. In trials judgements were accepted not as the unquestioned decisions of an autocrat, but as decisions in which the judge, if he failed to dispense straight justice, was bound himself to pay a fine. In state policy, external or internal, decisions were made by a council, sometimes even by an assembly, no longer by one man. The old phrase that the magistrates be elected 'according to birth and wealth' (ἀριστίνδην καὶ πλουτίνδην) shifted its original emphasis off birth to include a wider circle. We do not know whether others of the early aristocracies had practised endogamy as rigidly as the Bacchiadai of Corinth; but at least by the seventh century in many cities aristocrats brought wives into their families not only from other clans but also, for political reasons, from other states and even from non-Greek peoples. One famous example at the end of the sixth century was the Athenian Miltiades II, who governed the Thracian Chersonese and married a Thracian princess; their son, the great general Kimon, seems to have taken after his mother's side, being unusually large, shaggy, and simple by Athenian standards.[1]

The Lawgivers

Customary law, the rules which arise from traditional practices and beliefs, was called by the Greeks *ta patria*. What we would call common law, the law created by judges' decisions based on precedent, in Archaic Greece would find its nearest equivalent in the endorsement of *ta patria* by the authoritative pronouncement of a judge. In the *Odyssey* the *basileis* as judges pronounced *themistes* (dooms, things 'laid down' originally by divine authority, the *themistes* of Zeus); in religious laws this ancient word was still used in the first century A.D.

The king was aided by his council of elders, and here lay the germ of the law code, in the body of *themistes* stored in the collective memory; for a council whose members serve for life is a perpetually self-renewing organ, and has thus the continuity of memory which a succession of rulers cannot quite achieve. As magistrates took over the judicial duties of the *basileus* (though the council of elders might remain the supreme court of justice, as was the Areiopagos at Athens), so the old word *themis*, with its aura of divinity, started to give place to another from the same root: *thesmos*. *Nomos*, the most common word for a law in the fifth century, may have meant originally simply a portion or lot, as in the verb *nemein* (to distribute), and thus the natural lot appointed by the gods for beasts and men would come to mean 'natural law'. The adjective *eunomos*, 'of good habit', was applied to people and the abstract noun *eunomia*, 'the condition of good habits', came to mean law and order. *Nomos*, natural law, was now being used for man-made law, in that this *eunomia* must be the direct result of a just ordering of the city's administration. Tyrtaios, the seventh-century poet of Sparta, used the general term *eunomia* as a keyword to exhort the restive people in the crisis of a long war (below, pp. 117–18). This seems to be as far as the Spartans got in their legal development, for they never progressed to a written law code. A few essentials evidently were put into writing, such as the famous *rhetra* (pp. 117–18); but that word itself means a saying or verbal covenant. The same was true in conservative Elis; the importance of the sanctuary of Zeus at Olympia as an international repository for bronze plaques recording treaties and the like meant that the Eleans themselves drew up many such inscribed covenants, which are all called *rhetrai* in their preambles (below, p. 169). The fragmentary Laws of Chios in the sixth century (below, pp. 231–2) mentions some magistrate as 'guarding the *rhetrai* of the people', which here could mean either spoken or written decisions of a citizen-body.

Hesiod expressed the bitterness of those who had to live under a system of unwritten law. The high officials called Remembrancers in a city (above, p. 36) presumably included a specialist in the preservation and recitation of the unwritten *thesmia kai patria*, like the Icelandic 'law-sayman'; and the verbal pronouncements of such an official, whether judge's adviser or judge, would be supreme until, slowly or through some crisis, the weight of public opinion in the city insisted on a greater control of the legal system by the publication of the laws. A written code of laws and fixed penalties could (for example) dictate to the judge how he must decide in a conflict of evidence, prevent the imposition of irrational or sadistic penalties, and lay the judge himself under penalty if he failed in his prescribed duty.[2]

The double office of 'Remembrancer and Scribe' is first clearly attested *c.* 500, when the Cretan city Arkades (*Afráti*) appointed a man named Spensithios to be both Remembrancer and Scribe, as a paid expert with privileges equal to those of a *kosmos*, the highest magistrate (below, pp. 189–90); and legal inscriptions of the seventh century and later have been found elsewhere in Crete, enough to suggest that she may have been the earliest place in Archaic Greece to codify the law in writing, a claim supported by the literary evidence (below, p. 202, n. 7). The Western colonies may have been quicker than some of the mainland cities to publish law codes, in reaction against some injustice in the metropolis which had strengthened the original decision to emigrate: Katane's lawgiver Charondas and Rhegion's Androdamas are said to have been pupils of Zaleukos of Lokroi Epizephyrioi (below, p. 76). But their dates are uncertain, and by the late seventh century the mainland too could show at least one example, Drakon of Athens, who was to be superseded in the next generation by Athens' great lawgiver Solon.

Like Tyrtaios, Solon used the word *eunomia* to exhort his city in a time of rebellious disorder; then he went on to compile his great code which aimed at covering alike the fields of civil, criminal, and religious law. His lines in F 4, 18–20 W, are a fine plain statement of the principle of equality in justice, which was later called *isonomia*:

> Laws equally for low and high alike,
> according to each man unvarying justice,
> I have written.

Both Solon's code and that of Chios establish the right of appeal against the decision of a judge; possibly this great advance in the administration of justice came only with the written law codes.

The laws of Massalia on the south coast of France, a colony founded *c.* 600 from Ionic Phokaia, 'were Ionic, and written up in public'. This probably means not merely that they were in the Ionic dialect, but that they differed also in some more basic way from, for example, the laws of Doric Crete, or Zaleukos' Lokrian code, or the Chalkidic-Ionic of Charondas' laws for Katane; for as the *nomima* (customs, institutions) of different areas varied (below, p. 44), so their concept of the law will have varied too. Massalia indeed offers a fascinating picture of the type of constitution which must have existed in an Ionic aristocratic city *c.* 600, and was substantially preserved, even to the Roman period, by the tenacious communal memory of a small society descended from *émigrés* who had been transplanted half across the world to the Ligurian coast. Government was hereditary. Its structure was pyramidal and consisted of a basic council (*synedrion*) of 600 *timouchoi* (office-holders), who held their seats for life and were all heads of houses, the eldest son succeeding to the seat on his father's death – a rigid principle which may have been based on inalienable *kleroi* (allotments) which had been allotted to the original settlement of 600 males. This body had judicial powers, in that it could disfranchise a citizen for an illegal act and later re-enfranchise him; but the immediate administration of the city's affairs was in the hands of a committee of fifteen from the 600. Three of the fifteen headed the committee, and one of these was supreme. The basis of election to the 600 had widened somewhat by the fourth century B.C., but still in Roman times the laws of Massalia maintained a certain archaic severity. They banned any outrageous shows such as mimes, and any new and outlandish cults which might seem to cloak an unwillingness to work. The primitive details of the cult-statue of the Eastern ('Ephesian') Artemis, Massalia's chief deity, were faithfully transmitted to her own colonies in Iberia, and such was the civic zeal for preserving the antique in all things that criminals were executed by the original sword used since the foundation of the city, 'though corroded by rust and barely equal to the task'.[3]

Relations between States

The ancient Greeks were well aware of the mixture of ethnic elements within their country, though they did not always distinguish variety in dialects from variety in language. In the Peloponnese alone, Herodotos says, there were seven different races (*ethne*), which he classifies as: aboriginals still *in situ* (Arkadians), aboriginals who had changed their area (Achaians), Ionians (Kynouria), Dorians, Aitolians, Dryopes, and Lemnians (below, p. 133). The great distinction among the Greeks was between the Ionic and Doric races. The antipathy between them is often underlined in ancient literature. Propaganda must have heightened it during the wars between the Athenian and Peloponnesian Leagues in the fifth century, but surely did not create it. The roots went down much deeper, to those differences which in all times and places have always formed natural obstacles to any real community of interests: differences in speech, in social institutions, in religious rites. Differences in speech may blend in time, but institutions – above all, religious ones – are far less fusible. Dorians, for example, could not set foot in an Ionic sanctuary; the law forbade it. In colonial foundations it seems to have been accepted that Doric and Ionic should not, if possible, be mixed. Himera in Sicily, isolated on the north coast some way from the other Greek colonies, was an exception and, as such, described by Thucydides in some detail. Her settlers were Ionic speakers from Zankle, afforced by a band of Doric exiles from Syracuse; the dialects fused, but the Ionic institutions (*nomima*) obliterated the Doric.

· It is easy to see the centrifugal forces in ancient Greek society – the ethnic differences with their social and religious effects, the obvious geographic difficulties, and above all the dearth of arable land to feed an expanding population, so that boundaries were bitterly disputed. But there were also certain factors deliberately introduced to avoid war and promote understanding between states. The festival of Olympian Zeus in Elis was celebrated quadrennially by Games open to all Hellenes, which had become widely supported by the late seventh century. During the time of this festival (around August) the whole district of Olympia itself was declared holy ground by the proclamation of a traditional truce. No one could carry arms – nor, *a fortiori*, move an army – within its borders. Possibly the truce was established originally to stop local quarrels during the festival; but its terms were automatically required of other Greek states too when they began to send their *theoroi* (religious envoys) and athletes to participate. The truce was broken more than once (below, p. 136); but at least it existed, a visible symbol of the goodwill which can be implanted in individuals by a common festival, however much state ambitions may bedevil the athletics.

The office of *proxenia* provided another sort of channel for good relations between states. It was a later, technical development from the guest-friendship (*xenia*) of the great families illustrated in the Homeric epics. It resembled the modern vice-consulate, in which a resident citizen of state B is chosen as vice-consul through his familiarity with state A, whose citizens can thus apply to him for aid when visiting B. (The ancient Greek would probably have regarded the modern consulate system as little better than exile.) *Proxenoi* were normally men of high birth and wealth who had ties with similar households in the other state. The office was sometimes hereditary in a family, and the man could be selected also for any embassy to the state for which he was *proxenos*; for the office of professional diplomat did not exist in Archaic Greece, any more than those of professional priest or technical adviser on state financial policy.

In all Greek states citizenship was a privilege jealously guarded, carrying as it did not only the right to a share in the government (by office or at least by vote), but also material benefits, such as a share in any free distribution of surplus silver from the city's mines, or corn from a foreign monarch's bounty, as well as exemption from direct forms of taxation. The rare mutual concession of *epigamia* between two states, therefore, was a strong indication of their good relationship, for apparently it meant that in such a marriage, if the man wished to settle in his wife's city, he and the children born of the marriage rated as citizens there. (No problem arose if he stayed in his own city, for Greek citizenship normally descended through the father only, at least until the Athenian citizenship law of the mid-fifth century, which required the mother also to be of Attic descent.) Andros and Paros, for example, appear to have had *epigamia* in the mid-seventh century (below, p. 183).

The official alliances between cities in the Archaic period were mostly for military purposes, *epimachiai* (defensive) or full *symmachiai* (both offensive and defensive). But sometimes two states agreed by written treaty to an official 'friendship' (*philia, xenia*), i.e., at least a non-aggression pact. Sybaris, the great Achaian colony in south Italy, founded in the late eighth century, made such a pact during the sixth century with the Serdaioi (probably a lesser state in Italy), the parties binding themselves 'in faithful, guileless friendship perpetually' (below, p. 169). Nor should we forget that the mechanism of arbitration (*diallaxia*), long used to allay internal quarrels, was already used to prevent external wars in the seventh century. Sometimes a single city was asked to provide the independent board of arbitrators, sometimes the board was made up of individuals from three or more small states. Occasionally a single man, even a tyrant, might be called on to act as an adjudicator. And even if all these safeguards failed finally, hints survive that the cities often had their own Geneva Conventions. Chalkis and Eretria banned slings and arrows (below, p. 65), surely not only because they were outlandish but because they were deadly, the bullet-like slingstone and the arrow perhaps poisoned. The members of the Delphic Amphiktiony (below, p. 74) could and did attack each other, but poisoning of wells was forbidden. The Megarian villages likewise fought each other in the early days (below, p. 155), but their captives were called 'spear-guests' and treated well.[4]

Tyranny

Tyranny as a form of government appeared in mainland Greece shortly before the middle of the seventh century, and mostly in the cluster of cities around the Isthmus of Corinth. 'Tyrannos', a word thought by the Greeks themselves to be of Lydian origin, was used by them to define the man who had seized his power unconstitutionally and accepted the laws of his city only if he chose to: *de facto* he was above, that is outside, the law. The pattern for the Greek tyrant was the Eastern type of monarch who overthrew by force an existing hereditary ruling dynasty – as did Psammetichos I of Egypt (fl. *c*. 663–609) and Gyges of Lydia (fl. *c*. 680–650); both these men were contemporaries of Kypselos of Corinth, who was, if not the first, among the first of the mainland Greek *tyrannoi*. Moreover, Kypselos had been helped to start his revolution by his royal neighbour Pheidon of Argos, a hereditary king whose vigorous actions resembled those of a tyrant in more than one way (below, pp. 134–6). The example of Argos at this time may have been one factor among the reasons which produced the cluster of tyrannies in the area of the Isthmus: not only Kypselos in Corinth, but Theagenes in Megara, Kleisthenes (and Orthagoras before him?) in Sikyon, Prokles in Epidauros. These were all sea-coastal trading states, short of land and quick to see and copy a prospering tyranny next door. The mainland states which had no tyrannies in this century were not short of land, nor sea-coast traders (even in Attica a great many demes were inland). Thessaly, Boiotia, and Sparta, had no tyrannies, and Athens not until the mid-sixth century. The undoubted discontent among the poorest classes in seventh-century oligarchies cannot have managed to give any powerful support, or indeed incentive, to the would-be tyrant (though when once he was in power, he usually improved the general standard of living); but insofar as such discontent did have any chance of snowballing, this will have happened more easily in the smaller, busy states, in their shipyards and potteries and smithies, than in the big, rural districts where a field-labourer's dawn-to-dusk work would leave small leisure and few focal places for political discussion at the end of the day.

Thus the examples of power wielded in Argos, and seized in Lydia and Egypt, may have helped in causing these tyrannies to start when and where they did. But what were the fundamental causes for discontent? Perhaps the strongest lay in the drastic political situation wherein a small ruling class continued through hereditary right to monopolize all the magistracies – theoretically in perpetuity, actually until the build-up of resentment among those who felt equally qualified by ability, wealth, and even lineage (for some, like Kypselos, had an ancestry older than that of the ruling Doric clan in the city) was finally precipitated into action by some last-straw crisis, often economic. Then one of these able out-siders broke the closed ring and seized the power for himself – quickly and completely, with armed troops if necessary, before any others of his own social stratum who had been supporting the same cause could start up rivalry and the dread spectre of stasis (civil strife) for the new mastery of the state.

This same cause, a political grievance sparked off by other distresses also building up, is seen elsewhere in the seventh and early sixth centuries: at Mytilene (below, pp. 239–41), where the ruling clan (Penthilidai) was ousted by a non-Penthilid, and there was a flurry of stasis, and several attempts and short successes in tyranny, until at last the exhausted city elected Pittakos to be the *aisymnetes* (an old word of uncertain meaning, perhaps 'judge' or 'arbitrator'), which office he is said to have held for ten years. The poet Alkaios abused him as a tyrant among other more personal insults, but had to allow that the city did elect him. At about the same time Athens too avoided tyranny for a generation by electing an arbitrator (Solon) as archon, with *carte blanche* also as a *nomothetes* to frame laws which broke the traditional monopoly of the Eupatrid government there. Sparta too in the seventh century had avoided the explosion of resentment which could end in tyranny by distributing new allotments (*kleroi*), carved out of the conquered Messenia, to her poorer citizens, and ensuring for them certain rights in the document called the *rhetra* (below, pp. 117–18). The colony Kyrene solved a complicated political crisis which threatened revolution by down-grading her king and recasting the tribal basis of her citizen-body (below, p. 187).

NOTES

1 *Od.* 19. 107–14; cf. Walcot, *Hesiod and the Near East*, 72 f. A different view holds that this passage, with the similar picture in Hesiod, *WD* 225–37, reflects the outlook of the world of Hesiod; cf. M. Finley, *The World of Odysseus* (1956), 107. Archaic kingship: Thuc. 1. 13,1 and Arist., *Pol.* 1285b; Alkinoos' dues: *Od.* 6. 293–4; 7. 7–11; 8. 34–9; Kyrene, Hdt. 4. 161; Odysseus' speech, 7. 146–52; Telemachos', 1. 394–6. On the origin of the Eupatridai I have accepted the view of Wade-Gery, *Essays*, 86 ff. (= *CQ* 25 (1931), 1 ff.). Hellanikos and the Attic king-list: Jacoby, *Atthis* (1949), 126 f.; Thera and Apollonia, Arist., *Pol.* 1290b; Hesiod on the *basileis*, *WD* 258–62. Increased share in government for the hoplite class: Arist., *Pol.* 1297b. Kimon's appearance: Plut., *Cim.* 4,4 and 5,3.

2 *Themistes*: *Il.* 1. 238; 9. 99; *Od.* 16. 403; *IG* ii.3. 1364,6 (1st c. A.D.). *Thesmoi*: Solon, F36 West; Delphi, *DGE* 324 (4th c. B.C.). *Nomos* as natural law, cf. Hesiod, *WD* 276–8. *Eunomia* is first attested in *Od.* 17. 487, contrasted with *hubris*. Eunomia, Dike, and Eirene (Order, Justice, and Peace) are the children of Themis in Hesiod, *Th.* 901–3. On the whole question of these terms in Archaic Greece see most recently M. Ostwald, *Nomos and the Beginning of Athenian Democracy* (1969), and for *eunomia* esp. A. Andrewes, *CQ* 32 (1938), 89 ff. and V. Ehrenberg, *Aspects of the Ancient World* (1946), 70 ff. *Rhetrai*: *Od.* 14. 393; Elean *rhetrai*, Buck, 259 ff., nos. 61–4. The word is still used in an oligarchic decree of the late 5th c. from Thasos, Meiggs and Lewis no. 83,5. *Thesmia kai patria*: cf. the preamble of the old Attic law on tyranny, *Ath. Pol.* 16. 10 and Ostwald, *TAPA* 86 (1955), 106 ff. The 'law-sayman' in early Icelandic society recited the whole of the unwritten common law in the course of the annual assemblies held during his three-year term of office, and the part of most practical import (the Formulas of Actions) each year, presiding at the assemblies with a casting vote and answering all questions on the law, as final authority; see J. Bryce, *Studies in History and Jurisprudence* I (1901), 327 ff. Decision in a conflict of evidence: see the Gortyn Code, Buck, 317, 326 (no. 117, lines 30–5): 'If some of the heirs-at-law wish to divide the property, and others not, the judge shall decree that all the property belong to those wishing to divide, until they do divide it'. Judges penalized: cf. the law from Eretria, above, p. 38, n. 3: 'If a man does not pay [his penalty], the rulers are to do according to the law. Whoever does not do so is himself to incur [– – – –]'.

3 Spensithios at Arkades: see Morpurgo-Davies and Jeffery, *Kadmos* 9 (1970), 118 ff. and below, p. 203, n. 11. The first written codes: Ephoros, *FGH* 70 F 139; Arist., *Pol.* 1274a; cf. G. L. Huxley, *Early Sparta* (1962), 120, n. 282. The title of Lokroi's chief magistrate (*kosmopolis*) seems to echo the Cretan *kosmos* (Polyb. 12. 16,6,9); but Ephoros says that Zaleukos' code was compiled from Cretan, Spartan, and Areopagite *nomima*; he stresses elsewhere the connection of Cretan customs with Spartan (cf. Hdt. 1. 64). For the 4th-c. view of the Areiopagos as a primeval dispenser of the law cf. Isokr., *Areopagitikos*. Charondas and Androdamas: Arist., *Pol.* 1274a–b. On the Cretan lawgivers see below, p. 202, n. 7. Massalia's code: Str. 179. The council: Arist., *Pol.* 1305b, 1321a; succession possibly based on *kleroi*: L. Whibley, *Greek Oligarchies* (1913), 122 f. Judicial power: Lucian, *Tox.*, 24–6. The pyramidal structure of government: Str., loc. cit. (presumably the powerful 15 were elected for a term, not for life); later qualifications for citizenship: ibid. Laws of Massalia: Val. Max., *Dicta factaque memorabilia*, 2. 6,7. The cult-statue: Str., loc. cit.

4 The 7 races: Hdt. 8. 73. Dorians debarred from Ionic precincts: Hdt. 5. 72,3 (Kleomenes of Sparta, below, pp. 123–7), and *DGE* 773: 'It is not lawful for a Doric stranger or a slave to [be a spectator of] the [rites] of Kore of the City' (Paros, 5th c. B.C.). Colonies: cf. Epidamnos (Thuc. 1. 24,2), Herakleia-in-Trachis (Thuc. 3. 92,5), Himera (Thuc. 6.

5,1). E. Will, *Doriens et Ioniens* (1956), argues against the existence of any basic Doric-Ionic antipathy. The Olympic truce: cf. (e.g.) Plut., *Lycurg.* 1. 1, Thuc. 5. 49, and the action of Pheidon of Argos, below, p. 136. On safe-conducts for the heralds of the Games and their patrons see H. A. Harris, *Greek Athletes and Athletics* (1964), 155 f. *Proxenoi*: Menekrates of Oiantheia, below, p. 75. and Meiggs and Lewis no. 4; cf. the excellent commentary on *proxenia* before the 4th c. B.C. by M. Wallace, *Phoenix* 24 (1970), 190 ff. On the lack of professional diplomats in ancient Greece, D. Mosley, *Phoenix* 25 (1971), 319 ff. Distribution of surplus silver: *Ath. Pol.* 22,7; of corn-doles, Philochoros, *FGH* 328 F 119, and Plut., *Per.* 37,3. Athenian citizenship law: *Ath. Pol.* 26,4; Andros and Paros, Plut., *QG* 30. cf. Hdt. 4. 152,5 (Samos and Kyrene); Meiggs and Lewis no. 10 (Sybaris). Arbitration between states, see M. N. Tod, *International Arbitration amongst the Greeks* (1913), ch. 8; early examples are Athens and Mytilene, below, pp. 90, 239; Plut., *QG* 30 (Andros and Chalkis). For citizens appointed to allay internal strife cf. Solon and Pittakos (pp. 90, 239-40) and Demonax of Mantineia at Kyrene (below, p. 187). On the whole subject of ancient Greek tyrannies see esp. Andrewes, *The Greek Tyrants* (1956). 'Tyrannos' a Lydian word: Hippias, *FGH* 6 F 6; cf. Cuny, *REA* 24 (1922), 89 ff. and Andrewes, *The Greek Tyrants*, 20 ff. Cf. further R. Drews, *Historia* 21 (1972), 129 ff.

4 Colonization

Early Settlements: Motives

The treasuries at Olympia lie below the hill of Kronos, facing south into the sanctuary. As at Delphi, these small temple-like buildings were dedicated by those states whose citizens were steady supporters of the Games, states rich enough to give valuable gifts which needed special housing, and to build their own treasuries to house them. The best-preserved today are those at Delphi. Little now shows of the Olympic treasuries except twelve foundations and a profusion of architectural remains in the museum. Of the ten which Pausanias saw when he visited the site, two belonged to states of the Isthmus, Megara and Sikyon, and all the rest to colonial states: Byzantion in the north-east, Kyrene in the south, and from the west Syracuse, Gela, and Selinous in Sicily, Sybaris and Metapontion in south Italy, Epidamnos in Illyria. They demonstrate both the wide span of Greek colonization and the size of its contribution in athletes, chariots, and gifts to the importance of the Games.

The earliest Greek settlements in the West were Euboic, and the largest number of these were from Chalkis (below, pp. 63–4). Bred beside the narrow Euripos strait, where the current reverses direction about every three hours, these sailors were prepared to defy the far more formidable currents of the Messenian straits, and to push as far as the Bay of Naples before the middle of the eighth century. The early Oriental imports found alike at Lefkandi near Eretria and Pithekoussai near Naples remind us that Archaic Euboia was well placed to be a middleman between East and West (below, pp. 63–7).

Echoes from the early settlers are heard in the *Odyssey*. The Cyclopes are contrasted, these pre-polis cavemen in a rich countryside, with a nation of political thinkers and skilled mariners in a poor one. The Cyclopes never plant or plough, for the corn and vines grow unaided; they have no council meetings nor decisions based on law. And there is an island off their coastline, quite deserted. It has woods, water-meadows, vines, good deep-soiled arable land, wild goats for hunting, and a well-protected harbour with fresh water at hand. What more could settlers want?

> But the Cyclopes have no red-cheeked ships, nor any shipwrights to make them well-benched ships which would achieve all purposes, voyaging to the cities of men, as so often men sail across the sea to visit one another. Such men would have made a well-settled place of the island.

In other words, the Greeks would have put a colony there in a twinkling.

These extended descriptions of natural scenery in the *Odyssey*, which have no real counterparts in the *Iliad* or Hesiod, are one of the debts of literature to the colonial movement. The island of Ogygia, Kalypso's island, is even more enchanting, as well it might be: a climate where the water-meadows were full of parsley and wild violets and all kinds of trees grew, including splendid ones for shipbuilding, and in a cool autumn, fires were stoked with scented cedarwood (hoarded by sculptors back in Greece for making statues offered to gods), while the vine arbour rioted with grapes at the door. In the city of Scheria in Phaiakia, where Nausikaa's grandfather had led a band of settlers from Hyperia (Farland) to escape from the terrible Cyclopes, a real colonial site underlies the description by Nausikaa: a walled city with a good harbour on either side, the beached ships fringing the causeway which leads to the city gate. The Phaiakians have settled on a peninsula and fortified it, the join of neck and headland forming the two harbours. Such a position was easy to defend, and many Greek colonies followed this pattern, on a peninsular site or an island close offshore (as Kyme, Syracuse, Leukas). Inside the city the magic orchard of Alkinoos, where 'pear grows ripe upon pear, apple on apple', seems an echo from sites like Kyrene with her amazing triple harvests, first from the hot sea-plain below the city, then from the foothills where the city lay, and lastly from the high plateau behind. The poet Archilochos, grumbling in Thasos at about the time when Ionians of Kolophon, uprooted by Gyges of Lydia, were going out *c.* 675 to settle by the river Siris between Sybaris and Metapontion, seems to have read the prospectus:

> . . . but Thasos here, like a donkey's back,
> sticks up its crest of wild and bristly trees
> . . . it is not good, delectable, or lovely
> as is that country round the streams of Siris.

The familiar sound returns in the description by William Penn of his prospective settlement of Pennsylvania, with its vines and wild game in a climate like the south of France, or the report from Raleigh's first expedition to the coast of (later) North Carolina, a place 'the most plentiful, sweet, fruitful and wholesome of all the world'.

The commonest single reason for any emigration has always been bad economic conditions at home, usually building up slowly and then touched off by some sudden disaster such as the blight on the potato crops which finally precipitated the mass Irish emigrations to America in the 1840s. Another driving force is religious or political intolerance, as when dissenting Calvinists finally created the Puritan settlements in New England, or when after 1649 ex-supporters of the Stuarts emigrated to Virginia and invested in plantations. Another factor is the prospect of trade.

In Italy Rhegion, for example, was traditionally a famine settlement; and land shortage, which means near-famine conditions, sent out settlers from the narrow coastal strip of Achaia on the Gulf of Corinth to the wider Italian coast, where three of their colonies, Sybaris, Kroton, and Metapontion, soon ranked with the richest in the West, thanks to their arable land, timber, and trade. For the trading factor the north-eastern settlements at the other end of the Greek world, mostly founded from Miletos and Megara, are the best-known examples, especially those around the Euxine. Many of the sites had little to make them of themselves desirable to any settler who was simply in search of material or political elbow-room. The Thracian and Scythian peoples were to the Greeks unresponsive and untameable (the people *en masse*, that is, not the friendly philhellenes among their chiefs and wealthy families, whom Herodotos describes); and the climate was rigorous for those bred in mainland Greece or the temperate airs of Ionia (below, pp. 210–11). No one state ever managed to achieve a monopoly over the rich trade in these parts in the Archaic period; the nearest to this was Miletos, which seems to have founded more settlements there than any other single city, but even she was far from achieving any sort of economic stranglehold. The best examples of the free-for-all competition in this area occurred naturally at the respective bottlenecks at the western and eastern ends of the Hellespont and Propontis. At the Hellespont, settlements from Mytilene and Athens disputed for at least two generations in the late seventh and sixth centuries (below, pp. 238–9). At the far end near the Thracian Bosporos the rival settlements Selymbria (Megarian) and Perinthos (Samian) overlooked each other. In an early war the Megarians attacked Perinthos, and a fleet from Samos came north to defeat them (below, p. 156). This suggests that the trade from their daughters was important enough for the two mother-cities to guarantee them military protection when necessary: that is, Selymbria and Perinthos may have been in a dependent relationship to their *metropoleis*, as the Kypselid colonies apparently were to Corinth (below, pp. 147–8).

As for the political crisis – stasis, or the threat of it – a colony is, from the government's viewpoint, one way to rid the state of elements actually or potentially dangerous. The tradition said of Taras, Sparta's one colony, that the emigrants were men denied Spartiate status on grounds of birth (below, p. 115). With no prospects at home and suspected of plans for rebellion, those of doubtful claim were forced to emigrate.

Metropolis and Colony: Relationship

The important but complex problem of the relationship between emigrants and city before the settlers left home, and between daughter and metropolis after the new foundation, can only be briefly considered here, first by a look at the case of Kyrene, long accepted as our best example because Herodotos has carefully preserved the versions of each side. According to the metropolis – the barren island of Thera in the Aegean, the modern Santorin – the foundation was an official venture: Grinnos, 'basileus' of Thera, was ordered unexpectedly by the Delphic oracle to found a settlement in Libya, but old age made him hand over the leader's duty to one Battos in his entourage. (Herodotos shrewdly guessed that 'Battos' was the title given to him later, and Pindar says that his name was Aristoteles.) The city then decreed formally that a colony be sent out, using conscription to bring up the total to the minimum number of able-bodied men of military age thought necessary to make a colony viable in its early years, probably two hundred in this case. A fourth-century reissue, found in Kyrene, of a text which is stated therein to be that of the original decree says that Battos shall go out as *oikistes* and 'founder-leader' (*archagetas*), and that for the first five years the colony shall have protection rights from the metropolis – its members may return thither if the infant settlement fails (correspondingly, Theraians settling there shall have Kyrenaian citizenship; below, p. 186). After that, presumably, it was on its own, an independent colony which soon, like many others, far outstripped its metropolis in importance.

In the colony's version of the story the unofficial, independent aspect is stressed: Battos himself was the unsuspecting enquirer at Delphi, and the Pythia instructed *him* to be the *oikistes*. The political factor is hinted in Battos' ancestry. According to the colony's version his father, Polymnestos, was a prominent citizen, his mother, Phronime, a highborn Cretan who became Polymnestos' concubine after a dramatic rescue (below, p. 191). But the Theraian version said that his father was a Minyan of the Euphemid clan, i.e., not true Doric (compare the case of Kypselos at Corinth, below, pp. 147–8); it is also stated by a later source that Battos had led an unsuccessful faction in Thera. The *oikistes* of a colony, shepherd of his people as a king had been in earlier days, had to have wealth and some blue blood (below, pp. 56–7), and so his personal reason for going would probably be political or religious rather than economic.[1]

Winds, Currents, and Trade-routes: Naukratis

We return to other aspects of the mother-daughter relationship below (pp. 54–6). Meanwhile, Herodotos goes on to say that the settlers were guided to an island, Platea, off the Libyan coast by a Cretan murex-fisher. The winds and currents whereby a Cretan might know the route are described by other authors: off Cape Malea, the south-east tip of the Peloponnese, the prevailing north wind and the local current swept Odysseus' ships down to the Lotophagoi in Libya and, on another occasion, Jason's ship to Lake Tritonis; while the return journey could be made when the south wind Leukonotos blew, and ships sailed north again via the south-western tip of Crete. Against the headland west of Kyrene the current splits east and west. The western stream probably carried the Samian Kolaios right through the straits of Gibraltar to Spain. He had set out from Samos allegedly meaning to go to Egypt, but arrived at Platea instead. The direct route from Samos to Egypt would have been by another combination of wind and current southward past the southern tip of Rhodes (Vrouliá) to the Delta. Perhaps Kolaios had planned a round trip, from Samos across the Aegean to Cape Malea with some Eastern luxuries for Sparta (below, p. 217), thence to the Libyan coast for raw materials (gold, fleeces, silphion), and thence in the eastward current back along the coast to the Delta.

Ionic Greeks of Miletos were already settled at the west side of the Delta by the end of the seventh century, establishing the commercial feelers which were to lead *c.* 570 to the permanent recognition of Naukratis, the Greek trading-settlement (*emporion*) there, by permission of the Pharaoh Amasis. This was not a colony (though later Miletos claimed to be its original metropolis), but a joint establishment formed by twelve Greek trading states: Miletos, Samos, Chios, Teos, Phokaia, Klazomenai (Ionic); Rhodes, Aigina, Knidos, Halikarnassos, Phaselis (Doric); and Mytilene (Aiolic). Amasis' permit gave them the near-monopoly of all Greek trade in the Delta area, for all Greek goods must enter and leave via Naukratis. A common precinct, the Hellenion, housed the cults of nine members, but three had each her own precinct, Samos to Hera, Miletos to Apollo, and Aigina to Zeus Hellanios; possibly they already had precincts established there when the Hellenion was agreed upon. The presence of Aigina, the only state not from the eastern Aegean, is a significant reminder of her great reputation as a middleman; her hostility to Samos was doubtless precisely for this reason, that both were deeply concerned with the southern trade (below, pp. 150–1).

The affairs of Naukratis were arranged as carefully as those of a city-state, with *prostatai* (representatives) in charge of the markets. She got her wealth by supplying the Greek states with Egyptian raw materials (grain, gold, alum) and manufactured goods (papyrus, linen, faience, small bronze and wooden figures, jewellery); but most of the Greek goods which came in were for Naukratite consumption, since the Egyptian religion regarded all foreigners as unclean. Silver, which Egypt lacked, seems to have been the one great exception.

Types of settlement

Naukratis, then, was not a colony. How was a Greek colony defined? In his classic *Essay on the Government of Dependencies* Sir George Cornewall Lewis rightly observed that the English usage of the word 'colony' is inaccurate, because it implies dependency on the metropolis, and also loose, because it covers all types of settlement, from a great government-sponsored plantation like Virginia or Georgia to a single trading settlement formed originally by private enterprise, like Hong Kong. His own definition was:

> a body of persons belonging to one country and political community [modified in a later paragraph to allow a *small* admixture to the settlement], who, having abandoned that country and community, form a new and separate society, independent or dependent, in some district which is wholly or nearly uninhabited, or from which they expel the ancient inhabitants. (1891 ed., p. 168)

Basically this covers the Greek *apoikia*. The first requirement is roughly correct. The Greeks did not mix Ionic and Doric; the odd exception, as Himera in Sicily, merely proved the rule (above, p. 44). But if a city could not raise even by conscription a sufficient number of able-bodied men (*axiomachoi*)—for this anywhere between two hundred and a thousand are recorded—the venture was opened to other states. The added element might be political exiles from their own city, as was the Doric element in Himera. Thus joint settlements were not uncommon. Sometimes this meant two *oikistai* (as at Zankle and also Italic Kyme), but more often the city which had provided the bulk of the settlers and an *oikistes* was accepted as the metropolis. Nevertheless, joint settlement often meant stasis later, and the eviction of the smaller number, as the Achaian Sybaris evicted her Troizenian element. Political theorists like Aristotle emphasized this risk.[2]

The Greek colony was self-evidently 'a new and separate society', for its citizens took the name of the new place. In their choice of position, like all colonies, they settled either in empty country beside a river (Siris, Sybaris,

Selinous) or spring (Kyrene, Thourioi), or on a site whence, as excavations show, the natives had been evicted (Kyme in Italy, Syracuse), or on ground given to them by a friendly local chief (below, p. 57).

Which emigrations, if any, were not state-sponsored at their start? Which colonies, if any, were dependencies of their metropoleis? These are difficult questions to which only half-answers can be given here. It is probable that very few were wholly private projects. Zankle, for example, seems to have begun as a pirates' nest, regularized later by an official contingent of settlers sent out by Chalkis. But mostly even those described by ancient authors as purely private ventures led by disgruntled aristocrats are thought by modern scholars to have been at least semi-official. The Athenian Miltiades I took a band of settlers up to the Chersonese allegedly because he declined to live in Athens under Peisistratos (below, p. 96), and the same motive apparently made Dorieus later leave the Sparta of king Kleomenes for the West (below, p. 123). But Miltiades' settlement coincided with a Peisistratid one on the opposite bank of the Hellespont, and Dorieus, after a preliminary failure, returned to Sparta (which would have meant death, had he left originally without permission), and was granted ships by the government for his next attempt. Kypselos of Corinth 'drove out his non-friends' to settle at Leukas, Ambrakia, and Anaktorion in the north-west; but these places were governed by junior members of his own family. It may well be that in fact some of the very early foundations began in rather an irregular way; but every reputable colony could produce its Delphic oracle, the tomb of its *oikistes*, and the common cults which bound it in piety to its metropolis, and so any settlements which were conscious of a remote and hazy start would equip themselves later with fictitious traditions to crystallize it.

The fragmentary decree of a Doric settlement on Black Kerkyra (Korčula) off the Illyrian coast may be quoted, for, though it is of the fourth century, its terse simplicity probably repeats the pattern of the Archaic colonial arrangements.

The first settlers, [having taken over the] territory and walled the city, shall set aside and take within the city wall each man one house site with its plot; and of the district outside the city wall the same settlers shall set aside and take each man as his original allotment [πρῶτος κλῆρος] 3 pelethra [100 sq. feet] of the [nearest? or best? land] and of the rest of the land ?his due parts [τὰ μέρη]. It must be recorded publicly [how much land], and where, each man has got for portion; and 1½ pelethra per man is to be permanent [i.e., inalienable] for themselves and their [descendants]. Those who come and settle hereafter are to take 4½ pelethra of the [remaining] land. The magistrates are to take oath never to redistribute the city or the district at any time or in any way.

The descendants of the original settlers were thus to remain in possession of the best land, and the illegal demands of any later settlers' descendants to get shares within the wall by a redistribution must be resisted. We know that at least in some colonies the mainland aristocratic system of hereditary government was followed, all magistracies being confined to the descendants of the founding families, as here in Black Kerkyra. At Kyrene, constitutionally a monarchy, a crisis was produced by a secondary settlement *c.* 570, apparently because the newcomers claimed equality with the old, and the land of the surrounding

Libyans was encroached on and wars with them resulted. An Arkadian named Demonax was called in to arbitrate. He solved the trouble by recasting the old tribal system of the colony in some way which ameliorated the grievances, and transferring to the citizen-body all the secular powers of the king, though leaving his religious duties and privileges untouched (below, p. 187).

The law against alienation of property long remained in some colonies, for in the Archaic period before the advent of a democracy tenure of citizenship required the possession of land. In the fourth century at Lokroi Epizephyrioi a citizen still could only sell his property if he could prove in court some dire necessity; and in Leukas, though the law had been rescinded by the fourth century, citizenship had earlier been confined to the holders of the original allotments (kleroi).[3]

All colonies were bound to their mother-cities by religious ties. The emigrants had been forced to leave behind them their family burial-plots. They had broken their political relationship, ceasing to be citizens of the metropolis, but they must ensure that at least there was no spiritual disinheritance. So they carried to their new land a basket of barley-grains from the old one, and in a clay pot some brands from the hearth of their old Prytaneion which they kindled again in the new Prytaneion overseas; and by these actions they retained their family connection with the ancestral land and hearth of the place where their dead were buried. They sent their theoroi with due gifts to the chief festival of the metropolis, and gave special privileges such as front seats, and first cuts from the sacrifices, to the metropolitan theoroi who came in their turn to the colonial festivals. It was considered a shocking thing for a colony and mother-city to go to war.

The independent colony did not usually flout these traditional bonds of filial piety. Dependency meant not these but secular obligations, such as are attested for the northern and north-western colonies of Corinth: Corinthian officials in their administration (Leukas and Potidaia); ships or hoplites sent to help the metropolis in wars which did not directly concern the colony (Potidaia, Leukas, Ambrakia, Anaktorion); and coinage following the Corinthian types of Athena Chalinitis/Pegasos, with the city's initial letter alongside. This last, however, may have been a commercial asset rather than a grievance, as the Corinthian types were well known and accepted in foreign parts.

It may be hazarded that colonies which had come from an energetic trading metropolis, and which lay on trade-routes important to her, were apt to be dependencies—if, that is, they were not merely emporia, like some of the Milesian settlements (below, p. 210). But inferences on this are rash until more evidence comes from archaeology to help our interpretation of the literary sources.

Relations with the Local Population

Two lines on Nausithoos, founder of Scheria in the Odyssey, sum up the manifold duties of the oikistes as leader of the new city: to mark out its site and build a wall round it; to divide up the land within the wall into house plots; to set aside a proportion (normally a tithe) of these last for the precincts of the gods; and to divide the arable land outside the wall into allotments for the citizens. Throughout his life he was the ruler of his city. He led the wars or negotiations with the

native people, sometimes marrying the chief's daughter to preserve good relations. He was a man from one of the high families, sometimes an Olympic
victor. He might undertake the task for personal ambition, or from necessity
through political misfortune or religious pollution, or simply from the responsible feeling of the good aristocrat for the welfare of his people in an area hit by
famine. His reward was to receive heroic honours at his death. Unlike ordinary
mortals he was buried within the city walls, usually in the agora itself, and an
annual feast was held for him with chthonic rites. A fragment from these is
preserved in the *Aitia* of Kallimachos, the Calling Prayer for the dead *oikistai* of
Zankle:

> Whoever founded our city,
> kind may he come to our feast.
> Let him bring two guests and more,
> the bull's blood is poured unstinted.

In the wide expanse between the Iberians in western Spain and the Colchians
at the eastern end of the Euxine the Greek settlers met widely differing degrees of
civilization. Most of the foundation-stories which record the relations of
colonists and local peoples, both at the first influx and later, are types which find
their parallels in the colonial periods of other nations. A few examples will
suffice. Mandron, chief of the Bebrykes on the Hellespont, invited Phobos of
Phokaia to bring his settlers into his territory, to aid the Bebrykes against their
local foes; later the Bebrykes grew to resent the newcomers, but a plot to get rid
of them was betrayed and the Phokaians seized the place, massacring the natives,
and renamed it Lampsakos. The *oikistai* of Megara Hyblaia and Massalia both
had hospitable relations initially with the local chiefs, Sikel and Ligurian; but in
Massalia's case at least it did not last. Phalaris, tyrant of Akragas, is said (on a
lighter note) to have defeated a besieged company of the local Sikans by fixing a
temporary truce and bargaining with them to exchange their good standing crops
for army rations, the normal decayed state of which he had hastened by artificial
means. The Sikels called Killyrioi were reduced to serfdom by the Syracusans;
the Mariandynoi on the Euxine 'could be bought and sold [by the colonists of
Herakleia on Pontos], though not over their own border; those were the agreed
conditions'. But many of the Greek settlements along the fierce coasts of Thrace
spent much of their early days fighting not only for extension of their land but for
survival, as Archilochos testifies for Thasos (colonized *c.* 700) and Herodotos for
the Athenians in the Thracian Chersonese.

Nevertheless, despite the resolute Hellenism which kept the Greek language
and culture dominant in the colonies, there was evidently some friendship and
intermarriage, attested by the non-Greek names which occur in good Greek
colonial families: Brentes, Paibes, Smordos are found in Thasos; Alazir in the
royal family of Kyrene's colony Barke. There is no clear case, however, of a
native man holding Greek citizenship, let alone a magistracy, in the Archaic
period (though later there is no doubt that this happened). The names came into
these Greek families presumably from the fathers' names of the local women
whom Greeks had married, and were perpetuated by the custom of naming the
children after their grandparents on both sides.[4]

NOTES

1 The treasuries: Paus. 6. 19. The Cyclopes: *Od.* 9. 105–41; modern scholarship identifies the island with Jerba off the coast of Tunisia. Ogygia: *Od.* 5. 55–74. Scheria: *Od.* 6. 262–9. On the peninsular site see J. M. Cook, *BSA* 53–4 (1958–59), 12; the orchard, *Od.* 7. 126; Kyrene's harvests, Hdt. 4. 199; Archilochos, F 23–4 W. The solidest and most perceptive work on the Western colonies remains that of T. J. Dunbabin, *The Western Greeks* (1948). Friendly Scyths: Hdt. 4. 133. The fullest study of Kyrene is by F. Chamoux, *Cyrène sous la monarchie des Battiades* (1953). Grinnos 'basileus': i.e., in the hereditary oligarchy formed by the descendants of the original settlers from Lakedaimon the head of the Theran state evidently retained the title of 'king', but without Sparta's unusual feature of a dyarchy. Establishment of the Libyan colony: Hdt. 4. 150–8; 200 settlers, 4. 153, with Mahaffy's virtually certain emendation ἄνδρας <s'>. The 4th-c. inscription in Kyrene: Meiggs and Lewis no. 5. I follow here (against them and also myself in *Historia* 10 (1960), 137 ff.) the interpretation of line 35 which makes the guarantee of rights of return to be available for the *first* five years only, rather than for the period *after* the first five years; see on this A. J. Graham, *Colony and Mother-city in Ancient Greece* (1964), 53. Battos' proper name was Aristoteles (Pindar, *Pyth.* 5. 116); Battos was a Greek corruption of the Libyan word for a ruler, as Herodotos says (4. 155,2). His paternal ancestors were Minyans from Lemnos (4. 150,2; see below, pp. 185–7). Factions in Thera: Menekles of Barke (*FGH* 270 F 6).

2 Odysseus' ships: *Od.* 9. 67–84. Jason: Hdt. 4. 179. The wind Leukonotos: Str. 837. The divided current: Rhys Carpenter, *Folktale, Fiction and Saga in the Homeric Epics* (1946), 103. Early Greek settlement on the site of Naukratis: Str. 801 (Milesians) and Payne and Beazley, *JHS* 49 (1929), 1 ff.; Naukratis proper, Hdt. 2. 178–9; cf. in general R. M. Cook, *JHS* 57 (1937), 227 ff.; C. Roebuck, *Ionian Trade and Colonization* (1959), 134 f.; and F. Bernand, *Le Delta égyptien d'après les textes grecs* I (1970), chs. xi–xv. Organization of Naukratis: Roebuck, *CP* 46 (1951), 212 ff. He considers that Chios played a leading part in its trade, because her colony Maroneia in Thrace had access to the northern silver-mining area (*Ionian Trade*, etc., 136). For an excellent survey covering the whole ground see M. Austin, *Greece and Egypt in the Archaic Age* (1970). Numbers for colonies: Steph. Byz. s.v. Apollonia (200); Plut., *Per.* 11 (250, 500, and 1,000). *Oikistai* at Zankle: Dunbabin, *Western Greeks*, 11 (Thuc. 6 4,5; Callim., ed. Pfeiffer, I, 43); at Kyme, ibid., 6 f. (Str. 243). Sybaris and other examples of stasis: Arist., *Pol.* 1303a.

3 On state-sponsoring and dependencies see the excellent study by Graham, *Colony and Mother-city*, Pts I–II. Zankle's origin: Thuc. 6. 4,5. Miltiades I and the Chersonese: Hdt. 6. 34–6 and Wade-Gery, *Essays*, 155 ff. (= *JHS* 71 (1951), 212 ff.). Dorieus: Hdt. 5. 42–8 and Dunbabin, *Western Greeks*, 348 ff. Kypselos: Nic. Damasc., *FGH* 90 F 57. On early colonial traditions see esp. H. W. Parke and F. Wormell, *The Delphic Oracle* I (1956), 49 ff. and W. G. Forrest, *Historia* 6 (1957), 160 ff. Decree from Black Kerkyra: *SIG*³ no. 141. Magistracies confined to Founders' Kin: Arist., *Pol.* 1290b (Thera and Illyrian Apollonia). Demonax: Hdt. 4. 161. Lokroi and Leukas: Arist., *Pol.* 1266b.

4 The *Birds* of Aristophanes parodies some of these duties in the founding of Cloudcuckooland; the basket and pot (42–4), oracles to ensure good luck for the venture (959–91), the famous Athenian geometrician Meton, who arrives to measure out the air into *kleroi* (995–6), the peddler of decrees in place of the *nomothetes* to draw up a law code for the settlement (1035–55). Religious dues to the metropolis: Thuc. 1. 25,4; 38,1–3 (Corinth and Kerkyra). Secular obligations: Plut., *Them.* 24. 1 (Corinthian

officials in Leukas); Thuc. 1. 56,2 (*epidemiourgoi* in Potidaia; on their duties see C. Vatin, *BCH* 85 (1961), 253 n. 4). Troops and ships to support Corinth in the Persian War: see the Serpent Column, coils 9–11, Meiggs and Lewis no. 27. Nausithoos as *oikistes*: *Od*. 6. 9–10. *Oikistai*: diplomatic marriage, Athen. 576a (Protis of Massalia); high birth, Thuc. 1. 24,2 (Phalios of Epidamnos); Olympic victor, Phrynon of Sigeion, below, pp. 89–90; heroic honours, Pind., *Pyth*. 5. 93 (Aristoteles Battos), Callim., *Aitia* I F 43, 81–3 Pf. (the Calling Prayer at Zankle). Relations with natives: Lampsakos, Plut., *De mul. virt*. 18; Megara Hyblaia, Thuc. 6. 4,1; Massalia, Justin, *Epitome* 43. 3,4–13; Phalaris, Polyaen., *Strat*. 5. 1,3 and Frontin., *Strat*. 3. 4,6; Killyrioi, Hdt. 7. 155; Mariandynoi, Str. 542, Athen. 263d. Thracian battles: Archil. F 5W; Hdt. 6. 38–40. Non-Greek names: Thasos, see Meiggs and Lewis no. 3 (Brentes) and J. Pouilloux, *Thasos* I, 16 ff.; Alazeir, Hdt. 4. 164,4. Greek magistracy held by native Campanians at Neapolis in Italy after the early period: Str. 246.

II

Central and
Northern Greece

5 Euboia and the Lelantine War

Chalkis and Eretria: Colonies and Trade-routes

The first great clash of states in the Archaic period came from the actions at home and abroad of Chalkis and Eretria, the two chief cities in Euboia. They were almost part of the Greek mainland, facing Boiotia and north Attica across the narrow channel called Euripos. Chalkis had a traditional friendship with Thebes, and Eretria, at least in Classical times, with Athens. If the two cities wished to expand without collision, plainly Chalkis' immediate sphere of influence would lie in northern Euboia and onwards up the north Aegean coast, whereas Eretria's ambition would be turned to south Euboia and thence into the central Aegean; indeed, in her heyday she controlled Andros, Tenos, Keos, 'and other islands'.

Between the pair lay the plain called Lelanton, after the Lelantos river which traversed it. It grows olives, vines, and fruit-trees and has clay-beds; traditionally the area once had copper-mines too, but in Classical times they were said already to have been long worked out. The north-west end of the plain comes close to modern Chalkis, which partly overlies the ancient city; the south-east end is at Lefkandi, the modern name of a flourishing site – city and necropolis – abandoned by the end of the Geometric period. The site usually identified with Old (i.e., pre-490) Eretria lies further east, and excavations there show that this too was a powerful city from the eighth century onwards. The ancient city at Lefkandi, which, if not itself the original city of Eretria, must from its propinquity have been an Eretrian dependency, may well have been a victim of the war.

Like most of their neighbours at the time, the two cities were governed by horse-breeding aristocracies, the Hippobotai in Chalkis and the Hippeis in Eretria. In the *Iliad* they appear as the Abantes, great fighters 'raging with their outstretched spears'. They were also great seafarers; the preponderance of Euboic pottery at Al Mina shows that by the early eighth century they had settled in this site on the coast of north Syria, and, though Euboia lies on the east side of the Greek mainland, nevertheless Euboians were the first Greeks to plant settlements in the West, pioneers in Italy, and then Sicily, from the early eighth century (above, p. 50). The incentives were grain, timber, and above all metals, copper from Cyprus and central Italy, gold from the East and Etruria, iron from Elba. Eretria, with her eastern outlet, must have had the edge over Chalkis in getting to Al Mina; indeed, possibly the Euboians there were Eretrians only (below, p. 66), though the evidence is not conclusive. On the other hand, Chalkis probably found it less hard than Eretria to reach the West, because friendship with Thebes may have enabled her traders and settlers to start from one of the Boiotian ports on the Corinthian Gulf. If Chalkis and

Eretria were habitual friends, they could join forces in all these enterprises; but with their relations to each other the problem begins.

Pithekoussai (Ischia) was the first Euboic Western settlement early in the eighth century, a joint venture; but after civil strife and volcanic eruptions the survivors moved across on to the Italic mainland, to a tall cliff on which they settled. The site was named Kyme (Cumae); the bulk of its people were from Chalkis and Kyme in Aiolis. It is not clear whether these settlers were already there when the Pithekoussans moved over, or whether they came shortly after, to swell the ex-islanders' numbers and make the colony viable. But only one ancient author gives Eretria any part in Kyme; the rest call it a Chalkidic colony. So possibly any Eretrian element among the ex-islanders was soon submerged. Eretrians also made an early settlement on Kerkyra; it cannot have been large, because it was evicted *c.* 734 by a detachment of Corinthian emigrants *en route*

FIG I. Pithekoussai: sherd from a bowl painted in the local version of the Euboic Late Geometric style. Signature (*right* to *left*): '[. . .]inos made me . . .'; below, part of a frontal winged creature, perhaps a siren or sphinx. Date, about 700

for Sicily. But Chalkis' tracks in the West are indeed impressive. Besides Pithekoussai and Kyme there were: Naxos (*c.* 735?), the first Greek colony in Sicily; two Chalkidic place names (Ortygia and the spring Arethousa) on the site occupied *c.* 734 by Corinthian Syracuse; Leontinoi and Katane *c.* 733, inland from Naxos; Rhegion and Zankle, the two watchers which observed all ships toiling through the difficult Straits; and, presumably, the settlement called Chalkis on the coast of Aitolia which later became Corinthian.[1]

The War: its Nature, Date, and Terminus

Meanwhile, towards the end of the eighth century, the two mother-cities went to war, the first recorded large-scale war of post-Mycenean Greece. Thucydides notes its occurrence, and his context is significant. In the early days, he says, no empires or federations existed to enlarge the scale of warfare from border feuds to big expeditions: 'the war of Chalkis and Eretria long ago was the one which achieved the biggest division into allies by the rest of Greece'. He does not tell us the date or the victor, or even that they were seafaring cities, but implies by his context that this was a border war, blown up to abnormal size by the presence of an unusual number of allies. And indeed two ambitious cities with a good plain between them had an obvious cause for border strife. It was presumably their maritime activities east, west, and north which brought in their respective allies from the rest of Greece; for if either city was ruined by war, various other cities on these maritime routes which profited as ports of call would be the poorer. So both combatants found allies, and the war, instead of staying localized as a Euboic border feud, was long remembered.

Some details survive. Amphidamas, a renowned warrior, led Chalkis to victory in a battle, but fell himself, and the poet Hesiod (fl. *c.* 700, hardly later) competed in song at his funeral games and won a tripod as prize, which he dedicated to the Muse on Helikon upon his return to Boiotia. This suggests that all or some part of the war occurred in the last years of the eighth century. Two allies from the eastern Aegean were Samos for Chalkis and Miletos for Eretria. Another ally of Chalkis was Kleomachos of Pharsalos in south Thessaly, who brought horsemen to aid Chalkis against Eretria's superior force (below, p. 72). Generations later the Chalkidians still pointed out his tomb in their agora, 'with the big column still standing on it', though some ancient writers denied that his death was actually in that battle, and gave this glory to another ally named Anton from the Chalkidike (Sithonia?), the northern peninsula where both cities made settlements in the seventh century (possibly earlier; but cf. note 2). Both Pharsalos and the Chalkidike are explicable as allies. The men of Chalkis whose settlements gave its name to the peninsula will have gone there sometimes by sea, through the Sporades to avoid the long and dangerous Magnesian coast, but sometimes, perhaps, overland through Thessaly itself, which might well require friendship with Pharsalos, the southern gateway for the route through the Thessalian hinterland. Kleomachos presumably brought a levy of riders from his own estate (as did Menon of Pharsalos in the fifth century), and may have crossed on to the head of Euboia by the short sea passage from Trachis. If the column was indeed his memorial, this was a great honour. Burial or a cenotaph in the agora of a city was normally confined not merely to its own citizens, but to those who rated heroic honours—kings, *oikistai* in their colonies, or men who had been in some way saviours of their cities.[2]

Kleomachos is undated; we cannot be certain that he fought in the same battle as Amphidamas. Anton's provenance may date him later, that is seventh century (cf. note 2); and a fragment by Archilochos of Paros (fl. *c.* 680–640) also refers vaguely to war between Chalkidians and Eretrians: the lords of Euboia, he says, when they fight on the plain, will do it in the way wherein they excel, with swords at close quarters, not with bows and slings. The lords of Euboia were traditionally descendants of the Abantes with their thrusting-spears (above, p. 63), and surely it is the social point which Archilochos stresses here: close fighting has always been the nobles' way, slings and arrows the weapons of outsiders. An ancient stone stele stood in Eretria's famous precinct of Artemis Amarynthia, bearing the text of a pact between both sides not to use long-range weapons (μὴ χρῆσθαι τηλεβόλοις). Archilochos' lines might refer to hearsay of this unusual agreement, the prototype of a Geneva Convention; a written pact would be epigraphically possible in the seventh century, though hardly in the eighth. A further cryptic reference to trouble in the plain is in a quatrain ascribed to Theognis of Megara (c. 570–490?; below, pp. 157–8):

> Alas for cowardice! Kerinthos is lost,
> Lelantos' good vine-plain is being shorn,
> the gentry's exiled, base men run the place,
> damnation to the clan of Kypselids.

Kerinthos, a small port on the east coast of Euboia, was traditionally founded by the same *oikistes* as Chalkis, and probably, therefore, a dependant of the latter. The Kypselidai of Corinth may be included because Periander (below, pp. 148–50; a friend of Eretria's ally Miletos) set his colony Potidaia c. 600 on Pallene in the Chalkidike. This might well anger the Hippobotai ruling Chalkis, and if she turned against Corinth, Eretria might seize the chance to destroy Kerinthos, ravage the plain, and foment stasis in Chalkis so that the lower, anti-Hippobotic classes there temporarily gained the power. If the plain was being shorn for cavalry skirmishing, this poem might indeed refer to some flare-up of the war in the early sixth century; but if the phrase means only that the 'base' are now happily raking in the Hippobotic crops, then it need imply no more than trouble fomented for Chalkis by Periander, with no reference to an actual renewal of the war.[3]

We have now to face the problem: was this war a violent but short affair at the end of the eighth century, won by Chalkis (allied to Pharsalos, Samos, *possibly* the Sithonian part of the Chalkidike, and others)? Many scholars hold that the certain references in the literature to the war all belong to such a campaign: that both cities had begun their Western colonizing in amity ('they were friendly but for the war', says Strabo, and Pithekoussai was a joint settlement). But then, it is suggested, they quarrelled over their trade expansion in the West and went to war, and Eretria, beaten in the one great battle, lost her hold and hopes in the West thereafter; if they ever did fight again, it was only the odd border bicker. But the literary evidence implies equally that the war was *not* over after one great Chalkidic victory near the end of the eighth century, and the archaeological shows that Eretrian pottery was flourishing through the seventh century, but not Chalkidic. The tradition known to Thucydides held that the hostility had its roots in border trouble, which is very apt to smoulder and flare up over several generations. Strabo's remark (above) admittedly does not fit a picture of intermittent border fighting; but he may have projected a later amity to an earlier date (cf. n. 4). Eretria certainly lost one great battle, but what evidence is there that she had ever taken any real interest in the West? The Eretrians who joined Chalkidians to settle Pithekoussai might have been exiles from their city (as were possibly those in Kerkyra (above, p. 64), who were stoned out of Eretria when they tried to return). Eretria surely put her trading energy chiefly into her natural outlet east (Pl. 3): that is, she did not 'lose hold in the West', simply because she had never aspired to a hold there as Chalkis did. This view would not show Chalkis and Eretria as habitually friends but for a short war (lost by

Eretria), but as habitually border disputants from the eighth century into the seventh and even the sixth, each trying to push its boundary forward and attacking the other's ships, and the many allies joining either side because of their anxiety lest their good trade centre in Euboia should be wiped out.[4]

As for these allies: Miletos may have been Eretria's port of call *en route* for the south-eastern Mediterranean, a friendship which alone would suffice to make Samos ally with Chalkis (below, pp. 212–13). Modern scholars add Corinth to Chalkis (and so Megara to Eretria), because it was Corinthians who forced the Eretrians out of Kerkyra (though they seem also to have overlain some Chalkidic elements in Syracuse and Aitolia; above, p. 64), and also because Corinth's shipwright Ameinokles built four ships for Samos, perhaps at the end of the eighth century (below, p. 146). Pharsalos, the Chalkidike, and the central Aegean islands are all explicable, as we have seen. In view of their later history Athens, or at least the Aegean side of Attica, may have given support to Eretria, and Thebes to Chalkis. Less probable as allies, perhaps, are the Peloponnesian land powers, though Argos for Eretria and Sparta for Chalkis have been proposed.

Whatever was the final date and outcome of the famous war, Chalkis, whose men were called by an old verse 'the best fighters in Greece' (below, p. 134), did win one, possibly two, great battles in the plain. As for Eretria, her pottery market throve throughout the seventh century, and she was flourishing *c.* 575–570, when Lysanias of Eretria was among the ambitious suitors who hoped for a dynastic alliance through marriage to Agariste, daughter of Kleisthenes of Sikyon (below, p. 165).

Early Cavalry and Hoplite Warfare

One last detail of the war raises a matter of general interest concerning Archaic Greek warfare. Aristotle in the *Politics* emphasizes at one point that certain horse-breeding, i.e., wealthy, oligarchies in the old days used their horses against their neighbours – Chalkis against Eretria, for example, and several other such pairs are added. Later he returns to early cavalry, and offers a penetrating account of the rise of the hoplite: when kingship ceased in early Greece, the succeeding type of government was based on the warrior class (οἱ πολεμοῦντες), at first on the *hippeis*, because strength and superiority in war lay with them, for the hoplite element was useless without organization, and among the early Greeks the experience and ordering of such things did not exist; and so the strength was in the *hippeis*. But as the cities waxed greater and the hoplites got stronger, they did then get a greater share in the government. This makes sense to us: the *hippeis* class lost their particular prestige as battle-winners, and some of their entrenched political power with it, when it was realized that battles were best won by heavy-armed soldiers drilled in the mass formation of the phalanx (above, p. 41). Horses, unsuited in any case to the rough terrain of much of Greece, were basically status symbols, too precious to be sacrificed through breaking legs in a massed frontal attack or sustained shoving. The horse-breeding cities went on using them as, one supposes, they had always been used – for shock tactics, to scatter those on foot and then ride them down; for skirmishes with the enemy cavalry; for scouting; and for chasing the retreating foe. They were often used also simply as vehicles; arrived at the battle, the rider dismounted and fought on foot, while the mounted squire led off the horse.

Later History

Thus when the hoplite element in Chalkis and Eretria realized its potential political power, government by Hippobotai and Hippeis became less settled; we hear that one Tynnondas, whose name sounds Boiotian, became 'tyrant of Euboia' before c. 600. By the sixth century other Greek states had overtaken them in ambition and power. Eretria continued to flourish commercially thanks to her pottery, but the elegant series of black-figured vases once identified as Chalkidic by the lettering and Ionic dialect of their inscriptions is now thought to come not from Chalkis but from one of her Western colonies, Rhegion perhaps (Pl. 4). The swords called 'Chalkidic', however, continued to maintain their reputation.

About 556 Eretria gave asylum to the Athenian would-be tyrant Peisistratos, whose family property lay in Brauron just opposite the Eretrian end of Euboia; and a Naxian exile named Lygdamis, who may have been already sheltering in Eretria, the city which had once controlled the nearby islands (if not Naxos itself), also joined Peisistratos' party. Chalkis may have abstained or taken the opposite side, for some fifty years later she supported Boiotia in an attack on Attica (below, p. 79), and shared a serious defeat, which the victorious Athenians marked by using the ransom money to have a bronze four-horse chariot made (an emblem normally more appropriate to their opponents), which they mounted on a black Eleusinian stone base and dedicated on the Acropolis. The chariot-group was looted or destroyed by the Persians in 480–479; but it was renewed, with the same dedicatory epigram, about fifty years after the original occasion, to mark another victory over the same enemies; and fragments of both bases still survive. The Hippobotai, on the other hand, faded for a period after 506, for Athens confiscated their estates in the plain to share out among 4,000 Athenian settlers, and they went into exile. But the Eretrians continued meanwhile at peace with Athens. The gravestone of an Athenian there, dated (on script) perhaps c. 525, reads: 'Here lies Chairion, an Athenian of the Eupatridai'. This might imply an exile from Peisistratid Athens; but the Eretrians had supported Peisistratos, so the stone may only attest an old family *xenia*, with no political involvement. Eretria held aloof from Thebes and Chalkis in 506, and perhaps served as a corridor to connect Attica with the 4,000 Athenian settlers now in Euboia. Her disaster came in the early fifth century, when, after her support in 499 of her old ally Miletos, in 490 on its way to Marathon the Persian fleet under Datis sacked and depopulated her.[5]

NOTES

1 Thebes and Chalkis: Hdt. 5. 74,77: Athens and Eretria: Hdt. 6. 100. Eretrian control of islands: Str. 448. Lefkandi: M. Popham and L. Sackett, *Excavations at Lefkandi, Euboea, 1964–66* (1968); and cf. V. Desborough, *The Greek Dark Ages* (1972), 367. Old Eretria: K. Schefold, *Ant. Kunst* 7 (1964), 102 ff., 9 (1966), 106 ff., 11 (1968), 91 ff., 12 (1969), 72 ff. Copper-mines: allegedly including iron, Str. 447. G. Huxley (by letter) recalls *Ox. Pap.* 30. 2526 (Λήλαντον δ' ὅρος καὶ πόλις) as a possible identification of the site at Lefkandi, alternative to Old Eretria. Abantes: *Il.* 2. 536–7, 542–4. For Al Mina, the early Greek trading port at the mouth of the Orontes discovered by Sir Leonard Woolley, see most recently J. Boardman, *The Greeks Overseas*[2] (1973), 37 ff. Boardman first demonstrated that the early Greek pottery identified there as Cycladic is in fact Euboic (*BSA* 52 (1957), 5 ff. and *Anatolian Studies* 9 (1959), 163 ff.). Desborough (*Greek Dark Ages*, 199) notes that by the first half of the 9th c. gold, ivory, and faience objects – all imports from the eastern Mediterranean – appear in the tombs at Lefkandi. Pithekoussai, see G. Buchner in *Arch. Reports* (1970–71), 63 ff.; the ancient sources on this site and Kyme are collected in J. Bérard, *La Colonisation grecque de l'Italie méridionale et de la Sicile*[2] (1957), 37 ff. Eretrians at Kerkyra: Plut., *QG* 11. Naxos, Leontinoi, Katane, Zankle: Thuc. 6. 3; Rhegion, 6. 43. Ortygia and Arethousa: Str. 449, Schol. *Il.* 9. 557. Chalkis in Aitolia: Thuc. 1. 108.

2 The war: Thuc. 1. 15. The modern view that it was overseas colonizing and trade which brought in the large number of allies was first clearly stated by A. Blakeway in 'Greek Poetry and Life' (*Studies Presented to Gilbert Murray*, 1936), 47 ff., and is now generally accepted. Sources for the respective allies and the battle(s): Hesiod, *WD* 651–9 and scholia; Hdt. 5. 99; Str. 465; Plut., *Mor.* 153 f., 760e–761a; cf. also the helpful comments in M. L. West, *Hesiod: Theogony* (1966), 43 f. The *Certamen* alone calls Amphidamas 'basileus'; Hesiod does not, which I find decisive. On Chalkidic Pallene, the western prong, the settlers were mainly Eretrian. They *may* have come from Eretrian Methone (f. *c.* 733) across the Thermaic Gulf; we have no foundation dates. Sithonia, the central prong, was the part originally called 'the Chalkidike'; that is, these settlements were from Chalkis and thence the title spread in time over the whole peninsula. Torone, the chief settlement, is mentioned obscurely in Archilochos (F 89 West). Akte, the eastern prong, was chiefly Andrian (below, pp. 183–4), although Sane, the first settlement, was made jointly with Chalkis (Plut., *QG* 30); Akanthos and Stagiros, the next Andrian cities, were founded traditionally *c.* 655. No firm archaeological evidence for the Greek settlements in Chalkidike antedates as yet the 7th c.; see in general R. M. Cook, *JHS* 66 (1946), 77 f., and n. 94; Burn, *Lyric Age*, 93 ff.; Bradeen, *AJP* 73 (1952), 356 ff. (His suggested date for the first settlements (early 8th c.) rests on the inference that they *must* have preceded Chalkis' Western settlements.) On the importance of Pharsalos as the main southern entry to Thessaly, see Gomme in *HCT* i. 324 (on Thuc. 1. 111) and J. Morrison, *CQ* 36 (1942), 61 ff. On the route through Thessaly to Chalkidike, Thuc. 4. 78; on the short sea-passage Euboia–Trachis and the route thence up to Thrace, Thuc. 3. 92–3. Menon and his aid to Athens in 477(?): Dem. 13. 23 and 23. 199; see below, p. 72.

3 Archil. F 3 West. It is differently interpreted by those scholars who hold that the war ended with the battle *c.* 700 (see n. 4 below). *Ox. Pap.* 2508, a fragment of a poem in elegiacs ascribed tentatively to Archilochos, refers to a battle and to Eretria and Karystos. If Archilochos is indeed the author, one could use this as further support for a flare-up in the 7th c. and attach it to *FGH* 26 F 4.24 (Konon, 1st c. A.D.), which says that at some early date Leodamas of Miletos (Eretria's ally) defeated Karystos and Melos. The inscribed stele: Str. 448. Its authenticity was doubted by Forrest

(*Historia* 6 (1957), 163 f.), basically because he argues on other grounds that the war ended *c.* 700, an impossibly early date, as he rightly says, for an inscribed pact. Kerinthos: Theognis 891–4; *oikistes* Kothos, Str. 445, 447. Potidaia as cause of the strife: Wade-Gery, *Poet of the Iliad* (1952), 61. Plains cropped for cavalry charges: cf. Hdt. 5. 63.

4 Much of the groundwork for the picture of the trade connections between states was done by A. R. Burn in a basic article, *JHS* 49 (1929), 14 ff., and, for the extent and date of the war, by Blakeway in *BSA* 33 (1932–33), 202 ff., and 'Greek Poetry and Life' (n. 2 above). For the view, originated by Blakeway, that the war ended *c.* 700 (though he admitted the possibility of the odd border struggle for the plain in the seventh century) see for its most emphatic statement, with additional matter, Forrest, *Historia* 6 (1957), 160 ff., with references to earlier holders of this view; cf. also West, *Hesiod: Theogony*, 43 f.; Coldstream, *GGP*, 368 ff.; and (a judicious summing-up) Dover in *HCT* iv. 216. Chalkis and Eretria 'mostly in agreement': Str. 448; he may have been influenced by *Il.* 2. 536–44 (where Chalkis and Eretria are both led by Elephenor), and by their connections, to which he refers, with schools of philosophy in the 4th c. and later. The 'agreement' could well have existed in the 5th c. and later, when both places had lost their military importance; both (e.g.) were at one in revolting against Athens in 446. The other modern view (here maintained) of a long period of intermittent war was well argued by Boardman (*BSA* 52, 5 ff.), whose cogent study of Eretrian and Chalkidic pottery demonstrated that Eretria was influential still in the seventh and sixth centuries, whereas Chalkis made a much less impressive showing.

5 Allies: on Sparta see Forrest, *Historia* 6, 162; on Argos, Bradeen, *TAPA* 78 (1947), 226 ff. (cf. Forrest, *Historia* 6, 160 n.4). The Chalkis–Samos tie still held in the late 4th c. B.C., when Antileon of Chalkis rescued some Samians condemned in Athens, 'maintaining the existing friendship between Chalkidians and Samians' (Ch. Habicht, *AM* 72 (1957), 156 ff., no. 1). Aristotle on cavalry: *Pol.* 1289b, 1297b; on the latter passage see Andrewes, *The Greek Tyrants*, 34 f. Cavalry tactics in the 6th c.: Hdt. 1. 63; 5. 63; 8. 28, and in general J. K. Anderson, *Ancient Greek Horsemanship* (1961), P. A. L. Greenhalgh, *Early Greek Warfare* (1973), chs. 5–6, M. Frederiksen, *Dialoghi di Archeologia* 2 (1968), 1 ff. Tynnondas: Plut., *Sol.* 14. (Phoxos and Antileon, two separate tyrants in Chalkis (Arist., *Pol.* 1304a, 1316a), are undated.) 'Chalkidic' pottery: R. M. Cook, *Greek Painted Pottery*[2] (1972), 158. Swords: Alkaios F 167P (below, p. 239). Peisistratos' allies: Hdt. 1. 61–2; 5. 74–7. The Athenian victory and dedication: the base-fragments, Meiggs and Lewis no. 15. Athenian settlers: Hdt. 5. 77. Chairion: *IG* xii. 9, 926; cf. Raubitschek, *ÖJh.* 31 (1938), Beibl., 46, and J. Davies, *Athenian Propertied Families* (1971), 13. Datis and Eretria: Hdt. 6. 100–1.

6 Thessaly, Phokis, the Lokrides, Boiotia: the First Sacred War and its Aftermath

Thessaly and the Anthelan Amphiktiony

Thessaly, the largest fertile plain in Greece, is watered by the river Peneios and hedged by mountains, except at the Pass of Tempe in the north-east, where the river has breached the barrier and connected the plain with the Aegean coast.

The Thessaloi were north-westerners who had arrived in this rich land, dispossessing the Boiotoi, traditionally 'sixty years' (two generations) after the Fall of Troy. The Boiotoi moved south and found a settled home in another rich plain (below, pp. 77–8). Others of the existing population filtered across the Aegean and settled on Lesbos, extending thence to the adjacent mainland Aiolis. Others stayed and fused with the newcomers; others also stayed, but formed an extended populace (*perioikis*) round the newcomers by withdrawing into the surrounding hill country, that is, Perrhaibia, where Mount Olympos lay; Magnesia, the eastern promontory holding Pelion and Ossa; and Achaia Phthiotis, which had been Achilles' country, on the south.

Thessaly proper, the great central plain, was divided into four cantons called *tetrades* (quarters), controlled by ruling families. The Aleuadai of Larissa and the Skopadai of Krannon were in Pelasgiotis, which preserved the name of the Pelasgoi, an aboriginal people once more widely spread over Greece; in Phthiotis were the Echekratidai of Pharsalos, the first city encountered by those entering Thessaly from the south. Thessaliotis and Hestiaiotis, less central, were less important. Local tradition said that the original Aleuas I of Larissa, eponym of his clan and of uncertain date, had first quartered Thessaly, had laid upon each family's estate a levy of forty horse and eighty foot, and had been the first *tagos*, a Thessalian title which other Greeks translated as *basileus*. Exactly how this office arose we do not know. Possibly when the incoming clans first settled in the plain, they elected, or already had, a single leader; but the plain is very wide, and it may be that originally they all settled down in scattered clumps, each under its local headman, and only recognized a common *tagos* when the head of some family in one tetrad came to the top at a time of common crisis, and continued to hold chief authority for as long as the family could retain it thereafter. The *tagos* was essentially a war leader, who controlled the levies from all Thessaly. The *perioikoi* in the hill-country provided *peltastai* (light-armed soldiers carrying the *pelta*, a smaller shield than the *aspis*) and, at least in Classical times, paid taxes as did the *perioikoi* of other Greek states. The

Penestai, peculiar to Thessaly, are described by ancient authors as serf-types like the Spartan Helots or the Cretan Mnoia; they may have been survivors of the original Pelasgoi. Their labour enabled the Thessalian families to manage their big baronial estates. The local climate favoured the survival of aristocracy, for this great plain is subject to extremes of summer heat and winter cold, a severe risk for the small independent farmer without reserves to tide him over hard times. The Penestai were trained for war by their masters; in the fifth century Menon of Pharsalos brought 200 Penestai horsemen from his estate to help the Athenians fighting in Thrace (above, p. 65).

Thessaly, this loose federation of the four *tetrades* and the *perioikis*, was in effect a *dunasteia*, since a comparatively small number of families controlled everything – as in Bacchiad Corinth, pre-Solonic Athens, and indeed most of early Greece; the difference being that Thessaly was still a *dunasteia* late in the fifth century. In her retention of archaic customs she was a fine survival of the Homeric-type aristocracy (Pl. 6). Eastern Thessalians retained in their dialect -οι from the original -οιο for the second declension genitive as in epic; and in common with other Aiolic districts Thessaly continued to use the old patrony-mic adjective in -ιος, as, for example, Telamonios Aias in the *Iliad*. One festival included bull-baiting of some kind (*taurokathapsia*), a spectacle also preserved in some of the cities in Aiolis. The Thessalians were also famous charioteers, a skill for which they and the Boiotians were still noted in the fifth century; the chariots which other wealthy Greeks entered for the great Games were sometimes driven by a Thessalian or Boiotian professional (below, p. 78). Horses were their great interest; the proud title *dikaios* (the Just), elsewhere associated with statesmen or philosopher-kings, in Thessaly was borne by a good brood-mare of Pharsalos, whose foals all resembled their sires. The trailing chiton worn by charioteers in races and processions was said to be the old Thessalian dress, and the centaurs, bred among the high woods and fierce freshets on Mount Pelion, were Thessaly's great contribution to Greek mythology. 'Hospitable and magnificent' (φιλόξενος καὶ μεγαλοπρεπής) – that, according to Xenophon, was the typical Thessalian. Their Homeric outlook on life extended to their powers of cooking, eating, and drinking. Thessalian meals were famous for their quantity, but not their quality; indeed, a non-Thessalian once went so far as to regard this food as the Greeks' secret weapon against Persia in 480: a few more of those meals with the rulers of Thessaly on the way down through Greece, he said, and the Persians would have been past fighting any battles.[1]

By the end of the sixth century Thessaly was an active ally of Athens (below, p. 77). How had her ambition and influence spread so far south? We have seen that in the Lelantine War, about 700 (above, p. 65), the southern tetrad Phthiotis took some part, for Kleomachos of Pharsalos brought troops to aid Chalkis, where he was said to lie buried with all honours. This may well mean no more than that a guest-friendship (*xenia*) existed between the Echekratidai of Pharsalos and the family of Amphidamas of Chalkis (though this Thessalian aid has also been interpreted as a pan-Thessalian move towards expansion southwards). But certainly from early times Thessaly did have a share in an ancient Amphiktiony ('dwellers-round') centred on the cult of Demeter at Anthela. Anthela lay on the coast of Malis south of Thessaly, in Trachinian country; behind her rose Mount Oita, where Herakles had died. This was the locality of Thermopylai ('hot gates,' that is the place of hot springs and cavernous entrances to Hades). The twelve delegates to the Amphiktiony met in spring and autumn, and were entitled Pylagorai ('gate-assemblers'), perhaps a reference to the local Gates of Hades, since Demeter was a chthonic goddess in many of her oldest local cults. The immediate dwellers-round, presumably the original members, were the small states Ainis, Malis, and Doris. Achaia Phthiotis, almost as near, was also a member, and this was probably what paved the way for the entry of the body of which she was a perioecic limb, namely the four tetrads of Thessaly proper *plus* the other perioecic districts Perrhaibia and Magnesia. The Dolopes, further outside the circle, were also members, perhaps at Thessaly's urging; clearly she was the largest controller of votes. There was also an 'Ionic' member, presumably northern Euboia, which here ranges close to the Malian coast; eastern Lokris was also a member, and the two states south of her, Phokis and Boiotia. Thus the full number of voters was twelve; but the last two at least, the remotest, may have joined only during, or after, the First Sacred War.[2]

The War and the Delphic Amphiktiony

This war (*c.* 595–586) centred on Delphi, well to the south of Thessaly; but a Thessalian army was deeply involved. The alleged cause of the war was Kirrha (or Krisa), the Phokian city which controlled the port Itea on the Gulf of Corinth. To this port came most of those seeking the oracle. They disembarked to climb the winding road up to Pytho, the traditional name for the actual sanctuary. This was for long the obvious and simplest route from the south, east, or west, until the modern roads from Athens to Delphi were blasted over the spurs of the mountains. Kirrha throve on these visitors; indeed, until the war she was apparently in recognized control of the holy site itself, for the early Homeric *Hymn to Apollo* tells how Apollo in person and the Cretans whom he ordained to form his first priesthood there (below, pp. 191–2) all came up to Pytho from 'viny Krisa', having first made an altar to Apollo Delphinios on the shore of the port. Later authors add that Kirrha impiously harried pilgrims and defied the proper administrators of the oracle; whereupon a coalition of other states came to Delphi's aid. Eurylochos of Thessaly (city unspecified) led the joint attack with another Thessalian commander named Hippias. Athens also sent a force under Alkmeon, an aristocratic leader who earlier had been under a curse for sacrilege after murder by his clan (below, pp. 88–9). Kleisthenes, the tyrant of Sikyon, joined in and blockaded Itea with his ships, a feat for which he was later awarded a third of the war spoils. Kirrha fell in 591, and after five more years the last Kirrhaians were driven out of Kirphis, the sheer height which rises alongside the valley from Delphi to Itea. Kleisthenes had earlier been insulted by the oracle, which called him a 'stone-thrower' (common skirmisher) because of his anti-Argive policy (below, p. 164); moreover, the annihilation of Itea presumably benefited the port of Sikyon, opposite it on the Gulf. Athens too may have had a good reason to want Kirrhaian control ended and another local party set up to control the oracle, duly grateful and favourable to its Alkmeonid benefactors. The rich plain of Kirrha, which today is a solid sea of olive-groves in the Pleistos valley, was ravaged and declared to be sacred pastureland for ever, feeding the flocks which were to be sacrificed to Apollo. The Pythian festival, hitherto a simple affair of citharodes singing paians to the god, was developed by Eurylochos into an international contest rating second only to Olympia. For the first reorganized Pythia (586) valuable prizes were given from the war spoils. At the next (582) and thereafter the prizes were crowns of laurel, said in one tradition to be from the laurel-trees in Thessalian Tempe. In that year also they instituted chariot-races as at Olympia, and Eurylochos and Kleisthenes, both from horse-breeding states, won prizes.

The split within Phokis which had in fact caused one side to call in the Amphiktiony and thus to start the war is revealed to us in the *Hymn to Apollo*. The oracle at Pytho, with all its potential for prosperity, seems to have been originally in the hands of a Cretan priesthood with the local support of Kirrha, and the *Hymn* says (in lines presumably inserted after the outcome of the war) that vengeance will come on this priesthood and end it. Those who had favoured it were now disgraced, and the reformed Phokis was now a member of the Amphiktiony. Thessaly must have been a part of it before 595, for only this could explain her leadership in a war which was fought so far to her south; she and her *perioikis* had four votes in all, and the wishes of the small or straggling districts of Ainis, Malis, Doris, and the Dolopes will have followed discreetly on hers. As a result of the war the Anthelan body was known thenceforth as the Delphic Amphiktiony, and became the official overseer and military defender of the Pythian cult. Sikyon was worked in as a second Doric representative alongside Doris, and Athens as a second Ionic. It is said that this enlargement created the system attested in the Classical period, whereby each member state had two votes.

Phokis and her two neighbours, eastern Lokris and Boiotia, were now in an awkward position, for henceforth they could be pincered *en bloc* between Thessaly, whetted by her successful southern venture, and Athens on the Boiotian border. It may have been now that Phokis built a wall across the narrow defile at Thermopylai to keep the Thessalians out; and a strange and revealing reflection of anti-Thessalian feeling in these states survives in the short Boiotian epic falsely ascribed to Hesiod, called *The Shield of Herakles*, which modern scholarship has recognized as a pastiche, composed as propaganda. It was made to be sung at a Boiotian festival in midsummer, 'at the hottest time of the dogstar Sirios', and tells of an exploit of Herakles son of Zeus, born to Alkmene, wife of the Theban lord Amphitryon, whose troops were 'shield-bearing Kadmeioi [men of Thebes itself] and horsewhipping Boiotians blaring above their shields [that is, protected by their shields from chin to chariot-rail], followed by close-fighting Lokrians and great-hearted Phokians'. The poem tells how the Boiotian hero Herakles fought and killed a local Thessalian hero from Pagasai, Kyknos son of Ares, who had raided the cattle which were being driven south to Pytho for the hecatombs to Apollo. The Thessalian, interfering with the Phokian sanctuary, is killed by the Boiotian hero, whose mortal father had for allies Lokrians and Phokians. The date of the poem, therefore, may be shortly after the Sacred War, and its core an old story now deliberately given a contemporary political twist. The hostility of Thessaly to this cluster of states is amply attested later (below, pp. 76–9).[3]

The Lokrides and Phokis: Later Relations with Thessaly

The states of Phokis and the two Lokrides had been formed by the continuous pressure of the southward movement in these parts during the Dark Age. The Boiotians spoke a version of the Aiolic dialect of Thessaly whence they had migrated; but between Thessaly and Boiotia the Lokrians infiltrated, whose dialect was the north-western, and they in their turn were split permanently apart into an eastern and a western Lokris by the Phokians, who pushed between and settled in the valley of the river Kephisos. Eastern Lokris, pressed against the sea-coast, and by herself no match for the Phokians, usually sided with them, as the *Shield of Herakles* shows – and, indeed, the Phokian wall at Thermopylai, which was in Lokrian territory.

Once physically separated by Phokis, eastern and western Lokris diverged in further ways. The western Lokrians were mainly hill-dwellers living in independent settlements, but their modest harbours on the Gulf of Corinth had ties with the world outside. Of all these harbours that of Naupaktos was potentially the greatest asset, for whichever Greek power held this strategic point on the Lokrian boundary was in a fair way to control the western exit from the Gulf. We know very little as yet of the history of Naupaktos in the Archaic period; in the early fifth century the eastern Lokrians sent settlers there to consolidate the position, and about the middle of that century the Athenians, well aware of its military and commercial importance, seized it from the Lokrians, gave it to a force of Messenian hoplites who were exiles after a great revolt from Sparta, and thus secured for Athens an independent but devoted ally of the greatest value in the two Peloponnesian wars of the fifth century. In Oiantheia, another Lokrian harbour, a citizen named Menekrates son of Tlesias was *proxenos* for Kerkyra in the late seventh or early sixth century, which indicates some traffic with the Western colonies; indeed, Lokroi Epizephyrioi, founded *c.* 673 on the southern coast of Italy, used the local script of western Lokris, so the bulk of her settlers probably came thence. Menekrates was drowned off the coast of Kerkyra; the Kerkyreans sent for his brother Praximenes, and commemorated their *proxenos* with a splendid tumulus, still visible at Kastrádes, outside the modern city of Corfu, bearing a long and grateful epitaph inscribed on its stone revetment.

In eastern Lokris the settlements formed a kind of sympolity at some early date, as did the demes of Attica. Like Athens, one town, Opous, was the head and centre of government. Hence they were called sometimes Opountioi, or more generally the Lokrians 'under Mount Knemis' (Hypoknemidioi). Like the Attic Eupatridai, the aristocracy was formed by a select number of families, here called the Hundred Households. The assembly of all voting citizens was called the Thousand. Members from the Hundred were among the emigrants sent to Lokroi Epizephyrioi, and western Lokris too may have had an ancestral tradition of the Hundred, for eastern Lokris was regarded as the original source of *all* Lokrians. The Lokrian founding hero, Ajax Oïleus, had belonged to Naryka in eastern Lokris, where a family named Aianteioi still lived in the third century

B.C.; and in the fifth century the settlers sent from eastern Lokris to Naupaktos were exempted from paying any taxes to eastern Lokris, 'except in common with the west Lokrians'.

The hereditary oligarchy of the Hundred and the Thousand continued in the Classical period. Another survival said to be from early times was the savage custom whereby the Lokrian Maidens, two girls from the Hundred, had to be sent periodically to Troy in an appalling scapegoat ritual through 'a thousand years of atonement' for the crime committed by Aias against the Trojan Athena. The law code preserved in the Western colony of Lokroi Epizephyrioi was likewise very old. This colony was probably, as we have seen, a western Lokrian venture, but eastern Lokrians may well have swelled the number of settlers, particularly as 'Lokrians' are attested also at Abantis, a colony in Illyria originally founded from eastern Lokris' neighbour Euboia. The famous law code was the work of Zaleukos (fl. c. 660); and thus colonial Greeks produced one of the earliest Greek law codes. It was not the earliest, for one of its sources is said to have been Crete (see pp. 43, 202, n.7). We deduce from surviving accounts that the laws were simple and uncompromising, in the Archaic manner: for example, anyone who proposed to alter an existing law, or appealed against a judge's decision, was faced with death by strangling if he lost his case.[1]

Phokis, the state which separated the two Lokrides, continued her fierce resistance to Thessaly's encroachment through the sixth century. Herodotos says that she soundly defeated invading Thessalian forces, horse and foot separately, in two engagements 'not long before' 480. The horsemen were beaten in the pass into eastern Phokis at Hyampolis near Abai, where the Phokians had sunk wide-mouthed pots into the ground to bring down the horses. The soldiers were defeated below the eastern slopes of Mount Parnassos, where the Phokians had gathered for refuge; Tellias, an Elean seer acting for them in their campaign, advised them to whiten their bodies like ghosts and attack by night, thus recognizing their own side in the dark, but causing the Thessalian camp to panic. (Later authors offer more details of these, or else of a possible third campaign: that Phokis had actually been a dependency of Thessaly under governors, whom they rose against and massacred, thus provoking an invasion by the Thessalian army, which they met and defeated under two Phokian leaders and the seer Tellias, after suffering a sharp defeat themselves under Gelon, another leader.)

We are not told how long they had been subject to Thessaly before these great victories. Another late account says that one Lattamyas of Thessaly led a force southward as far as the hill-fort Keressos near Thespiai in southern Boiotia, where he was repulsed and killed. This is dated in one version 'over 200 years before the battle of Leuktra' (371 B.C.), which, if right, would mean that, to get into Boiotia, Thessaly had subdued Phokis before 571. But an alternative view puts this Boiotian victory at Keressos not long before 480. This seems preferable, for it could then be a prelude to the bigger Thessalian disaster in Phokis, recorded by Herodotos. He adds that in 480 the Thessalians still tried to make the Phokians obey them and let the Persians through; at which the Phokians, though pinned between the Medizers Thessaly and Boiotia, immediately determined to resist the Persians.

In the second half of the sixth century, before the disasters mentioned above, Thessaly had evidently felt that she could now command a passage down through central Greece whenever necessary; for at some time between 546 and 510 she made an alliance with the tyrannic dynasty of Peisistratos and his sons in Athens, and one son was named Thessalos. The Thessalian ruling families would be sympathetic with the principle of one-family rule in a city, and Athens was a member of the Delphic Amphiktiony. Shortly before 510, when Sparta was threatening to evict the Peisistratid dynasty, the Thessalians honoured the alliance. A thousand Thessalian horsemen under the *tagos* Kineas arrived in Attica, and when the Spartans duly came in by ship to Phaleron and landed there, the Thessalians heavily defeated them in a charge across the plain. But the next Spartan force to arrive, led by their king Kleomenes and marching up by land, routed the horsemen, who withdrew swiftly back to Thessaly. The Phokian and Boiotian victories over Thessaly may have followed soon afterwards, for by this time many of the Boiotian cities were banded in a federation under the leadership of Thebes.[5]

Boiotia

The Aiolic-speaking Greeks of Boiotia had moved there from Thessaly 'sixty years after the Fall of Troy', to this area whose early wealth and power is shown by the reputations and visible Mycenean remains of several of the cities, notably Orchomenos in the north and Thebes in the south. There was some poor hill-country here too; the poet Hesiod, born in Askra on Mount Helikon, illustrates the hardness of peasant life there in his *Works and Days*, and his father had once tried emigration across to Kyme in Aiolic Asia Minor. But parts of Boiotia have good arable soil of a dark purplish colour, a contrast for travellers coming from the red Attic countryside. Lake Copais, drained in 1909, now provides more flat, rich plains. In ancient times it supplied abundance of eels and other fish. Moreover, from the several modest harbours on her two coasts Boiotia could tap three routes to great foreign markets – one through the Corinthian Gulf to the Greek West, and two from the Euripos channel, either northward to Macedon and Thrace or south-eastward through the Cyclades for Cyprus or Egypt.

But Boiotia as a whole remained an agricultural state. Thebes held the dominant position, for here the chief road down from northern Greece, having come through Phokis, branched several ways, one route going down to Megara and the Peloponnese, another to Attica, another eastwards to Aulis and the short crossing to Chalkis. A series of coins struck by many of the cities, starting (at earliest) in the late sixth century, shows the 'Boiotian' figure-of-eight shield on the obverse, and on the reverse the initial letter of the city's name. This clearly implies a league coinage of some kind, whether the coins were struck for the festival of the Pamboiotia at the old sanctuary of Athena Itonia near Koroneia or to denote a secular federation. We cannot date the start of the Pamboiotia; Athena Itonia should be a very early deity, since her epithet betrays the Thessalian origin of the cult, though the earliest surviving records of the festival belong to the third century B.C. But even if this coinage was merely a festival issue, it is highly likely that Archaic Thebes, given her geographic position and her Bronze Age fame, took every chance which arose to gain influence over the other cities, especially those nearest to herself, for many years before she succeeded in forming a lasting federation towards the end of the sixth century. Such efforts probably took up most of her energies through the century, with little time to spare for any active foreign policy. Indeed, much of that policy in the Archaic period must have concerned Boiotia's northern border and the encroaching power of Thessaly. Moreover, quarrelling among the Boiotian cities was proverbial, a state of affairs in which none would care to send her troops to some state beyond the Boiotian borders, if thereby she risked denuding her own walls of defenders. Thebes played no part in the Lelantine War of the late eighth century and perhaps later, though certainly she and Chalkis had a military alliance in 506, if not earlier (above, p. 68). Though far from Anthela, Boiotia may have been an early member of the old religious Amphiktiony because her people had originally dwelt in Thessaly; later she was certainly a member of the Delphic Amphiktiony. But even if she belonged to either (or both) at the time of the Sacred War waged over Delphi in the early sixth century, she seems to have played no part in the fighting and power politics on that occasion. Possibly the Boiotians already distrusted the Thessalians at the time. Certainly they had no particular reason for visiting the Delphic oracle, for in Boiotia itself there were many old and famous cults of Apollo (Pl. 7) with many epithets – Ismenios at Thebes, Ptoios at Akraiphia, Karykeios at Tanagra – and some famous oracles too: Trophonios at Lebadeia, Amphiaraos at Oropos, as well as the oracular Apolline cults (the Ismenian and Ptoian). Thebes herself certainly supported Kleisthenes of Sikyon, a leader of the Sacred War, in his anti-Argive policy, by sending him on request the sacred relics of her Bronze Age hero Melanippos, who in the saga of the Seven against Thebes had killed the Argive champions Tydeus and Mekisteus; but this was diplomatic support, not military. Again, about 556–546 Theban individuals gave more wealth than any others to the Athenian ex-tyrant Peisistratos when he was collecting troops and funds to force his way back to Attica (below, p. 95); but they sent no troops themselves. Among Peisistratos' Attic opponents, duly exiled when he secured Athens again about 546, were the clan of the Alkmeonidai. One of these, Alkmeonides son of Alkmeon, made a dedication in the Ptoion at Akraiphia in the hill-country north of Thebes, to commemorate a chariot victory won by him at the Panathenaia at Athens, in which his charioteer had been a Boiotian named Knopion or Knopiadas. If the dedicatory inscription is correctly dated *c.* 540–530, this suggests that Akraiphia was not yet dependent on pro-Peisistratid Thebes – that is if we infer that Alkmeonides only made his dedication at Akraiphia because he was in exile from Peisistratid Athens. But not many years later Akraiphia was evidently on the Theban side, for Hipparchos (killed in 514), son of Peisistratos and brother of the tyrant Hippias, also made a dedication there. In any case, not all Alkmeonids were anti-Peisistratos, for at least one (Kleisthenes) was back in Athens and elected archon in 525 (below, p. 96).

Thus Thessaly and Thebes both appear to have backed the tyranny at Athens, but Thebes only unofficially. She was forming the Boiotian League probably by the last quarter of the sixth century, and Thessaly's aggressive attitude may have been one reason why Thebes found cities willing to join. Tanagra, Thespiai (the area of the Thessalian defeat at Keressos), and Koroneia were certainly members at this time; but in 519 Plataia defied her and joined Athens. This could not but turn Thebes to an anti-Attic policy. She was clearly hostile by 506, four years after the tyranny had fallen at Athens, for she joined Chalkis then to attack Attica. The end of this campaign was a great victory for Athens (below, p. 104); but the Thebans then made alliance with Athens's old enemy Aigina, and harried the northern Attic border while Aiginetan ships harried the coast. In the Persian War of 480–479 Thebes sided with Persia. Two generations later she offered the defence that at the time she had still been governed in the Archaic manner by a small circle of families (*dunasteia*), whose natural affinities, like those of the Thessalian leaders, had been with the horse-breeding aristocrats of Persia[6] (Pl. 5).

The Heroic Tradition of Funeral Games

Among the 'Homeric' customs preserved in these Aiolic aristocracies and their close neighbours, including Euboia, funeral games deserve a special mention. Many Greek states held periodic sacrifices with games (ἀγῶνες ἱππικοὶ καὶ γυμνικοί) in honour of past heroes, renowned or shadowy, of the time of the Trojan War or even earlier; indeed, the four Panhellenic festivals were all said to have such an origin, although the sixth-century establishers of the Pythia, Nemeia, and Isthmia may have simply copied the older Olympic tradition (below, p. 152). Perhaps it is only by chance that the two famous Games for dead heroes which survive in early Greek poetry both have a Thessalian connection (those held for Patroklos by Achilles in *Iliad* 23, and those for Pelias father of Alkestis in Stesichoros' poem *Athla epi Peliai*) and that the first games commemorating a mortal man of which we hear are those held for a leader killed in the Lelantine War – Amphidamas of Chalkis, a place with strong Thessalian connections at the time (Hesiod, *Works and Days* 654–9; cf. above, p. 65). But it is certain that the surviving epigraphic and literary records of games held to commemorate the deaths of real persons come nearly all from the Greeks north of the Corinthian Gulf and from their settlements overseas; and the earliest and most remarkable of these are some fragmentary bronze cauldrons or tripod-bowls bearing Boiotian inscriptions and dating from c. 700 into the sixth century. Tripods, cauldrons, and other bronze vessels were standard prizes for various contests in these games, as both epic and vase-painting make clear. The descriptive formula inscribed on them is recognizable from the key-words and phrases: ἆθλον (a prize), or τὰ ἆθλα (the games), ἐπί + dative, *over* the (dead) man. One fragment appears to list the names of several dead warriors, and others give also the name of the donor of the prize; and, as Hesiod on his return from Chalkis dedicated his tripod to the Muses on his native Helikon, so five of these Boiotian cauldrons were dedicated on the Athenian Acropolis, presumably by Athenians who had crossed the Boiotian border to compete – perhaps at Thebes, as did a man from Troizen across the Saronic Gulf, whose epitaph, perhaps c. 550 or some years later, says that his

mother set on the pillar marking his grave the tripod 'which he won in a race at
Thebes'. Outside mainland Greece a tomb in Chalkis' colony Kyme in Italy has
produced a bronze bowl (*c.* 500), a prize from the games for one Onomastos; in
the Aiolic parts flanking the Hellespont, Lampsakos (a Phokaian colony) had
games for one Leophantos in the fifth century (perhaps earlier), and in the
Thracian Chersonese, whose earliest Greek settlements were both Aiolic and
Attic, the Athenian Miltiades I was honoured by funeral games *c.* 525(?), as was
also the Spartan general Brasidas in 422 at Amphipolis in Thrace. Miltiades and
Brasidas were regarded as *oikistai*, and so would receive the chthonic sacrifices
due to heroes; but not all *oikistai* had funeral games as well. In these two cases,
however, perhaps the Thracian barbarians retained the primitive notion not
only of honouring but also of placating the dead by these observances.[7]

NOTES

1 Arrival of Thessaloi: Thuc. 1. 12,3. Aleuas I: dated *c.* 700? by Wade-Gery, *JHS* 44 (1924), 57 ff.; *c.* 630, J. Morrison, *CQ* 36 (1942), 61 and J. Larsen, *CP* 55 (1960), 229 ff.; but in the late 6th c. by M. Sordi, *La Lega tessalica fino ad Alessandro Magno* (1958), 65 ff. Larsen holds that a feudal kingdom of all Thessaly was established at the time of the settlement, and that the office of *tagos* 'was probably elective from the start, or at least by the last part of the seventh century'; he suggests further that under this 'strong elective kingship' was 'an assembly controlled by the nobles, to elect the king and other high officials and to decide important questions of foreign policy' (*Greek Federal States* (1968), 14,20). I have preferred the view that in the Archaic period the office of *tagos* was not necessarily permanent, but rather the product of emergency. *Tagoi* of all Thessaly: see Hdt. 5. 63,3; 7. 6,2. In Thetonion in the 5th c. (Buck, 225 f., no. 35) 'the *tagos* in charge' is to enforce a law when necessary. This might imply that the office at least was permanent, whichever powerful family might monopolize it at the time; but some scholars see this phrase as referring to a local, not a pan-Thessalian, official; see Buck, loc. cit. Menon of Pharsalos: see above, p. 69, n.2. *Dunasteia* in 424 B.C.: Thuc. 4. 78,3. Dialect: Buck, 88, 151 (genitive) and 202, no. 32 (patronymic adj.). The *taurokathapsia* ('bull-grasping'): see Schol. Pind. *Pyth.* 2. 78 (Thessaly), *CIG* 3212 (Smyrna), *IGRom* 4460 (Pergamon). Thessalian horses: Hdt. 7. 196. *Dikaia*: Arist., *Pol.* 1362a. Hospitality: Xen., *Hell.* 6. 1,3.

2 Early pan-Thessalian drive for power southwards: this is especially the view of Larsen (*CP* 55 (1960), 229 ff.; *Greek Federal States*, 108 ff.), to whom the reconstruction of early Thessalian history owes much. His interpretation of Kleomachos' aid (which, however, he dates in the early 6th c.) hinges on the belief that the Thessalians came right down by land to Boiotia and thence across to Chalkis, because obviously they could not have brought their horses all the way from Pagasai to Chalkis by sea; but see above, p. 69, n. 2 for the short, easy sea-passage from Trachis to northern Euboia. *Amphiktiones* = 'dwellers around (a cult-centre)'. On the Anthelan Amphiktiony see in general Glotz-Cohen, *Histoire grecque* I (1926), 254 f. The connection between hot springs and entrances to Hades was well shown by J. Croon, *The Herdsman of the Dead* (1952).

3 First Sacred War: ancient evidence and date, Kallisthenes, *FGH* 124 F 1; Aeschin. 3. 107–12; Marm. Par. *FGH* 239 ep.37. I follow here the interpretation of the war by Wade-Gery, *Essays*, 17 ff. and W. G. Forrest, *BCH* 80 (1956), 33 ff., the latter esp. on the motives of the states which fought it. Pythian festival: Marm. Par., loc. cit. For the view that Delphi, if not Phokis as a whole, was a member of the Anthelan Amphiktiony already in the 7th c. see H. W. Parke, *The Delphic Oracle* I, 117 ff. Early connection of Crete with Delphi: below, pp. 191–2. Phokian wall at Thermopylai: Hdt. 7. 176,3–5: 215; Burn (*Lyric Age*, 200) holds that it was built *before* the Sacred War. For the interpretation of the *Shield* see R. Ducat, *REG* 77 (1964), 283 ff. A TAQ for the poem is provided by Stesichoros (if his date is *c.* 600–550), who ascribed it to Hesiod.

4 For the view that Phokis tried to hold the eastern Lokrians actually in subjection see Larsen, *Greek Federal States*, 41 f. Eastern Lokrians in Naupaktos: Meiggs and Lewis no. 20; Messenians settled there by Athenians, Thuc. 1. 103,3. Menekrates of Oiantheia: Meiggs and Lewis no. 4 and M. Wallace, *Phoenix* 24 (1970), 190 ff. The Hundred Houses: Polyb. 12. 5,7. The Thousand: see Meiggs and Lewis no. 20, lines 39–40. Larsen (*Greek Federal States*, 53) rightly insists that the Thousand came from all eastern Lokris, not from Opous only. The Aianteioi: *DGE* 366, a decree setting forth the ritual for the Lokrian Maidens *c.* 275–240 B.C. Taxes paid to eastern Lokris: Meiggs and Lewis no. 20, lines 10–11. For a full discussion, with the earlier

bibliography, of the historical background of the ritual of the Lokrian Maidens see G. Huxley in *Anc. Soc. and Inst.*, 147 ff.; he concludes that the maidens were chosen from both the Lokrides, and that the start of the custom was roughly between 750 and 675, its end shortly before Plutarch's time (*Mor.* 557c). Abantis: R. Beaumont, *JHS* 56 (1936), 164 f. Zaleukos' code: cf. Dem. 24. 139–40; Polyb. 12. 16; and for a full discussion Dunbabin, *The Western Greeks*, 68 ff.

5 Phokis against Thessaly: Hdt. 8. 27–8; Aesch. 2. 140; Plut., *De mul. virt.* 2 (=*Mor.* 244a-e); Paus. 10. 1–2. Lattamyas' campaign: Plut., *De Her. mal.* 33 and *Camill.* 19 (which dates it 200 years before 371 B.C.); and (possibly) Paus. 9. 14. Advocates for the late date of these events (end of 6th or early 5th c.) are M. Sordi, *Riv. Fil.* 31 (1953), 235 ff. and *La Lega tessalica*, 85 ff.; Larsen, *CP* 55 (1960), 229 ff.; Moretti, *Ricerche sulle leghe greche* (1962), 97 ff.; Stadter, *Plutarch's Historical Methods* (1965), 34 ff.; R. Buck, *CP* 68 (1972), 94 ff. (*c.* 520?). For the opposing view see Burn, *Lyric Age*, 203 f., who would date both Lattamyas' campaign and a first battle at Hyampolis (separate from that described by Herodotos) to the first half of the 6th c., *c.* 571. Phokian defiance of Thessaly and Persia: Hdt. 8. 30. Athenian alliance: Hdt. 63–4; the epithet Koniaios given there to the *tagos* is perhaps his patronymic (cf. above, p. 72), since no Thessalian town Konia is known (Kondaios emend. Kip). Thessalos son of Peisistratos: Thuc. 1. 20, 6; 6. 55,1.

6 60 years: Thuc. 1. 12,3. On Theban history in general see P. Cloché, *Thèbes de Béotie* (1952); P. Roesch, *Thespies et la confédération béotienne* (1965), and esp. on the federation J. Ducat, *BCH* 97 (1973), 59 ff. For the dating of the federal coinage see B. Fowler, *Phoenix* 11 (1957), 167 f.; R. Buck, *CP* 68, 94; Ducat, *BCH* 97, 61 f. Both the latter argue that the federation under Thebes was not created before the last quarter of the 6th c. The Pamboiotia: Moretti, *Ricerche*, 97 ff. Cult of Athena Itonia: Sordi, *La Lega*, 6 ff. Theban cults and oracles of Apollo: Ismenios, Paus. 9. 10,2; Ptoios, 9. 23,6; Kerykeios, Buck, 228, no. 38,1 (=*LSAG*, 94 no. 5). Other oracles: Paus. 9. 39 (Trophonios); Hdt. 1. 46,49 and Paus. 1. 34,4–5 (Amphiaraos). Theban support to Kleisthenes of Sikyon: Hdt. 5. 67,2–3; to Peisistratos, Hdt. 1. 61,3. Alkmeonid dedication at the Ptoion: see most recently Ducat, *Les kouroi du Ptoion* (1971), 242 ff., no. 14, pl. 72 and M. Ebert, *Griech. Siegerepigramme* (1970), 38 ff., no. 3. For the root Knop- in Boiotian names see Ducat, *Kouroi*, 245 and for a Theban named Herodotos who drove his own chariot to victory in the Games see Pindar, *Isthm.* 1, 15. Ptoion (Akraiphia) belonging to Thebes: Paus. 9. 23,5. Archonship of Kleisthenes: Meiggs and Lewis no. 6. Dedication of Hipparchos son of Peisistratos I at the Ptoion: most recently, Ducat, *Kouroi*, 251 ff., no. 142, pls. 73–4. Tanagra, Thespiai, and Koroneia: Hdt. 5. 79,2. Plataia: ibid., 6. 108 (dated 519, Thuc. 3. 68,5 and Gomme in *HCT* ii). Thebes and Chalkis: Hdt. 5. 74,2 and 77. Aigina: ibid., 5. 80–1. *Dunasteia* still in early 5th c.: Thuc. 3. 62,3.

7 Boiotian inscriptions on cauldrons: *LSAG*, 91, nos. 3a-e (five, from the Athenian Acropolis); ibid., nos. 2a-c and 9 (from Thebes and Delphi). Troizenian epitaph: ibid., 176, no. 2; Kyme, ibid., 238, no. 8; Lampsakos, ibid., 367, no. 47. Miltiades: Hdt. 6. 138,1. Brasidas: Thuc. 5. 11,1; cf. K. Meuli, *Der griech. Agon* (1968), 57 ff.

7 Athens and Attica

The Early State and its Constitution

The Attic peninsula, forming the Athenian state, contains about one thousand square miles, an area spacious enough to enclose a great variety of persons and properties, and therefore of interests and even factions. In many parts there was good material for wealth: the rich silver-mines around Laurion, the marble of Pentelikos, excellent potter's clay from the streams of Ilissos and Kephisos, flourishing olive-yards, good timber on the mountains, and many harbours or small shelters for ships all round the long coast. But there was also poorish soil for crops everywhere except in the fertile plain which lay between Athens and Eleusis.

The variety of the countryside was echoed in the population. The inhabitants claimed Attica to be 'the oldest Ionic land', and certainly the evidence of their dialect, tribal names, and religious cults indicates that their ethnic ties overall were not with the Aiolic-speaking Boiotians on their northern boundary nor the Doric Megarians on their south, but with the Ionic company in the Aegean; they linked up with southern Euboia and the Cyclades. On the other hand, there was still no intermarriage officially between the Attic demes Pallene and Hagnous even in the Classical period; while four others – Marathon, Oinoe, Trikorythos, and Probalinthos (below, pp. 101–2) – were bound by a common cult into a unit, the Tetrapolis, whose existence, perpetuated by the cult, may well have originated in some real tribal or even ethnic distinction from the area around them. When the Mycenean civilization had fallen, Attica served as a catchment area for *émigré* families from the Peloponnese, Boiotia, and else-where, who either settled in Attica or continued eastwards across the Aegean to colonize what came to be called Ionia, the Ionic Dodekapolis (below, p. 208) on or just offshore from the coast of Asia Minor. The Archaic Attic aristocracy had some interesting blends, judged by their own family cults and traditions. The Peisistratidai were Neleids from Messenia; the family of the tyrant-slayers Harmodios and Aristogeiton came originally from Euboia or Boiotia; and Miltiades' ancestry was believed to go back originally to Aiakos of Aigina, and thence to Philaios of Salamis, which became part of Attica in the sixth century, after long disputes with Megara.

More directly, the sheer size of the peninsula must have produced discrepant interests. The long west coast looks across the Saronic Gulf towards the Peloponnese, and perhaps it was the Athenian families living on this side who fostered the traditional connection with Troizen and the fierce rivalry with Megara for Salamis. But the families on the even longer eastern seaboard would

naturally look for expansion to the Aegean, as did their Euboic neighbour
Eretria. The process whereby the demes of Attica were fused into a general
sympolity with Athens as the official capital and seat of government seems to
have been mostly completed by *c.* 700. Athenian tradition in the late fifth
century maintained that it had been done by Theseus in the Mycenean period;
but modern scholarship suspects that, irrespective of what was Athens's actual
position in that period, the great build-up of Theseus as the Athenian national
hero was in fact a counter to the older Doric propaganda about Herakles and
does not antedate the late sixth century. However, despite the natural differences in local attitudes, the affair of Kylon in the 630s (below, pp. 87–9), our
first closely dated event, shows that by then Attica was a political unity, 'the
Athenians'.

Ancient authors tell us very little of Athenian history before Kylon's time.
We depend chiefly on the interpretation of the visible remains, and here recent
archaeological research has cast new light on the early period. Already in the
ninth century and increasingly through the first half of the eighth the current of
development had turned seawards, with new deme settlements made along the
coast, and Attic Middle Geometric pottery (*c.* 850–750) exported widely, even to
Cyprus and Syria, whose products in their turn appear occasionally in rich
Athenian graves; the Eastern imports in the graves of Euboic Lefkandi, just
across the Euripos straits from Attica, provide an instructive parallel. But a
change starts to show around the middle of the century. During the next
half-century (Late Geometric) the population in Athens went on increasing, for
her cemeteries expanded steadily and the wells dug almost doubled in number;
but outside Athens the new settlements apparently went into the countryside at
least as much as down to the coast. Many of their graves show as much wealth,
even in gold, as any contemporary grave in the city. It is as if aristocratic
families had moved from the city to settle in the country. Yet now, from the
mid-eighth century onwards, the export of Attic pottery (Late Geometric II)
declined sharply, in face of a great expansion abroad of Corinthian Late
Geometric ware. Corinth was already profiting from the demands for pottery
from the Western colonies; but Athens had planted no colonies as yet, having
space still to spare in Attica. Yet, given the first-class quality of much Attic Late
Geometric ware, this cannot be the sole reason why the Euboic as well as the
Corinthian colonies were taking Corinthian ware now. Was the Attic trade
affected by any events happening in Attica itself at the time? Herodotos says
that in the late sixth century there had long been an 'ancient hatred' between
Athens and her neighbour Aigina; could this go back to the second half of the
eighth century? Or could the first rumblings of the Lelantine War between
Chalkis and Eretria have started already and affected Attic exports, *if* the
Eretrian traders had been concerned in any way with the shipment of Attic
pottery? There is no literary evidence that Athens was an ally of either side in
the war when it came, whether it was short or long; but the eastern demes at
least, if not the whole peninsula, may well have been affected in some way by
this trouble which concerned Aegean ports as distant as Samos and Miletos.

Athenian Protoattic pottery was not exported either (*c.* 700–625). From this
some scholars have inferred that an Attic-Eretrian combine must have lost the

Lelantine War about 700; but Attic pottery had declined abroad drastically for over a generation before the war broke out. As we have seen, Eretria's pottery went on flourishing in the seventh century; and in the Attic countryside even more than in the city the graves of the wealthy continued to be richly stored with Attic pottery through the eighth and seventh centuries. Even if the 'ancient hatred' with Aigina was going strong in the seventh century, and Aiginetan tip-and-run raids were harassing the coasts, the rich in Attica continued to do well on their country estates. For they were evidently exporting a product still more valuable than painted pottery, the fine Attic olives and olive-oil, stored in the plain, ballooning Attic 'sos' amphorae which have been found in every quarter of the Mediterranean, from Spain to Cyprus. As for the Protoattic pottery of the early seventh century, it could be argued that it failed to recapture the external markets simply because its decoration could not equal that of the Protocorinthian. The Corinthian artists could draw much better than the Attic. But then they had a head start. The Near Eastern models of draughtsmanship which inspired the Greek Orientalizing tradition (above, pp. 28-9), being on luxury goods of metal, ivory, cloth, and so on, were of modest scale. Protocorinthian pot-painting moved smoothly into the new style, being itself the descendant of a Corinthian Geometric tradition which had concentrated mainly – though not wholly – on elegant ware for the dining-tables of men and the dressing-tables of women. But the finest achievements of the Attic Late Geometric potters, beyond their elegant table- and toilet-ware, had been the huge amphorae and kraters used mainly for funerals. In the seventh century the technique of building up and firing such large works was still as skilled as ever; but the Attic pot-painter was now faced with a new fashion for outline figure-drawing, and this great blank surface to cover. Thus many early Protoattic drawings are basically small-scale concepts, arbitrarily blown up to disproportionate and straggling size by hands as yet unskilled in drawing big human or animal figures (Pl. 12).[1]

So during the years c. 700-640 Attica seems to have been slowly working up to the kind of economic and social background from which eventually tyranny may erupt. With no strong maritime or commercial outlets to encourage trade or find good spots abroad for the safety-valve of emigration, the poor grew poorer and the rich stayed rich. The soil was presumably getting steadily less productive, since there was no systematic rotation of crops or conservation of trees on the hillsides, or use of fertilizers; and politically the whole government lay in the hands of a hereditary caste termed the Eupatridai (high-born). The old tribal system which produced this situation, common to many early societies, is described below (p. 100).

In this government three archons ('rulers') divided between them the three main functions of the old Greek kingship, the religious, military, and judicial (above, pp. 39-40). The *basileus* continued to administer the ancestral cults of the city, and judged such lawsuits as were connected with them. The *polemarchos* commanded the four Attic tribes (Geleontes, Hopletes, Argadeis, Aigikoreis) in their tribal regiments. The third office, where the real secular power lay, was that of *the* archon, sometimes called the archon *eponymos*, for his name was used to date the year. It is this third office which marked the end of real kingship, the replacement of the civil power of the *basileus*, a power to be confined henceforth to those families which could claim to be closest in blood and authority to the ex-royal family.

That such a coveted office should have been ever held for life, or thereafter regularly for a ten-year period (as the tradition said), is perhaps unlikely. The close aristocracy of the Bacchiadai at Corinth elected their *prytanis* annually, and in Cretan Dreros in the seventh century the man who had once been *kosmos* was ineligible for ten years to hold office again (below, pp. 189–90). Oligarchic society was fully aware of the possibilities offered for tyranny if a high office could be extended by its holder over successive years. The later Athenian tradition said that the annual archonship began in 682–681 with one Kreon; conceivably this marked the first year in which immediate iteration of office was forbidden – at least, that would be a practical reason for starting an official record of the names. The literary evidence shows that a Miltiades was archon in 664–663 and again in 659–658, which could suggest that in seventh-century Athens a five-year interval had to elapse. In Classical Athens a single tenure only was allowed; but in the Archaic period the supply of qualified persons would surely have run short, had not iteration after an interval been allowed.

The great power wielded by the early archon cannot be fully discovered now. Probably he presided over the Assembly when it met; but the most important duty must have been the judging of all non-religious lawsuits except the special cases tried by special bodies such as the Areiopagos or the *thesmothetai*. Litigation has always formed much of the daily life of small societies, modern as well as ancient, usually over property – land, buildings, dowries, livestock, wills in general – and in ancient societies at least the amiable principle of a gift to the judge whose decision has recognized the righteousness of one's case could easily be extended to a gift to the judge who *might* decide in one's favour. To be a judge in Archaic societies everywhere meant prestige to the uncorruptible, prestige and wealth to the corruptible, though for those who were charged and convicted the law against bribery was severe. The six lesser members of the board of nine archons, the *thesmothetai* (law-stablishers), may have begun as three pairs of lesser judges, flanking each archon as he sat in judgement. They presided over certain types of case, and must have looked after the law in some manner; but they were not a college of lawgivers, for the law codes drafted in Athens in the late seventh and early sixth centuries were the work of individuals, Drakon and then Solon.

The deliberative body was called the Council of the Areiopagos, for it met on the 'hill of Ares', the low hillock near the western approach to the Acropolis. As in most Archaic cities, it consisted of past holders of the high magistracies (in Athens, the ex-archons), who then became councillors for life. The tenure of the magistracies, and thus the right to be a councillor, was confined to the Eupatridai. Presumably these were certain families to whom the right had been confined long ago by some qualification, as the *Libro d'Oro* of Venice confined the right of government to those families whose ancestors had been members of the Great Council before A.D. 1297. Perhaps Eupatridai were those directly descended from the 'royal' families of Athens and of the other old settlements in Attica. At all events, it was a closely-knit ring until the lawgiver Solon broke it.

In Lakedaimon the Spartiates made no secret of holding all governmental power, though the Lakedaimonioi (*perioikoi*) were allowed to look after themselves in their daily life. In pre-Solonic Athens perhaps things did not work out in practice very differently; clearly the principle of heredity excluded some at least of the prosperous Attic families from ever holding office, and the *ekklesia* (assembly) of citizens in Archaic Athens, if it was summoned only irregularly for specific business, may have been difficult for peasants in distant areas to attend, even though legally as Athenaioi they had the right to attend and vote. Perhaps, busied with the immediate work of maintaining a tolerable living for his household, the peasant demesman thought of himself as Attic and, for example, Rhamnousian, not as 'Athenian'. It was the country nobles who held office, or those who hoped for eligibility thereto one day, to whom the latter title was important.[2]

Kylon and Drakon

Attica may thus be seen as a big area of irregular fertility, with her population here scattered, there clustered, like pebbles on a board, which lay between the large, stolidly aristocratic and agricultural state of Boiotia and the cramped, unfertile, maritime state of Megara on the Isthmus. She bridged these two extremes, partaking something of both geographically, and this compromise is reflected in the pace of her early historical development. The cramped Isthmus states were colonizing already in the eighth century, and had exchanged aristocratic government for tyrannic already by the mid-seventh; whereas Boiotia's combination of a rich agricultural nobility and a scattered peasantry never produced the internal stresses to bring about either of these events. Attica was big enough not to feel the need for more space until the late seventh century, but poor and vigorous enough to feel it acutely, like Megara, when it came. Very late in the century she started her colonization near the Hellespont, and in the mid-sixth century she arrived at her tyrannic phase, when the Isthmus states had already ended theirs. But in the third quarter of the seventh century the combination of powerful nobles and obedient peasantry was still strong enough to make an Attic would-be tyrant fail.

This man was Kylon, an Athenian Eupatrid who had won the *diaulos* (middle-distance) race at Olympia in 640–639. Later he married the daughter of Theagenes, tyrant of Megara (below, p. 156), and in an Olympiad year somewhere between 636–635 and 628–627, backed by other Eupatrid sympathizers and by troops from his father-in-law, he seized the Acropolis. We are not told his motive for the attempt. As a Eupatrid, he was not debarred from holding office. Was he a simple-minded son-in-law, used as a pawn by Theagenes to extend Megarian power into Attica? Or a disinterested reformer, attacking the whole Eupatrid system of control? Or was he as head of a leading family exasperated by the greater power of another family at the time? At all events, he had consulted the Delphic oracle as to his chances, and had been assured that he would capture the Acropolis 'on the greatest festival-day of Zeus'. This probably meant the Diasia to Zeus Meilichios, an Attic festival which was held outside the city; to make one's military *coup* on a holy day which emptied the city of men was an established practice. But Kylon took it to mean an Olympic festival, in compliment to himself; and had he succeeded, the oracle would doubtless have claimed that that was what it meant. He and his followers seized the Acropolis, but the people of Attica did not support them. They rallied in from the countryside and besieged them. The archon of the year was the Alkmeonid Megakles, and he and his board were given – or perhaps had *ex officio* – power to deal summarily with the conspirators when they should be starved into surrender. Kylon and his brothers somehow got out and away; but quick action was needed over the starving remainder, for death would pollute the holy precincts on the Acropolis. So they were lured out on promise of a trial, and immediately killed, some of them even at the precinct of the Eumenides near the Acropolis entry, where they had fled for sanctuary. The continual troubles which beset Athens for some years thereafter were finally agreed to be due to the polluting presence in the city of those who had impiously slain the suppliants, and who must now be cast out themselves. The tradition said that Solon, who in 594 was to be created archon, now persuaded the current Alkmeonidai to stand trial before a special court composed of their peers, 300 Eupatridai. They did so, were condemned, and exiled. It may well have been a political affair, created by the then surviving Kylonidai and any other *dunatoi* (leading men) who hated the Alkmeonidai. Solon, who in general seems to have been pro-Alkmeonid, may have misjudged the situation. But – to come back finally to Kylon's motive for his attempt – the fact that only one clan was exiled for the pollution could mean that the nine archons at the time had all been Alkmeonidai, just as in Crete it was legal for one clan to fill the board of *kosmoi* in any year. If an inner circle of this kind was possible within the Eupatrid government at this time, it might well goad other Eupatridai to rebellion.

In 621–620 the first written Attic law code was drawn up by the lawgiver Drakon, and the modern interpretation sees this, surely rightly, as one result of the failed conspiracy. Some Cretan and colonial cities had their written codes already, all presumably produced in the stress of some crisis, for in early societies this drastic and laborious task was not undertaken merely on theoretic grounds. Most of Drakon's code was superseded by that of Solon later, which indicates that (as indeed the later tradition said) much of it was still cast in the harsh terms of a society like that of the gift-taking *basileis* against whom Hesiod protested, terms which may have seemed all the colder for being set down in the visible permanency symbolized by writing. Under the death penalty now, if not before, stood the crime of attempted tyranny, with lesser crimes such as theft and vagrancy alongside. Other offences were punished by fines, the unit of value for assessment being the ox ('a 20-ox fine'); so at least the size of the penalty no longer depended on the personal whim of the judge. The clauses on homicide were not revoked by Solon, and the surviving fragments indicate that here at least Drakon may have made a great advance. Homicide of all types (premeditated murder, unpremeditated, and manslaughter) was no longer left to the primitive system of tribal self-help; the four *basileis* of the four tribes were to hold the trials, and the verdicts were to be given by the *ephetai*, who appear to be a special body chosen *aristinden* (by birth) to pronounce on matters of blood-guilt. Under the old system, whereby the next-of-kin or phratry (below

p. 100) were responsible for exacting retribution for homicide, the Kylonian affair must have touched off more than one family vendetta, a situation fatal to stability of government; but under Drakon's code the state itself judged the killer henceforth. Thus Athens won free from at least one of the conventions of primitive society. But others persisted. There was as yet no right of appeal from the judgements of the Eupatrid courts. This and a whole nexus of primitive custom concerning property remained for Solon to face in the next generation.[3]

The North-eastern Settlements

The next event in Attic history which may well be causally linked both backward to the failure of Kylon and forward to the reforms of Solon was the foundation of two colonies up in the north-eastern Aegean, in an area which had been regarded hitherto as the preserve of Mytilene in Lesbos – the Aegean entrance to the Hellespont. Two Lesbian settlements had looked out on these straits since the early seventh century: Sestos on the Thracian side, and Ilion on the Asian mainland in the district of Old Troy, whose name she perpetuated. The commercial potential of this position was great. Sestos was called 'Mistress of the Hellespont', because of the current. This poured out of the Euxine and down the narrower Propontis at the rate of 4–5 knots, and finally swung the fish and the ships to Sestos' shoreline in the Hellespont. A like good fortune built the prosperity of Byzantion. Further material benefits must have come to the two Lesbian cities as ports of call; for in summer, when the prevailing wind blows steadily down the Aegean from the north, there are on average about eight days in a month when it changes and blows from the south, and then the ships, using oars and sail, could beat the current and get into the Hellespont and Euxine. So sailors must have paid out sometimes on harbour dues and treats ashore while they hung about waiting for the wind to change.

The Athenian emigrants arrived at Sigeion, a fortified position on the Trojan coast. Phrynon led them, an Olympic victor of 636–635; presumably he was no longer in his first youth when undertaking the responsible tasks of an *oikistes*, so the colony will have arrived *c*. 620–610. The Mytilenaians reacted strongly and sent troops across to the Troad under Pittakos, who finally killed Phrynon in 607–606. But before his death Phrynon had also founded Elaious (Olive-place), another Attic colony, on the opposite shore of the straits; tradition said that Solon was the agent in this, persuading the Athenians that they must get a footing there too if this colonial venture was to be viable.

This emigration, the first sent out from Attica since the old days of the Ionic Migration, may have followed the common colonial pattern: economic hardship drove the rank-and-file, and political or personal troubles produced one or more aristocrats who headed the project, one being accepted as *oikistes*. Conceivably Phrynon may have been one of Kylon's surviving sympathizers, who felt it advisable to emigrate after the failure. If this were so, the choice of the Hellespont area would be readily understandable, for Megara, which had provided the main support for Kylon's attempt, had been colonizing up in the north-east ever since the early seventh century – perhaps even earlier – when she had founded Kalchedon and later Byzantion, the pattern for such straits settlements as Phrynon attempted at the Hellespont. The sites of Elaious and Sigeion were fertile, and the Attic pot-painters had long passed the experimental stage in freestyle drawing and were starting to produce the Black-Figure style proper, a style destined to defeat all other competitors abroad in the sixth century. The two colonies might well be expected to further the sale of this excellent ware. Hitherto (and indeed well into the sixth century) the Attic ware often found abroad was the sos amphora (above, p. 85). Some have men's names scratched in Attic letters on the shoulder. The buyers doubtless put these big-bellied jars to all manner of uses afterwards, but the commodity shipped out in them originally was most probably the famous Attic olive-oil. (Wine was certainly exported in Archaic times, but by and large people reckoned on drinking the produce of their own holdings, and those travelling, like Odysseus (*Odyssey* 5. 265–6), usually carried their personal nips in wineskins.) If they did carry oil, this would indicate only that the owners of large estates – not the small farmers – were doing well, for only the big owners could produce enough excess oil to be worth exporting, and could afford the olive-presses to make it, and the risks involved in shipping it overseas.

After Phrynon's death the Mytilenaians continued to harass the Troad colony, and their poet Alkaios reported unblushingly that after a skirmish his shield now hung in Athena's temple in Sigeion. Periander, the tyrant of Corinth, was appointed by both sides as arbitrator, and confirmed the Athenians in possession of the site. Nevertheless, it must have reverted later to Lesbian hands, just as Elaious seems to have lost her Attic identity among the Thracian dwellers in the Chersonese; for we find that in the next generation Peisistratos and Miltiades I renewed the Attic holdings at the Hellespont (below, p. 96).

The Reforms of Solon

Meanwhile, as the archaeological evidence from the cemeteries shows, there were still many wealthy families in Attica at the end of the seventh century. The pottery is copious and splendid, and the fashion had arisen for costly marble works to commemorate the dead in family burial-grounds: kouros (Pl. 8) and kore, types which may have come to Attica from the Aegean islands (above, p. 31), and the kore-faced sphinx sitting on top of a tall marble stele which usually bore the figure of the dead in profile relief. But Eupatrid monopoly was now being challenged; the safety-valve of emigration had not worked, and indeed could not help those who were tied in Attica by any kind of debt or obligation (below, pp. 91–2). All this could end only in civil war (stasis) or else, as in other Greek cities already, the rule of one man, whether a tyrant, as in Corinth and her neighbours, or an elected dictator (*aisymnetes*), as in Mytilene (below, pp. 239–40). The Athenians entrusted the situation to Solon son of Exekestides, a man who upheld the concept of law and order throughout his career, and elected him as archon and arbitrator in 594.[4]

Solon was a Eupatrid, a man of foreign family friendships before and after his reforms – he visited both Egypt and Cyprus – and a scholar who could turn out elegiac and iambic verses with a pleasant facility which publicized his policy and its justification in a forthright and easily memorable form; indeed, his poetry was the main source whence later historians got their evidence for the economic crisis which he sought to solve. The fragments quoted tell us something of the situation as he saw it and of his actions. They give an impression overall of an honest, disinterested, and prudent statesman, who hoped to cure the city's present ills by abolishing certain primitive laws and practices which had long outlasted their original setting, sources by now of resentment and desperation which threatened to erupt in tyranny or civil war. The ruling *dunatoi* had now so bad an image, according to his verses, that their very existence was threatened. He describes the rat-race for more wealth ('the very men who now have greatest wealth/scramble the harder'), and the office-holders who are embezzling the funds of gods and state alike, while the poor

> go off in their numbers to a foreign country,
> sold and shackled in their shameful chains.
> The bane comes fast upon every household,
> no doors, walls, inner rooms now can keep it out.

In fine, he says, this is riot (*dusnomia*); they *must* have law and order (*eunomia*). Another fragment describes the poor whom his laws have rescued, the victims of the debt-laws, as (1) those sold over the border as slaves; (2) those who avoided this fate only by fleeing into exile, 'no longer speaking Attic Greek, / as wanderers abroad'; and (3) those who remained in Attica 'in shameful slavery [*douleia*], / trembling before their masters' whims'. Distraint upon the debtor's body, to sell him as a chattel slave if his other possessions had failed to cover the debt, was an accepted practice in many primitive societies. Solon's two drastic economic reforms were to enforce a blanket cancellation of all outstanding debts (the *seisachtheia*, 'shake-off-burdens') and to forbid distraint upon the body. Hence debtors of type (1) who could elude their masters and get back over the border into Attica were free once more, and debtors of type (2) could return openly without fear. The technical status of (3) is not clear. I find it hard to believe that these were chattel slaves like (1), for surely it would be risky for the creditor to sell a man as a slave to labour still in his own district where he might have friends and kindred; and *douleia* need not bear the literal meaning. Can (3) have been the people who are described in the ancient sources as *hektemoroi*, 'sixth-parters'?

> For this rent they tilled the fields of the rich; for the whole land was in the control of a few men; and if they failed to pay the rent [that is, one *chous* (jugful) from each *medimnos* (bushel, the standard grain-measure)], they became liable to seizure for slavery.

Subsistence farming for the average smallholding family in early Greece must have been always very near the bone. If each year, come what might, one had to set aside from one-fifth to one-quarter of the harvest to be seed-corn for next year's crop, even one bad harvest could mean near-starvation for two years, unless one could borrow seed-corn from the local lord, the only person likely to have enough land to be able to make loans in hard years from his grain-stores.

Thus the *hektemoros may* have been not literally a 'shameful slave', but what in Cretan law was called the *katakeimenos*, a debtor who offered himself to his creditor as a bond-servant until such time as the full debt and interest should be repaid. It might profit some creditors to take the debtor's services and sixth part, holding over him the threat of outright slavery if he failed in this, rather than to take his bit of land (supposing it were alienable; cf. below, p. 100) or, lastly, his person to sell once and for all. The *horoi* (markers), 'which I pulled out of the black earth: / she was slave once, now free', will have been stones or posts bearing the creditor's family device or some such simple sign, which marked his right (*de iure* or merely *de facto*) to the land. A recent interpretation of the *hektemoros*, however, sees him not as a man compelled to pay the sixth part *because* he was a debtor, but as a man whom some hereditary obligation, contracted long ago by his ancestor with the local lord's family (e.g., for protection of some kind), still constrained to pay the sixth part as agreed generations ago, on pain of slavery if he defaulted; this is not quite what the ancient writers describe, but since Solon's act abolished the system, whatever it was, they might have misunderstood its true nature.

Thus the economic reforms seem to have been chiefly negative, that is, the abolition of unjust and long-rooted hardships. He did not use the tyrant's methods. A tyrant, being outside the law, could enforce a redistribution of the land (γῆς ἀναδασμός), or, less drastically, he could tax the citizens and use the tax in loans to needy farmers. But Solon rejected the tyrant's methods. By the *seisachtheia* he enabled a good part of the population to breathe again – with current debts remitted, distraint upon the body forbidden, and the abolition of hektemorage, the obligation which had involved in some way an unfair claim on the *hektemoros'* land. Furthermore, he forbade the export of any crops except the olive; this action released for internal use the surplus grain which the rich had been selling outside – to Megara and Aigina, presumably, since Boiotia and Euboia were richer agriculturally than Attica itself. He also did something to the weights and measures (and, the fourth-century writers assert, to a monetary system), but none of this is clear to us; and he encouraged foreign craftsmen to settle in Attica – potters from Corinth, for instance, who helped to raise still higher the standard of Attic black-figure ware.[5]

On the legal side too he brought reform by the abolition of primitive practices. He 'gave the right to any third party to claim redress on behalf of any wronged person', which suggests that (as Drakon appears to have done for cases of manslaughter) he abolished a bad result of the primitive law of self-help. He also introduced the right of appeal; the archons were to be no longer supreme in their own courts. No doubt one thought twice before lodging an appeal, since the penalty for losing it was probably severe (cf. above, p. 78; below, pp. 231–2). The court which heard appeals under Solon's new law was either the assembly of the people or the new second council (below, pp. 93–4).

His great political reform was to grade eligibility to office henceforth purely in terms of wealth. This broke the Archaic caste-system of hereditary Eupatridhood by giving rich non-Eupatridai the right to stand for the nine *archai* and thus the right thereafter to life-membership of the Areiopagos council. To those citizens who formed the rest (i.e., the majority) of the hoplites, being men of sufficient substance to possess their own bronze panoply, he gave the right to stand for the lesser offices.

His four grades or ratings were called *pentakosiomedimnoi, hippeis, zeugitai,* and *thetes.* The last three titles existed already as social-military classes. *Thes* was the old title for men free-born but of no substance, day-labourers who counted for little politically or militarily. The *zeugitai* (yoke-men) seem to have been the hoplites, for the front rank of a unit was called the 'first yoke', men of some substance. 'Horsemen', those rich enough to breed horses, was also an old title used in many cities (as Chalkis and Eretria) for the *aristoi*; and of these Attic *hippeis* the cream, the richest, were now graded as the *pentakosiomedimnoi* (500-*medimnoi* men), those whose annual wealth in terms of grain was not less than that amount. (This title may have been Solon's invention. He is said to have assessed the latter three classes also on this standard, *hippeis* at not less than 300; *zeugitai* not less than 200; anyone below that was a *thes.* But he did not alter the existing names.) His use of these four classes as criteria for the grades of office, simple though it was, must have seemed drastic to the Eupatridai. Most authorities, ancient and modern, take the dry measures literally and believe that Solon was encouraging a back-to-the-land policy by requiring that aspirants for the high offices should have their wealth in an essential product, grain (and, if the parallel wet measure, the *metretes*, was regarded as equivalent, in the olive and vine as well); in other words, one must possess, or acquire, a large holding of land. But perhaps Solon simply used the *medimnos* here as a standard unit of value, meaning that a man's wealth, from whatever sources it came – farm-produce, timber, silver-mines, gifts of gold-dust from generous barbarian rulers – all should be assessed in terms of *medimnoi* of barley, just as it would have been in coins, had Attica been producing her own coinage at the time. In the same way the Cretans for long used the bronze cauldron as a standard unit of value (below, p. 191).

It is disputed whether Solon's nine archons were still, as heretofore, elected, or whether he introduced the system of the lot (*klerosis*), out of forty candidates previously elected from the four tribes. If he did introduce the lot, presumably to lessen the chance of graft, his law must have been annulled by Peisistratos later (below, p. 96); but the source which attributes the lot to him may have been misled by some necessary rewording of the old laws later.[6]

After office the archons automatically joined the Areiopagos council. The reformed system would slowly dilute the hundred per cent Eupatridhood of that body, but a unified state – city and countryside – which had now been freed from primitive restrictions and encouraged to expand commercially and increase its population was going to need some extra body to function between the supreme control exercised by the Areiopagos and the decisions made at the infrequent, even if regular, meetings of the citizens' Assembly. Solon created a second council, the Four Hundred, one hundred elected annually from each tribe. According to Plutarch it was a probouleutic body: that is, it was the sieve through which matters were passed before they came to the Assembly for decision. A democratic sieve has large holes, an oligarchic has small. We are not told what were the duties and powers of Solon's new council, but a sixth-century inscription found on Chios may provide a parallel (below, pp. 231-2).

In Chios the 'Citizens' Council' is to be elected, is to 'transact the affairs of the *demos*', and, in particular, is *either* to hear appeal cases *or* to prepare them for the Assembly to hear (the stone breaks at a crucial point). As for the Assembly, Solon himself says that he confirmed the proper rights of the *demos*, but gave it no new ones; which might imply that he did *not* give it the right to judge these new cases of appeal from the archons' courts. If it did not, probably the Council of Four Hundred did. It is also said that he first allowed the *thetes* to vote; but they were freeborn Attic men, so perhaps he merely reaffirmed a traditional but lapsed right of *thetes* to be present and cast their votes at least on matters which concerned them.

So Solon in Athens abolished a caste-system which had inevitably slowed down her political and economic development in bottlenecks behind which the pressure had built up. He claimed that he was doing by law what other states had to pay for with a tyranny. The supreme overseeing powers of the Areiopagos remained as before, but he dented the power of the archons by recognizing the right of appeal, and the day-to-day powers of the Areiopagos by creating a second, assembly-elected council, a body whose powers are not recorded, but whose very existence implies that the Assembly was now acknowledged to be beyond the stage where it could be satisfied by the Areiopagos as sole handler of 'the affairs of the *demos*'.

Judged by the surviving fragments, barely touched upon here, his complete code of law was for its time a monument of even-handed justice, weighed out by a shrewd commonsense which hoped to get the oligarchic government working fairly and reasonably when freed from all the archaic uses, now become abuses, which had clogged it. But clearly he knew well the suicidal tendency of oligarchies stressed later by both Herodotos and Thucydides: oligarchs will not consent to be equal one with another; each thinks that he ought to be leader, and hence comes stasis. Solon can hardly have hoped for a stable oligarchy beyond the next few decades; they would surely bring the tyranny which he had staved off, unless mass apathy and individual greed for power could alike be broken.

> A city's fall comes through its leading men,
> through folly the people come under a tyrant;
> it's easy to raise him, but not to pull him down.

The Tyranny

The resentful Eupatridai now disputed for the *archai* with those newly qualified, and so the dynastic struggling continued as before; there were even two years of *anarchia*, and one Damasias had to be removed by force from the archonship after retaining it illegally for a second and part of a third term. The oldest families, most of whom farmed the fertile plain between Attica and Eleusis, were called collectively the Pedieis (plainsmen) and led by Lykourgos of the ancient clan Boutadai. Their rivals were the Paralioi (coastmen), led by Megakles son of Alkmeon, many of whose clan, the Alkmeonidai, farmed the coastal parts south of Athens down to Sounion. Solon himself appears to have been of this party; late authors describe them as more moderate than the Pedieis, and Solon as a supporter of the middle way; both he and the Alkmeonidai claimed to have saved Athens at different times from tyranny. Now, after his reforms, he warned the citizens sharply of the dangerous aims of Peisistratos son of Hippokrates, who was a younger relative (born *c.* 600) of his own on the mother's side.

Peisistratos had won fame and popularity by seizing Megara's port Nisaia (*c.* 570–565?) when the Megarians still held Salamis, the island which Solon earlier, standing in the agora garbed as a herald and crying his verse to the people, had urged them to capture for Athens. He now became leader of a third faction: his followers were called the Hyperakrioi (overhill-men), because his family's land was at Brauron on the east coast beyond Hymettos. Modern historians surmise that this group was a hive-off from the Paralioi; hence the bitter attacks by Solon, who rightly saw him as a future tyrant. By *c.* 561, however, Peisistratos had enough support in the city for the Assembly to vote him a bodyguard of citizen club-bearers upon his fictitious plea that his enemies had assaulted and wounded him. Clearly the club-bearers were carefully picked, for he used them to seize the Acropolis; but not long afterwards the original two factions united briefly to drive him into exile. By the mid-550s he was back in Athens, again with a dramatic and fictitious plea – that an Amazonian beauty named Phye from the country deme Paiania, dressed in full armour and occupying his chariot, was Pallas Athene come to restore him to her city. Megakles had helped him in this, needing his alliance once more against the Pedieis. The alliance was cemented by a dynastic marriage between Peisistratos and Megakles' daughter; but soon the marriage and alliance had both collapsed, and Peisistratos with his family had to withdraw once more from Attica.

For the next decade he concentrated his interests on the Aegean area, as was natural for a native of the east coast. He moved across to Eretria; thence he went up to Rhaikelos in the Chalkidike, not far across the Thermaic Gulf from Eretrian Methone; and finally to the silver-mining area inland around Mount Pangaion, whence came much of the wealth which financed his return later to Athens. Money came also from Thebes, money and men from a Naxian exile named Lygdamis, mercenary troops from Argos (his second wife's city), and help evidently from Thessaly, for his son Hegesistratos was also called Thessalos. About 546 he led a force which landed at Marathon, the best spot for an invader who was based on Eretria. There he was joined by many Athenians who supported his cause. The rest gathered and marched north-east to intercept his course, but were defeated decisively at Pallene in the pass between Pentelikos and the north end of Hymettos. Megakles and his followers went into exile in their turn. Peisistratos governed Athens thereafter until his death in 528–527, and his son Hippias succeeded him.

Athenian tradition said that he was a wise and benevolent ruler. His foreign policy entailed no leechlike border wars; it concentrated, as before, on the Aegean side. He emphasized Solon's claim for Athens as the mother-city of Ionia, undertaking to purify the central Ionic sanctuary, that of Apollo on Delos, by reburial elsewhere on the island of all the dead whose graves were in sight of the precinct. He secured Naxos, potentially the most powerful of the

Cyclades, by setting up Lygdamis as tyrant. More important still, he revived the earlier Attic ambition of control at the Hellespont by capturing Sigeion. The Mytilenaians again disputed it bitterly, but Hegesistratos, put in by his father to rule there, succeeded in holding it as a property of the family, to be regarded as a dependency of Athens as long as their rule prevailed in Attica. Herodotos' elliptic narrative of this event (below, pp. 238–9) leaves it unclear whether Peisistratos won Sigeion thus before or after his return c. 546. The Chersonese, where Elaious had been also occupied (above, pp. 90–1), had been resettled by Miltiades I of the Philaid clan, apparently before 546, for Kroisos of Lydia (defeated by Persia in that year) had helped him in some trouble with Lampsakos after his settlement. Herodotos says that Miltiades left Athens to occupy the Chersonese (at the request of the Chersonesian Dolonkoi, who were at war with the other natives of the peninsula) because he could not endure life under Peisistratos in Attica (during the first or second tyranny, we suppose). But as Hippias later aided Miltiades II to regain his uncle's dominion when the Chersonese had reverted temporarily to Thracian hands, it is possible that Peisistratos and Miltiades I had some kind of mutual understanding when the occupation of Sigeion was undertaken.

At home, though his mercenaries were always there to remind the people that they were under a ruler who was not bound to obey the law, Peisistratos strove to avoid openly flouting it; he appeared duly to defend himself on a charge of manslaughter (the accuser did not appear), and the annual archons went on —elected, for the holders were always his own relations or men favourable to his government. Under his son Hippias men were elected actually from families formerly opposed to his rule; the fragmentary archon-list (above, p. 35) shows Kleisthenes the Alkmeonid, evidently restored from exile, in 525–524 and Miltiades II in 524–523. When the tyrant did flout law or custom, it could be in a good cause; he created a citizens' property-tax of 5 per cent, from which came subsidies to poor farmers to avoid debt, an evil which Solon's reforms had been unable to cure. The links between the city and country demes were strengthened by an improved road-system, the work of his sons; its hub was the altar of the Twelve Olympian Gods in the Agora, whence the distances were measured along routes spaced out by inscribed herms as milestones. Part of one survives, which marked the halfway point between Athens and the deme Kephale. Peisistratos son of Hippias erected the altar; Hipparchos contributed the herms, some of which bore also improving mottoes for the wayfarer, as 'Think justly as you walk' and 'Never cheat a friend'. By these roads the circuit-judges must have travelled. They were a board created by Peisistratos himself, to judge disputes in the demes which could be settled on the spot, thus saving the country people from loss of time and money in journeying to the city for their cases to be heard.

Peisistratos was already in his fifties when he became tyrant, and over seventy when he died; Hippias' son Peisistratos, archon in 522–521, was born not later than 551, so Hippias himself was born probably in the 570s. Much therefore of the home and foreign policy of 546–527 may have been really the work of the family as a whole, particularly in the spectacular building programme, where the later tradition is sometimes unclear whether the tyrant himself or one of his sons or his grandson was responsible for a work. On the south-east side of the Agora lie the remains of the famous spring-house Enneakrounos (Nine-jets), noted there by Pausanias the traveller 'still as it was adorned by Peisistratos' (1.14,1). The water was channelled in clay water-pipes from the abundant spring Kallirrhoe (Fairstream), which up to modern times still poured out beside the bed of the Ilissos south of the Olympieion. This huge temple of Zeus Olympios and the precinct of Apollo Pythios, both lying south of the Acropolis, are associated with Peisistratos the younger. As a memorial of his archonship in 522–521 he dedicated to Apollo a marble altar whose capping-slab survives, bearing the faint but finely-cut inscription:

> This token of his archonship Hippias' son Peisistratos
> offered in the precinct of Apollo Pythios.

The traces of a little temple in the precinct have been tentatively ascribed to his grandfather. The foundations of the unfinished Olympieion near it are dated *c.* 515 by the sherds found in association. This building was over 100 × 40 metres, of local poros stone in the Doric order, and overlay a smaller temple. (Building ceased after the family was exiled in 510; many of the column-drums were re-used later, mostly in the city's defences. With new Corinthian columns it reached the stage of entablature by the efforts of the Syrian ruler Antiochos Epiphanes in 174 B.C., and was at last finished by Hadrian *c.* A.D. 132.) At the southern foot of the Acropolis, under the fourth-century theatre of Dionysos, are traces of buildings dated in the late sixth century: a simple half-circle hollowed out for the seating, a round orchestra (dancing-floor) in front for the singers and dancers, and behind them the small shrine of a cult-statue. Peisistratos senior is held to have created the state festival of the City Dionysia in 534, when the old cult of Dionysos, originally at Eleutherai, north of Eleusis, was brought to Athens. At Eleusis itself excavation has indicated that in the time of Peisistratos the *telesterion* (Hall of the Mysteries) was rebuilt on a larger scale, the sanctuary protected by a strong wall, and the town by fortifications.

The steep Acropolis with its old 'Pelasgic' walls remained the military base of the tyranny; and scattered bits of evidence suggest that Peisistratos popularized the worship of the patron goddess in various ways, not only to stress his position as her protégé (above, p. 95), but to enhance also the greatness of Athens as the centre of a united Attica, and of Attica *vis-à-vis* the outside world. The Great Panathenaia, a quadrennial festival which was started in 566 when Hippokleides (below, p. 165) was archon, is associated by a late authority with Peisistratos. His son Hipparchos is said to have introduced the recital of the Homeric poems as the rhapsodic contest – even, in one version, to have had the poems written down. Details should not be pressed too closely; the many components of such a festival – the actual sacrifices, the great procession escorting the animal victims, the gathering of the people – are distinct from particular contests, which might be introduced by different patrons at different times (athletics, four-horse and two-horse races, flute-playing, reciting, etc.). But the general impression survives of a propagandic drive for culture. Illustrations of Homeric episodes do increase on Attic vases after *c.* 550, and the

Attic elements in the dialect of the epics are marked. The silver coinage which bears for the first time the helmed Athena's head/owl-in-incuse is now generally ascribed to the tyrannic period, specifically to Hippias – not (as formerly thought) to Solon. Many of the fragmentary limestone buildings on the Acropolis with brightly painted pedimental groups must belong to Peisistratos' day; the remains from a superb marble pediment showing Athena downing a giant in the Gigantomachy are dated in Hippias' time, *c.* 515. The existence of a precinct for the Brauronian Artemis in the south-west corner of the Acropolis also suggests a Peisistratid patron. Finally, the marble statues dedicated to Athena increased greatly in number from the 540s onwards, and the most popular became the Ionic version of the gift-bearing kore. She no longer wore over her shift the sober 'Doric' chiton with its scanty overfold, short sleeves, tight belt, and fullness pulled rather heavily to sides and back, but simply the long, loose, wide-sleeved Ionic shift of linen or some such thin crinkly stuff; when belted, it could hang or drape – or trail in pleats which fluted vertically or fanned out sideways as she held it up to walk – and was crossed by the pleated Ionic himation, a shawl slung under one arm and fastened over the other shoulder like a small Scotch plaid. Sculptors from the Cyclades and Ionia came to encourage the Attic artists on these delightful lines; Aristion of Paros made several funeral statues, and Archermos of Chios a dedicatory kore (Pl. 11).[7]

The economic and social benefits for Attica under the Peisistratidai were many. The links across the Aegean encouraged trade, and the fine pottery of Attica now eclipsed all rivals. Other states had produced good black-figure ware (Corinthian, Lakonian, 'Chalkidic'), but none of a standard so consistently high as the Attic; and Attic red-figure, developing from *c.* 530 onwards, was unique. To us too its charms are obvious; it gave the good draughtsman a better chance to show his skill, and the beautiful black glaze over the body of the pot silhouetted its absolute symmetry and vied in burnish with the far more costly bronze vessels. The potteries and building works increased employment, and the Great Panathenaia brought in Greeks from other states, though admittedly these games never equalled the great four founded earlier. Rhapsodes and other poets came to the tyrants' court, Anakreon of Teos, who had been with Polykrates at Samos (below, pp. 217, 227) and Simonides of Keos – professionals undertaking court poems for their livelihood. (Pls. 9, 10)

But the tyranny fell in 510. The great families of Attica, exiled or not, could hardly tolerate the prospect of a steady Peisistratid succession. Hippias may well have been efficient, but he had had no authority from the city to take over the rule in 527. Hipparchos, the next son, had a reputation for dissolute arrogance. Hegesistratos was abroad as tyrant of Sigeion under Persian authority; we know no details of Iophon, a fourth son. The crucial factor was to be the power of Sparta's League under king Kleomenes (below, pp. 123–7). In 519 Spartan diplomacy turned the military power of Thebes against Athens by encouraging Plataia, the Boiotian border-town then under Theban pressure, to ally herself to Athens. In 517 the same diplomacy reached the Cyclades and evicted Lygdamis from his tyranny at Naxos (below, pp. 180–1). An oligarchy succeeded him, and presumably the Athenian aristocratic families deposited there by Peisistratos as hostages renewed their hopes of return. Three years later the Persian Great

King Darius brought the shadow of Persian power closer to the mainland Greeks by mounting an expedition against the Thracian and Scythian tribes on the northern side of the Hellespont and Aegean. In the Chersonese Miltiades II was prepared to join the Scythians in breaking the bridge across the Danube, to cut off Darius' return; but no support for this came from the other Greek petty rulers of the northern Greek and Ionic cities mustered there as part of Darius' subject forces. The Persians returned safely after what was clearly a military fiasco against the skilful nomad Scythians. Hegesistratos in Sigeion had evidently been loyal to Darius, and Hippias linked the Peisistratidai further with Persia by marrying his daughter Archedike to Aiantides, son of the Greek quisling ruler of Lampsakos, not far from Sigeion. Hers was the famous epitaph which said that, though she was daughter, sister, wife, and mother of tyrants, she showed no haughty pride. Then, in 514, Aristogeiton and the young Harmodios, both of the old family of the Gephyraioi (which hailed in the far past from Eretria or, as Herodotos believed, from Tanagra in Boiotia), struck down Hipparchos at the beginning of the Panathenaic festival, as he was marshalling the procession at the start of the Sacred Way. Harmodios was killed by the guards, and Hippias had Aristogeiton tortured to death in the vain hope that he would reveal any accomplices; for it seemed clear that the attack had been directed primarily against the tyrant himself. A strong tradition remembered the men as martyrs, and after the tyranny fell, *skolia* were sung in their memory at aristocratic club dinners 'because they slew the tyrant, and gave Athens *isonomia*' once more (cf. below, pp. 229–30). So this was one manifestly anti-Peisistratid family, and outside Athens was a still more dangerous one. Kleisthenes, the Alkmeonid leader, re-exiled at some time after 525–524, had gone to Delphi and secured the support of its controlling priesthood (the tradition said, by rebuilding mainly at his own cost Apollo's temple, inadvertently burnt down *c.* 548), so the Pythia now gave one reply only to all Spartan enquiries, official or personal: that Sparta must free Athens from the tyranny.

The death of Hipparchos had turned Hippias into a harsh and suspicious ruler. He took the opportunity caused by the Gephyraians' act to disarm the Athenian people, not knowing how many more families might foment this restiveness in Athens, and having for his own defence only his mercenaries and the promise of a cavalry force from his allies in Thessaly. In 513 came a border attack by exiles under Alkmeonid leadership, who held to the death the frontier fort Leipsydrion; though unsuccessful this was a fresh threat, and another song went the rounds, a lament for the dead, 'Alas, Leipsydrion, comrade-betrayer . . .'

Stasis and the Reforms of Kleisthenes

In 510 the Spartans, having first sent a force which was routed by the Thessalian cavalry, succeeded in driving out at last the tyrant and his family. King Kleomenes had thus obeyed the commands of Delphi, clearly hoping that oligarchic Athens, once freed, would become a member of the Peloponnesian League (below, p. 125). Battened behind the wooden defences of the steep

Acropolis, the tyrant's party could have withstood a siege, but by a mischance the Peisistratid children, in a convoy smuggling them out of Athens, were captured and used as hostages. Hippias capitulated and the family went into exile in Sigeion, as subjects now of Persia; if Sparta did attack for anti-Persian reasons, she was now fully justified.

But the situation did not improve immediately for Athens. The vacuum left by the tyranny was filled instantly by aristocratic stasis, the party of Kleisthenes against that of Isagoras son of Teisandros, leader of a high-born family concerning which Herodotos, enquiring two generations later, could only find out that it administered the cult of Zeus Karios (or, on a modern suggestion, Ikarios). It seemed that the clock had merely been put some forty years back; and Isagoras at least was trying to do this, for his party must have engineered the *diapsephismos* which followed the fall of the tyranny. This was a comb-out of the citizen-lists, which disfranchised many who had been untroubled, perhaps even enrolled, during the tyranny. But Kleisthenes, whose previous actions show him as a politician both energetic and sagacious, was well aware that the city and countryside, after two generations of economic improvement and the repression of aristocratic ambitions over leadership, would never submit again to oligarchic government in the old pattern. Against Isagoras' 'solution' he set his own project – far bigger and more complicated, but drafted and administered on the principle of *isonomia*: a complete tribal reorganization with all its political consequences, an event probably long overdue in the Attic system.

The population, citizen and metic, had expanded greatly during the century, but the citizens were still divided into the four ancient kinship-based tribes of Geleontes, Aigikoreis, Argadeis, and Hopletes. A tribe consisted of a number of phratries (*phratriai*; the name implies a blood-relationship, in this case 'brotherhood'; in some other states these units were called *patrai*); each phratry was composed of a number of clans (*gene*). Within a clan the members of the high-born families controlled for good or ill the lives of the clansmen; for they provided the leaders in war and politics, the judges, the priests of all cults, the kindly protectors, and the harsh exploiters. Nobody, high or low, could have produced title-deeds to the land which he occupied; however he had come by it, it was inalienable in the sense that it belonged to his children also, born or unborn; as in all ancient communities, it was his lifeline: it grew his food, supported his four walls, and represented his substance, his position, his freeman's rights. When Hesiod tells Perses to work hard for prosperity 'so that you may get another man's land, not he yours', it shows that in the last straits a man might have to watch a creditor take over his land, but not, I think, that the land was alienable in the ordinary sense (cf. above, p. 55).

Outside Athens the people lived in settlements of all sizes; many were well-established demes, some large, some declining. Some did not rate as demes until Kleisthenes' reforms upgraded them. The council created by Solon was formed by one hundred men elected from each tribe, and the tribal army must have consisted of four regiments of varied size and training, led by four commanders under the polemarch; but we do not know how scattered geographically the members of each tribe were by the late sixth century. Kleisthenes' scheme was in theory straightforward, though it might well take some years to put into action. For religious matters the old tribes were retained, each still under its *phylobasileus*; but for all secular purposes he divided the people into ten new tribes, each called after a Tribal Hero. (To avoid complaints over the choice of heroes a hundred names were sent to the Pythia, who selected ten by lot.) Each tribe was to be geographically a microcosm of all Attica, for Kleisthenes divided the state into three areas, City, Coast, and Hinterland. Each area was itself divided into ten sections called *trittyes* (thirds, 'ridings'), because each tribe was an artificial compound formed by three *trittyes*, one from each area. Any rational person could see the sense of such a division. Under the new reforms each tribe would be contributing its regimental commander and its quota to a reorganized city council of 500 members, fifty per tribe. The City, with its attached arc of the old 'Plain', obviously contained the highest number of men who could (*a*) attend the *ekklesia*, held in the Agora; (*b*) give full-time attendance to the council when necessary; and (*c*) supply capable, experienced generals, ambassadors, and the like; for here dwelt the biggest proportion of the old and wealthy families. Hence each tribe must have its slice of the City – and correspondingly its slice of the Hinterland, to avoid the embarrassing consequences to the state of possibly having one commander among the ten who was distinctly below standard, or one *prytany* (executive committee of the council; see below) formed of hill-country farmers who had no clear idea of how such a committee should go about its work.

A further intention was also clear. By making his new tribe an artificial body of members from different parts of Attica, bound together by a new tribal cult with no kinship ties (real or believed) or other such obligations of the Archaic tribe, Kleisthenes evidently meant to weaken any over-strong influence which the heads of the old families, or certain among them, held over the rest of the local population. The extremes of civil turmoil which this influence could inflict had been shown before the tyranny. The new tribal system did not change anyone's residence, but it could change his mental attitude. Men would live at the gates of the 'local squire' as before, and attend the local festivals; but they would also assemble at fixed times with a new cross-section of the population as their colleagues, to worship a tribal hero and to elect the tribal commander (*strategos*) and also the fifty councillors, who would have the special duty of acting for one-tenth of the year as the *prytany*, a body consisting of each tribal contingent in a sequence chosen by lot, which met daily, prepared the agenda for meetings of the whole council, received foreign embassies, and generally acted as an executive committee.

The most remarkable instances of Kleisthenes' intention to weaken the influence of the 'squire-class' are the freak enclaves which were deliberately created by the boundaries of the *trittyes* in certain places. For instance, the Marathon Tetrapolis, four old demes bound by an ancient cult (above, p. 83), lay in the coastal *trittys* of Tribe 9 (Aiantis), yet Probalinthos, one of the four, was split off and assigned to the coastal *trittys* of Tribe 3 (Pandionis) much further down the coast, thus becoming – politically speaking – a wedge of Probalinthian loyalties driven in to split what had hitherto been a long run of the old Hyperakrioi, i.e., of solid influence from the *genos* of the recently ejected tyrants. So far in Kleisthenes' intentions we may safely go. Further modern research has suggested the rather cynical view that at some points he drew his *trittys*-boundaries in such a way as actually to help the influence of one *genos* – his own, the Alkmeonidai. Herodotos certainly believed that in his struggle against Isagoras he only favoured the *demos* in order to get his support against his powerful foe. In this he was successful, the reforms were passed; but Isagoras then shocked the Athenians by actually calling in Kleomenes and the Spartan troops and prompting the king to demand that the accursed Alkmeonid should be exiled and that three hundred of Isagoras' followers should govern Athens. The citizens supported the council in resisting this, and after being besieged on the Acropolis for two days Isagoras' whole party capitulated. The Spartans were allowed to leave Attica together with Isagoras, and Kleisthenes' tabled reforms were started as soon as he and his supporters had returned from the exile which Kleomenes had briefly enforced on them.

The basic reform was the tribal. This brought in its train an enlargement of the council to five hundred. If the *prytany*-system was part of the original design (as was assumed above), and not a fifth-century development, we may deduce that he saw this council as a responsible, indeed important, body in the government of the state. The *Ath. Pol.* says that the 'modern' conciliar oath was first sworn in Hermokreon's archonship (501–500). This could mean several things: that the reforms were proposed piecemeal between 508–507 and 502–501; or that the first meeting and swearing-in of the new council was some six years after the passing of the reforms because the actual work of establishing all the demes (about 140, as far as is known), creating the *trittys*-boundaries, and producing the new deme-registers took some years; or that the original formula of the oath proved unsatisfactory after a few years. Then, says the *Ath. Pol.*, they began electing the *strategoi* – the military board which was to produce the great statesmen of the fifth century – by tribes, one from each tribe, with the polemarch still as leader of the army. The first two explanations above could cover this also; or it has been suggested (though the Greek text does not encourage this) that 'they' means specifically the Assembly: that now began the method certainly used later by the full democracy, whereby the Assembly, not the tribe, selected a general for each tribe from those of its members who were put forward as candidates. The ancient sources, though doubted in this by some modern scholars, say that after the expulsion of the tyrants Kleisthenes enrolled in the tribes many 'metics, foreigners, and slaves'. Certainly the enlargement of the citizen-body by the enrolment of foreigners, as craftsmen or helpers in other ways (including safe voters), was characteristic of ancient tyrannies, and since a comb-out of the citizen-rolls followed the fall of the Peisistratidai, it is possible that the Athenian tyrants first enrolled these people, Isagoras cast them out, and so Kleisthenes enrolled them again. The *Ath. Pol.* says that he 'distributed everybody into ten tribes instead of four, wanting to mix them so that more could share in the citizenship', and that he called the citizens *demotai* (demesmen) lest by using patronymics to identify themselves they should show up the *neopolitai* (newly-made citizens). The foolishness of suggesting these reasons as the sole motives for the tribal reform need not mean that the enrolment itself never happened; a citizen was required now to give his demotic, but not his patronymic unless he chose (as many aristocrats naturally did, whereas those with non-Greek parents need not reveal this).[8]

Lastly, the famous law of ostracism. According to this, any citizen who had broken no law, but was considered by a sufficiently large number of his fellows to be a real danger to the state, could be exiled from Attica for ten years (without confiscation of his property), *if* in the main Assembly held during the sixth *prytany* (in January, approximately) the people were asked whether they wished to hold an *ostrakophoria*, and agreed; debate was not allowed, only a straight vote. Then, in the seventh *prytany*, when the special assembly for the purpose was held, a minimum of 6,000 citizens must cast a vote – a sherd on which was written the name of the man whom he desired to see banished. The man whose name polled highest was exiled. Evidently, when the question was first put to the Assembly in the sixth *prytany*, everybody knew already that A or B, whose public views were diametrically opposed, was the candidate aimed at, although in the event there was often a large scatter-vote, revealed to us by the number of different, often unknown, names among those on the sherds dumped after the *ostrakophoriai*.

The basic reason for ostracism in the 480s was probably the same as that held to justify the modern system of party government: that it is better to let one pilot steer even an erratic course than to risk certain shipwreck of the state by stasis, if two *dunatoi* are determined each to wreck the other's proposed policy at every point. The *Ath. Pol.* offers a different reason. The existing old law against tyranny said: 'if any men seek to set up a tyranny, or if [anyone] helps to establish the tyranny, he and his seed are to be *atimos*' (the word here carries its archaic meaning 'outlawed', i.e., to be killed with impunity; 'deprived of citizenship' is the later, milder meaning); but since suspicions alone were not enough to invoke it, this law was useless if these were proved right only when the citizens, back from the local festival outside the city walls, found a tyrant with a bleak-faced force of mercenaries awaiting them. According to the *Ath. Pol.*, Kleisthenes' law was passed as a prophylactic measure to remove suspects in high places – popular leaders in war, persuasive speakers in the Assembly – whence the step to tyranny was easy. Popularity with the fickle crowd might not save a candidate from ostracism on the day, especially if his opponent had an active and unscrupulous *hetaireia* (political club) behind him. Tyranny remained a possibility after 510, as Isagoras was to show in 506 and Hippias in 504; so the reasons cited above may both be right, given the twenty years' development between 508–507 when it was passed and 488–487, when the first ostracism, that of Hipparchos son of Charmos, took place (App. I).

After Kleisthenes' reforms the Areiopagos remained as before, a body which as supreme judge and Guardian of the Laws stood above them (though an individual Areiopagite was liable to prosecution like any other citizen). The archons were still elected, but the members of the new board of ten generals, appointed annually and re-eligible for office immediately, had won so much political power by 487 that in that year sortition was introduced for the archonship, a tacit admission that not only the *basileus* and polemarch but the eponymous archon himself now needed no special skills or brain to carry out his duties. The *demos* was recast in a new mould by the tribal reform. All Attica, including the city itself, was now divided into demes, the newly created alongside the old, each with its *demarchos* and deme-register of citizens, each a clear-cut unit but cross-linked by the *trittys*-system.

Foreign Policy: Sparta and Persia

The foreign policy of Athens in this last decade of the sixth century naturally veered with the leaders in power at the moment. Isagoras had encouraged the Spartans to believe that after the fall of the tyranny Athens, like many other places, would become a member of the Peloponnesian League. The first Spartan attempt had failed, but about 506 a bigger one was launched. Attica was to be pincered between three enemies, the Boiotians from the north and west and their allies the Chalkidians from the east, and the League forces from the south-west, via Eleusis; and Isagoras was to be installed as tyrant. But this concerted project failed. Kleomenes had kept the plan secret, relying too much on his forces to follow the Spartans wherever they went; at Eleusis, where the goal became clear, the contingent from Corinth, which had no quarrel with Athens, baulked and withdrew. Damaratos the co-king supported them, and the League army broke up and retired to the Peloponnese. The Boiotians meanwhile moved eastward to support the Chalkidians, for the Athenian army was already mustered. It now followed up, caught the Boiotians, and inflicted a crushing defeat, taking 700 prisoners. Then, crossing the narrow Euripos, it won an equally decisive victory over the Chalkidians. The visible memorial of the double victory was a bronze quadriga dedicated on the Acropolis (above, p. 68); but the richest prize was the estates of the Hippobotai, the ruling aristocracy at Chalkis, which were carved up into plots for Attic settlers. As long as Eretria was friendly to Athens, she would provide a bridge between Attica and this new piece of territory.

The Thebans soon returned to the attack. They were again pressed back by the Athenians, but found an ally in Aigina, an enemy of Athens since the seventh century (cf. pp. 84, 150). Aiginetan ships raided the Attic coast in an 'unheralded' (? truceless) war off and on until the common danger of Persia halted it in the 480s; and c. 504 the Spartan authorities made a last attempt to get Athens into their sphere of control. Their published reasons were that they had wronged the Peisistratidai – for they had now discovered that the Pythia had been bribed – and that they had read many oracles foretelling disaster from the Athenians, which king Kleomenes had stolen from Athena's temple on the Acropolis. They invited Hippias from Sigeion to come and resume the tyranny; but this plan died even faster than the previous one, for in the congress called to discuss it the Corinthians again led a unanimous opposition, and the allies bade the Spartans leave the government of a Greek city alone.

The threat of Persia seems to have divided the opinion of post-tyrannic Athens. In 508–507, when Kleisthenes was in power, an Athenian embassy to Susa had agreed to give earth and water – symbolically, to submit their territory – to Darius if he would help them against Kleomenes and the League; but on its return the Athenians were angered at this submission and c. 504, defying the satrap Artaphernes at Sardis, they refused to recall the resentful

Hippias. About 499, at the start of the eastern Greeks' revolt against Persia, the Athenian Assembly had voted to send twenty ships to Ionia for the sake of their old 'colony' Miletos, a solid contribution from a fleet with an estimated total of only fifty; but after an initial defeat on land at Ephesos the force returned home without delay. Five Eretrian triremes had accompanied them, honouring the Milesian help sent to Eretria in the old Lelantine War. The archon of 496–495 was Hipparchos son of Charmos, whose career suggests a pro-Persian attitude; Kleisthenes had suspected him of tyrannic ambitions after 510, and he was ostracized in 487 and then (significantly) convicted *in absentia* of treachery. In 494, when Miletos was sacked by the Persians, the playwright Phrynichos produced a play which openly lamented this, and he was fined. The reason for his punishment given to Herodotos later (that it distressed the Athenians to be reminded of the Ionians' misfortune) is so odd that few modern writers have accepted it; the anxiety of a peace party not to twist the Persian tail gratuitously seems more likely. However, the anti-Persian party were soon to get a powerful leader. Mardonios the Persian general was mopping up pockets of resistance along the north Aegean coast after the Ionic Revolt, and Miltiades, who had supported the Ionians, left his dependency in the Chersonese, came south to Athens, survived an (Alkmeonid?) attempt to get him out of the way by a prosecution for 'tyranny over Greek subjects', and evidently convinced the waverers at last; for in 491 Athens, like Sparta, rejected a final demand from Persia for earth and water, and in 490 Miltiades was the tactical commander against the Persians at Marathon.

Art

Little has been said here on Attic art and its quality. It has been analysed in many excellent and detailed studies, and in any case it speaks very clearly for itself; more than any others, Attic sculpture and vases alike succeed in conveying the power of shape, the black-and-red pottery by its pure outlines and the continual balance between dark and light, the marbles because their delicate surfaces and shadows are undisturbed now by the original paintwork. Among the sixth-century sculptors whose names survive, Aristion and Archermos were from the islands (below, pp. 185, 233), Endoios worked much in Ionia, Gorgias was probably Lakonian; Phaidimos, Aristokles, and Antenor, as far as we know, were Athenians. Among the many potters and painters, some personal names are non-Greek ethnics (Lydos, Skythes, Sikanos and Sikelos, Brygos, Mys), which may denote either a foreigner or one of foreign ancestry; but they all learnt their skill in Attic potteries, identifying their work if not their names with that of Attic artists.[9]

NOTES

1 'Oldest Ionic land': Solon F 4a W. Pallene and Hagnous: Plut., *Thes.* 13. The Tetrapolis: see esp. D. M. Lewis, *Historia* 12 (1963), 30 f. Early emigration: Thuc. 1, 12,4. Families: Hdt. 5. 57; 65,3–4; 6. 35,1; of Miltiades, see most recently G. Huxley, *GRBS* 14 (1973), 137 ff. Discrepant interests: cf. R. J. Hopper, *BSA* 56 (1961), 214 ff. Theseus tradition: Jacoby, *Atthis* (1949), 219 and n. 23. 9th and 8th cc. settlements inland: Coldstream, *GGP*, 344 ff., 348 ff., 360 ff. Lefkandi: see above, p. 69, n. 1. Athens and Aigina: Hdt. 5. 82–8; Coldstream, *GGP*, 361 (late 8th c.?); Dunbabin, *BSA* 36–7 (1936–37), 83 ff. and Bradeen, *TAPA* 78 (1947), 223 ff. (first half of 7th c.?). For the decline of Attic pottery from Late Geometric II onward see Coldstream, *GGP*, 360 ff. sos amphorae (so-called from the neck-pattern, a circle between double zigzags), distribution: see most recently J. De Hos Bravo, *Madrider Mitteilungen* 11 (1970), 102 ff., with bibliography.

2 Early archonship: length of appointment, *Ath. Pol.* 13; annual archon-list in the Archaic period, J. Cadoux, *JHS* 68 (1948), 70 ff. (Miltiades' archonships, 120). Bribery: *Ath. Pol.* 7. 1 and 55,5; Plut., *Solon*, 25. 2; the archon was required to dedicate a lifesize(?) gold image, apparently at Delphi. Origin of Eupatridai: the fundamental discussion is still that by Wade-Gery, *Essays*, 86 ff. (=*CQ* 25 (1931), 1 ff.).

3 Kylonian conspiracy: Hdt. 5. 71; Thuc. 1. 126; *Ath. Pol.* 1; Plut., *Solon*, 12; for recent discussion and bibliography, M. Laing, *CP* 62 (1967), 243 ff. Seizure of cities during an extramural festival: Hdt. 1. 150 (Smyrna); Polyaen., *Strat.* 1. 23 (Samos). Boards in Crete filled by one clan: R. Willetts, *Aristocratic Society in Ancient Crete* (1955), 28 (=Gortyn Code, col. V, 5.). Drakon's code: I have followed here the recent excellent exposition and interpretation by R. Stroud, *Drakon's Law on Homicide* (Univ. of California Publication 3, 1968).

4 Sestos: Str. 591. Byzantion: Polyb. 4. 38 ff. On winds and currents: Rhys Carpenter, *AJA* 52 (1948), 1 ff. and B. Labaree, *AJA* 61 (1957), 29 ff. On Elaious and Sigeion see Wade-Gery, *Essays*, 155 ff. (=*JHS* 71 (1951), 212 ff.) and below pp. 238–9. Evidence for wealth in Attica: cf. (e.g.) the Vari cemetery, S. Karousou, *AA* (1940), 125 ff. Grave-sculpture: G. M. Richter, *Kouroi*² (1960); *Archaic Gravestones of Attica* (1961); *Korai* (1968).

5 Solon's reforms in general: cf. A. Andrewes, *The Greek Tyrants*, ch. 7 and *The Greeks* (=*Ancient Greek Society*), 104 ff.; Forrest, *Emergence*, ch. 6. Ancient evidence: Solon's poems (those here quoted, F 13.72–3, F 4.23–9, F 36. 8–15 West). On hektemorage: *Ath. Pol.* 2, here cited; Plut., *Solon* 13.2; M. Finley, *Rev. internat. droit français et l'étranger* 43 (1965), 159 ff. $\frac{1}{5}$ to $\frac{1}{4}$ is the proportion of seed-corn as quoted in the records of France before the Revolution: C. B. A. Behrens, *The Ancien Régime* (1967), 32. The *katakeimenos*: Willetts, *Aristocratic Society in Ancient Crete*, 54 ff. Horoi: Solon F 36.5–7 West. The recent interpretation of hektemorage is that of Andrewes, *The Greeks*, 105 ff. and M. Finley, op. cit.; cf. also Forrest, *Emergence*, 147 ff. Law on exporting: Plut., *Solon*, 24. Weights, measures, and monetary system: *Ath. Pol.* 10; Plut.. *Solon*, 15.3–5. For the most recent discussion and suggested solution to the weights and measures, C. Kraay in *Studies presented to E. S. G. Robinson* (1973), 1 ff. I follow here his view (*Num. Chron.* (1956), 43 ff.; (1962), 417 ff.) that the first Attic coinage showing the Athena/owl is not earlier than the last quarter of the 6th c. (above, p. 98, but that Peisistratos may have introduced the 'Wappenmünzen' (*Archaic and Classical Greek Coins* (1976), 56 ff.). Citizenship to alien craftsmen: Plut., *Solon*, 24.2; see Dunbabin, *BSA* 45 (1950), 193 ff., on Corinthian potters working in Solonic Athens.

6 The legal reforms: *Ath. Pol.* 9; Plut., *Solon*, 18.5. *Zeugitai* = hoplites rather than the alternative suggestion, those owning a yoke of oxen: see in general Busolt-Swoboda, *Griech. Staatskunde* (1926), 820 n. 2 and 822 f. n. 1; Andrewes, *Greek Tyrants*, 87. The 'first yoke': Thuc. 5. 68,3. For the possibility that the 'pentakosiomedimnoi' too was a very old rating see E. Smithson, *Hesperia* 37 (1968), 77 ff. Old Attic laws assessed property in terms of *medimnoi*, cf. Isaios x. 10 and Plut., *Solon*, 23.3. Archons chosen by lot: Forrest, *Emergence*, 164, prefers this view (*Ath. Pol.* 8.1) marginally. Hignett, *Hist. Ath. Const.*, 323 f., accepts the other view (Arist., *Pol.* 1273a-b), which says that it was by election; he notes that the *Ath. Pol.* may be inferring the use of sortition for archons simply from the wording of the 'old law' which it cites in this context, namely that the stewards of Athena must be chosen *by lot* from the Pentakosiomedimnoi. If so, this would of course be inadequate as evidence, for even if these stewards *were* chosen by lot in Solon's time, it would not follow that the archons too were chosen thus. The necessary qualification for these stewards was thought to be common to all Pentakosiomedimnoi – viz., just to be rich beyond the dreams of temptation; whereas the archons needed more 'technical' qualifications.

7 Council of 400: *Ath. Pol.* 8. 4; Plut., *Sol.* 19. 1. (Its existence was denied by Hignett, on grounds generally agreed now to be inadequate.) Voting by *thetes*: Solon F 5 West; *Ath. Pol.* 7.3. Self-destruction of oligarchies: Hdt. 3. 82,3; Thuc. 8. 89,3. Solon on tyranny: F 9 West. *Anarchia* and Damasias' years: *Ath. Pol.* 13.1–2. Factions and Peisistratos: Hdt. 1. 59–61,2. Solon on Salamis: Frr. 1–3 West. Hyperakrioi a hive-off: Hignett, *Hist. Ath. Const.*, 110; Forrest, *Emergence*, 176 f. Peisistratos in exile: Hdt. 1. 61,2–64; Rhaikelos and Pangaion: *Ath. Pol.* 15.1–2. His good rule: Hdt. 1. 59,6; Thuc. 6. 54,5–6 (of the family in general); *Ath. Pol.* 16.7. Sigeion: Hdt. 5. 94–5; Chersonese: Hdt. 6. 34–40. Charge of manslaughter: Arist., *Pol.* 1315b and *Ath. Pol.* 16.8. Archonship, property-tax, and the two altars: Thuc. 6. 54 (Meiggs and Lewis no. 11). Subsidies and circuit-judges: *Ath. Pol.* 16. Road-systems and herms: [Plat.] *Hipparch.* 228b-e; *IGi²* 837 (= *SEG* XV. 53). Buildings: cf. J. Travlos, *Pict. Dict. Anc. Ath.* (1971), 100, 458 (altars), 204 (Kallirrhoe), 402 (Olympieion), 537 (theatre of Dionysos). Eleusis: G. Mylonas, *Eleusis and the Eleusinian Mysteries* (1962), ch. 4; N. J. Richardson, *Hom. Hymn to Demeter* (1974), 9 f. Possible Peisistratic cult of Herakles: Boardman, *Rev. Arch.* (1972), 57 ff. The Great Panathenaia: J. A. Davison, *JHS* 78 (1958), 23 ff.; Boardman, *Rev. Arch.* (1972), 58 n.5. Attic coinage: see above, n. 5. Aristion of Paros: Jeffery, *BSA* 57 (1962), 152; E. Mastrokostas, *AAA* 5 (1972), 298 ff.; N. Kontoleon, *Aspects de la Grèce préclassique* (1970), 53 f., 89 ff. Archermos of Chios: Raubitschek, *DAA*, 484 ff. Architectural fragments: cf. J. S. Boersma, *Athenian Building Policy from 516/0 to 405/4* (1970), chs. II–III; Boardman, *Rev. Arch.*, 69 ff. (Acropolis); Agora area, E. B. Harrison, *The Athenian Agora* XI (1965), 3 ff., 31 ff.

8 Scythian campaign: Hdt. 4. 1–143. Archedike: Thuc. 6. 59,3. Motives of the tyrannicides: Hdt. 5. 57–62,1; Thuc. 6. 54–8. The *skolia*: Bowra, *GLP²*, 373 ff.; for a thorough discussion of the political background see M. Ostwald, *Nomos and the Beginnings of Athenian Democracy* (1969), esp. 126 ff. Loose use of word 'tyrannos' for the active members of a tyrant's family: see below, pp. 229–30. Delphi, Leipsydrion, and the fall of the tyranny: Hdt. 5. 62–5; *Ath. Pol.* 19. Aristocratic stasis: Hdt. 5. 66,1. Zeus Ikarios: D. M. Lewis, *Historia* 12 (1963), 26. *Diapsephismos*: *Ath. Pol.* 13,5. On Athens's early tribal system see the excellent discussion in Forrest, *Emergence*, chs. 2 and 8. Hesiod's advice: *OD* 338–41. Alienability of land, see esp. Andrewes, *The Greeks*, 97 f., 275. The interpretation of the enclaves and the tribal reforms in general (cf. Arist., *Pol.* 1319b) is that of Lewis, *Historia* 12 (1963), 22 ff., a fundamental treatment which also gives credit to Kleisthenes essentially as a reformer rather than a manipulator of the divisions through personal oligarchic ambition; for the latter view see Forrest, *Emergence*, 199 ff.; for a differing viewpoint see now P. J. Bicknell, *Studies in Athenian Politics and Genealogy* (1972). Conciliar oath and election of the *strategoi*: *Ath. Pol.* 22.2; cf. Hignett, *Hist. Ath. Const.*, 166 ff. New citizens: Arist., *Pol.* 1275b and *Ath. Pol.* 21.2,4; for a sceptical view see Wade-Gery, *Essays*, 148 ff. (= *CQ* 27 (1933), 25 f.); admittedly the text of the *Pol.* is disturbed here.

9 Date of the law of ostracism: for the modern dispute as between 508–507 (implied by

the *Ath. Pol.*) and 488–487 (implied by a quotation from Androtion) see Appendix I. The political use of the *hetaireiai* is well attested, even for *ostrakophoriai* ([Andok]. 4.4), cf. most recently W. R. Connor, *The New Politicians in Fifth-century Athens* (1971), 25 ff. The campaign of 506: Hdt. 5. 74–7; Thebes and Aigina, 77; Spartan failure to restore Hippias, 90–3. Embassy to Susa: Hdt. 5. 73; to Sardis, 96. Aid to Ionia: 5. 97–103. Treachery of Hipparchos: Lycurg., *In Leocr.* 117. Phrynichos' punishment: Hdt. 6. 21,2. Miltiades' flight to Athens and prosecution: Hdt. 6. 41,4; 104. Attic sculpture: the specialist studies of Payne, Langlotz and Schrader, and Richter need no mention; for recent work cf. Deyhle and others in *AM* 84 (1969), a tribute to the wide knowledge of E. Homann-Wedeking in this field also.

III

The Peloponnese

8 Sparta: The Messenian Wars, and the Peloponnesian League

The Background

During the seventh and sixth centuries the Greeks of the Eurotas valley, whom we call commonly the Spartans, built up a reputation as the strongest power in Greece. But their system failed in the new epoch created by the final Greek victories against Persia in 479 B.C. That war had shifted the axis of the Greek world to a more realistic balance between the mainland and the Greeks of the Aegean and western Asia Minor. Attica, facing both ways, was now the true pivot. Although Sparta did finally win the Peloponnesian War of 431–404 by a mixture of luck, hard fighting, and the mistakes of her opponent, she showed herself incapable of leading Greece, and from the fourth century onwards what most interested ancient authors about her was her way of life. The unlimited admiration which many of them showed for her institutions has been chiefly responsible for the over-simple generalizations by many later writers, who have seen Sparta variously as the epitome of paleo-Nazism, noble savagery, the English public school before 1939, and so on.

Broadly speaking, the favourable ancient view centred on the word excellence (*arete*). Sparta's citizens, it said, had long been the best living models of the law and order (*eunomia*) for which every city-state strove. Her army was the pattern for all other armies, her valiant simplicity the model for all codes of behaviour; Spartan products – shoes, Army Issue mugs, wine-bowls, wet-nurses – were each the best of its kind for its purpose. But for modern scholars the keyword to explain what Sparta created and represented is conservatism. Her institutions were not necessarily peculiar in themselves, but as survivals of a primitive type of society which anthropological research has made more familiar to us than it was to the Greeks and Romans.

The springs of the Eurotas rise in the Arkadian mountains, and flow south down the long valley called 'hollow Lakedaimon', formed by the towering range of Mount Taygetos on the west and on the east the lower, less abrupt Mount Parnon. At the north end of the valley lay Sparta, a straggling unwalled city formed by four adjacent villages named Pitana, Mesoa, Limnai, and Konosoura. These were the four *obai* of Sparta itself, an ancient noun meaning some kind of settlement. The site dominated the valley, because here converged the main passes to and from the rest of the Peloponnese. West of Taygetos were the Messenians, occupying a still richer area than Lakedaimon, whom the Spartans conquered, probably in stages, between the years *c.* 735–600 (below, pp. 114–20).

East of Parnon lay the Kynouria, a narrow strip where the mountainside sloped down to the sea, broken by flat, fertile plots at points on the coast where the rivers emerged. This area was always claimed by Argos as hers, but it too had become Spartan property before the end of the sixth century.

The Lakedaimonioi were part of the general influx of Hellenic tribes from the north-west beyond the Pindos range, tribes which settled in stages in the Peloponnese after the end of the Mycenean civilization, a process called loosely 'the return of the Herakleidai' by the Greeks and 'the Dorian invasion' by modern convention. The dialect is termed generically north-west Greek, Doric being specifically the speech of Lakedaimon with her north-eastern neighbours Argos, Corinth, Sikyon, and Megara. In Lakedaimon the Spartiatai, holding the dominant position and (possibly) with some tribal tradition to back them, came to control the whole valley before the end of the eighth century. Under Spartiate leadership the other Lakedaimonians, the *perioikoi* (dwellers-round), became a formidable army which lived its civilian life in peaceful villages, offering a fixed homage to the kings in Sparta and managing most of the technical matters for which the Spartiates had little time – shipbuilding, metal-work, commerce, and so on. They were freemen, but not policy-makers. Sparta's officials made the decisions, and the other Lakedaimonians minded their own business and answered the call-up when required. So did the other perioecic settlements which were later settled in the defeated Messenia and Kynouria. It may be that all the *perioikoi* felt genuinely that Sparta's interests and their own coincided. The cynical reply to this is that they had always the example of the Helots (below, pp. 114–15) before them. But even in the great Messenian-Helot revolt of the 460s, which seriously threatened Sparta's existence, only two perioecic villages (Thouria and Aithaia, both in Messenia) joined the rebels.

Thus the Spartans (the term commonly used to include both the Spartiates and the other Lakedaimonians) lived in their river valley, obtaining free from Taygetos and Parnon the protection which Athens only achieved in the mid-fifth century with her costly Long Walls. The insularity of their geographic position influenced their temperament and every aspect of their lives – political institutions, educational system, religious beliefs, and cult of the Muses in general. They did not like new ideas. Inbreeding both intellectual and physical meant that by the fourth century their population had dwindled, their culture was sterile, and even their traditional quality of steadiness had bogged down into sluggishness, a characteristic attacked by Thucydides already in the fifth century. The barrack-room outlook must have been always present potentially in their lives, if it is correct that their educational system (*agoge*) was indeed a very ancient institution; and it must have grown openly after the conquest and permanent overseeing of Messenia. But other factors than military necessity also turned them from the paths of culture. Because they would not or could not adapt themselves to economic innovations, even to one so important as coinage, by the second half of the sixth century Sparta must have been losing her outside markets, though at the same time her army was making her the acknowledged head of a large federation.

Yet something did emerge on the credit side which is often forgotten. If all the creative instincts of a people are channelled into courses which have been fixed for them – by tradition, convention, but sometimes too by external necessity – such channelling may make these instincts concentrate their power into an unusual intensity of vision and purpose, so that within a limited framework they create a result which draws its own severe excellence from the powerful combination of undissipated force with long-practised sureness of touch, as in many examples of primitive art. Something of this phenomenon may be allowed to Archaic Sparta. She produced at least one first-class poet (Alkman), a series of outstanding artists (below, pp. 127–9), and the famous Spartan dancing, solo and choral, in which both sexes excelled. The military system was, as a system, greatly superior to those of its (not unmilitaristic) neighbours; the constitution gave its citizens a sufficient say in things to avoid the dangers of tyranny; and a larger share of the rights and pleasures of life fell to the women there than anywhere else in ancient Greece.

The *agoge*, the training which produced the whole system, was roughly as follows. A male infant born to a Spartiate was carried before the elders of the tribe. If deformed or ailing, he had to be abandoned at once in a ravine on Taygetos called Apothetai; but if deemed healthy, he was returned to his family and reared at home until his seventh year. Then his schooling began. For the first age-class he was enrolled in a 'herd' (*boua*) consisting of a number of boys of his own age under a herdsman (*bouagos*). Dancing, singing, and learning obedience probably formed most of the instruction. The herds moved up annually, and the thirteenth year marked the start of the second age-class – the start of the rigorous training which, graphically described by the later historians and antiquarians, has implanted on the minds of successive ages a fixed meaning for the term Spartan (pallet-beds of Eurotas rushes, cold baths daily in the river, one garment only, and no complaints allowed). Dancing and singing continued in the training, but probably the boys began their military drill in this period and were trained to live off the land like soldiers, i.e., to steal the food for their daily mess from the countryside. Each herd was now in charge of an older leader, called an *iren*; a group of herds formed a (?)drove (*ila*), commanded by 'the best *iren* of the group'. In charge of them all was the *paidonomos* (regulator of the *paides*), a man over the age of thirty. The boys of each year-class apparently had a descriptive title, some of which have survived: *rhoïdas* (fourteenth year), *prokomizomenos*, *mikizomenos*, *propais*, *pais* (eighteenth year). 'Boy' (*pais*) may seem to us the wrong title for a seventeen-year-old, but it was also the name at Olympia for the junior competitors, those in their seventeenth to twentieth years (above that came simply 'men'). In his nineteenth year the youth became *melliren* (*iren*-to-be), and *iren* in his twentieth. The final ten years of training, when he was now also a full soldier, were the toughest of all. Probably the title of *iren* (etymology unknown) applied throughout them, though only the terms *protiren* and *trietires* (first *iren*, third-year *iren*) chance to be attested. The irens seem to have formed the front ranks of the phalanx, and from them came the '300 *hippeis*' who formed a royal bodyguard. In his thirtieth year the soldier became a full citizen, entitled to vote in the Assembly and stand for the ephorate (below, pp. 118–19); he could marry before this age, it seems, but would not be entitled to a house and estate (*kleros*). (An alternative view holds that he became a full citizen at twenty, though candidateship for the ephorate began at thirty.) The *perioikoi* went through a similar training, being equally liable for the call-up; so did the young near-Spartiates of differing social status – the excluded and resentful element from which the Spartiates had to face trouble more than once.

The Cretan system was the only one with which the Greeks, including the Spartans themselves, compared the *agoge*. Modern scholarship, accepting this connection as valid because Crete too had been repopulated by Doric incomers (below, p. 188), sets both places in the light of anthropology and finds the same practices, *mutatis mutandis*, reflected in the training by age-classes of the youths in other warlike tribes: thus the Dorians of the Eurotas valley will have preserved, through conservatism as much as military necessity, a type of system commonly developed in primitive times by an incoming race which has to maintain its dominance over any survivors of the existing population and to fight for its position among independent neighbours.[1]

Constitution and Early Wars

Sparta was ruled by a dyarchy. The two royal families dwelt each in one half of the city, the Agidai in the western *obai*, Pitana and Mesoa, the Eurypontidai in the eastern, Limnai and Konosoura. It is possible that originally two separate leaders ruling their respective settlements agreed to merge their people and hold joint rule thereafter. The Spartan tradition alleged that Agis and Eurypon were the sons of Eurysthenes and Prokles, who were twin great-great-grandsons of Herakles, so that the dyarchy had existed from the start; and later writers describe even the very early kings as already campaigning separately outside Lakedaimon. But the first joint action which they mention (which *may* therefore mark the generation when the dyarchy in fact began) was *c.* 775–750, when the Agid Archelaos and the Eurypontid Charillos defeated Aigys, a town on the Arkadian border, which became thereafter a perioecic dependency. The succeeding Eurypontid Nikandros actually crossed the north-east border and ravaged Argive territory. He was supported by Asine, an Argive city whose ties appear to have lain eastwards with the cities across the Saronic Gulf, for her eighth-century pottery is influenced by Attic rather than Argive Geometric. For this act of defiance Eratos, king of Argos, afterwards besieged Asine, a long siege which apparently took place during or after the First Messenian War; for when the Asineans finally gave in and emigrated, the Spartans gave them a new Asine in the conquered area of Messenia (below, p. 135). Meanwhile Nikandros' colleague Teleklos had campaigned southwards. He reduced three settlements in Lakedaimon – Amyklai, Pharis, and Geronthrai – but not drastically; Amyklai became an *obe* like Sparta's four, and Pharis and Geronthrai seem to have been left as perioecic. He also – a momentous act – first invaded Messenia round the south end of Taygetos. He planted perioecic settlements in the rich southern plain called Makaria on the river Nedon, and finally was killed by the Messenians at the shrine of Artemis Limnatis on the border. His successor Alkamenes, continuing the drive south through Lakedaimon, sacked the town of Helos, which had got Argive support, and reduced the people, not to perioecic dependence, but to the serfdom which was called Helotry after them, according to tradition.

Meanwhile the first war against Messenia started. It lasted twenty years (*c.* 735–715), a long span, which may possibly have been reckoned as starting from Teleklos' actions in Messenia. The Spartan army now attacked round by the north end of Taygetos, circling down into the fertile plain called Stenyklaros. This area was Messene proper, 'the midland', traditionally the home of the Messenian royal family, between Taygetos and the massive Mount Ithome. The name of the whole country means 'the land of Messene'.

This long First War was won by the Eurypontid king Theopompos, according to the fragment of a verse by Tyrtaios, poet of the Second War (F 5W):

> . . . . to our king Theopompos, dear to the gods,
> through whom we took the wide-floored Messene
> . . . [through] the spearmen, fathers of our own fathers.
> In the twentieth year they left their rich farms,
> and began their flight from the heights of Ithome.

Born *c.* 750, the king probably inherited a dragging war, and achieved a decisive victory. The later authors believed that in this war the Spartans took all Messenia. Even if they took only Messene proper (as Tyrtaios says, and is perhaps more likely), they now had a pincer-hold on both north and south. The conquered land was parcelled out in *kleroi* for Spartiates, and the defeated Messenians remained on it as Helots, working the fields on the system of *métayage* (50 per cent of the produce to their new masters). That this war had any direct connection with the Lelantine War (above, pp. 66–7) is perhaps unlikely; but the border states Argos and southern Arkadia must surely have been involved as allies. Argos and Sparta, equals in military power and ambition, were inveterate enemies until the Battle of the Champions *c.* 545 (below, pp. 122, 138–9) docked Argos of her *perioikis* east of Parnon.

About the end of the First War factions developed between the Spartiates proper and the so-called Maidens' Sons (Partheniai), an insulting catchword for men debarred from full citizenship perhaps for various reasons of lineage, not all for bastardy. The centre of rebellion was the *oba* Amyklai, which held the venerable precinct of Apollo Hyakinthios, a famous cult which had its roots in the Bronze Age. The rebels were forced out of the country, and founded a settlement at Taras in southern Italy. This was Sparta's only colony in the Archaic period – a body of embittered men who had not qualified for *kleroi* in the prospective share-out of Messene, and were led by an *oikistes* named Phalanthos, whose name-ending, like that of Hyakinthos in the cult, suggests a non-Doric but high-ranking background, like that of men who were elsewhere to seize power as tyrants in their cities (cf. pp. 46–7, 147). Taras prospered in an idyllic setting of long springs and warm winters, dear to the poet Horace as a holiday retreat. Her political system rejected dyarchy in favour of single rule, but some of the Spartan customs, such as the skilled dancing and the primitive cults, were long preserved there.[2]

The fifth-century Spartans admitted that their early history had been beset continually by riot (*kakonomia*), one facet of which was clearly this resentment over the qualifications needed for full citizenship. A further source of trouble was inherent in the governmental system itself. The dual kingship prevented the dangers of unbridled monarchy, but only at the cost of perpetual friction between the two royal families, a friction often increased by the one house creating or exacerbating quarrels within the other, usually over the succession. The *gerousia* (council of elders), the city's only council, might have been a stabilizing influence, but its composition makes one doubt this. It numbered thirty, that is, the two kings as members *ex officio*, and twenty-eight *gerontes* over sixty years old, with life tenure. Election was confined to certain families only: an oligarchic trait, and in Greek oligarchies the quarrelling for power between heads of families was proverbial. Two at least of the *gerontes* had to be an Agid and Eurypontid, next-of-kin to the kings. Were the 'certain families', one wonders, perhaps the descendants of those men who had been the members of the two chiefs' councils at the time when the dyarchy was formed? If so, there would be a built-in tendency for one-half of the *gerousia* thereafter to side with one king. This state of affairs would admittedly have one possible advantage, that of saving the citizens (the *damos*) from the autocratic control which might be achieved by a united council; thus, perhaps, the *damos* won the more easily its right to decide on the proposals of policy laid before it by the *gerousia* (below, pp. 117–18).

The duties and privileges of Spartan kings are expounded by Herodotos, whose high-born Spartan friends were manifestly *au fait* with all the details and scandals of life in the royal households. The kings had the right of levying war 'against whatever land they chose', and led the army, always being last to leave the field. They had rights over all flocks and herds to feed their troops, and they kept the hides and chines of all victims sacrificed during the campaign. (The right of levying war was vestigial by Herodotos' time, the ephors being the real force in this as in much else; and joint leadership of the army was stopped before the end of the sixth century.) They also retained certain judicial powers: they judged all cases concerning the marriage of heiresses (unless the father had himself arranged the betrothal) and concerning the routes of public roads; and they witnessed all adoptions. They chose the Spartan *proxenoi* for other states, and they maintained a special liaison with Delphi, having four Pythioi (king's messengers to Delphi) and custody of all the oracles given. Each lived in his family house; there were no kings' palaces in Sparta. Each had special honours at public festivals, making the libations and having front seats; but they were expected to dine in the common messes with the other Spartiates, and only got their 'royal' double portions of the food if they did so.

In general the Spartan kingship suggests the primitive tribal leader rather than the sceptre-bearing Agamemnon; Pausanias says that except for a couple of epigrams no poet ever immortalized the deeds of any royal Spartan. Yet they retained a few vestigial traces of divinity. A king should be one begotten by a king, not merely by a crown prince, so the king's heir was not simply the eldest son, but – if possible – the eldest son born to him *after* he himself had succeeded to the throne. If the two kings ever made a joint official decision, they could not be gainsaid. When a king died, each perioecic village had to send its quota of men and women to join with Spartiates and Helots in public mourning of a wild primitive kind with wailing and laceration of cheeks, such as was usually the convention for the women mourners only. There were no public meetings or elections for ten days afterwards, and the new king proclaimed a cancellation of all debts to himself or the state, a kind of *seisachtheia* (above, p. 91).[3]

The Second Messenian War and the Rhetra

The Second War – the revolt of Messenia – broke out during the second quarter of the seventh century; the exact date is uncertain. In 669–668 a Spartan army was severely defeated by the Argives at Hysiai in Argive territory (below, p. 136). This defeat might well encourage a Messenian revolt, whereas it seems unlikely that *after* becoming embroiled with Messenia the Spartans would go looking for trouble by invading Argive territory. This Second War lasted many years, like the first. Tyrtaios' part seems to have been that of the official minstrel, maintaining morale by patriotic songs. Surviving fragments of his elegiacs show that both sides were fighting in some kind of hoplite armour and tactics (F 11W): also, judged by his passionate admonitions, that at some time the Spartan morale was near cracking (F 10W). Stasis was looming again; a fairer share-out of the land was being demanded; and Tyrtaios composed his song *Eunomia* to cope with the emergency. One fragment (F 4W) insists upon the maintenance of Sparta's Three Estates – the kings, *gerousia*, and *damos* (citizen-body) – within their respective spheres of graded power. Its generalizing statements correspond closely with the particular clauses defining the power of the *gerousia* and *damos* which are preserved in an old Spartan text quoted by Plutarch (almost certainly from the lost Aristotelian *Lakedaimonion Politeia*), 'which the Spartans call a Rhetra' (saying, ordinance; above, p. 42). Allegedly an oracle from the Pythia concerning the *gerousia*, it orders that, *having established a cult of Syllanian Zeus and Athena, having done the 'tribing and obing', and having established a* gerousia *of 30 members including the kings,* (1) *season in, season out they are to hold Apellai* (the monthly Apolline festival, after which, while the people were still gathered in from the countryside, the assembly of the *damos* would be held); (2) *the* gerousia *is both (a) to introduce proposals and (b) to stand aloof;* (3) *the* damos *is to have power to* —— (a badly garbled Doric phrase here is glossed by Plutarch (=Aristotle, *Lak. Pol.*) as '*to give a decisive verdict*' (*epikrinai*); (4) (a later addition, according to Plutarch) *but if the* damos *speaks crookedly, the* gerousia *and kings are to be removers*, which last is glossed as '*they are wholly to stand aloof and dismiss the assembly*, as perverting and altering the proposal contrary to the best policy'. Plutarch says, presumably quoting from the missing part of Tyrtaios' poem, that Theopompos and Polydoros added clause 4, and the poem's surviving lines apparently ascribe the whole document to the kings. A joint action by old Theopompos and young Polydoros in the second quarter of the seventh century is chronologically possible, and so is the inscribing of a *rhetra*, perhaps on a bronze plaque like the sixth-century examples of *rhetrai* found at Olympia (below, p. 169). The content could well have been formulated to cure a political crisis, just as Tyrtaios' poem *Eunomia* was said to have done. (For the 'tribing and obing', cf.

below, pp. 119–20; a tribal reform is possible.) The *gerousia* as a body, of course, existed already. Had it previously been thirty (ten per tribe) *without* the kings? If so, did their inclusion now downgrade them slightly, as well as lowering by two the total of the others? Whatever the interpretation, the crucial clauses are clearly 2–4, and their meaning is much disputed. The view here taken is that (2) the *gerousia* alone had the authority (*a*) to lay a proposal before the *damos*, and (*b*) to decline, i.e., to quash, the proposal. For (*b*) the *gerontes* did not have to be unanimous (as they did in more democratic Carthage), so presumably for (*a*) too a majority sufficed. The *damos* heard the proposal put before them (3). They had the right to decide, but *not* to discuss. If the composition of the *gerousia* was indeed as suggested above (p. 116), then it may sometimes (even quite often?) have been deadlocked 50-50 about a proposal, and the people had a real 'casting vote'. In such a situation each side in the *gerousia* must surely have put its own case at the assembly; perhaps even, after a bare majority had introduced a proposal, the minority which had opposed it could make its case too. For the *damos* itself could not discuss; it is described (above) as 'giving a decisive verdict'. Thus the 'crooked speech' in (4) would mean simply criticism and argument (in contrast with '*straight* sayings', the phrase used in Tyrtaios' poem); and then the *gerousia* would close its ranks, wholly decline to continue with the meeting, and dismiss the assembly (thus giving both bodies, one hopes, time to cool down and reflect).

Thus the *rhetra* defined firmly the probouleutic authority of the *gerousia* and, in the last clause (whether or not it is a later addition), its final authority if the *damos* transgressed the authority assigned to it. The latter too was absolute: the decision of the *damos* was to be final upon the proposals laid before it. On the *damos qua* army rested the safety of Sparta, and this concession could go far to explain why she was untouched by the revolutionary winds which created the tyrannies in the Peloponnese now or shortly afterwards.

The *rhetra* may have been the work of a historical Lykourgos, a Spartiate arbitrator of Solon's type, or of a committee, or of the two kings or even one king – for Polydoros was labelled 'philodemos' by later authority. However conceived, it was taken to Delphi for the Pythia to issue as a spontaneous oracle given to Lykourgos, a holy writ which the pious Spartans would not disobey.[4]

Government and Army System

The Three Estates in the *rhetra* and Tyrtaios do not include the ephorate. As yet this office is attested only in Sparta and her offshoots. Some scholars hold that it had always consisted of five members, the ephors ('overseer') being the headmen of the *obai* of Sparta and Amyklai; other pentads are known in the Spartan system. On this view the function of the ephorate as representing the *damos* will have been inherent in the office from the start. The ancient view (possibly influenced by royal propaganda) was that originally they were royal appointments like the Pythioi, and created by Theopompos (according to Aristotle) to sit in judgement as aides to the kings. Certainly much of their duty later concerned the enforcement of the law. In Classical times they were elected by and from the assembly, served for a year, and were not re-eligible. It is not clear which of their judicial powers went back to the Archaic period. Their well-known annual command to the citizens sounds ancient: 'to keep their moustaches shaven and obey the law'; and so does the first half at least of their monthly oath: 'to keep the kingship untoppled – if the kings obeyed the laws'. Divination by the stars, a primitive-sounding aspect of their authority, could be used as a weapon against the kings, for if, in the course of watching, an ephor saw a shooting star, it signified that a king had sinned against the gods. The insertion of an intercalary month to keep the calendar roughly accurate, another ephoral duty, may have been a development from the same powers.

At the time of the *rhetra*, then, they may have been still merely kings' servants. Chilon, the first famous ephor, was eponym in 556. The list of the *eponymoi* seems to have been first officially published, like the Athenian archon-list, in the second half of the fifth century. The late chronographers said that it began with one Elatos in Ol. 6 (756–752 B.C.); but this date may be just an educated guess, stemming from their presumed date for the *floruit* of king Theopompos. If indeed the record went back so far, it certainly was not written down.

The Spartan governmental system retained the Homeric pattern of hereditary kingship, a council of elders, and a warrior assembly. But whereas other cities reduced their kingship to a magistracy, and created a second council from the citizen-body as that body increased its size and its claims to more rights for the assembly, the conservative Spartans left their kings still hereditary war-leaders; stuck to one deliberative body; and gave the assembly power of decision, but not necessarily of initiating proposals too. But Sparta also developed the peculiar office of the ephorate; and whatever difficulties surround our reconstruction of this office, at least it is clear that, had it not developed into a safety-valve for the *damos*, the kings and council would have lost much more power to the assembly than they did.

The 'tribing and obing' in the *rhetra* (above, p. 117) is interpreted to mean a reform of the previous army system. The old Doric division of the people into its three tribes, Hylleis, Dymanes, and Pamphyloi, which hitherto had formed an army of three brigades, perhaps of unequal size and cumbersome to assemble for the harder drilling now required for phalanx-fighting, was retained for general purposes, but the *obe*, the geographic unit, was made the basis of the army for mustering and drilling, each *obe* now serving as a brigade. The total number of the *obai* is unknown; nine is an attractive suggestion, because this is the number of the main divisions which the Spartiates had to form when mustering in 'the pattern of war' for the Karneia, the great and ancient festival to Apollo Karneios, a festival which traditionally was first properly organized in 676. The brigades were undoubtedly divided into smaller sections, and on this new basis the Spartans produced a flexible army of well-drilled units which in the fifth century was acknowledged to surpass all other armies in manoeuvring. Thucydides describes it as an army of officers. Every order could be passed rapidly from the king right down to the young sub-lieutenants (*enomotarchai*), whereas instructions for other armies depended mainly on the single voice of the herald or commander. So the Spartan army was unique in that in any battle all of it knew more or less what it was going to do before doing it. Moreover,

Spartan officers did not always follow the custom of the formal exhortation (*parainesis*) before action. If the commander was a good speaker, this may have raised the morale, but sometimes possibly it merely frayed the nerves. In any case, Thucydides notes astringently, at this stage of the encounter it was less useful than a sound previous training.

In broad terms the effect of this change may be compared with the military reforms made in Europe by Prince Maurice of Orange and expanded in the next generation by Gustavus Adolphus of Sweden, when (based on the old Roman army system) a flexible citizen-army of small units each under a trained and responsible commander replaced the old standard force, an unwieldy square of pikemen, mostly mercenaries, often sixteen ranks deep, and led by a general whose highest flight of skill might be no more than the knowledge of how to 'embattle by the square root' (to draw up a given number of men into a square formation). To get an efficient fighting-machine was undoubtedly the chief idea behind the Spartan reform; but possibly here (as was later the case in Kyrene, Athens, perhaps also Corinth and Sikyon) this reordering of the citizen-body also satisfied some politico-social unrest, the resentment over inequalities inherent in any rigid social system: for example, were some families over-influential in the Doric tribes? Had the four *obai* of Sparta city higher standing than the others? Be that as it may, Xenophon's description of this well-articulated force manoeuvring is full of interest, despite our uncertainty on some details. One point does seem clear, that here – as probably in other Greek states too – the front ranks were formed from the lower age-groups; the heaviest casualties will have been among the year-classes under thirty. Tyrtaios (F 10W) calls on the young men not to retreat and leave the front line to be held by the old men; and Herodotos records the names of the three Spartiates who won Sparta's highest commendation for valour at Plataia in 479, and had two other things in common, that all were irens, and all were dead.[5]

Post-war Development: the Peloponnesian League and the Expulsion of Tyrants

In the end the Spartan army won the Second Messenian War. The main struggle probably ended not long after the mid-seventh century, but the clearance of all pockets of resistance throughout all Messenia may have lasted many years more, with a last flare-up of resistance at the northern border, in Hira. The list of allies seems credible: Sparta had support from Samos (perhaps in ships to mop up along the coast), Elis, Bacchiad Corinth (i.e., before 657; below, pp. 146–7), and Lepreon – evidently from Argive Nauplia too (as in the First War from Asine), for Argos evicted the Nauplians after this war (below, p. 138), and Sparta settled them at Mothone on the Messenian coast. Messenia was aided by the Arkadians, Sikyon, and Argos (at this time under king Pheidon), Pisa, and some Eleans (below, pp. 136, 162, 168, 171).

A whole rich country had now been added to Spartan territory. Some places were settled with *perioikoi*, but most were parcelled out into Spartiate *kleroi*. In the reign of the Eurypontid Latychidas near the end of the century the poetry of Alkman gives a bright, sharp glimpse of a Sparta freed from stress. Alkman was famous for his *Partheneia*, songs for bands of girls from the high Spartiate families to sing at festivals to a goddess or heroine. Half the choir might sing alternate verses, or some might be sung solo. The lyrics profess to be the thoughts of the girls themselves, praising the beauty of their leaders with the emotional attachments of adolescence expressed in the language of court poetry:

> Astymeloisa answers nothing.
> She holds out Hera's wreath,
> and like a star falling through the bright heaven,
> or a gold wand, a downy feather . . . (F 2P)

Astymeloisa, Megalostrata, Agido, Klesimbrota and Timasimbrota: the names of the leaders remind us that they were the daughters of a warrior aristocracy (citadel-care, great army, leader, renown to man, honour to man).

Sparta continued to extend her power in the sixth century, for the aftermath of this war developed into a fresh one under the kings Leon and Agasikles, starting from the reprisals made against the allies of Messenia. Many exiled Messenians had found safety across the border in southern Arkadia. This area had as yet no important state, but it lay within the expanding aims of two other Arkadian powers, Tegea and Orchomenos to the north-east. Spartan forces moved up into the area, initially perhaps in pursuit of Messenians, and were defeated by Orchomenos, it seems, in a campaign of which very little is known. Later, but still in the first half of the sixth century, they trusted in an ambivalent oracle from Delphi and actually advanced into the Tegeate plain to seize it for more *kleroi*. Here they met with a famous defeat, and their survivors were held as serfs to labour there until their ransoms came – wearing meanwhile the chains which they themselves had brought for the Tegeates.

In the long run Tegea would have had little hope against Sparta; but about the mid-sixth century the Spartans altered their policy. Delphi advised them to turn mythology to propagandic use: to acquire somehow for Sparta the bones of the hero Orestes son of Agamemnon, which lay in Tegeate territory. An impressive grave, presumably of the Bronze Age, was located in an ironsmith's yard in the plain and rifled secretly for the Spartans by one of their trained Special Service élite known as the Agathoergoi. The Spartans now had on their side the great hero who had hitherto preserved the country in which he was buried; and would he have gone with them willingly unless they too had some right to call themselves his descendants? The Tegeates accepted this after some losses in further fighting, and a treaty was inscribed on stone at the border between Tegeate and ex-Messenian territory, in which Tegea undertook not to enfranchise or harbour Messenians thereafter. She was then taken into military alliance with Sparta, and thus became an early member of what developed into a military league of Peloponnesian states under Spartan hegemony.

This new and ambitious policy of welding the Peloponnesian states together into a league rather than continuing the primitive pattern of subjection by conquest is best associated with the lifetime of the kings Anaxandridas and Ariston, in whose reign Tegea was brought in, and of Chilon, traditionally ephor in 556, who, says an ancient authority, first 'yoked the ephors alongside the kings'. Based on the account of the bones of Orestes, modern research has reconstructed a credible picture of the propaganda given out by Spartan diplomacy from *c.* 550 onwards; it claimed that the Spartans should lead the Peloponnese by right as well as might, because they too, no less than the Argives, their rivals, were Achaioi, heirs of Agamemnon as well as of the Dorian hero Herakles. In addition to this 'philachaian' policy the Spartans gained further credit and authority during the sixth century by sending forces on request to rid Greek states of their tyrants. The names of Anaxandridas and Chilon are linked in a papyrus fragment which says that 'Chilon the Lakedaimonian, having been ephor and [?]commander, and Anaxandridas pulled down the tyrannies in Greece: in Sikyon Aischines, Hippias [at Athens], Peisistrat[os' son? ——]'; and another, fuller source adds the tyrannies in Corinth and her colony Ambrakia, and in Naxos (with four others whose evictions suggest a date in the early fifth century). Corinth's last tyrant fell in 583 (below, p. 151); the Spartans may well have abetted the descendants of the original Corinthian (Bacchiad) exiles – some of whom had settled in Sparta – to return and depose this tyrant, but they are not likely to have begun their League so early, and with so remote an ally, before they had settled their own northern border by securing Tegea. Corinth certainly joined Sparta's League, but probably after the mid-century; both had common ground in a mutual distrust of Argos. The event of 583 may, however, have germinated the policy which Anaxandridas and Chilon developed in the next generation. The Sikyonian was evicted *c.* 556 (possibly he had succumbed to Argive propaganda; below, p. 165). The Athenian and Naxian tyrants fell later, in the reign of Anaxandridas' son Kleomenes (below, p. 125); but about 546, when the Persians under Cyrus I had advanced westward and were indirectly threatening Lydia, Kroisos, the Lydian monarch, sought alliance with Sparta as being the chief military power of the time in Greece. Clearly the efforts of Anaxandridas and Chilon were bearing impressive fruit, whether or not they had quarrelled (as a modern view holds) over the philachaian policy. Sparta accepted the alliance. When Kroisos, after a defeat by Cyrus, called on her urgently for aid, she prepared (Herodotos says) to send a fleet, but news of the final collapse of Lydia came before it could be dispatched. It is doubtful if in fact she would have embarked on an expedition overseas, because she had just invaded Thyrea in the Kynourian district which Argos also claimed. An Ionian plea for help after the fall of Lydia received equally restrained support. Meanwhile the Argives were heavily defeated in the Battle of the Champions (below, pp. 138–9), and gave Sparta no further trouble for over a generation.

About 525, near the end of Anaxandridas' reign, Sparta attacked another tyrant, Polykrates of Samos. This time she did send a naval force across the Aegean, at the request of Samian oligarchs whom Polykrates had exiled. There is evidence that oligarchic Samos had had artistic and trading ties with Sparta (below, pp. 216–17), so Sparta may have had a practical motive for her support. The Corinthians readily joined the expedition – and presumably contributed a good part of the ships – which again suggests commercial motives, as well as indicating that Corinth was by now a member of the League. The attempt was a complete and costly failure.

The cases of Samos and Athens, which are well documented for us by

Herodotos, suggest strongly that what the later writers referred to as Sparta's great achievement, the expulsion of tyranny from Archaic Greece, was derived from Spartan propagandic wording for the extension of her sphere of influence by means of her military League. The pattern revealed at Athens and Samos alike was probably characteristic of the method: a resentful oligarchic party, within the city concerned or in exile, called in a Spartan force, sometimes through family ties of hereditary friendship (*xenia*) with the family of one of the Spartan kings. If the tyrant was ejected and the oligarchy restored, this meant that the city would now be added to the League. Sparta had a natural sympathy with aristocratic rule rather than despotism, and the bias of oligarchies towards internal quarrelling helped her to keep a city within the League on the simple principle of 'divide et impera'. If there was any one interest common to the League members, it was probably distrust of Argos. The hostility between Sparta and Argos dated back at least to the eighth century, and increased in the seventh when the Argive Pheidon was king. As long as Sparta claimed some kind of control over the southern Arkadian area and – worse still – tried to seize the land beyond Mount Parnon, this hostility was bitter. So Sparta may have profited from the antagonism roused in other cities by the claims of Argos to control them as part of the Heritage of Temenos (below, pp. 134–9). Large and small places alike – Sikyon and Epidauros, Corinth, Mantineia, Tegea – whose borders marched with those of the Argive *perioikis* might all hope for some protection by joining a common military League led by the largest anti-Argive power.[6]

The Reign of Kleomenes

The death of Anaxandridas *c.* 522 left two sons with claims to his throne. This happened because of a political crisis earlier in his reign. His wife had borne no male child and he had to yield to pressure from the ephorate and take a second wife to get a royal heir. This wife was of Chilon's family, and she bore him a son, Kleomenes. Then he left her – at least, she had no more children – and returned to the first wife, who bore him three sons in all, Dorieus (a name which stresses his Heraklid rather than his 'Achaian' ancestry) and then Leonidas, who was later to lead the Greek forces at Thermopylai, and Kleombrotos, who may have been Leonidas' twin. Thus Kleomenes was the eldest son, but Dorieus the eldest by the first, true queen. Doubtless rival parties within the Agidai and Chilon's family fostered the dispute. Kleomenes' claim prevailed, and to Dorieus fell a role commonly offered to a failed leader in stasis (above, pp. 52–3); he led out a colony. Doric propaganda had long stressed the renowned route westward of the great Herakles from the Peloponnese across Sicily and the shores of the western Mediterranean to far Erytheia (identified by the Greeks as Tartessos in Spain) to win the cattle of the triple-bodied herdsman Geryon – a route for the heirs of Herakles to follow. Dorieus led his colony first to the Kinyps river in Libya, west of Sparta's 'granddaughter' Kyrene; and when this settlement failed through local Carthaginian and Libyan hostility, he returned to Sparta, redeployed his forces upon oracular advice, and tried in Sicily, where many Doric colonies had succeeded. But here also he failed, and was killed in battle.

Thus Kleomenes had succeeded to the Agid throne. Herodotos tells us enough anecdotes to make it clear that, after this unhappy start as the only son of a cast-off morganatic wife, reared presumably in a childhood atmosphere of hatred and ambition, he grew up with some severe kind of neurosis. Modern scholarship has interpreted his character and career diversely: either as an ambitious and powerful ruler who followed his father's policy and tried to make Sparta's leadership of the League develop into a leadership of all Greece, until at last, after ominous signs of self-aggrandisement, the depressive side of his complaint won and he went mad; or as one who, even at his sanest, was an ineffective bungler and went far towards losing the power which his father had won for Sparta.

Nearly all our knowledge of his reign (c. 521–491) comes from Herodotos, and (inevitably in a non-consecutive narrative covering so wide a range in space and time) the account is disjointed, one piece apparently from a favourable source, another from an unfavourable ('a most upright man', 3. 148,2; 'verging on madness, whereas Dorieus was all that a Spartan should be', 5. 42,1). The most hostile sources would be the true queen's Agid next-of-kin, and the family of the Eurypontid king Damaratos, who was exiled through Kleomenes' agency (below, p. 125); the most favourable, his mother's family and the Eurypontid next-of-kin of Latychidas, who succeeded Damaratos. One asks naturally: did Kleomenes follow his father's policy—enlarge the scope of Spartan hegemony, continue hostile to Argos, and hold a watching brief on the movements of Persia?

On the first point, it seems clear that Kleomenes would accept no long-distance commitments which involved any sustained use of Lakedaimonian or League troops. Thus c. 519, when he was in Boiotia (reason unspecified) with a force of men, Plataia, then under attack from Thebes, offered herself for membership of the League; but he refused her on the score of distance, and urged her instead to apply to her southern neighbour Athens, which she did, and became one of the several small independent allies who served Athens so well through the fifth century. So, at no cost to his city, he won Athenian gratitude at the time, while ensuring that, if Spartan-Athenian relations should worsen later (as they did), Sparta would have a valuable ally in a Thebes now fiercely anti-Athenian. Again c. 517, backed by the ephors, he refused to let Sparta be drawn into another involvement overseas with Samos. Syloson, nephew of Polykrates, had brought Persian control into Samos as the price of his own assumption of rule there. Maiandrios, the caretaker governor, had bowed before the Persian show of force; but rather than see Syloson in his own place, says Herodotos, he fled to Sparta and tried vainly to bribe Kleomenes to restore him to power – whether under Persian rule or not is unclear. Again, after the Persian king Darius had failed in his invasion of Scythia, a Scythian embassy tried without success c. 513 to get Spartan aid for a proposed pincer movement to catch the retreating Persian army. Herodotos recalled this because the Spartan tradition said that Kleomenes was a heavy drinker, and that he had learnt this from the embassy. Lastly, a second appeal for aid from Ionia at the turn of the century was refused. Aristagoras, tyrant of Miletos, was heading a revolt by the Greeks of Asia Minor against the rule of Persia, and a Milesian embassy made a direct appeal to the king, hoping to persuade him by promises of untold wealth for the conqueror of Persia; but Kleomenes, on hearing that it involved not only the sea-voyage to Ionia but three months' march inland to reach Susa, refused point-blank. Tradition said that his small daughter Gorgo stiffened his resolution when he might otherwise have yielded to temptation, and so the Ionians got no help from the League. A further reason for refusing might have been that Sparta as a friend of oligarchic Samos was not keen to back an enterprise headed by Miletos, Samos' chief enemy. Certainly Samos' participation in the revolt was distinctly half-hearted (below, pp. 219–21).

But Kleomenes took vigorous action in commitments nearer home. About 510 there came a chance to enlarge the northern border of the League by bringing in Attica. Kleisthenes the Alkmeonid and the other leading men who opposed the rule of the tyrant Hippias had bribed the Pythia to persuade the Spartans into sending an army to put down the tyranny, a course which would subsequently bring Athens into the League. The first League force, led by a Spartiate commander, went up by sea, landed on the shore at Phaleron, and was repulsed by a thousand horsemen sent from Athens's ally Thessaly. Kleomenes himself led the next attack, by land through Megara and Eleusis. He evicted the tyrant and his family, made (or possibly renewed) a *xenia* with the family of Isagoras, the leading oligarch, and soon afterwards returned to Attica with a small force – i.e., this was not a League decision, one supposes – and tried to support Isagoras in the dynastic struggle which broke out between his party and that of Kleisthenes. This attempt, which sought to change the constitution to a narrow oligarchy of 300, failed completely, and Isagoras fled to Sparta; but *c.* 506 he returned with the whole League army, this time under the two kings Kleomenes and Damaratos. The compact was that Kleomenes should set him up as *tyrannos* of Athens. But when the plan became known, Damaratos objected (for which Kleomenes later engineered his deposition), and so did the contingent from Corinth, which had as yet no cause for quarrel with Athens, and, as a city, was powerful enough to stand up to Sparta if she chose. So the League force disintegrated, and the plan with it; and when *c.* 504 a final Spartan project was started, this time actually to bring back Hippias the Peisistratid as tyrant, it did not even survive the meeting of League deputies called to discuss it at Sparta. Again Corinth led the opposition. Oracles uttered in the past to Athens, which were brought back by Kleomenes from his first attempt with Isagoras, figured in this abortive project. But Herodotos never mentions the king's name as a planner here, and it seems unlikely that he would have agreed to Hippias, his past foe whom he had driven from Athens, as ruler there once more. Isagoras, now in exile, was perhaps more likely to have put the Spartans up to this.

Athens, then, was one area where he was prepared to take action. Another was Naxos; *c.* 517 the Spartans evicted Lygdamis, the tyrant there, demonstrably to help oligarchy, but perhaps also to remove a possible supporter of Persia (below, p. 181). Another was Argos, the perennial enemy. Kleomenes mounted a major attack *c.* 494, about fifty years after the Argive defeat at Thyrea, which implies that a fifty-year truce had been signed at that time. Now he invaded Argive territory by sea, and defeated her army so heavily at Sepeia near Tiryns that she took another generation, it was said, to recover her manpower. Tradition also said that he made this attack because the Pythia had foretold that he would capture Argos. She had earlier given a joint reply to a joint embassy from Argos and Miletos (allies of old), an embassy sent probably in the years between 499, when Miletos was starting her revolt and seeking allies (below, p. 139), and 495, when the revolt was weakening. The riddling oracle suggested to Argos the danger of a future defeat by some trickery, and to Miletos, unequivocally, defeat and slavery if she opposed Persia, a power which the Delphic oracle clearly feared to offend, both then and later in 480–479.

Kleomenes did not capture the city itself. He massacred many of the leading oligarchs who had sought sanctuary in a holy grove named Argos after its hero-inhabitant, and burnt down the grove. Put on trial by his enemies, says Herodotos, before the ephors for not capturing the city, he claimed that the grove was the Argos meant by the Pythia; this had been revealed to him by the portent of a light flaring from the breast of Hera's cult-statue in the great Argive Heraion outside the city, when he went there to sacrifice and ask if the deity meant him to sack Argos itself. The story of this campaign illustrates the complexity of his character: an able commander, but savage to the defeated foe; a subtle planner who evidently had some compact with those inside the city *not* to reduce it; and a cynic who, despite his proclaimed respect for oracles and portents, was prepared to blast his way to his objectives by open sacrilege at times; for, though very diplomatic once to Athena's priestess on the Athenian Acropolis (p. 48, n. 4), he had the priest of Argive Hera scourged for opposing him, cut down a sacred grove in the plain of Eleusis, and bribed the Pythia to support by an oracle his allegations against his co-king Damaratos. Like the able but unscrupulous general Lysander a century later, he was prepared to 'patch the Heraklid lion-skin with the fox where necessary'.

The reign of Kleomenes spanned the period *c.* 520–490, when the power of Persia, now solidly based in satrapies stretching from the Bosporos down to Cilicia, was probing for further moves westward. There were always Greek exiles like Syloson of Samos at the court at Susa ready to give the Great King information on the situation in Greece and, if exile had made them very bitter against the government in their city, to offer that city as a dependency if he could provide the troops to put the exile back in power. Sparta had been a mouthpiece for the mainland Greek states in defying Persia earlier, but it is hard to say whether her foreign activity under Kleomenes was geared to any declared or consistent anti-Persian policy. Certainly the Peisistratidai in Athens were technically Medizers, through intermarriage and their ownership of Sigeion (above, pp. 98–9); and Lygdamis, tyrant of Naxos, was their friend and supporter. The Argives were certainly pro-Persian by 480–479. But the appeals to Sparta for aid from Maiandrios (who had fled from the Persians in Samos, though admittedly not having resisted them), the Scythians, and Aristagoras had no results. The Spartan policy seemed to be to expend no troops until the menace was much nearer and clearer. Here Kleomenes' last recorded action as head of the League is interesting. About 492–491 Aigina, Athens's perpetual enemy and never a popular member of the Peloponnesian League either, upon demand gave earth and water, the tokens of submission, to the Great King's envoys; this was presumably to ensure the safety of her trade-routes through the southern and south-eastern Aegean. At Athens's request Kleomenes swooped on Aigina with an armed force to displace her Medizing government. Damaratos, trying once more to thwart his co-king's project, was deposed as a bastard on Kleomenes' contriving, which was backed by an oracle given by a bribed Pythia named Perialla; and his cousin Latychidas succeeded him as king. He left Sparta not long after and went over to Persia, settling there on an estate granted to him and his descendants, and accompanying Xerxes on the campaign against Greece. But according to Herodotos he warned the Spartans in advance of the invasion, and never spoke against Sparta and her ways to Xerxes. He gave one piece of military advice in 480: to split the united resistance of Athens and Sparta by threatening Kythera, the vitally strategic island off the south-east cape of Lakedaimon, and so bringing the Spartans down from the Isthmus and central Greek waters to defend it. But this meant also splitting the Persians' fleet and depriving Xerxes, with the land army, of the support of 300 ships.

Damaratos' advice was not taken, for good or ill (and we cannot tell which he meant it to be). As for Kleomenes, his action in delivering the Aiginetan Medizers as hostages to Athens was defiantly anti-Persian. But not long after this the supporters of the exiled Damaratos roused such feeling against him that he too fled into exile, first to Thessaly and then to Arkadia, where he tried to raise rebellion against Sparta as head of the League. Yet he returned to Sparta when the government hastily called him back to be king once more; but now, according to Herodotos, his madness had taken a firm hold, and when his family confined him in wooden stocks, he hacked himself to death with a knife borrowed from his Helot guard. He was succeeded by his half-brother Leonidas, whose stand at the pass of Thermopylai in 480 informed the world once more of the best qualities of the Spartans, valour and obedience. Damaratos had told Xerxes that the only thing which they feared was the Law, which told them to keep their ranks (*menein en tei taxei*).

> Report to Sparta, passer-by,
> *Orders obeyed: here we lie.*

The epitaph written by Simonides, using for 'orders' *rhemata*, an echo of the old word *rhetra*, rightly has the terseness of a military dispatch.[7]

Art

The surviving sculpture, pottery, and bronzes of Archaic Sparta are now well-known through many specialist studies. Her art is discussed here in some detail only because the references in ancient sources are less known, and bring out well its remarkable character. Like that of other countries before the Renaissance, it was necessarily shaped by two basic factors: the materials available in the area; and the social and religious conventions of the society for which the artists worked. The local stone is a hard bluish marble, and Lakedaimon has so far yielded no fine stone sculpture earlier than the mid-sixth century. Wood was the obvious material. Taygetos must have been well-wooded then, for it was a great place for game. (The Spartiates were keen huntsmen; in this way they kept fit when their compulsory military training had ended, and provided the additional luxury of meat for their public messes.) The famous Lakedaimonian artists were wood-carvers and workers in bronze, a skill which also needs wood – brushwood and charcoal for the furnaces and wood for the cores of the plate-bronze images. Pausanias at Olympia noted particularly two archaic groups (probably statuettes) made of gilded cedarwood, both by Lakedaimonian sculptors, Sikyon-trained. By his time the figures were scattered in the Heraion and treasuries. Both groups showed labours of Herakles, Sparta's great hero; the *Apples of the Hesperidai* was by Theokles son of Hegylos and his son (unnamed; possibly also Hegylos), and the *Wrestling with Acheloös* was by Dontas and Medon(?), brother of Dorykleidas.

The second basic factor, that of convention, was especially potent in Sparta. The primitive type of aniconic or part-iconic cult-image was persistent there. As a start, there were the *dokana* (beams), two wooden uprights joined by a crossbeam, which represented the twin Dioskouroi, Castor and Pollux, and accompanied the army on campaigns to bring good luck. As for Apollo, whose worship was everywhere in divers tribal or local cults, there were ram-headed pillars typifying his aspects as Karneios: columns before house-doors (like the equally primitive Attic herms) for him as Agyieus (of Crossroads); the weird Apollo Tetracheir, four-handed and four-eared; and above all the identical Apollo-colossi, Hyakinthios at Amyklai and Pythaieus at Thornax, each a great bronze-plated and gilded wooden mast some 45 feet high, with feet, a helmed head, and hands holding a bow and spear. A fifth-century statue of Zeus dedicated by Sparta at Olympia was almost certainly in the same part-iconic style; it was particularly apt for female statues, whose tubular bronze tunics could be decorated with bands of figures in relief as elaborate as the woven or embroidered strips on their real clothes. This was probably the type of the famous bronze Athena Poliouchos (Citadel-holder) at Sparta made by the renowned bronze-sculptor Gitiadas, who made also the bronze reliefs which covered the walls of her temple, thus giving her the added title Chalkioikos (Bronze-housed). He also composed poetry, we are told, including a Hymn to Athena in Doric.

But cult-statues alone would never be the true mirrors of a people's art, based as they are on canons other than the purely visual and technical – even the great Athenas of Pheidias, the Promachos and Parthenos, were somewhat conventional in their stance. The secular bronzework of Sparta was among the best in Greece. It has been recognized in a variety of utensils which were widely exported: mirrors, hydriae, and other vases, their handles formed by naked boys or girls, long-haired and long-legged, often with added decorations of small couching lions or sheep (Pl. 14); statuettes of hoplites and soft-slippered women with skirts pleated at the back like kilts; and the wine-kraters noted especially by Herodotos, of which the splendid Vix krater at Châtillon-sur-Seine is surely an example.[8]

The characteristic Spartan stone relief-stelai probably start after the mid-sixth century. On the best-known example a male and female sit side by side in profile. He holds out a chalice (kantharos) and his face is frontal, as if he asks directly for drink-offerings from the viewers. She holds a pomegranate, while veiling (or unveiling) her face. Two worshippers are shown in miniature as in the medieval artist's convention, the man offering a hen and egg, the woman a flower and pomegranate. A great snake – a chthonic symbol like the pomegranate – crawls up the throne-back. Six planes in all are shown, flattening as they recede into the background. The sliced effect suggests a knife on wood; perhaps earlier examples were wooden. The type continued into the fifth century, showing pairs or single figures, seated or standing. The most likely interpretation suggests that they are funerary, in that they show dead mortals rather than gods, but are also dedicatory in a sense, because in conservative Sparta dead citizens could be heroized, i.e. worshipped as chthonic spirits, when other cities had long ceased this practice except in the special cases of kings or founders of colonies (Pl. 16).

The pottery ('Lakonian') flourished through the years c. 580–510 (Pl. 15), and was exported to Taras; Katane in Sicily; Kyrene, Sparta's granddaughter; Samos, her oligarchic friend; Naukratis (via Samos or Kyrene?); and elsewhere. The potters borrowed the black-figure technique from the experts of Corinth, but were satisfied with simpler background decoration than the carpeting style of the Corinthians. Three workshops have been identified for c. 570–530: those of the Arkesilas Painter and his gifted pupils the Naukratis and Hunt Painters. The Arkesilas and Hunt Painters even labelled their figures, the Hunt Painter achieving the neat, square lettering which predominates in the stone inscriptions of Lakedaimon, suggesting that all these crafts may have been confined to small guilds or even families, as Herodotos says of heralds and cooks in Sparta.

One further factor may have limited the development of Spartan art – not merely concentrated it in certain pathways, but stopped it even there from reaching the highest peaks. Perhaps this was not simply, as some critics hold, because Sparta stifled her development by her barrack-room outlook, but also because, within their self-imposed military and religious discipline, the well-to-do Spartiates lived *too* safely and securely. If that sounds somewhat Victorian, it may not be inapposite; for, however much we may appreciate the craftsmanship of the safe Victorian epoch, plainly its products will never be ranked for genius near those of some north Italian city-states in the fifteenth century, achieved amidst the throes of external and internal strife. The well-born Spartiates of the Archaic period lived comfortably on their estates and their hunting; but their wealth was not of the material, ready-cash kind which could demand, and get, higher and higher standards of work from artists competing fiercely for commissions. Moreover, the Spartans did not have the world on their doorsteps (as did the Athenians or the Venetians), bringing in new ideas and objects by the boatload. Lastly, they never experienced that mental fervour or stress which, in a sudden extension of the frontiers of learning, boils out in the great art of a Renaissance. The Spartan was trained as a soldier not to break ranks to pursue either the beaten foe or the paths of learning.

NOTES

Recent and basic studies of Spartan history, here referred to by author's name only:
G. L. Huxley, *Early Sparta* (1962); W. G. Forrest, *A History of Sparta 950–192* B.C.
(1968); A. Toynbee, *Some Problems of Greek History* (1969).

1 Spartan institutions: Xen., *Lak. Pol.*; Arist., *Pol.* and Frr. 532–45 Rose; Plut., *Lycurg.*;
   FGH 581–98. Shoes and mugs: Kritias, F 34D[4]. Wine-bowls: Hdt. 1. 70. Nurses:
   Plut., *Alcib.* 1. Thouria and Aithaia: Thuc. 1. 101,2. Spartan sluggishness: 1. 70–1.
   Coinage and economy: G. Stubbs, *CQ* 44 (1950), 32 ff. Dancing: Pollux, *Onomast.* 4.
   102–8; Athen. 14. 630–1. The classic articles comparing the Spartan system with those
   of the Zulu and Masai are H. Jeanmaire, *REG* 26 (1913), 121 ff., and W. S. Ferguson,
   Harv. Afr. Studies 2 (1918), 197 ff. The *agoge*: Xen., *Lak. Pol.* 2–4; Plut., *Lycurg.*
   16–17. The technical terms are often baffling and the details disputed, but the general
   lines seem clear. Dances and the Gymnopaidia festival: Wade-Gery, *CQ* 43 (1949),
   79 ff.; for the year-classes I follow the Strabo gloss ap. A. Diller, *AJP* 62 (1941),
   499 ff. *Trietires*: J. Bingen, *Ant. Class.* 27 (1958), 105 ff. (on *IG* v.1. 1120). For the
   term 'pais' in the Games, see H. A. Harris, *Greek Athletes and Athletics* (1964), 154 f.
   Citizenship at 20: M. White, *JHS* 84 (1964), 41.
2 Other early dyarchies: H. Mitchell, *Sparta* (1952), 101 ff. For a 20th-c. example, E. M.
   Forster, *The Hill of Devi* (1953), 37 ff. For the alleged actions of the early kings before
   c. 600 (when Herodotos' account takes over) the chief source is Paus. 3. 2,1–3,5 and 7.
   1–6 (probably mainly from the Spartan writer Sosibios, *FGH* 595); see the reconstruc-
   tions in Huxley, chs. 1–2; Toynbee, 172 f.; and esp. Forrest, chs. 3–4 and *Phoenix* 17
   (1965), 176 ff. Asine: Paus. 2. 36,4; 3. 7,4; 4. 14,3. Her pottery: P. Courbin, *La
   Céramique géometrique de l'Argolide* (1966), 61; Coldstream, *GGP*, 132 f.; cf. further
   W. S. Barrett, *Hermes* 82 (1954), 421 ff. and Kelly, *Historia* 16 (1967), 422 ff. Telekles
   in Messenia: Str. 360. The absolute dates for the First War's 20 years (Tyrt. F 5W) are
   estimated (1) from the Olympic victor lists (below, p. 168), which show seven
   Messenians between 776 and 736, thereafter only one (Phanas, killed in the Second
   War). A Spartan first won in 720; thereafter they proliferate, and to get to Olympia the
   Spartans had to go via northern Messenia or Arkadia. Paus. 4. 15,1 sets the end of the
   war (the capture of Ithome, in his account) *c.* 724, i.e. 10 years too high. (2) The
   foundation-date of Taras (above, p. 115) is estimated by the pottery as *c.* 710. The date
   of king Theopompos' birth should be *c.* 750 or slightly later, if three kings per century
   is a realistic average. Messene proper = Stenyklaros, see Ephoros, *FGH* 70 F 116 and
   F. Kiechle, *Messen. Studien* (1959), ch. 4, who argues that Sparta only conquered the
   whole of this large country in the Second War, a view here accepted. Taras: Antiochos
   of Syracuse, *FGH* 555 F 13; Eph., *FGH* 70 F 216; D. Sic. 8. 21; and in general P.
   Wuilleumier, *Tarente* (1939).
3 Royal friction: Hdt. 6. 52,8; 61–6. *Gerousia*: restricted election, Arist., *Pol.* 1306a (in
   Sparta as in Elis; I do not see how the passage is to be otherwise interpreted); royal
   next-of-kin, Hdt. 6. 57,5; a straight split in the *gerousia* at the trial of king Pausanias in
   403, Paus. 3. 5,2. Kings: duties and privileges, Hdt. 6. 56–60; epigrams, Paus. 3. 8,2;
   supremacy when both in unison, Hdt. 6. 73,2 and 86,1; heir, Hdt. 7. 7,3; on Leonidas'
   death in 480 the successor was his own son Pleistarchos – not Euryanax, son of
   Leonidas' dead elder brother Dorieus, for Dorieus had never been a king. This
   succession does not imply, against Herodotos, that Dorieus was in fact younger than
   Leonidas (A. H. M. Jones, *Sparta* (1967), 49).
4 The ancient dates for the Second War are contradictory. Pausanias, as for the First
   War, is dependent on a late poet's version, and reliable only in patches. He gives the

date as 685–668 (4. 15,1 and 23,4), but in 29,9–11 says that it ended in 657, i.e., he continues to lower things by about 10 years (675–657); this version may be deduced from the reordering of the Karneia, the great local festival, in 676 (below), if it was thought to be connected with the start of the war. Some scholars believe *c.* 668 to be in fact the most likely date for the start, after Sparta's defeat by Argos at Hysiai (Paus. 2. 24,7). According to Plutarch (*Mor.* 194b) the end was *c.* 600; this could imply (as accepted here) that after the organized resistance had collapsed, the final reduction of all Messenia still took a long time. Tyrtaios and the threat of stasis: Arist., *Pol.* 1306b–07a. The *rhetra*: see Appendix II. Evidence on Polydoros: Appendix II.

5 Only A. H. M. Jones, *Sparta*, has argued that the *damos* in the *rhetra* stands for the ephorate. Ephors at Thera: *IG* xii. 3,322; Herakleia, *IG* xiv.645; Kyrene, Chamoux, *Cyrène*, 214–16. Pentads: *agathoergoi*, Hdt. 1. 67; arbitrators, Plut., *Sol.* 10; *lochoi* (with archaic names), Schol. Thuc. 4. 8; note also that Dorieus' expeditions (above, pp. 123–4) were led by himself and four other captains, which suggests 5 contingents. Election of ephors: Arist., *Pol.* 1265b, 1270b, 1294b. Monthly oath: Xen., *Lak. Pol.* 15. Theopompos as creator of the office, and the ephoric judgement-seats: cf. *Pol.* 1313a; Xen., *Lak. Pol.* 15; Plut., *Agis and Kleom.*, 8–11; *Ages.*, 4. The ephor-list: Apollodoros, (D. Laert., I. 3,1 (68)); date of its publication in the 5th c., see *LSAG*, 60, 196. The muster system at the Karneia (a copy of the war-muster, D. Skepsis ap. Athen. 4. 141e–f, our only informant on this) was clearly ancient. The Karneia was traditionally refounded by the poet Terpander, summoned in 676 to allay disputes in Sparta. The three tribes were mustered into 9 'tents', i.e., each tribe contained 3 units, which in the muster at Kos (cf. Appendix II) were called 'thousands' (*chiliastyes*). Each tent itself had 3 phratries (also at Kos). We therefore equate each tent with an *obe*, and postulate 9 *obai* in all, which in war produced x (27??) regiments. Cf. Huxley, 48–9 and Forrest, 42–6, a brilliant reconstruction of the Archaic tribal/obal army system to which the reader is referred. Thuc. on the Spartan army, 5. 68–9. Military reforms in Holland and Sweden: for everything cited above see the Inaugural Lecture before the Queen's University, Belfast by Professor M. Roberts, *The Military Revolution of 1560–1600* (1956), a reference I owe to Dr E. A. O. Whiteman. Xenophon on manoeuvring: *Lak. Pol.* 11. 5–10. Age groups under 30 (*ta deka aph' hebes*) ranked in front: cf. Toynbee, *JHS* 33 (1913), 49. Irens at Plataia: Hdt. 9. 71,2 and 85,1.

6 Allies: Spartan, Hdt. 3. 47,1 (Samos), Paus. 4. 15,7–8 (Corinth and 'some men' from Lepreon, enemy of Elis); Messenian, Paus. ibid. (Arkadia, Elis, forces from Argos and Sikyon), Str. 362 (Pisa, Elis(*sic*) and Argos, Arkadia). If Pausanias and Strabo are right, Elis was not on Sparta's side (where she would normally be expected): see Huxley, 57 and nn. 365–71; and for the date of Aristomenes, leader of the Messenians, and the final resistance at Hira, see Wade-Gery in *Anc. Soc. and Inst.*, 289 ff. For the reconstructed history of *c.* 600–550 see esp. D. M. Leahy, *Phoenix* 12 (1958), 163 ff. and Wade-Gery, op. cit. Orchomenos: Theopompos, *FGH* 115 F 69; Tegea, Hdt. 1. 66–8. Spartan-Tegeate treaty: Plut., *QG* 5; cf. Jacoby, *CQ* 38 (1944), 15 f., Leahy, *Phoenix* 12, 163 ff., and Wade-Gery, op. cit. Unless 'on the Alpheios' in Plutarch means the Alpheios where it edges the precinct of Olympia (i.e., Plutarch's source, Aristotle, would then be speaking of the copy of the treaty which must in any case have been set up at Olympia; cf. below, p. 169), this should mean somewhere on the Spartan-Tegeate border; for the geographic problem see Leahy, *Phoenix* 12, 163 and Wade-Gery, op. cit., 297 f., 302. Philachaian policy, evidence: bones of Orestes, Hdt. 1. 68, and of Teisamenos, cf. Leahy, *Historia* 4 (1955), 26 ff.; Stesichoros' poetry, cf. Bowra, *GLP*[2], 112 ff.; king Kleomenes 'the Achaian', Hdt. 5. 72,3. (The name Philachaios on a bronze plaque *IG* v. 2. 159 (= *LSAG*, 212 no. 27) is less useful as evidence than is sometimes stated. Epigraphically it should not be earlier than the mid-5th c., which implies that Philachaios, father of the man Xouthias concerned in the inscription (who may in any case be a Tegeate, NB), was born in the late, not middle, 6th c., as is usually claimed.) Tyrant-evictions: Chilon and Anaxandridas, *FGH* 105 F 1 (= Pap. Rylands 18), and for a fuller record for 'the Spartans', Plut., *De Herod. malig.* 21. The Spartan thalassocracy: see Appendix III and (most recently, on

the composition of the whole list) Forrest, *CQ* 63 (1969), 95 ff. Sparta, Kroisos, and the Argives: Hdt. 1. 69–70, and 82–3; and the Ionians, 152; and Polykrates, 3. 44–56.

7 Anaxandridas and Dorieus: Hdt. 5. 39–48; Dorieus in Libya, below, ch. 12, p. 186. Modern interpretations of Kleomenes' career: the first (and standard) view, of a powerful ruler, has been challenged by Forrest, ch. 8. Kleomenes' actions: Plataia, Thuc. 3. 68,5 (on the date see Gomme in *HCT* ii, 358); Maiandrios, Hdt. 3. 148; Scythians, 6. 84; Aristagoras, 5. 49–51; Lygdamis, Plut., *De Her. mal.* 21; Athens, Hdt. 5. 63–6, 69–70, 72–7, 90–3; Argos, 6. 76–82 (the Pythia's joint oracle, 6. 19 and 77,2) and 7. 150–2; the Eleusinian grove, 6. 75,3; bribery of the Pythia, 6. 66; Aigina, 6. 49–51, 61–73. Lysander's remark: Plut., *Lys.* 7,4. Damaratos and Xerxes: Hdt. 7. 3, 102–4, 209, 234–5, 239. Kleomenes' exile and death: Hdt. 6. 74–5; on his plotting in exile, see W. Wallace, *JHS* 74 (1954), 32 ff.

8 Olympia groups: Paus. 5. 17,2; 6. 19,8,12–13. The Acheloös-group at least were statuettes (*xoïdia*). Dorykleidas also made a chryselephantine Themis in the Heraion (5. 17,2). This technique – a wooden core, faced with carved ivory for the important flesh-parts and gold plates for the dress, hair, etc. – needed the skills of both carving and metalwork. The *dokana*: Plut., *Mor.* 478a-b. Columnar Apollo: Eumelos, F 11 K. Karneios: cf. C. Leroy, *BCH* 89 (1965), 371 ff. Agyieus: Dieuchidas, *FGH* 595 F 25 and Jacoby, ad loc.; Pythaieus, Hdt. 1. 69,4; Paus. 3. 10, 8. Hyakinthios: Paus. 3. 19,2. Sparta's Zeus at Olympia: Paus. 5. 24,3 (Jeffery, *JHS* 69 (1949), 26 ff.); another, by the 6th-c. Spartan sculptors Ariston and Telestas, *c.* 18 ft. high (i.e., surely a columnar type), Paus. 5. 23,7. Gitiadas (fl. late 6th c. ?, cf. Jeffery, *JHS* 69, 27 f.): Paus. 3. 17,2–3 and 18,8. Lakonian bronzes: E. Langlotz, *Frühgriech. Bildhauerschule* (1927), 86 ff., pls. 44–8; Richter, *AGA*, 88; Kirsten, Rumpf, Karousos in *Charites* (1957), 110 ff., 127 ff., 33 ff. Kraters: Hdt. 1. 70,1 and Rumpf in *Charites*, 127 ff. Vix krater: as Lakonian, Rumpf, ibid.; Jeffery, *LSAG*, 191 f.; M. Stoop, *Bull . . . Ant. Beschaving te 's-Gravenhage* 39 (1964), 83 ff.; as Corinthian, H. Gjødesen, *AJA* 67 (1963), 344; C. Rolley, *BCH* 82 (1958), 168 ff.; as Syracusan or Lokrian, Guarducci, *Rend. Linc.* 13 (1965), 3 ff. We do not know whether Sparta learnt her bronzeworking from Corinth, Sikyon, or even Samos, a notable centre for early bronzework. She certainly profited from eastern Greek architects, e.g. Theodoros of Samos and Bathykles of Magnesia (Paus. 3. 12,10 and 18,9).

9 'Hero-reliefs': see esp. M. Andronikos, *Lakonika Anaglypha* (1956; = *Peloponnesiaka* I, 253 ff.), where the dedicatory side is stressed. Heroized mortals: Chilon, Paus. 3. 16,4 and A. Wace, *AE* (1937) I. 217 ff.; Maron and Alpheus, Paus. 3. 12,9. Cf. also the family burial-plot of *c.* 600 B.C. found *inside* the city, in Mesoa (Chrestos, *ADelt* 19 (1964), 123 ff.): four graves (two men, a woman, and a child) under a great ash-mound interspersed with the bones of oxen, boars, and horses. To sacrifice horses to the dead implies some kind of ancestor-worship. On Lakonian pottery see Lane, *BSA* 34 (1933–34), 128 ff.; B. B. Shefton, *BSA* 49 (1954), 299 ff. and in Arias-Hirmer-Shefton, 308 ff. Crafts hereditary in Sparta: Hdt. 6. 60; cf. *LSAG*, 187.

9 Argos: the Heritage of Temenos

The Background

The eastern part of the Peloponnese was inhabited mainly by Hellenes originally from the north-west of the Greek peninsula, who had filtered down and along the shores of the Corinthian Gulf after the collapse of the Mycenean power. The countryside was reasonably fertile; there were many city-states, and their fortunes intersected continually, for here the mountains were not rugged enough to hold mutual friends or foes apart.

Herodotos says that seven races still inhabited the Peloponnese in his time, and although some of his divisions contain problems, his picture seems roughly true: as well as Doric-speaking states such as Argos, Sparta, Corinth, and Sikyon, and the 'north-west Greek' of Elis and Achaia, there was a pre-Doric 'Mycenean' element penned into Arkadia and further pre- or at least non-Doric elements holding on in the district between Elis and Messenia, and round the Gulf of Argos, from the Kynouria on its west side ('Ionians, though time and the Argives have Dorized them') to the Dryopes once in Asine, and in Hermion to its east. This helps to explain why many, if not all, Doric states contained racial elements outside the three standard Doric tribes of Hylleis, Dymanes, and Pamphyloi. Sometimes these outsiders were given citizenship or at least some kind of status within a fourth tribe (as the Hyrnathioi at Argos); some of them remained virtual or actual serfs. Some were *perioikoi* ('dwellers around'), a status which may have included downgraded Doric cities which had been defeated by a larger Doric neighbour.

By the end of the eighth century Argos ranked high in the Peloponnese. Her easiest route for expansion was north past Mycenae into the Corinthia, and so from early times her relations with Corinth were nearly always bad. Her hostility to Sparta also started early, because between them lay the Thyreatis, which was a fertile pocket at the head of the Kynouria, the long strip south of Argos, east of Sparta, and coveted by the Spartans. Most of the other cities stood or were pulled behind one or other of these three big states.

Argos city lay flat in the plain of Argos, very near a low round hill called from its shape Shield (*aspis*). She was overshadowed by the Larisa, her acropolis, a sheer and rocky height towering directly above the city and retaining even now the remains of archaic precincts to Zeus Larisaios and Athena within the medieval battlements which follow the line of the old citadel wall. Though the modern town overlies most of the ancient city, the excavations of the French Archaeological School in the environs are doing much to illuminate our picture of the aristocracy who lived in Homer's horse-pasturing

Argos at the end of the Geometric period. One of the graves excavated is now famous as the Panoply Grave (*c.* 710–700). It held the body of a man aged about twenty-five to thirty – that is, within the front-ranks age-groups according to the later hoplite standards – whose grave-goods included a bundle of iron spits (cf. below, p. 135), a pair of iron fire-dogs of Eastern type with finials shaped like ships' prows, a bronze bell-shaped thorax, and a conical bronze helmet of 'Assyrian' type. At this date, then, an Argive aristocrat could already own the essential parts of what was to become the standard hoplite panoply: helmet, thorax, greaves, and big round shield protecting the body from neck to knees. This was the bronze sheathing which enabled a rank of fighters, their overlapping shields forming a solid breastwork, to charge through a barrage of missiles and either to rout a less-protected foe or come to close fighting with thrusting-spear and short sword against a similar rank (Pl. 17; cf. Pl. 29).

It is not yet clear whether the hoplite phalanx was a Greek invention or borrowed from Near Eastern tactics. Nor is it clear which Greek state first adopted it; but the claim of Argos under her great king Pheidon would seem as good as any. The round shield, the *hoplon*, was also called the 'Argolic shield'. Moreover, Argive tradition said that Proitos and Akrisios, twin heroes of Argive saga who fought each other for the kingdom, invented the shield, and – significantly – that this was the first battle in Greece in which leaders *and troops* all carried shields. The warriors of Argos are praised in an early gnomic verse of Homeric colouring, sometimes referred to as an oracle, whose first three lines run:

> Of all the land the best's Pelasgic Argos,
> the mares of Thrace, the girls of Lakedaimon,
> the men who drink fair Arethousa's water . . .

Then a qualification, presumably therefore a later addition:

> But better still are those who dwell between
> Tiryns and Arkadia rich in flocks –
> Argives in linen breastplates, goads of war.

And its final distich could be adapted to fit whatever city was due for an insult at the time of recital:

> But you Megarians [e.g.] aren't third or fourth
> or twelfth – or in the tally or count at all.

When lines 1–3 were made, the best warriors came from Chalkis, by the spring Arethousa; but when 4–6 were added, Argos had outstripped her – presumably, had eclipsed the reputation which Chalkis had gained after her victory over Eretria at the end of the eighth century (above, pp. 65–6).[1]

Pheidon and the Heritage of Temenos

The military renown of Argos reached its peak under her king Pheidon (fl. *c.* ?680–657), thanks to his insistent claiming of 'the Heritage of Temenos' with a powerful army to back him. What was this Heritage? Argive propaganda had early annexed Agamemnon, king of Mycenae according to the *Iliad*, and had claimed him as ruler of Argos. Roughly speaking, therefore, the Heritage consisted of the cities listed as under Agamemnon of Mycenae and Diomedes of Argos in *Il.* 2. 562 ff. They comprised virtually all the northern and eastern Peloponnese: for Diomedes, Argos, Tiryns, the eastern cities (Asine and Hermion, Troizen and Epidauros), and Aigina; for Agamemnon, Mycenae, Corinth, Kleonai, Orneai, Phleious, Sikyon, and five of the small towns of Achaia. The Argives claimed that at the Return of the Herakleidai, Temenos, a son of the Heraklid Aristomachos, had with his children won all this kingdom. The eastern cities came through his daughter Hyrnatho's marriage. Sikyon was taken by Phalkes son of Temenos, and Phleious by Rhegnidas son of Phalkes; possibly Rhegnidas was said to have got Kleonai too, for another tradition recorded that after the Return of the Herakleidai some men of Kleonai and Phleious fled from the Dorians and settled Klazomenai in Ionia (below, p. 225). Hippasos of Phleious, who was said to have opposed Rhegnidas and fled to Samos, was great-grandfather of the philosopher Pythagoras (fl. *c.* 540). If this piece of the story is correct, it could make Rhegnidas historical and a younger colleague of Pheidon, rather than a grandson of the mythical Temenos. Nevertheless, Kleonai was still a faithful supporter of Argos (mainly, perhaps, through fear of Corinth) in the fifth century (below, p. 137).

Asine did not outlast the eighth century. Her interests were not Argive; she supported Sparta in the First Messenian War (above, pp. 114–15), and for this the Argive king Eratos besieged and sacked her. Argos herself had supported the city of Helos in Lakedaimon which had vainly resisted Sparta during the second half of this century. But the great Argive-Spartan collision evidently came during the second quarter of the seventh century, in the reign of Pheidon.

Pheidon son of Aristodamidas was a hereditary monarch, though it is possible that a powerful Argive aristocracy had reduced the kingship to a shadow before he succeeded – which, if true, might help to explain why Herodotos and Aristotle classed him in the genus tyrant. Certainly his deeds, good and bad, were on such a scale as to make this classification understandable. He established a standard of weights and measures in the Peloponnese. Late authority said that he dedicated sets of iron spits in the great sanctuary of Hera between Argos and Mycenae, where in fact several corroded sets have been excavated: also that he had controlled Aigina and had coined there the first Greek silver coinage – the spits, it said, were the obsolete coinage, called in. Iron spits (*obeloi*) were certainly a common unit of barter in early Greece, for the first Greek mainland states to coin silver gave the name *obelos/obolos* to the basic coin whose value equalled one spit, and drachma (handful, i.e., set of six) to the bigger coin which equalled 6 obols. Sparta indeed went on using spits for barter long after the rest had switched to coinage. About 575 is the rough date given to the first Aiginetan coins, which typologically are indeed the earliest issues in the mainland area. If Pheidon were involved in their issue, his reign would lie beyond the end of the seventh century; but if a date *c.* 680–657 is preferred for him on grounds thought more cogent, then his spit-offering must be explained otherwise: for example, was it simply meant as bullion, since in the days of barter a mass of iron was a good nest-egg for any temple? Or – perhaps more likely – did he standardize the length and weight of spits among his measures, and offer a standard set in the temple for reference?

Economic reforms like this were one mark of the good tyrant. Defiance of the gods marked the wicked one, and Pheidon qualified for the title on this count also; for he marched his army westward into Elis when the holy Truce for the Games forbade all armed men within the area of Olympia. He seized control of the festival, claiming the right to hold all those Games which Herakles had held. This was not mere megalomania. Elis itself lay a long way north of the sanctuary; but an Elean family maintained a hereditary control over the Games, and Pheidon was probably supporting a rival faction centred on the district called Pisa around Olympia itself. Clearly he hoped that, if this Pisatan party got control of Olympia, Argos could add this great centre of influence to her own sphere of control. In the official Elean list of victors the year 668 was marked as an Anolympiad, a year in which no legal Games were held; and in 669–668 the Argives heavily defeated a Spartan force, which was probably making for the Thyreatis, because it was caught at Hysiai just inside Argive territory. Strabo says that Pheidon 'took the leadership of the Peloponnese from Sparta', so it is tempting to see him as the victor of Hysiai and even, perhaps, a pioneer in the development of the hoplite phalanx during his reign. Other details suggest Argive control of smaller places at this time. In the Second Messenian War among Messenia's allies were Argos, Sikyon, and Pantaleon, ruler of Pisa. Sikyon is far from Messenia; and Pisa, as we saw, owed gratitude to Pheidon. Again, *if* we reject the coinage story as an anachronism, but accept that Pheidon did control Aigina as part of the Heritage, he must have controlled Epidauros too (below, pp. 149–52); for the route Argos–Epidauros–Aigina would be easy, but Argos–Aigina direct could only be done by a fleet, and Argos was never a sea power.[2]

Pheidon's death occurred, apparently, in an attempt to bring Corinth too into his sphere of influence. Corinth always maintained that her Heraklid founder was one Aletes, no connection with Temenos' family. Pheidon went there 'to assist one side through friendship, during stasis'. A detailed version, full of romantic embellishment, says that Pheidon plotted to bring Corinth under Argive control by murdering a thousand young Corinthians whom he had summoned to Argos. Melissos, an Argive, betrayed this plot to his Corinthian *xenos*, and prudently shifted his own family to Corinth. His young son Aktaion was killed in a lovers' brawl there, and this caused stasis in Corinth, which finally drove the current Bacchiad government into exile. We know that this eviction was in fact achieved by Kypselos of Corinth. Thus it seems possible that Pheidon twice supported opponents of the Bacchiad rule, once when Melissos betrayed his plot, and again, perhaps no more than ten years later, in support of Kypselos, when he himself was killed.

On balance, therefore, it may be inferred that the Argive claim to the Heritage of Temenos, if not actually invented by Pheidon, was first worked up by him intensively as propaganda, and became thereafter a basic factor in Argive foreign policy.

Kleonai and Nemea

Those who, as here, accept the years *c.* 680–657 as the most likely for the reign of this colourful figure – with his strong line in propaganda, his military superiority to Sparta, and his economic reforms – have then to explain why Herodotos says that his son Lakedas wooed Agariste of Sikyon about a hundred years later (*c.* 575–570). We know that Lakedas' successor, Meltas, was deposed, thus ending the line of Temenid kings. The ex-royal family must have gone somewhere to live, and it could be posited that Herodotos' Lakedas was in fact a Lakedas (II), the son of a Pheidon (II), brother of Meltas; Pheidon (II) could then be the coin-minter, settled in exile in Aigina. A dedicatory epigram from the Games at Nemea by a pankratiast named 'Aristis son of Pheidon of Kleonai' is dated around the mid-sixth century on its letter-forms; and it has also been suggested that the wooer Lakedas son of Pheidon was in fact the brother of this Aristis, their exiled father Pheidon (II) having been given citizenship by the faithful Kleonai.

The loyalty of Kleonai to the Argives may seem surprising, since she lay much nearer to Corinth, on the main road which ran south past Mycenae to Argos. But she had cause to dislike both Corinth and Sikyon; for at the Pythian Games the Sikyonians once claimed for their city a Kleonaian boy-victor named Teletias, and killed him in the ensuing fight; and in the rival claims of Phleious and Kleonai to control the important cult of Zeus in the valley of Nemea which lay between them, Corinth always backed Phleious. Thanks to the support of Argos, however, Kleonai won the dispute, which gave her the control of the Nemean Games. They were founded formally in 573, and were biennial. Traditionally they had a far older origin, like the Games at Olympia and the Isthmus, in the funeral games to a hero. In Nemea's case this was Opheltas-Archemoros, infant son of a priest-king Lykourgos; two grave-barrows in the precinct were said to be theirs. Pindar says that Adrastos of Argos first celebrated the Nemean Games, but that they belonged to Kleonai. In historical terms this may mean that the cult of the Argive hero Adrastos, when Kleisthenes banned it in Sikyon (below, p. 164), was established at Nemea by the Argives in retaliation and secured under the control of Kleonai, with the story (perhaps invented then) that Adrastos and the rest of the Seven against Thebes had marched through the valley and drunk at a spring there (known thereafter as the Adrasteian); and that the infant's nurse, lured by the military like her counterparts in Victorian London parks, had put him down on the ground, where a snake had killed him. (The tradition that Herakles had founded the Games after killing the Nemean lion is undated; the lion's cave was identified with one in the hills about 2 miles away.)[3]

The Sixth Century: Clashes with Sparta

In the course of Sparta's Second Messenian War – which could mean roughly at any time in the second or third quarters of the seventh century – Argos supported Messenia. Her view would be steadily anti-Spartan, whether her leader at the time was Pheidon himself or Lakedas or Meltas. But Nauplia, the seaport on the Gulf of Argos, supported Sparta, as Asine had done in the First War. Meltas must have been exiled before the end of the war, because the Argive king who evicted the Nauplians near its end was Damokratidas. (Sparta gave them a new city, Mothone in the conquered Messenia.) Thus the monarchy continued after the expulsion of the Temenidai. It was still confined, if possible, to those who could claim to be Herakleidai of some kind, but it was now elective. Damokratidas may have been the first elected king; if so, his name and the novelty of election may have helped to create the later, anachronistic story that democracy had succeeded Meltas. Another king named Aigon (undated) was remembered because he was a non-Heraklid, elected abnormally 'when that line failed whence it was traditional for the Argives to get their kings'. There was still an annual 'king' in the fifth century.

Meltas may be further commemorated in an anecdote of an unnamed king who was exiled. At a time when Argos had suffered greatly 'in the war against the Lakedaimonians' (the Second Messenian War? or some more direct Argive-Spartan collision?), so that the Argives were feeling bitter in any case, the Argive army had aided some (unnamed) Arkadian cities to get their territory back (presumably from Sparta's clutches, she being the obvious foe; below, p. 171); and the Argive king had not then done what Argos expected – he had not mopped in the rescued land as *kleroi* for Argives: in other words, had not required dependency on Argos as the price of Argive help. The king fled to Tegea, evidently one of the grateful cities, and died there. It is economical to identify him as Meltas, though of course some one of the elected kings might also have been exiled. At all events, it must have happened before c. 550, when Tegea became an ally of Sparta. Another glimpse of Argive foreign policy comes from Sikyon in the early sixth century, where the bitter anti-Argive actions of the tyrant Kleisthenes (below, p. 164) suggest that Argos was continuing her claim to the Heritage of Temenos. This supports the inference drawn from the anecdote of the exiled king, namely that at some time between the Second Messenian War and c. 550 the Argive state showed those Arkadian cities which lay uncomfortably between the Argive and Lakedaimonian borders that any aid from Argos might entail dependence thereafter. So Sparta found it correspondingly less difficult to gather first Tegea and then Mantineia and the other cities into her Peloponnesian League. They were between the devil and the deep; and so Argos lost any chance she might have had to form and lead a solid anti-Spartan bloc on Sparta's northern boundary.

Sparta was now regarded by external powers like Lydia as the biggest military force in mainland Greece; and c. 545 she and Argos, set on their collision course over the Thyreatis once more, engaged there in a battle of 300 champions on each side. It was an out-of-date way of deciding a dispute and proved useless, for at its close the full armies engaged nonetheless. Sparta won this battle of Thyrea, wiping out the old disgrace at Hysiai, and deprived Argos thereafter of the places to her south, that is the country east of Mount Parnon, from the Thyreatis through Kynouria and right down to include the island of Kythera. The vital position of this island as a base alike for trading ships from the rich South and East and for attacks on the adjacent mainland made her so valuable for her holder, and correspondingly dangerous when in the wrong hands, that the ephor Chilon had once said that really it would be best for Sparta if Kythera were sunk beneath the sea.

Thus in the late sixth century Argos suffered from the loss of manpower, territory, and influence in face of Sparta's advance under her Agid kings Anaxandridas and then his son Kleomenes (above, pp. 122–6). Possibly a tyrant called Perilaos or Perillos took control at this crisis, though the evidence for his date is shaky. At any rate, Argive troops helped Peisistratos of Athens to seize tyrannic power there at about this time. But if the Argives hoped for a military alliance thereby, the hopes were unfulfilled.

Relations with Persia

After the Persian forces had reached the Aegean coast and reduced the Greek cities there to subjection by c. 540, the attitudes of the mainland states towards Persia were bound to harden one way or the other. The tyranny at Athens (c. 527–510) was friendly to Persia. Argive foreign policy may have been set on a similar course already, for when Sparta began her anti-Persian declarations c. 545, one might infer that this would drive Argos on to the other side. Her attitude crystallized more clearly in the decade c. 500–490. At some date between 499 and 494, when Miletos was leading the Ionic Revolt against Persia (below, pp. 219–21), Argos and Miletos sent a joint embassy to the Delphic oracle, presumably because the Argives were uncertain whether to answer an Ionic appeal for aid. The joint oracle delivered to them prophesied doom to Miletos if she opposed Persia, and gave a wholly ambivalent reply to Argos:

> But when the female conquers the male,
> evicts him and wins fame among the Argives,
> she will make many Argive women mourn,
> so one of men born in years to come will say:
> 'the dread three-coiled snake was killed by the victor-spear'.

So Argos sent no help to the revolt. But c. 494 Kleomenes of Sparta landed on the Argive coast with a large army and heavily defeated the Argives at Sepeia south of the city, massacring 6,000 soldiers, including most of the oligarchs who formed the government. The Argives assumed then that the oracle had foreseen this disaster, and that Miletos, already in straits, had now no hope against Persia. In 481–480 they refused to join the anti-Persian coalition unless their one king were ranked as commander equally with the Spartan dyarchy. Faced with the Spartan refusal, says Herodotos, they said: 'Better be ruled by the Mede than yield to the grasping Spartans'; and in the Persian War they stayed neutral, having brushed up their Bronze Age tradition of Argive Perseus and made him an ancestor of the Persians also.[4]

The Constitution

We know little of the Argive constitution in the Archaic period. The change from a hereditary to an elected king probably stressed the chief duty of kingship as war-leading rather than policy-making. An inscription from one of the precincts on the Larisa, dated about the mid-sixth century on lettering, lists 'the following *damiorgoi* who ruled', and gives nine names; and another not much later lists additions made to the temple of Athena while 'the following were *damiorgoi*' – six names. These lists show that Argos, like many other oligarchic cities, had high officials called 'public workers', and that hers were in multiples of three, which implies that their election was confined to the three Doric tribes. The Greek *demiourgoi* may have been a board annually elected, like the archons at Athens; or, if a comparison on philological grounds with Sparta's *agathoergoi* (above, p. 121) and Athens's *leitourgoi* is valid, they may have been a 'pool' of those best qualified by birth and wealth, whence individuals or boards were selected for specific services, religious or secular. The difference in number in the two Argive lists would be explicable thus; but most scholars see the *damiorgoi* here as a single board, and the drop from nine to six as some kind of tightening-up.

The fourth tribe, the Hyrnathioi, were non-Dorians, or at best not full Dorians, the name being taken from Hyrnatho, the local deity or heroine of the eastern Argolid whom propaganda had grafted on to Temenos' family as a daughter. This tribe is first attested, indirectly, in the first half of the fifth century, when inscriptions show officials in fours, implying that the Hyrnathioi were now on equal terms with the others, and the Argive democracy established. As a social and military unit the fourth tribe surely existed earlier, though presumably without full citizenship. As well as *damiorgoi*, oligarchic Argos must have had a council and assembly; but we know nothing of their powers.[5]

Art

In the Archaic period the art of the city-states in the north-east Peloponnese seems to have been based on a tradition common to the area of the Saronic Gulf and the Aegean islands, even as far as Crete (below, pp. 192–3). Each modified it according to her contacts, and developed the result according to her available materials. In pottery Corinth had led the way from the eighth century onwards; no others could match her pace, but Argos had her own handsome style of Geometric, and c. 700 B.C. her pot-painters, though still producing their Late Geometric II alongside the new styles of painting developed in Corinth and Attica, have left us some engaging miniatures of big horses led haltered by their tamers. Her seventh-century style developed as that of Attica and the islands had already done, into linear paintings of scenes from myth and epic, embellished by added colours of white, brown, or purplish-red; indeed, Argive letters

FIG. 2. Bronze relief from the armband of a hoplite shield dedicated at Olympia: Adrastos in centre (his name below, *right* to *left* in Argive letters) separates two warriors, perhaps Amphiaraos and Lykourgos (cf. Pausanias 3.18, 12), both held back by friends. Date, about 575-550

are used in the inscriptions on some figured sherds found on Kalymnos and a decorated plate from Rhodes, suggesting an early contact of some kind between Argos and these eastern Doric islands (Pl. 34).

Although their pottery remained provincial, the Argives were renowned for their bronzework, a skill to which the armour in the Panoply Grave bears early witness. By the second half of the seventh century Argos was evidently a centre for shield-making, for the round hoplite shield was called 'Argolic', and many bronze appliqués have survived from armbands (*porpakes*) of shields once dedicated at Delphi and Olympia. They are little relief-panels, impressed from moulds showing scenes from myth or saga (above); the style is fully equal to the Corinthian, and the names of the figures are nearly all written in Argive letters. Bronze was long to remain the sculptors' chief medium, for, like Sparta, Argos had no stone both handsome and tractable. But *c.* 600–575 (?Poly)medes of Argos made the colossal twin kouroi of island marble which were dedicated, and still survive, at Delphi, to commemorate the brothers Kleobis and Biton (Pl. 18). Herodotos tells how Solon of Athens (above, pp. 90–4) advised the great Kroisos of Lydia to call no man happy till he was dead, and instanced this Argive pair, who died in the Heraion after pulling a waggon bearing their mother (the priestess, according to a later source) all the way there from Argos. Since the statues were dedicated during Solon's lifetime, Herodotos' tale may possibly be founded on some poem of Solon's addressed to the young Lydian prince on this moral theme. (?Poly)medes did not survive in the literary tradition; apparently Argive stone-sculptors did not achieve the fame of their Sikyonian neighbours Dipoinos and Skyllis, trained in Crete (below, pp. 166, 194). But small statuettes show that the bronzeworkers flourished in the sixth century, and Pausanias at Olympia quotes the verse-signature of two bronze-sculptors, Eutelidas and Chrysothemis, members of an established Argive school (*technan eidotes ek proteron*), who had made the statue of Damaretos of Arkadian Heraia, a victor of 520 B.C. The great Ageladas followed them, a worthy forerunner of Polykleitos.[6]

NOTES

1 Seven races: Hdt. 8. 73. Panoply Grave: Courbin, *BCH* 81 (1957), 322 ff.; A. Snodgrass, *Arms and Armour of the Greeks* (1967), 41, 43, 50. Argolic shield: Paus. 8. 50,1 and Snodgrass, op. cit., 53 ff. Proitos and Akrisios: Paus. 2. 25,7, describing a pyramidal building with Argolic shields in relief, believed to mark the mass grave (*polyandrion*) of the combatants; it is briefly referred to by R. Tomlinson, *Argos and the Argolid* (1972), 36, describing a similar building known as the Hellenikon, probably of the 4th c. B.C. Armour: cf. also E. Kunze, *Olymp. Forsch.* 2 (1950), 215 ff. 'Oracle', first cited by Ion of Chios (mid-5th c.): see H. W. Parke, *The Delphic Oracle* I, 424 f.; Andrewes, *The Greek Tyrants*, 39 f. Pelasgic Argos is in Thessaly; the mares recall Diomedes' team, and the girls, Helen of Troy; the men are of Chalkis, site of the original spring called Arethousa. Origin of the hoplite: see Snodgrass, *Arms and Armour*, 59 f.; he sees it as 'largely an original creation of Archaic Greece'.

2 Agamemnon's kingdom: *Il.* 2. 562 ff. and cf. Str. 372. Temenos and the Argive claims to the north-east Peloponnese: Argos, Paus. 2. 18–19 and 38,1; 4. 3,3–6; Str. 358. Hermion, Troizen, Epidauros, Aigina: Paus. 2. 26,1–2 and 28,2–8 (Epidauros); 29,5 (Aigina); 29,10 (Troizen); 34,5 and Str. 371 (Hermion). Sikyon: Paus. 2. 6, 6–7; Str. 390. Phleious: Paus. 2. 13,1–2 (Hippasos) and 7. 3,9 (with Kleonai). Orneai: Hdt. 8. 73,3 and Andrewes in *HCT* iv, 106 ff. Mycenae: Str. 377. Asine: see above, p. 130, n.2. In the late Archaic period the Argeadai of Argos Orestikon, the ruling family in Macedon, wishing to establish their people as proper Greeks by attaching themselves to a venerable Greek pedigree, naturally chose the Argive (Hdt. 8.137–9; Theopompos, *FGH* 115 F 393; Ephoros, *FGH* 70 F 115). 'Temenos' need not be a Macedonian fiction, but the Argive royal stemma is only preserved for us in its 'Macedonized' form; above Aristodamidas we cannot test the names, and king Eratos (Paus. 2. 36,4) is not included there. See further Andrewes, *CQ* 45 (1951), 39 ff. Hdt. on Pheidon: 6. 127,3. Aristotle, *Pol.* 1310a, solved the dilemma between the Argive tradition and Herodotos' 'tyrannos' by classing Pheidon as a king who became a tyrant. The Heraion spits: Arist. F 480/1 R; for full details, Ll. Brown, *Num. Chron.* (N.S.) 10 (1950), 177 ff. and cf. M. Oikonomidou, *AAA* 2 (1969), 436 ff. Pheidon and the Games: Ephoros, *FGH* 70 F 115; his leadership of the Peloponnese: ibid. The Anolympiads: Str. 355, Paus. 6. 22.

3 Pheidon's death: Eph., *FGH* 70 F 35 and Nic. Damasc., *FGH* 90, F 35; cf. Andrewes, *CQ* 43 (1949), 70 ff., still the best discussion of the evidence for his date. The plot: Andrewes, ibid.; E. Will, *Korinthiaka* (1955), 344 ff.; I have differed slightly from their interpretations. Huxley, *BCH* 82 (1958), 588 ff., supports the Anolympiad as being in 728, and reminds us of the Panoply Grave, a fitting background for an 8th-c. Pheidon. Lakedas and Meltas: Paus. 2. 19,2; Plut., *Mor.* 89e. Aristis of Kleonai: see M. McGregor, *TAPA* 72 (1941), 275 and Meiggs and Lewis no. 9. Kleonai: Paus. 7. 3,9 says briefly that men of Kleonai and Phleious formed the majority of the settlers in Ionic Klazomenai, having emigrated there when the Dorians returned to the Peloponnese (below, p. 225). Teletias: Plut., *Mor.* 553a-b. The modern view (cf. Bury, *Nemean Odes* (1890), 250 f. and refs. ap. Skalet, *Ancient Sicyon* (1928), 58; McGregor, *TAPA* 72) that Kleisthenes of Sikyon seized Kleonai and held it until Argos regained it in 573 rests on the story of Teletias, and discounts the statement (Plut., *Mor* 553a-b) that Kleonai never knew the bad but necessary medicine of a tyrant.

4 Nauplia and Damokratidas: Paus. 4. 24,4; 27,8; 35,2. 'Democracy' in early Argos: Paus. 2. 19,2. Aigon: Plut., *Mor.* 340c, 396c. Argive king in 480: Hdt. 7. 149; in the mid-5th c., see Meiggs and Lewis no. 42. The unnamed king: D. Sic. 7. 13; cf. Forrest,

History of Sparta, 73. Battle of Thyrea: Hdt. 1. 82. Chilon's saying: 7. 235. Perilaos: Paus. 2. 20,7 and 23,7; cf. H. Berve, *Die Tyrannis bei den Griechen* (1967), 35 and Tomlinson, *Argos and the Argolid*, 92. Aid to Peisistratos: Hdt. 1. 61. The joint oracle: Hdt. 6. 19 (Miletos) and 77 (Argos). Sepeia: Hdt. 6. 76–82; 7. 148,1. Refusal to serve under Sparta: Hdt. 7. 148,4. Medizing in 480–479: Hdt. 7. 150–2.

5 Larisa inscriptions: *SEG* XI 336, 314; *LSAG*, 156 ff., nos. 7–8; M. Wörrle, *Untersuchungen zur Verfassungsgeschichte von Argos im 5 Jhdt. v. Chr.* (1964), 61 ff.; Jeffery, *Arch. Class.* 25/26 (1973/4), 319 ff. (Festschrift M. Guarducci). The *demiourgoi* as a regularly elected board: cf. (e.g.) Hammond, *CQ* 54 (1960), 33 ff.; Wörrle, *Untersuchungen*, 61 ff.; Tomlinson, *Argos and the Argolid*, 189, where the change of numbers from 9 to 6 is seen as suggesting 'the substitution for monarchy of a closely-controlled oligarchic system'. *Agathoergoi* as a 'pool': Jeffery, *Arch. Class.* (above). Status of Hyrnathioi: Hammond, *CQ* 54, 36; Wörrle, *Untersuchungen*, 12 ff.; Tomlinson, *Argos and the Argolid*, 189 f. Evidence for the Argive constitution in the 5th c. has been admirably assessed by Andrewes in *HCT* iv, 58 f., 121 ff. The officials called *artunai* (arrangers) are not attested before the 5th c.; cf. Wörrle, *Untersuchungen*, 70 ff., who suggests that they may have replaced the *damiorgoi* at the beginning of that century.

6 Argive LG II pottery: cf. P. Courbin, *La Céramique géometrique de l'Argolide* (1966) and (for date and the horses) esp. N. Coldstream, *GGP*, 129 f., 145 f., pls. 29–30; 7th-c. style, Courbin, *BCH* 79 (1955), 1 ff. Inscriptions on eastern Greek ware, cf. *LSAG*, 153 f., 353 f. Argolic shields: see above, n.1. Armbands: E. Kunze, *Olymp. Forsch.* 2 (1950), 212 ff.; *LSAG*, 158 f., no. 10; Kunze, *ADelt.* 17 (1961–62), *Chron.*, 120 (Corinthian script). Kleobis and Biton: Hdt. 1. 31–2; Richter, *Kouroi*[2] nos. 12A-B. Pausanias at Olympia: 6. 10,4. Ageladas: Overbeck, *SQ* nos. 389–99; Stuart Jones nn. 42–6; B. S. Ridgway, *The Severe Style in Greek Sculpture* (1970), 88, quoting from *Enciclopedia dell' arte antica, classica e orientale* (1958–66), s.v.

1   Ivory writing-tablet (waxed surface vanished), from an early
Etruscan tomb near Marsiliana d'Albegna. The Euboic
alphabet, model for the Etruscan and (via Roman) our own, is
cut as exemplar along the rim, retrograde as in the original
Semitic. *c.* 700–675? (pp. 25–6)

2   Gold strip from a site of the eighth or seventh century in
western Iran; exact provenance unknown. Grazing deer, two
flanking central plant (Tree of Life), guilloche border –
traditional Eastern motifs copied in early Greek art. (pp. 28–9)

3(a) Colossal ovoid krater with lid; Euboic, almost certainly Eretrian ware. Found in a tomb at Kourion (Cyprus), it may illustrate the Euboic trade-line both east to Syria and west to Italy. (Potters at Pithekoussai copied such patterns.) (b) [right] Detail from back: motifs as in front (goats nibble 'Tree of Life', horses graze), taken ultimately from Eastern artefacts. Late eighth century. (pp. 28–9, 66; cf. Pl. 2)

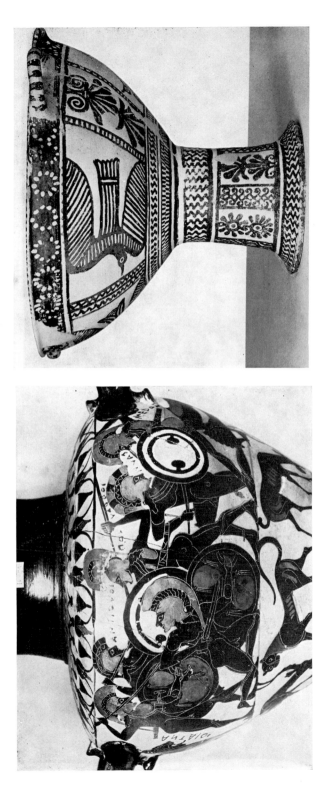

5 Drinking-bowl from Boiotia: a popular type with panels of flying birds, often shown upside-down as if the bowl was usually inverted – whether stored on the shelf, or in use at drinking-parties. Mid-sixth century. (p. 79)

4 Main zone of a 'Chalkidic' hydria: battlefield with three duels; names (*left to right*): Antaios, Antiochos, Polydoros, Fachys, Medon. Below, grazing goats and panther. These potters copied the Attic BF style, but used the script and dialect of Chalkis and her colonies. *c*. 540. (p. 68)

6   Bronze statuette of a helmed and belted god or hero (?),
aiming spear (lost), with 'Dipylon' shield as shown on
Geometric pots. From Thessaly (Karditsa), provincial style.
Early seventh century? (p. 72)

7   Large bronze statuette of a belted Apollo(?); eyes once
inlaid, cranium scored and drilled as if for a crest(?), spear or
bow once in left hand. Inscribed vertically up and down thighs:
'Mantiklos offered me to the far-shooting, silver-bowed one, as
part of the tithe; do thou, Phoibos, give him a happy exchange'.
Boiotian script and dialect. *c.* 675. (p. 78)

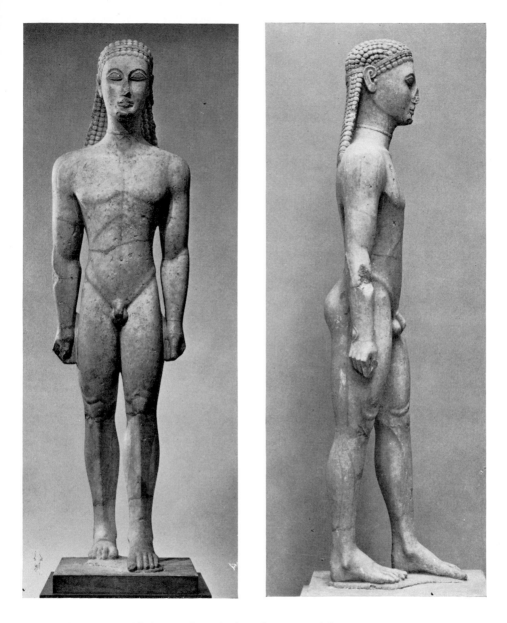

8(*a-b*)   Colossal marble kouros from Attica, almost certainly
funerary. The stance is derived from Egyptian sculpture. *c.*
625–600. (pp. 30, 90)

9 Attic BF amphora: Dionysos, holding ivy-trails and a goblet (kantharos), faces his son Oinopion, who wears a myrtle crown and offers the wine-jug. Signed (retrograde) 'Exekias made [this]'. *c.* 530. (p. 98)

10 Attic RF plate by, or in manner of, the Cerberus Painter. Rider in barbarian dress. The inscription 'Miltiades is fair' may either label the rider, or merely remind the viewer of Miltiades' Thracian estates. *c.* 520–510. (p. 98)

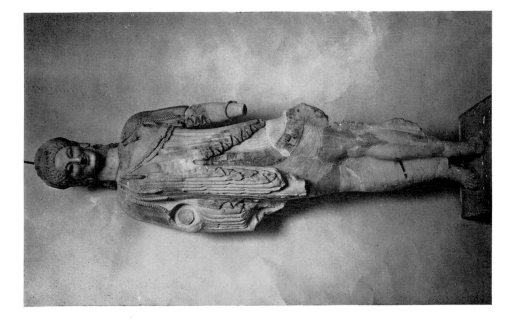

11(*a–b*) Colossal marble kore of Cycladic style, dedicated on the Athenian Acropolis. Her left hand held up her trailing skirt, her right offered a gift to Athena. Neck and other parts restored; eyes originally inlaid. *c.* 525. (pp. 98, 241)

12 Neck of a big Protoattic amphora from Eleusis: Odysseus and two companions blind the drunken Polyphemos; below, lion attacks boar. *c.* 660. (p. 85)

13 Base of a small Attic RF cup found at Olympia in the workshop where Pheidias made his chryselephantine statue of Zeus. Inscribed 'I am Pheidias'. *c.* 440. (p. 32)

14(a–b) Small bronze lion, once attached to a bronze vessel. Found in the Heraion at Samos, inscribed on the mane: 'Eumnastos, a Spartiate, to Hera'. c. 550. (pp. 128, 217)

15 Inside of a Lakonian BF cup (kylix). Rider on a stallion; a winged spirit (Victory?) swoops down with two crowns; water-birds and an eagle around, lotus-pattern below. c. 550–540. (p. 129)

16[opposite] Marble relief-stele from Chrysapha near Sparta; the heroized dead pair receive offerings from the living. c. 540–525. (p. 129)

17[opposite] Armour from the Panoply Grave, Argos. c. 710–700. (p. 134)

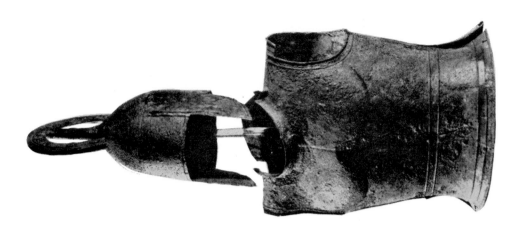

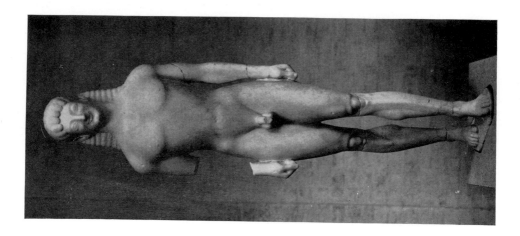

18 Colossal marble kouros, one
of a pair dedicated at Delphi by
the Argive state to commemorate
Kleobis and Biton. Signed on the
footplinth (not shown here):
'[?Poly]medes of Argos made
[this]', it retains traces of the
Daedalic style. *c.* 600–580.
(cf. Pl. 26, *left*; pp. 30, 141)

19 (*a*) and (*b*) [*opposite*] Parian
marble kouros, under lifesize, from
the cemetery of Tenea near
Corinth. *c.* 560–550. (p. 154)

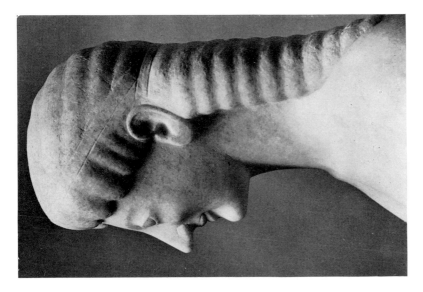

20[*left*] Detail of toilet-box (pyxis). The alert charm of the girl's face survives the careless painting, which is very plain in the standardized siren-and-rosette ornament below. Middle Corinthian. *c*. 575. (p. 154)

21　Bronze statuette from Arkadia: a countryman in felt cap, heavy cloak, and boots. *c.* 500. (p. 170)

22   Miniature polychrome oil-flask ('Macmillan aryballos') from
Corinth: hoplites overtaking and spearing the enemy, riders
galloping, a hare-hunt. Protocorinthian, c. 650. (pp. 28–9, 154)

23 Corinthian jug (olpe). Lions and stag, scale band, lions and
goat. Transitional to Early Corinthian. *c.* 650–625. (p. 154)

24[*opposite*]   Delphi: limestone metope almost certainly from
the early Treasury of Sikyon. The Dioskouroi and their twin
cousins herd cattle from a raid. *Right* to *left*: Polydeukes,
Kastor, Idas (Lynkeus was on the lost fragment to left). *c.* 560.
(p. 166)

25   Polychrome votive plate (pinax) from Thasos: Bellerophon
on Pegasos swoops on the Lycian monster the Chimaira (*Il.* 6.
180–3); hunting dog below. Cycladic ware, possibly Naxian. *c.*
650. (p. 179)

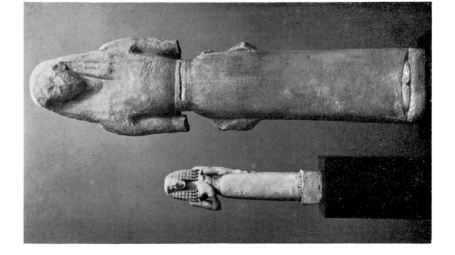

26 Two 'Daedalic' korai (casts).
Left, small limestone kore, almost
certainly from Crete; note the
wiglike hair with tagged ends.
Right, colossal kore of Naxian
marble, dedicated on Delos by
Nikandra of Naxos. The fists are
pierced, perhaps to hold metal
wreaths; the inscription, not
visible here, runs vertically up
and down the left flank. *Left, c.*
625–600. *Right, c.* 650–625. (pp.
179, 194)

27 Amphora from an Aegean
island, perhaps Paros. It shows
the grazing-stag motif taken
originally from Eastern art and
here developed in a sweeping
style enhanced by its linear
frame. *c.* 650. (pp. 28–9, 179)

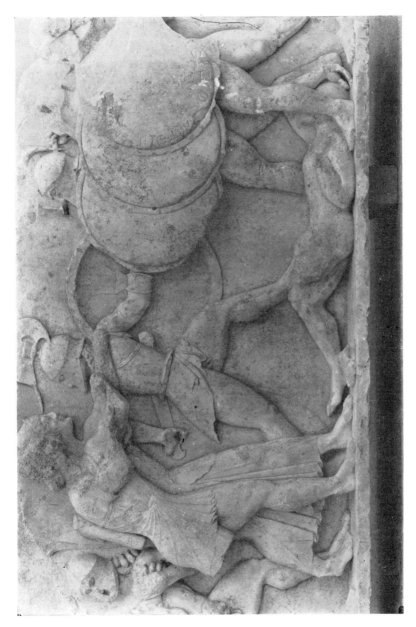

28 Delphi: part of the marble north frieze of the Treasury of Siphnos. Battle of gods and giants. *Left to right*, giant clutched in the paws of Kybele's two chariot-lions: the twin archers Apollo and Artemis: giant fleeing; dying giant: three giants face the twins, the righthand shield bearing the concealed signature of the sculptor. *c.* 530–525. (pp. 184–5)

29(*a*) Large storage-jar (pithos), front decorated with relief-figures modelled and then stuck on. A standard type, perhaps made in Tenos (this example was found on Mykonos). The Sack of Troy, showing mostly the massacre of Trojan children.

29(*b*). The wheeled Wooden Horse, with armed Greeks
swarming out. *c.* 675. (pp. 134, 179)

30   Upper face of a flat gravestone from the main cemetery of
Thera; names in the 'primitive' local script, Rheksanor (*right* to
left), Arkhagetas Prokles, Kleagoras (*right* to *left*), Peraieus. *c.*
600? (p. 186)

31 Clay vase, almost certainly from Crete. The bull's pose derives from Near Eastern art (cf., for example, Mallowan, *Nimrud and its remains* II (1966), fig. 386). Early sixth century. (pp. 28–9, 193)

32[*opposite*] (*a–b*) 'Fikellura' amphorae from Kameiros, Rhodes (the style is named after the area where its first examples were found); white slip, BF motif repeated on each side. (*a*) Running man, *c.* 550–540. (*b*) Hunting dog, *c.* 525. (pp. 241–2)

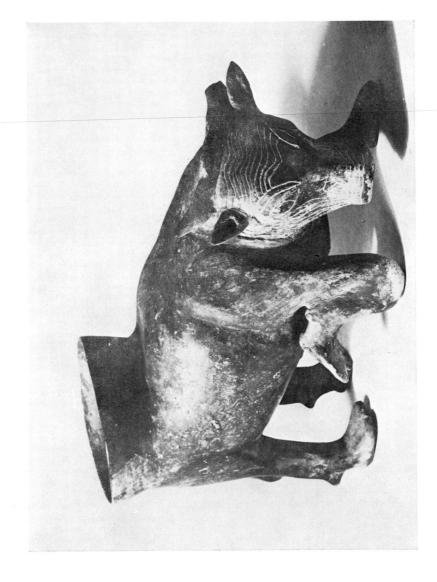

34   Polychrome votive plate from Kameiros, Rhodes. Hektor (*right*) opposes Menelaos for the body of Menelaos' victim Euphorbos (*Il.*17. 59–113). The script is partly Argive (note *lambda* and sibilant *san*); the painter may have copied the group from an Argive bronze shield-strap (cf. fig.2).c. 600. (pp. 141, 241)

33   Part of a small Subgeometric cup from Rhodes, with owner's graffito *right* to *left*: 'I am Qoraqos' cup'. c. 700. (p. 26)

35[*opposite*]   Lifesize marble statue, one of a series lining the Sacred Way to Apollo's temple at Didyma near Miletos. Dedication on right leg of throne: 'I am Chares son of Kleisis, ruler of Teichioussa [a dependency not far off]; the statue is Apollo's'. He wears the sleeved Ionic chiton and a heavy cloak draped round his back and over his knees. c. 560–550. (pp. 31, 211)

36[*opposite*]   High relief from the sculptured base of a column from Didyma. The girl wears a close-fitting chiton, a heavy veil held by a double (woollen?) headband, and under the veil what might be a close coif. The 'Venus rings' on her plump neck, though abnormal in Archaic Greek art, occur in Egyptian sculpture; for the round face and narrow eyes cf. also Pl. 38 (Samos). c. 540–530. (p. 241)

37 Marble lion from Miletos, probably from a tomb. The recumbent pose harks back to an Egyptian original, but not the perceptive treatment of the wrinkled hide and drooping head. *c.* 525. (p. 211)

38(a–b) Head of a colossal marble kouros, recently identified as Samian work when parts of the body were excavated in the Heraion. Note its east Greek traits: plumpness, narrow eyes (cf. Pl. 36), and (on men) the front hair cut short and brushed back from the forehead. c. 550. (pp. 213, 215)

39(*a–b*) Ivory kneeling boy, wearing a metal belt and soft ankle-boots, from the Heraion at Samos; perhaps one of a pair carved as supports for the frame of a lyre, the work of a Greek craftsman trained in this Oriental skill of ivory-work. *c.* 625. (pp. 212–13)

40 Electrum coin (stater) showing (obverse) a dappled deer grazing, (reverse) 3 punchmarks. Inscribed *right* to *left*: 'I am Phanes' [name misspelt] mark', signature of the official(?) who had it struck. Found in Halikarnassos, but the coinage is Ephesian. *c.* 600? (p. 222)

41 Sherd used for a deft graffito sketch, perhaps a pleasant touch of Kolophonian-Smyrniote humour. A youth ('an Arimaspian?', J. M. Cook), with caduceus and satchel, is sped smartly on his way by a small griffin. From Smyrna. *c.* 600–575? (pp. 224–6)

42 Marble flying Victory (Nike), traces of large wings behind, small pair on shoulders in front; originally mounted above eye-level. Dedicated to Apollo at Delos by Mikkiades, made by Archermos of Chios. *c.* 550–540. (p. 233)

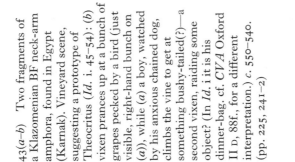

43(a–b)   Two fragments of a Klazomenian BF neck-arm amphora, found in Egypt (Karnak). Vineyard scene, suggesting a prototype of Theocritus (*Id.* i. 45–54): (*b*) vixen prances up at a bunch of grapes pecked by a bird (just visible, right-hand bunch on (*a*)), while (*a*) a boy, watched by his anxious chained dog, climbs the vine to get at something bushy-tailed(?)—a second vixen, raiding some object? (In *Id.* i it is his dinner-bag. cf. *CVA* Oxford II D, 88f., for a different interpretation.) *c.* 550–540. (pp. 225, 241–2).

44   Chian chalice from a tomb at Marion (Cyprus). (*a*) Outside, sphinx on white ground; (*b*) inside, purple and white lotus flowers on a black ground. *c.* 600–575. (pp. 231, 241–2).

45 Small marble statue of a recumbent feaster holding a
tankard, dedicated in the precinct of Apollo Termintheus at
Myous; the pose was popular in sixth-century east Greek art.
Inscribed boustrophedon: 'Ermonax and [his sons??] offered me
jointly[?], a tithe of their works, to Apollo'. c. 550–525? (p. 222)

46 Jug (oinochoe), polychrome on white slip, guilloche
neck-pattern; spotted deer and wary griffin, wild goats
browsing, lotus chain. From Rhodes (Kameiros), but this east
Greek 'Wild Goat' style was probably made at several centres
notably Miletos, Samos, Chios, as well as Rhodes. *c.* 600. (pp.
28–9, 241–2)

10 Corinth, Epidauros and Aigina; Megara

Corinth, Epidauros, Aigina

CORINTH UNDER THE BACCHIADAI

The stock epithet for Corinth was *aphneios* (wealthy), because of her profitable site. She was a north-south corridor for land-travellers and her two ports looked east and west on to the Saronic and Corinthian Gulfs. The river-plain between her and Sikyon was very fertile also, though we do not know exactly where the boundary lay.

Traditionally in 747 a hereditary kingship ended when the royal clan, called Bacchiadai after their distant ancestor king Bacchis, took over the rule of the city. This is a classic example of the earliest type of aristocracy, formed when the royal kin of an ineffective monarch took the power from him, but kept it wholly in their own hands. The Bacchiadai, like the Spartan and Argive royal families, professed to be descended from Herakles, their original Doric 'founder' being one Aletes. They forbade exogamy. This must have built up steadily a ring of well-born and resentful outsiders, for in Corinth there were not only non-Bacchiad Dorians, but also non-Dorians of very ancient stock; for example the family of Action, whose son Kypselos was to make himself tyrant in 657, traced its descent from the Lapithai of Bronze Age Thessaly, either directly or via Gonoessa in eastern Achaia.

The Bacchiadai elected one of themselves annually to be the *prytanis* (? 'ruler'; an old word of unknown derivation, used also by Ionic states). They had also a *polemarchos* and a council. The clan itself is said to have been 'over 200 in number', which suggests that the Corinthian oligarchy was of the archaic type best attested in Phokaia's colony Massalia (above, pp. 43–4) – the type which, consisting of a round number of households (*oikiai*), a number which became fixed and traditional, gave to the head of each household (and in some cases to his eldest son at the same time) the right to be a councillor. Possibly, therefore, about 200 families traditionally made up the Bacchiad clan; for it is said that an early Corinthian lawgiver named Pheidon enacted that the number of households must remain constant and the number of citizens also, even if their properties were unequal in size. He was, we suppose, the Bacchiad who first defined the ruling caste as consisting of about 200 (or a hundred?) specified families. The number of citizens should mean *all* the adult males of these households, though those eligible to serve on the council would be kept fixed to the paterfamilias (and his eldest son?), and the enforcement of adoption on sonless households would ensure that the clan's numbers were maintained and thus their rule also. Certainly adoption was introduced in archaic Thebes *c.* 728 by an exiled Bacchiad lawgiver named Philolaos, who enforced it 'to preserve the number of the estates' (*kleroi*), that is, the households.[1]

Early in their rule (*c.* 735) a Bacchiad named Archias led a band of emigrants westward. The band split, one part settling in Kerkyra. The population there was Illyrian, except for an Eretrian settlement, which the Corinthians ejected (above, p. 64). The other part went on, and settled in Syracuse. These became two of the greatest Western colonies, and it has been claimed that there the Bacchiadai showed a farsighted statesmanship; but the evidence is indecisive. The tradition said that Archias had to leave because he was polluted by manslaughter, and that the settlers were mostly from Tenea in the inland part of the Corinthia – which suggests that they were humble subsistence farmers. But the Euboians of Chalkis had demonstrated the potential of Italy and Sicily, Corinth's cramped neighbour Megara was following them, and Corinth herself at this time was apparently a pioneer in improvements to shipbuilding (perhaps through Phoenician instruction, since she had trade connections with the Near East), *if* Ameinokles of Corinth built four warships (triremes?) for the Samians *c.* 704 (but cf. below, p. 159, n. 2). Whether the Bacchiadai originally foresaw it or not, however, the Western colonies greatly increased the wealth of Corinth as the years passed; for the biggest expansion of her pottery, the Protocorinthian and its successors, began early in the seventh century, which suggests that the colonies, then in their second generation, were creating a fast-growing demand.

THE KYPSELID TYRANNY: COLONIES AND DIPLOMACY

Corinth is held by modern authority to have supported Sparta against Messenia in the late eighth century (above p. 120), and (again a modern inference) Chalkis against Eretria in the Lelantine War (above, p. 67). Aid to far-off Sparta in the eighth century sounds less probable than in the seventh; but Corinth may well have helped Chalkis for trading reasons. Her own perpetual foes, however, were Argos on her southern and Megara on her northern border, the small Doric corridor-state squeezed between two bigger powers. In the eighth century Megara seems to have been actually a dependency of Bacchiad Corinth; the saying 'Megarian tears' for false grief traditionally arose because the Megarians as subjects were forced to send duty-mourners to the funeral of a Bacchiad ruler, just as the *perioikoi* of Lakedaimon did at the death of a Spartan king.[2]

The Bacchiadai controlled Corinth 'for ninety years', a round number perhaps derived from a calculation of three (thirty-year) generations. Then they were overthrown in a revolution. Various factors seem to have combined to produce the passions needed for such an event – a combination of long-mounting grievances with some sudden crisis which touched off the explosion. Abroad, Megara had evidently regained her independence by the seventh century (whether or not her hero Orsippos did win back much of her borderland; below, p. 156); and *c.* ?664 (below, p. 159, n. 2) a Corinthian fleet in Kerkyrean waters fought Kerkyra's fleet in the first recorded Greek sea-battle, which suggests either that

Corinth was having to protect her trade-ships from Kerkyrean obstacles, or that she herself was trying to annex Kerkyra – unsuccessfully, if so, for Kerkyra was not annexed until the time of Periander (below, p. 148–9). In either case, Corinth was evidently in trouble in this area shortly before her government fell. At home, what happened to the wealth got from the tolls and dues and middle-man profits accruing to this city which occupied the central crossroads of mainland Greece? If most of the tax-collectors were Bacchiadai, other Corinth-ians might see all too little of the profits. Lastly, Kypselos, the leader of the revolution, was a non-Bacchiad on his father's side; and thus, as in Athens before Solon, so perhaps in Corinth too there were other proud families which could no longer tolerate exclusion from the government of their city. The ambition of king Pheidon of Argos at about this time (above, p. 136) may have been the wedge finally introduced to split a crumbling façade; for he went to Corinth 'through friendship' at a time of stasis there. So probably he hoped to add another member to his Heritage of Temenos by helping a new government into power there.

Thus in 657 Kypselos, encouraged by a favourable oracle from Delphi, over-threw the Bacchiad rule. Late sources say that he was *polemarchos* at the time, which sounds illegal for a non-Bacchiad; possibly the rulers were trying, too late, to quieten things by broadening the basis of government. His mother, Labda, was indeed a Bacchiad; but, says Herodotos, she was lame, and so no one within the clan would marry her. The success of some dictators in later times has been ascribed to the early influence of ambitious mothers; if Labda did educate her child for revenge, we may remember the brutality of the law in an endogamous society, as it is laid down in the fifth-century Cretan code at Gortyn concerning the heiress (who, as an heiress, must naturally be married to her nearest available male relative within the tribe, or, failing any such relatives, to another tribesman):

> but if no one in the tribe wants to marry her, her relatives shall proclaim throughout the tribe: 'Does no one wish to marry her?'; and if anyone will marry her then, it must be within the thirty days; but if no one does, then she is to marry whomsoever else she can . . .'

– which last meant that effectively she was proclaimed a social outcast.

The deposed Bacchiadai fled, some to Kerkyra, others to Etruria, others to Sparta, where, a later story implies, the long-haired Spartans laughed at their cropped heads. But 'Herakleidai' were still available in Corinth later to serve as *oikistai* for Western emigrants; so either some of the clan made their peace with the new régime and stayed in Corinth, or else not all Herakleidai were Bacchiadai.

Kypselos was one of the earliest *tyrannoi* of the Greek mainland (above, pp. 46–7). The dynasty founded by him lasted seventy-four years, for thirty of which he himself ruled. The surviving accounts of his régime give the impression of an able merchant-prince, harsh to his aristocratic enemies but free-and-easy with the people, and working to create a permanent line of dependent colonies for Corinth which would link her more closely to the sources, or the middlemen, for the valuable materials in the West: iron from Elba, corn and timber from Sicily and south Italy, gold and copper from Etruria, silver from Illyria, and much else. Many ports like Chalkis and Molykreion in Aitolia (above, p. 64) may have been appropriated by Corinth during the tyranny. The foundations of Leukas and Anaktorion are credited to Kypselos; the numbers required were made up by citizens hostile to the régime, who were anxious or compelled to leave Corinth, and the *oikistai*, according to some accounts, were his bastard sons Pylades and Echekrates. At Delphi, in gratitude to the Pythia for encouraging his accession, Kypselos built and dedicated a treasury which became known simply as the Corinthian treasury after his dynasty fell. Here were stored not only Corinthian offerings but the rich gifts of barbarian rulers, Phrygian and Lydian, with whom the Corinthian tyrants may have had *xeniai*. In Herodotos' time it still held a judgement-seat given by one of the Midas dynasty in Phrygia, probably a masterpiece of fretted woodwork like the screens and tables found in the 'Midas' tomb of the Phrygian dynasty at Gordion, the capital city. There were also many gold, silver, and elektron vessels and statues from Gyges and Kroisos of Lydia. Of all this treasure, by the second century A.D. there remained still a famous bronze palm-tree with frogs and snakes round its roots, said to be one of Kypselos' own gifts. This may remind us faintly of the taste in table-centres and *épergnes* of English nabobs retired from India in the early nineteenth century, and doubtless the Kypselid dynasty did grow very wealthy through their rule. It is said that Kypselos made the land and goods of the Bacchiadai public property, and that he was so popular with the commons as to need no bodyguard in the streets; so he may well have reallocated the Bacchiad estates into *kleroi* for the landless. The later tradition apparently preserved two views of him, the one as a sort of ogre, the other in kinder colours.[3]

His son Periander succeeded him and also ruled till his death *c.* 585. He pressed on with the extension of Corinthian power abroad. 'He built triremes and used both the seas': that is, at Kenchreai on the Saronic Gulf and Lechaion on the Gulf of Corinth, where extensive dredging and piling now made a proper harbour. This was followed by the construction of the famous *diolkos*, a paved way across the Isthmus scored with two grooves like tramlines for the wheels of a vehicle which transported the ships; traces of a wooden construction at the western end, before the grooves begin, have suggested some kind of hoist. Parts of the paving belong to the fifth century, but underneath lies an original pavement thought to be of Periander's date. At least two dependent colonies were also settled. One extended Corinthian influence to the north Aegean, for it was planted *c.* 600 on the neck of the western prong of the Chalkidike, which was already occupied by some Eretrian settlements. A route ran west thence inland to Lynkestis, where imported Greek bronzes of the sixth century have been found, and where a link-up could be made with traders coming eastwards from the Corinthian settlements on the Illyrian coast. Among the bartered goods along the route may have been essence of the local wild iris, for re-export in elegant Corinthian alabastra and aryballoi. The colony bore the Doric name Potidaia after Poseidon, chief deity of the sea-riding, earthquake-ridden Isthmus of Corinth.

The second dependency was Ambrakia, ruled by Periander's brother Gorgos, at the head of the Ambrakiot Gulf near Leukas and Anaktorion. Furthermore, Periander actually got control of Kerkyra (above, pp. 146–7), and put in as regent his son and heir Lykophron.

On the diplomatic side also he cast his nets widely. He made a *xenia* with Thrasyboulos, tyrant of Miletos (below, p. 213), thus reversing the previous Corinthian record of friendship with Samos. Such changes of policy often happened when a city came under a tyrant, and help to remind us how much the military and commercial alliances of the Archaic period depended on the nexus of guest-friendships and personal contacts in the cities. In this instance, obviously no Kypselid could inherit goodwill which had been built up in oligarchic Samos by the Bacchiadai. Periander gave the Milesians useful information in their long war with Alyattes of Lydia; indeed, he seems also to have had a *xenia* with Alyattes, for not only did the Corinthian treasury at Delphi house the Lydian gifts to Apollo, but Periander had access once at least to an important oracle which the Pythia had given to Alyattes. He reported its content to the Milesians; one wonders if he had taken on the diplomatic task of 'agent' for the Lydians at Delphi. And again, when the Kerkyreans rose against Corinthian rule and murdered Lykophron, Periander in vengeance sent 300 boys from the leading Kerkyrean families as a gift for the court of Alyattes. (The boys were rescued on the way and brought back finally to Kerkyra by the Samians, or, according to another version, by the Knidians.) With Egypt also, another wealthy non-Greek empire on the fringe of the Aegean, he had presumably a *xenia*, for Kypselos II, the nephew who briefly succeeded him at Corinth, bore also the Pharaonic name Psammetichos (Psamtik).

On the Greek mainland Periander's policy evidently favoured Athens. When asked to arbitrate between Athens and Mytilene for the possession of Sigeion in the Troad, he awarded it to Athens, though geographically it belonged rather to Mytilene (pp. 89–90, 238–9). And in the late seventh century this rare name Kypselos appeared in Athens in the family of the Philaidai, indicating a dynastic friendship through marriage to some aunt or sister of Periander. We do not know his attitude to Corinth's traditional border enemy Argos, where the hereditary monarchy of the Temenidai must have ended during his reign, if not before (above, pp. 136–8). Some of the late sources imply that he was hostile to Corinth's western neighbour Sikyon, where the powerful tyranny of Kleisthenes largely overlapped in time with his own; 'the Kypselidai' are said to have plotted with Isodemos, the brother whom Kleisthenes ousted from the rule of Sikyon, and Periander's friend Thrasyboulos once seized its harbour (below, p. 213). Nor does Periander's name occur in the events of the First Sacred War, in which Kleisthenes was a leading light. Yet Herodotos, our earliest source here, says that at the wooing of Kleisthenes' daughter Agariste an Athenian suitor was initially favoured because he was 'ancestrally related to the Kypselidai' (below, p. 165).

Again, we know nothing of his relations with Megara on the northern border, where in the 630s Theagenes was tyrant. But a dynastic alliance certainly existed between Kypselid Corinth and Epidauros in the eastern Argolid, for Periander had married Lysida (also called Melissa), daughter of Prokles, tyrant of that city. Lykophron was her son, and about her untimely death fearful stories were reported later against Periander, causing a cruel estrangement between father and son. On the pretext that his father-in-law had spread these tales, Periander arrested Prokles and took control of Epidauros, a city which, with her remarkable daughter Aigina, deserves consideration at this point.[4]

EPIDAUROS AND AIGINA: THE KALAUREIAN AMPHIKTIONY

At this time (*c.* 600) Epidauros was a smallish Doric coastal state with a good harbour and a modest sanctuary of Apollo Maleatas on Mount Kynortion inland, in the area where late in the sixth century the cult of Asklepios, god of healing, was to be introduced – it was said, from Trikka in Thessaly – and brought wealth and fame to the city. Her natural connections lay seawards, among the other places on the Saronic Gulf. Indeed she had an ancient obligation to send offerings annually to Athena Polias and Erechtheus on the Athenian Acropolis – traditionally because her holy statues of Damia and Auxesia, goddesses of fertility, had been made of Attic olive-wood. Her chief road inland lay through the hills to Argos, where an interested tradition said that when the Dorian Temenos took over Argos, his daughter Hyrnatho married one Deiphontes (also a Heraklid, according to one source), who seized and held Epidauros for himself, having quarrelled with his in-laws. The tale implies some strong local Epidaurian traditions which made it difficult for Argos to fudge up another son of Temenos for a direct claim to control of Epidauros, so that the pre-Doric deity of Hyrnatho at Epidauros had to be grafted on to the story as a Temenid daughter. The Epidaurians who rejected Deiphontes were said to have fled and settled in Samos, with similar refugees from Phleious near Corinth.

The island of Aigina was originally settled from Epidauros. Regarded by her metropolis as a dependency, she broke away to independence probably in the first half of the seventh century; indeed, she stole the sacred images of Damia and Auxesia, an act clearly designed to transfer to herself all the fertility and prosperity of Epidauros. She was then attacked by raiding Athenian ships, allegedly because Athens had now lost Epidauros' annual offerings; and in this struggle an Argive force helped the Aiginetans to kill nearly all the Athenians who had landed. It came to Aigina via Epidauros, so evidently Argos controlled Epidauros at the time; the inference is that all this happened in the reign of Pheidon of Argos (fl. *c.* 680–657?), who was said by a late source to have controlled Aigina in his day.

The antagonism between Athens and Aigina, thus started, continued throughout the Archaic period and was still active in the fifth century. Indeed, in the scattered data which remain from Aigina's history in the Archaic period, her enemies are more obvious than her friends. Like her neighbours at the Isthmus she was an oligarchic state whose revenues came mainly from trade – in her case, as a middleman, for the island had no attractive commodities to export. Most of her population, Aristotle says, were seamen. She was the first 'mainland' state to issue a coinage (*c.* 575?), silver with a sea-turtle as its device, and this priority may have happened because she was also the only 'mainland' state which had its share with the eastern Greeks in founding Naukratis, the *emporion* in the Nile Delta (above, pp. 53–4). It was presumably through her sea passage southward that she got a trading foothold in Crete, where many Aiginetan coins have been found; in 519 she founded a colony, Kydonia, on the north coast of Crete not far from its western end, where the cliff called the Ram's Head overlooked the sea-route down to Egypt. She ejected the previous occupants of the site, a band of Samians, for Samos and Aigina had been enemies since early days, 'when king Amphikrates ruled Samos' (below, p. 213). Amphikrates is otherwise unattested, but doubtless the feud concerned the southern sea-routes, for Samos too was a founder member of Naukratis. Aigina is said to have made a settlement somewhere in Umbria also; and one of her greatest traders, Sostratos, noted by Herodotos as the richest Greek of all time, dedicated an aniconic Apollo Agyieus, about the end of the sixth century, in a precinct recently excavated on the western coast of Italy near Caere. At some date after the death of Pheidon she evidently detached herself from Argos. She may have joined Sparta's Peloponnesian League; certainly c. 491 the Spartan king Kleomenes, alerted by her enemy Athens, disciplined her for giving earth and water to the heralds of Darius in token of submission to Persia, but this does not of itself prove membership of the League, since Sparta could have done this simply as recognized leader against the growing danger of Persia.

For painted pottery Aigina relied on her neighbours or trade partners. The precinct of her chief goddess, Aphaia, contained much fine seventh-century Attic and Corinthian ware, and also many of the exquisite Chian white-ground chalices – these doubtless from her Chian contacts at Naukratis, where quantities of these chalices have been found. Her artistic fame rested on her sculptors in wood and bronze. One Smilis of Aigina made a wooden cult-statue of Hera at Samos 'when Prokles ruled', replacing an earlier, plank-like figure. (If the seventh-century Prokles of Epidauros is meant, this may have been before Aigina broke away from Epidauros, and might account for what otherwise is surprising, the employment of an Aiginetan by the Samians; for Epidauros was friendly to Samos in the early days, having traditionally sent settlers there (below, p. 212) under an earlier Prokles son of Pityreus.) Her great school of bronze-casters belongs to the early fifth century, and so does not concern us here; but it may be noted that the famous sculptor Kresilas, one of the younger rivals of Pheidias, came from the colony Kydonia.

In Epidauros itself, the history of Prokles, who became tyrant there c. 650, shows no positive Argive links; but he married Eristhenia, daughter of Aristokrates, ruler of Arkadian Orchomenos, which suggests that Epidauros was then in the pro-Argive rather than the pro-Spartan camp. His daughter Lysida (Melissa) married Periander, an event which, as we have seen (above, pp. 149–50), subsequently brought Epidauros under the control of Corinth. Probably she became free again after the fall of the Kypselid dynasty in 582–581, but nothing is known of her political history during the rest of the sixth century. The arrival and development of the cult of Asklepios may have concentrated the channel of her energy. She was also one of an Amphiktiony of seven cities which administered the cult of Poseidon on the island of Kalaureia (modern Poros) offshore from Troizen. Of these seven, Epidauros, Hermion, and Aigina were true 'dwellers around'; Athens, Nauplia, and Prasiai were an outer ring, and the last two were later replaced de facto by their respective controllers, Argos and Sparta. Oddest of all, because remote and inland, was 'Minyan' Orchomenos, the Boiotian, not the Arkadian, city. Because of her presence modern scholars have suggested a Bronze Age origin for the Amphiktiony, though the surviving traces of dedications begin only *c.* 700. A recent theory sees its effective start in an anti-Pheidon coalition.

Archaic Epidauros was an oligarchy with a ruling class of 180 men (i.e., heads of families?) whence her council was selected; the councillors were called *artunai* (arrangers; cf. a similar body at Argos; above, p. 144, n. 5). She had the usual three Doric tribes. There is no positive evidence in our period of any Hyrnathioi (as at Argos) as a fourth tribe, for non-Dorians; but this may be by chance. It is unlikely, at least, that they were the Konipodes (dusty-feet), a title which Plutarch says was given to the country peasants, plodding into the city from their fields.

OLIGARCHIC CORINTH AND THE PELOPONNESIAN LEAGUE

Meanwhile at Corinth the dynasty had faded after Periander, who died in 585. Because his son Lykophron was already dead, his nephew, Psammetichos Kypselos, succeeded him, and was deposed after two years, at about the time when the Isthmian Games to Poseidon were officially founded. Possibly these were established by the oligarchic families to celebrate the return of constitutional government; possibly too they were meant to rival the successful Pythian Games at Delphi, recently inaugurated by Kleisthenes of Sikyon – just as the Argive build-up of the Games to Zeus at Nemea (above, p. 137) may in its turn have been prompted partly by the new Corinthian spectacle at the Isthmus. The Isthmia were held at some distance from the city, near the east coast of the Isthmus. Excavations have shown that the old temple was built during the seventh century; but the cult of Poseidon was established earlier, for at least one bronze male statuette of the late eighth century was found. The sanctuary flourished through the seventh and sixth centuries (and indeed later; the temple was burnt down *c.* 500–475, but was rebuilt almost at once). The Games were officially said – as at Olympia – to be funeral by origin, established in the Bronze Age over the dead princeling Palaimon-Melikertes, to whom chthonic rites were performed in an underground precinct on the site.

In the north-western colonies the cadet rulers seem to have lasted longer. Timonassa, ex-wife of Archinos of Ambrakia, married Peisistratos of Athens about the mid-sixth century, and the last tyrant in Ambrakia, another Periander, is said to have been succeeded by a democracy, which, if true in any sense, can hardly have happened before the end of the century. Kerkyra had won independence again before 480, but the exact date is unknown. A broken Argive inscription of *c.* 330 B.C. shows that the family did not all leave these parts; there was still a Periander then in (Anakto)rion (he was a host there (*theorodokos*) to Argive religious embassies), and also Kypselidai in either Kephallenia or, more vaguely, 'the [Pelop]onnese'.[5]

The Kypselid dynasties, home and colonial, are part of a long list of places which later Spartan propaganda claimed that the Spartans had 'rescued' from their tyrannic rulers; but it is hard to see what would persuade Sparta in the early sixth century, when entering on a struggle with her strong neighbour Tegea, to send troops as far afield as Corinth. Perhaps she merely abetted the descendants of her Bacchiad refugees (above, p. 138) to return now to their city. At all events, after her last tyrant Corinth returned to oligarchy. Later sources indicate that she enlarged the number of her tribes to eight; evidently here, as elsewhere in the sixth century after a tyranny, the actual number of citizens had increased, perhaps through higher live birth-rates thanks to economic prosperity, and through grants of citizenship to skilled alien artisans; and so a tribal reorganization was needed to regularize a situation for which the existing tribal system was no longer sufficient. According to recent research, it seems likely that the Corinthia was now divided geographically into three groups, each of eight thirds or 'ridings', one group being formed out of the city itself, the other two out of the Corinthian land north and south, respectively, of the Isthmus: and that each of the eight new tribes was formed by three thirds (as later in Kleisthenes' tribal reforms at Athens), one taken from each group. A council of eighty members was formed, ten from each tribe; within this eight men (one from each tribal decad?) formed a college of *probouloi*, the apex of the council, and the highest authority in the state. The whole was apparently a blended oligarchy, partly landed proprietors of noble birth, partly newer men who had risen in the prosperous atmosphere of the colonial empire created by the Kypselidai. (Athens also, under Solon, was showing now that plutocracy was challenging ancestral aristocracy.) Certainly we do not hear of political revolution at Corinth in the sixth century; and the ending of the tyrannic government first in the metropolis and later in her north-west dependencies seems to have left the latter places still tied to Corinth by certain commitments: to supply ships and men for her wars, to follow her system of coinage, and to receive annually Corinthian officials as administrators of some kind.

In 525-524 Corinth was a ready ally of Sparta in an expedition across the Aegean to eject Polykrates, tyrant of Samos, and restore an oligarchy there (below, p. 217). As an oligarchy herself, she may simply have wished to put down the tyrant and restore the old Samos-Corinth *philia* (cf. pp. 146, 212), especially if her own trade now was suffering in any way from the piratical fleet of Polykrates; in any case, the expedition failed utterly. By this time she was presumably a member of the Peloponnesian League, though the date when she joined it is not attested. Whenever the alliance was formed, it must have been a fairly loose one, for Corinth – as well she knew – was too large and too far from Sparta for the Spartans ever to force their wishes easily on her against her will. In 507–506 and again *c*. 504 her troops led the other dissidents of the League's army in refusing to follow Spartan troops against Athens (above, pp. 102, 104). Corinth showed no animosity towards Athens in the Archaic period; they shared a common border hostility against Megara.

ART

Clay-modelling – both pottery and moulded figures – and drawing were the chief artistic skills of early Corinth. The literary tradition said that both were 'invented' there: Boutades, a Sikyonian modeller working in Corinth, made the first clay relief by building up the outline of a young man's shadow-profile, which his lovesick daughter had traced on the wall, while the first linear draughtsmen were Kleanthes and Aridikes of Corinth and Telephos of Sikyon. Ekphantos of Corinth had first made paint from powdered clay, and Corinthians exiled by Kypselos had brought painting and modelling to Etruria. There was once an old painting of Helen and the Dioskouroi in the Corinthian colony Ambrakia, and some fragmentary paintings on large clay metopes have survived from the late seventh-century temple of Apollo at Thermon in Aitolia. They should perhaps be regarded as provincial work under Corinthian influence rather than actual Corinthian products (the clay is said to be local, and the inscriptions are partly in the local Aitolian script); but they offer some idea of the bold scale of Corinthian work, and in any case no one need go further than the vases to realize the amazing power of linear control even in the miniature-painting.

The development of the vase-painting from Protocorinthian and Transitional (c. 675–625) to Early Corinthian (c. 625–600; Pl. 23), Middle (c. 600–575), and Late (c. 575–550; the lower limits in all cases may be slightly extended) was analysed and illuminated so powerfully by Payne in *Necrocorinthia* that little will be said here. The potters' original models were the line drawings of figures, animals, plant-motifs, etc. on imports from the Near East about the end of the eighth century (above, pp. 28–9, 84–5); the pottery varies in size from normal table-ware to tiny flasks (aryballoi, alabastra) for oil or scent. The fusion of the old Greek Geometric black silhouette with the new line drawing produced the first Greek black-figure style, with incision for the inner lines. Attic potters took this over later and developed it (above, p. 92); in Corinth it continued into Late Corinthian, in decorative 'Orientalizing' patterns, mostly friezes of animals against a background thickly sown with rosettes and other filling-devices, a style that lost its quality finally in hasty routine work to meet the increasing demands of outside markets. But by c. 650–625 the pot-painters were also working in a quite different style, of outline figure-drawing in polychrome (black, red, pale brown; orange and white too by the sixth century) – scenes from saga and mythology. The influence of the picture-painters has been recognized here. Late Protocorinthian aryballoi can show a crowded battle-scene in a frieze 2 cm. high (Pl. 22); and the mythological scenes on a fine series of kraters through the first half of the sixth century show us faces in profile which seem to be characteristic – neat, cheerful, slighter-featured than the contemporary Attic. Indeed, the heads of girls in high relief added at the rims of pyxides (powder or trinket boxes) often look like portraits (Pl. 20), occasionally even with names attached. The same alert, spruce look appears on the heads ornamenting the clay revetments for temples which were exported elsewhere, and also on two marble grave-statues dated near the mid-sixth century, a kouros from Tenea (Pl. 19) and a seated sphinx recently found near Old Corinth. Stone sculpture as yet is sparse. Much may have been destroyed when L. Mummius sacked Corinth in 146 B.C.; but no names of Archaic sculptors survive in the literary tradition either. Certainly the Corinthians built stone temples, and traditionally they 'invented the pediment' – not, presumably, the mere idea of the triangular fill-in, but the idea of decorating it with a big design, probably at first painted on terracotta. The colony at Kerkyra provides perhaps our earliest example of a stone pedimental relief (c. 580?), from the temple of Artemis – the huge flying Medusa flanked by two couching spotted panthers, with her offspring (Pegasos and Chrysaor) and gods or giants all distributed puppetlike in the remaining spaces.[6]

Megara

COLONIAL SETTLEMENTS: THE TYRANNY

Megara, originally (it is thought) an offshoot from Doric Argos, occupies the narrow, mountainous isthmus between the borders of Ionic Athens and Doric Corinth. A short stretch of her northern border edged Mount Kithairon on the southern border of Boiotia, but there was no tradition of hostility there. The possession of these strategic entries from the Peloponnese into both Attica and Boiotia condemned Megara to all the miseries of a small corridor-state cramped between bigger powers. This showed strongly in the two great wars of the fifth century between the Athenian and Peloponnesian Leagues, and overshadowed her history already in the Archaic period; for to Corinth, exposed on her own southern border to the power of Argos, Megara was the easier problem, while on Megara's Attic border lay the sacred land of Eleusinian Demeter, the 'Orgas'. The Megarians always contested Athens's right to this and raided the border intermittently.

Five districts originally formed the state of Megara: Heraia, Peraia, Kynosoura, Tripodiskos, and Megara town with her port Nisaia on the Saronic Gulf. In the early days they were hampered by age-old rivalries (often fostered by Corinth), but still followed the aristocratic code in their conventions. They never fought à outrance; farmers and their crops were spared, and captives were well treated as 'spear-guests' (doruxenoi) and rarely failed to pay their ransoms honourably. In the eighth century Bacchiad Corinth claimed Megara as her dependency (above, p. 146), and held her for at least a generation. About 728, after Corinthian settlers had founded colonies in Kerkyra and Syracuse, a band of Megarians led by Lamis went out to the district near Syracuse. Here, after settling first at Trotilon and then leaving it to join the Chalkidian settlers inland at Leontinoi, they were ejected by the Chalkidians, settled on the peninsula Thapsos, left it on the death of Lamis, and settled finally on a site given to them by the local Sicel ruler Hyblon, after whom the colony was renamed 'Hyblon's Megarians', or Megara Hyblaia.

Whether or not these Megarians had emigrated to escape from the domination of Corinth at home, the initial setbacks imply that theirs was not a powerful body but one driven by poverty rather than by ambitious thoughts of trade; in any case, territorial expansion in Sicily was blocked for them on the north by Chalkis' colonies, and on the south by Syracuse. However, by the end of the eighth century Megara herself appears to have regained her independence, allegedly under the leadership of an Olympic victor named Orsippos (stadion, 720), who is said to have won back 'much of her lost borderland' (most probably on the Corinthian, not the Attic, side). But at some time still in the early period Heraia and Peraia had become Corinthian territory for good.

If Megara was involved at all in the Lelantine War between Chalkis and Eretria (above, p. 67), it was presumably on the side of Eretria and her friend Miletos; for Chalkis' colony Leontinoi had first accepted but then ejected the

Megarian settlers in Sicily. Friendship with the Eretrian-Milesian side could also explain why the Megarians, in a second bout of emigration about the start of the seventh century, switched over to Asian territory, where the Milesians were also expanding. There is no evidence of opposition from the Milesians there; on the southern shore of the Propontis the Megarians founded Kalchedon (*c.* 680; and traditionally a few small places earlier), Selymbria (662), and then crossed the Propontis to settle at Byzantion (*c.* 660). Byzantion became a great trading city, queen of the narrow entry to the Black Sea with all its riches; but at home the Megarians were ruled by a country aristocracy which by the mid-seventh century must have overreached itself, for *c.* 640–630 one Theagenes, himself an aristocrat according to his name ('god-descended'), won the people's support, it is said, by killing the flocks of the rich, who had enclosed the common grazing-land; and with this support he became tyrant of Megara, following the adjacent examples in Corinth and Sikyon.

Theagenes built a famous spring-house for his city's water-supply. He may also, conceivably, have been the ruler who first attached the island of Salamis to Megara. In the poet Hesiod's time (fl. *c.* 700?), Salamis was still an independent pirate's nest with a friendship for Attica, if we may judge by the poet's picture of her heroic ruler Ajax winning his worldly wealth by looting all the states on the west side of the Saronic Gulf, including Megara – but not the eastern, Attic, side. Geographically, Salamis perhaps goes with Megara rather than Attica; and by the early sixth century she was certainly in Megarian hands, for Solon was exhorting the Athenians to get her by force. Theagenes therefore, the first notable Megarian known to us after Orsippos, may have been the leader who first seized the island from the pirates, and doubtless helped thereby to lessen the population problem which his small and hilly city-state had always to face. If it was indeed he who won Salamis, this action perhaps preceded the disastrous attempt which he made about 631 to create a pro-Megarian tyranny in Attica by marrying his daughter to Kylon, a leading Athenian aristocrat (above, pp. 87-9). This would have made a strong bloc across the top of the Saronic Gulf; but the abortive *coup* failed utterly. Theagenes ended his career in exile.[7]

THE RENEWED OLIGARCHY: THEOGNIS

In the next generation the intense struggle for Salamis began. Oligarchic government had returned to Megara after the tyranny fell, and the first part of the sixth century was full of trouble abroad. Selymbria, the valuable Megarian dependency near Byzantion, became embroiled with her neighbour Samian Perinthos, and in a defeat there Megara lost the services of some 600 Megarian citizen-soldiers (below, pp. 214–15). Athens had produced a brilliant young general, Peisistratos, who later became tyrant, and *c.* 570(?), in the struggle to win Salamis, he actually seized Megara's port, Nisaia, and held it for a time. (Salamis was ceded finally to Athens on the arbitration of a board of five Spartans, but we do not know whether this happened before Peisistratos' death in 527, or nearer the end of the century.) The power of the oligarchy began to crack, and was finally ended by a frightening revolt of indebted peasants, which later writers called 'the lawless democracy'. The peasants demanded and got a *palintokia* (return of the interest paid on their borrowings), plundered the houses of the rich, and even held up and ki'led pilgrims and deputations to Delphi who were travelling thither via the Isthmus and Boiotia. Since the Megarian authorities took no action over these crimes, the Delphic Amphiktiony punished the offenders with exile or death.

This was in the lifetime of Megara's one outstanding poet, Theognis (c. 570–490?). His elegiacs, mostly addressed to his young friend Kyrnos son of Polypaos, reflect the convictions of the diehard oligarch. Like Alkaios of Mytilene he spent much time in exile, railing not only against 'goatskin-wearers who once lived like herds of deer outside the city, but are now the gentry', but against the mixed marriages whereby a new generation of wealthy men gained entry to the élite:

> We hunt for purebred asses, rams and horses,
> to breed their like; but now the noble's happy
> to wed a lowborn slut, if she brings riches . . .
> Don't wonder that the city's stock is failing –
> it's mating good with bad . . .

But he returned, and the 'democracy' was finally displaced by a moderate oligarchy before the end of the sixth century. A short verse sums up his view of the old aristocracies now disappearing:

> Citadel and steeple
> for his foolish people,
> so stands the lord
> without reward.

Herakleia Pontica on the south shore of the Euxine was Megara's next colony (c. 559), and it began with a 'democracy' whose excesses soon provoked an oligarchic reaction. If the colony was founded by evicted Megarian 'democrats', 559 would mark roughly the end of the 'lawless democracy'; but it might equally have been the foundation of some desperate peasants fleeing from the previous oligarchy. The colony included some men from Tanagra, an early instance of Megarian-Boiotian friendship (above, p. 155). The native dwellers round Herakleia, the Mariandynoi, were reduced to serfdom and worked the estates for their new overlords; the law protected them, Strabo says, from being sold over the border. Late in the sixth century one more colony, Mesambria, was settled on the western shore of the Euxine.

LATER HISTORY: THE CONSTITUTION

We know very little of Megara's history between the late sixth century and the Persian War. In the intermittent border quarrelling with Corinth she won one battle, aided by Argos. This appears to have happened near the end of the century, according to the remains of a Megarian treasury at Olympia. Pausanias saw this building, and says that above the pediment (which showed a battle between gods and giants) was an inscribed shield, recording that the Megarians dedicated the treasury from the spoils of a victory over Corinth; he adds that the Argives were said to have aided Megara in the campaign. The sculpture-fragments are dated *c.* 510–500. By that time Corinth was certainly a member of the Peloponnesian League, but evidently she got no help in this war from any other member – for the inscription would have mentioned this also. The Megarians too must have been in the League by 480–479, for they fought at Artemision, Salamis, and Plataia; but not being geographically part of the Peloponnese, Megara may have been one of the latest members to join.

Equally little is known of her constitution. Late inscriptions show that, like Argos, she had an eponymous *basileus*; possibly, as in Argos, his duties were chiefly military. The deliberative body was a council, within which representatives called *aisymnetai*, succeeding each other like the *prytaneis* of the Athenian council, formed a subcommittee which in oligarchic Megara probably carried considerable authority. A citizen-body (*damos*) existed, but we hear only of the standard three Doric tribes; if a fourth, non-Doric, tribe existed, it achieved no political standing, for no multiples of four are apparent in the numbers of her officials, even those recorded in late inscriptions.

The staple product of Megara was the Megarian cloak, a hard-wearing garment like the modern shepherd's capote. She had no marble quarries or good clay-beds. Her name means 'halls'; this may refer mainly to sanctuaries of Demeter, which sometimes bore this title, but evidently building was indeed her chief skill. Quite apart from Theagenes' spring-house and the great tunnel made by the Megarian Eupalinos for the water-supply of Samos (below, pp. 217–18), Megara was still said in the fourth century to own 'the biggest houses in Greece'. Her people, said a proverb, ate as if they were going to die tomorrow, and built as if they were going to live for ever. A verse by Theognis puts their philosophy rather more realistically:[8]

> My corpse will not require a royal bed;
> I'd rather have my comforts while I'm well.
> Planks are the same as quilting to the dead,
> wood may be soft or hard beneath his head.
> He cannot tell.

NOTES

1 History of early Corinth: see in general Dunbabin, *JHS* 68 (1948), 59 ff. and Will, *Korinthiaka* (1955); on the period before the late 8th c., most recently J. Salmon, *BSA* 67 (1972), 158 ff.; on the Bacchiadai and Kypselos' background, Will, op. cit., 295 ff. and Andrewes, *The Greek Tyrants*, 43 ff. Bacchiad stemma: Paus. 2. 4, 4; Dunbabin, *JHS* 68, 62 f.; by genealogical reckoning Bacchis himself would live in the first half of the 9th c. Endogamy and Aetion's story: Hdt. 5. 92. Bacchiad government and duration: D. Sic. 7. 9; Will, op. cit., 260, 298 ff.; P. Oost, *CP* 67 (1972), 10 ff. Pheidon and Philolaos: Arist., *Pol.* 1265b, 1274a-b; cf. Will, op. cit., 317 f.

2 Syracuse: Dunbabin, *The Western Greeks*, 13 ff. Tenea: Str. 380. Archias: Andrewes, *CQ* 43 (1949), 70 ff., with a sceptical comment on the tradition of the manslaughter. Near Eastern connections: Will, op. cit., 60 ff., 169 ff., 231 ff. Date of first Corinthian triremes: J. S. Morrison and R. T. Williams, *Greek Oared Ships 900-322 B.C.* (1968), 157 f., put this tentatively in the 7th c., but before the tyranny; cf. also Forrest, *CQ* 19 (1969), 100; if Thucydides' '*c.* 300 years before 404' (1. 13,2-3) was merely based on a 40-year generation taken from Hellanikos (e.g.), then Ameinokles' real date, on a 30-year one, would be mid-7th c. If Ameinokles' date *was c.* 704, then Thucydides' 'ships' were not triremes. For the 7th-c. date see most recently L. Casson, *Ships and Seamanship in the Ancient World* (1971), 80 f. and A. Lloyd, *Journ. Egypt. Arch.* 58 (1972), 268 ff., who argues that the Pharaoh Necho's triremes (Hdt. 2. 159, 1; Necho ruled *c.* 609-593) were probably built for him by Greeks, not Phoenicians (L. Basch, *Mariner's Mirror* 55 (1969), 139 ff. argues the opposite). Megarian tears: Schol. Pind. *Nem.* 7, 155; Zenob., *Paroim.* 5. 8.

3 Sea-fight off Kerkyra: Thuc. 1. 13, 4. If the date is scaled down (above, n.2), this battle would be dated near the end of the 7th c., which would fit well with Periander's annexation of Kerkyra, above, pp. 148-9. Kypselos' parentage and accession: Hdt. 5. 92; D. Sic. 7. 9; Arist., *Pol.* 1315b. Gortyn code: *IC* iv, col. viii, lines 14-21. Bacchiads to Kerkyra: Ephoros, *FGH* 70 F 57; to Sparta, Plut., *Lysand.* 1,2; Damaratos, a Bacchiad, to Etruria, cf. A. Blakeway, *JRS* 25 (1935), 147 f.; J. Bérard, *La Colonisation grecque ... dans l' antiquité*[2] (1957), 138. About 625 a Corinthian Heraklid went from Corinth as *oikistes* for Epidamnos, Thuc. 1. 24,1. Oost (*CP* 67) suggests that Kypselos claimed to be restoring in his own person the legitimate Bacchiad monarchy. The 74 years: Arist., *Pol.* 1315b; Chalkis and Molykreion, Thuc. 1. 108, 5 and 3. 102, 2. Leukas and Anaktorion: ancient sources vary on the *oikistai*; see Graham, *Colony and Mother-city* (1964), 30, n.3. Kypselid gifts to Delphi and Olympia: cf. *LSAG*, 127, n.3. Lydian and Phrygian gifts: Hdt. 1. 14; wooden furniture in the 'Midas tomb', see R. Young, *AJA* 62 (1958), 150, 153 f., pl. 27; the palm-tree, Plut., *De Pyth. Or.* 12 (= *Mor.* 399 f). The bad tradition of Kypselos: Hdt. 5. 92,5; the good, Arist., *Pol.* 1315b and Nic. Damasc., *FGH* 90 F 57.

4 The triremes (cf. above, n. 2) and both seas: Nic. Dam., *FGH* 90 F 58. Dredging of Lechaion: J. Salmon (unpublished thesis). Diolkos: N. Verdelis in *Ergon* (1960), 117 ff.; (1962), 77 ff. Trade-route via Lynkestis and the goods exchanged: R. Beaumont, *JHS* 56 (1936), 166, 188 ff.; Wade-Gery, *CAH* III, 552 f. Ambrakia: Str. 452; Periander's control of Kerkyra, Hdt. 3. 52, 6. There is no ancient evidence for the modern view that Kerkyra was originally a dependency which had broken free before Periander's time; for its refutation cf. G. Rodenwaldt, *Korkyra* II (1939), 170; Graham, *Colony and Mother-city*, 146 ff.; Hammond, *Epeiros* (1967), 414 ff. Periander and Thrasyboulos, Hdt. 1. 20 and 5. 92z; and Alyattes, Hdt. 3. 48. Knidian rescuers: Plut., *De Her. mal.* 22 (= *Mor.* 860b). Arbitration over Sigeion: Hdt. 5. 95, 2; Kypselos an Athenian name, Hdt. 6. 34,1; Meiggs and Lewis no. 6, p. 11. Isodemos: Nic. Dam., *FGH* 90 F 61. The tales of Prokles, Melissa, and Lykophron: Hdt. 3. 50-3: 5. 92; cf. also Ephoros,

FGH 70 F.

5 Epidauros: Hiller v. Gaertringen in *IG* iv 1², pp. ix ff.; J. Papademetriou, *BCH* 73 (1949), 361 ff. Temenid tradition: see above, pp. 134–5 and Hdt. 7. 99,3. Aigina, Epidauros, and Athens: Hdt. 5. 92–8; 8. 64,1; cf. Dunbabin, *BSA* 37 (1937), 83 ff. Prokles' family: D. Laert. 1. 7,1 (94); Paus. 8. 15,3 (cf. above, p. 151). Kalaureian Amphiktiony: Str. 374; cf. T. Kelly, *AJA* 70 (1966), esp. of the possible coalition against Pheidon. Konipodes and *artunoi*: Plut., *QG* 1. Psammetichos Kypselos: Arist., *Pol.* 1315b; Nic. Dam., *FGH* 90 F 59. Sanctuary of Poseidon and the Isthmian Games: see the reports by O. Broneer of his excavations there, *Hesperia* 22–31 (1953 to 1962); 8th-c. statuette, 28 (1959), 327 f.; Palaimon/Melikertes, Paus. 2. 2,1; the cult, Will, *Korinthiaka*, 169 ff.; the buildings and finds excavated there date from the Roman Imperial period (Broneer, op. cit. (1958), 15 ff.; (1959), 312 f.). Timonassa: *Ath. Pol.* 17,4. Periander of Ambrakia: *Pol.* 1304a, 1311a. Argive inscription; Charneux, *BCH* 90 (1966), 190 (= *SEG* 23. 189).

6 Sparta's eviction of tyrants, Plut., *De Her. mal.* 21 (= *Mor.* 859b). The interpretation given above of the post-tyrannic reforms was brilliantly deduced by R. Stroud from a series of tribal boundary-markers at Corinth (*Calif. Studies in Class. Antiquity* 1 (1968), 233 ff., with earlier refs). Specialities of the tyrants' colonies to Corinth: see in general Graham, *Colony and Mother-city*, ch. 7. They had to supply ships and men when called upon (against Persia, see Meiggs and Lewis no. 27; against Kerkyra (e.g.), Thuc. 1. 46,1 and 2. 9,2–3); to receive Corinthian officials in their government (Potidaia ?and Leukas: Thuc. 1. 56,2; Plut., *Them.* 24,1); and to carry a Corinthian device on their coinages. Expedition against Polykrates: Hdt. 3. 44-56. The motive given by Herodotos for Corinthian participation (anger at Samos' defiant action over the Kerkyrean boys; above, p. 149) has been generally rejected from Plutarch's time onwards (*De Her. mal.* 22 = *Mor.* 860a–c): why should oligarchic Corinth in 525 resent an ancient Samian insult to a long-departed tyranny hated in retrospect by the Corinthians themselves? Jealousy of one great trading state against another is a possible motive, but Samos' only Western settlement was Dikaiarchia, founded *c.* 533–531, near Chalkidic Kyme. Art: H. Payne, *Necrocorinthia* (1931; *NC*) remains fundamental for the study not only of the vases but of all Archaic Corinthian art. Literary tradition: Pliny, *HN* 35, 15, 151–2 and 17, 152; Str. 343, 382; Athen. 346b–c (= Overbeck, *SQ* 259–60, 262, 375, 382–3). Corinthians in Etruria: Blakeway, *JRS* 25 (1935), 147 f. Ambrakian painting: Ampelius, *Lib. Mem.* c. 8, 2. Thermon metopes: Richter, *AGA*, 16; *LSAG*, 225 f.; M. Robertson, *Greek Painting* (1959), 48 ff. Polychrome vases: see (e.g.) Arias-Hirmer-Shefton, pls. VI–XII. Heads on trinket-boxes: see *NC*, pls. 47–9; names attached, Milne, *AJA* 46 (1942), 217 ff. Within the MC-LC period comes the painted Chest of Kypselos at Olympia; Paus. 5. 17, 5-19, 10; *NC*, 351. Exported revetments: *NC*, 248 f. Tenea kouros: Richter, *Kouroi* no. 73; sphinx, E. Protonariou-Deilaki, *AAA* 6 (1973), 181 ff. Pediment invented: Pind., *Ol.* 13, 21–2. Kerkyra pediment: *NC*, 240 ff.; Rodenwaldt, *Korkyra* II (1939), 9 ff.; Richter, *AGA*, 15.

7 The 5 districts and their early quarrels: Plut., *QG* 17 (= *Mor.* 295b–c); cf. J. Salmon, *BSA* 67 (1972), 192 ff. Sicilian settlements: Thuc. 6. 4,1; Dunbabin, *The Western Greeks*, 18 ff. On Orsippos' victory see Salmon, op. cit., 198 ff., who observes that it might have been the Attic or Boiotian boundary rather than the Corinthian; for he holds that Heraia and Peraia were lost not later than the early 8th c., since (he argues from the offerings) the Heraion at Perachora was already Corinthian at that time. Northern settlements: E. Highbarger, *History and Civilization of Ancient Megara* (1927), 109 ff.; Kr. Hanell, *Megarische Studien* (1934), 119 ff. 'Megares' for 'Kares' has been attractively restored by Burn (cf. *Lyric Age*, 217 f., n. 29) in the 'Thalassocracy-list' following Miletos; for the list see below, Appendix III. Theagenes: Thuc. 1. 126,3; Arist., *Pol.* 1305a, *Rhet.* 1357b; Paus 1. 40,1 and 41, 2; the Springhouse (rediscovered), see G. Gruben, *ADelt* 19 (1964), 37 ff.; his exile, Plut., *QG* 18 (= *Mor.* 295c). Raiding from Salamis: Hesiod F 204 M-W; Ajax' Salamis as Athens's ally, cf. the interpolated passages *Il.* 2. 557; 7. 198–9; 8. 224-6; Hdt. 5. 66, 2; 8. 64,2 and Highbarger, op. cit., 128 ff.

8 Selymbria and Perinthos: Plut., *QG* 18 (= *Mor.* 295c–d). Peisistratos and Nisaia: Hdt.

1. 59, 4; arbitration, Plut., *Sol.* 10. The Athenian decree concerning settlers on Salamis (Meiggs and Lewis no. 14) is dated by its lettering *c.* 510–480, which gives a TAQ, but not closely, for we cannot be sure (since it is damaged) whether it is creating a system, or altering an existing one. The lawless democracy: Arist., *Pol.* 1302b, 1304b; Plut., *QG* 18 and 59 (= *Mor.* 295c–d, 304e–f); cf. Burn, *JHS* 47 (1927), 171 ff. for a survey. Theognis: for the date here given, cf. Campbell, *Greek Lyric Poetry*, 345 f.; lines translated here, 183–92, 233–4, 1191–4. Herakleia: Arist., *Pol.* 1304b; Tanagraian settlers, D. Sic. 14. 31,3; Ps.-Skymn. 981–2; Paus. 5. 26,7; cf. Nymphis, *FGH* III p. 13, F 2; Highbarger, op. cit., 113 f. The Mariandynoi: Str. 541; Paus., loc. cit.; Nymphis F 9. Treasury at Olympia: Paus. 6.19,12–15. Megarian contingents, land and sea against Persia, Hdt. 8. 8, 1 and 45,1; 9. 28,6. Burn, *Lyric Age*, 265, suggests that Kleomenes of Sparta, who in 519 was leading some troops 'near Plataia' (Hdt. 6.102,8), brought Megara into the League then. Her constitution: *IG* vii, 1 (*basileus*); 15 (council and *aisymnetai*); 70–1, 73 (three tribes). Cloaks: Ar., *Acharn.* 519, *Pax* 1002. Sanctuaries of Demeter: Paus. 1. 39,5. Houses: Isoc., *De Pace* 117; the proverb, Diog. Stoic. ap. Tertull., *Apolog.* 39. Treasury: see now P. C. Bol, *AM* 89 (1974), 65 ff.

11 Sikyon; Elis, Arkadia, Achaia

Sikyon

Sikyon, or Sekyon in her own dialect, was part of the Shore (*aigialos*), a name for the south side of the Corinthian Gulf in early times. Late authority cited a king-list of remarkable antiquity but dubious authenticity. Traditionally she was Dorized when Phalkes son of Temenos the Argive seized her from her king Lakestadas; which means that in Pheidon's time at least, *c.* 680–657(?), Argive propaganda regarded her as a dependency of Argos (above, pp. 135–6). Certainly the Argive hero Adrastos, one of the Seven Champions, was said to have ruled Sikyon in the Heroic Age because he had married a daughter of Polybous, the reigning king; and there was an ancient *heroön* of Adrastos in the agora of Sikyon, which means that traditionally he had been buried there, a form of honour reserved for kings, *oikistai* of colonies, great war-leaders, and such benefactors.

Sikyon was indeed a dependency worth claiming, for here the Shore was very fertile: well-watered, well-timbered, rich in fruit, olives and vines, vegetables (a kind of cucumber was called *sekyon*). Like the Argive plain it bred fine horses, all doubtless claiming descent from fair-maned Aithe (Flash), the Sikyonian mare which, yoked with the great Podargos (Fleetfoot) himself in the chariot-race for the Funeral Games of Patroklos, raced so fast that only illegal crowding by Nestor's son Antilochos deprived the pair of second prize. Classical Greece had a notable breed called *samphorai* (= *san*-bearers; i.e., branded with the letter *san*, M), which may have come from Sikyon; for this sibilant letter, used in the Sikyonian alphabet, was Sikyon's device on the reverse of her coins, and in the famous chorus in Aristophanes' *Knights* (545 ff.), which pictures the knights' horses – each with his standard-issue mug and ration of garlic and onions – boarding the horse-transports and rowing manfully for a landing and assault on Corinth just next door to Sikyon, the *samphoras* is rated for not pulling his weight.

Pausanias says in his romanticized version of Sparta's two Messenian Wars that picked Argive and Sikyonian troops helped the Messenians in both wars. Sikyonian aid sounds doubtful for a war in the eighth century which did not concern her own borders; but in the seventh-century campaign Pheidon of Argos might well have levied a draft from Sikyon if she was then part of his 'Heritage of Temenos' (above, p. 136).

KLEISTHENES THE TYRANT: RELATIONS WITH OTHER STATES

In the next generation, however, an able tyrant transformed Sikyon's position in the power politics of the Peloponnese. The later (post-Herodotean) tradition said that the Pythia had prophesied to a Sikyonian embassy at Delphi that their city needed, and would get, a hundred years' chastening, and that this tyrannic dynasty which arose subsequently did indeed last a hundred years, because it was mild and popular. It began, said the tradition, with Orthagoras, son of a cook (*mageiros*) named Andreas, who rose to military fame in border warfare against Pellene, Sikyon's Achaian neighbour – for trouble on this border was probably perennial. At the same time or later Donoussa beyond Pellene was subjected to Sikyon and destroyed; and beyond Donoussa, Aigeira – which faced the port of Itea across the Gulf – was once threatened; but its people tied torches to the horns of their goats and drove them through the dark to counterfeit the arrival of a supporting army; hence allegedly came the city's name, and a sanctuary made in gratitude to Artemis Huntress.

Orthagoras became tyrant, but we hear no more of him. His sons succeeded him as tyrants – first Myron, a debauched type who after seven years was killed by his brother next in succession, Isodemos; and then 'the other brother, back from Libya' (*sic*), Kleisthenes, who was too crafty for the simple Isodemos, and after a bogus dyarchy ousted him on a charge of conspiracy with the Kypselidai in Corinth, and ruled Sikyon for thirty-one years. But Pausanias' version makes another and older Myron, apparently another son of Andreas, into a tyrant too, and winner of the chariot-race at Olympia in 648 (Ol. 33). Certainly Pausanias saw at Olympia in the treasury of the Sikyonians two bronze *thalamoi* (chambers), one Doric and one Ionic, the smaller bearing two inscriptions stating that the bronze weighed 500 talents and that the dedicators were 'Myron and the Sikyonian *demos*'. The modest formula – no title, and the citizens included – agrees with that used by the fifth-century Sicilian tyrants: 'Hiaron son of Deinomenes and the Syracusans', for example. Pausanias is wrong in saying that the treasury itself was built by Myron, for it is of fifth-century date; but the date of the victory may be correct, for presumably it came from the records at Olympia. It is possible that Myron, the Olympic victor, was never tyrant, but regent for his nephew Myron, and so the dedicator of the *thalamoi* could have been either one of them.

Whatever were the intricacies of the succession before Kleisthenes, we do best to follow Herodotos' statement that he was son of Aristonymos son of Myron son of Andreas; and he was certainly the tyrant who brought Sikyon into prominence and whose deeds were therefore remembered. The rule of Periander of Corinth overlapped his own. They may have been hostile, if the Kypselidai had really supported Isodemos, and if it is true that Periander's friend Thrasyboulos of Miletos once seized the harbour of Sikyon (below, p. 213). On the other hand, Kleisthenes is said to have favoured one of the Kypselidai's kinsmen by marriage (below, p. 155). His first large commitment abroad, however, was in the First Sacred War (above, pp. 73–4), in the coalition of central and northern Greek states which, allegedly to protect the holy site of Delphi, attacked the people of Kirrha, who at that time controlled the oracle and the plain below it with the port of Itea. Kleisthenes' ships crossed the Gulf and blockaded Itea, and in 586, when Kirrha had been destroyed, he received one-third of the war-spoils and also gained for Sikyon a 'Doric' vote in the re-formed Delphic Amphiktiony. He won a chariot-race in the second festival of the newly organized

Pythian Games in 582; the remains of two small early buildings at Delphi may be the first Sikyonian treasury erected there. No other Peloponnesian state appears to have joined in the Sacred War; but presumably Kleisthenes had some practical reason. It may have benefited Sikyon's Western trade to annihilate Itea, for, though not herself a colonial power, she appears to have had some connection with Aitolia at the western end of the Gulf, so perhaps her traders had followed the Corinthians to those parts. A few objects bearing the Sikyonian script have been found near Thermon in Aitolia. Tradition said that the famous sculptors Dipoinos and Skyllis (below, p. 166) went from Sikyon to Aitolia after an altercation at Sikyon about a contract for some temple sculpture, namely a group showing the famous Delphic story of Herakles, backed by Athena, trying to wrest the tripod from Apollo, backed by Artemis. Plague at Sikyon followed the departure of the offended artists and the Pythia foretold that it would continue until they returned and finished the group; which, Pliny says, 'was achieved by huge rewards and prayers'.[1]

Furthermore, the Delphic oracle when under Kirrhan control had insulted Kleisthenes. It had called him a mere skirmisher (*leuster*, a stone-thrower) when he tried to get Delphic approval to extirpate the cult of Adrastos from his city. This was another important aspect of his foreign policy – an unremitting hostility to Argos which made him try to stamp out all Argive connections from Sikyonian history. Pheidon was long dead, but the 'Heritage of Temenos' policy which he had maintained so powerfully was still evidently the policy of Argos. Kleisthenes fought the Argives in battle, and tried to root out any Sikyonian cults or local traditions which could give a foothold to Argive propaganda for a claim to Sikyon. All sacrifices to the Argive hero Adrastos, who was irretrievably buried in the agora, were transferred to his greatest foe, the Theban hero Melanippos, whose relics were now brought from Thebes and solemnly buried inside the Prytaneion (one better than burial in the agora); and the ritual miming dances once held for Adrastos were now transferred to the cult of Dionysos. (For the theory that Kleisthenes once seized Kleonai in defiance of Argos see above, p. 143, n. 3.)

To use myth for purposes of propaganda was common in ancient Greece, and indeed is not unknown to nations today. But Herodotos, our informant, adds that through hatred of Argos Kleisthenes changed the standard Doric names of the three Sikyonian tribes to Pigmen, Assmen, Swinemen (Hyatai, Oneatai, Choireatai), while a (new?) fourth tribe, his own, he named Archelaoi (Leaders of the people; perhaps, indeed, he first created it). Some scholars see behind this megalomaniac-sounding act a serious attempt to give prestige to the non-Doric element there; possibly, they argue, this element had supported the family's rise to power – if, that is, like Kypselos of Corinth, the Orthagorids, descended from a cook, were outside the ruling Doric circle. But it is hard to believe that Kleisthenes ruled for the rest of his life over a people who minded these insulting names so little that (according to Herodotos) they continued under them for sixty years after his death. Were the names perhaps quite rational originally, but travestied in some anti-Kleisthenic lampoon which was the historian's source? Did Kleisthenes, like his famous Athenian grandson, recast the Sikyonian tribal system on some other basis, perhaps a local one? Hya, Orneai, and Choireai are all place-names attested elsewhere in Greece; but such speculation is idle until we know more about the district-names in the territory of Sikyon.

Kleisthenes' third stroke of foreign policy was the dynastic alliance made between his own family and the richest Athenian one at the time, told in one of Herodotos' most famous digressions. Kleisthenes had won the chariot-race at Olympia, and took the opportunity to proclaim there his wish to betroth his daughter Agariste to the claimant deemed most suitable after a year's stay at the court (c. 575 or slightly later). So the party which gathered there presumably shows us a cross-section of the places which sent competitors, or at least rich spectators, to the Olympic Games at this time. From Italy came Smindyridas of Sybaris and Damasos of Siris: from Epidamnos, Amphimnestos: from Aitolia, Males: from the Peloponnese itself Lakedas son of Pheidon from Argos, Onomastos from Elis, and two Arkadians, Amiantos from Trapezous and Laphanes from Azania: from Athens came Megakles and Hippokleides: from Eretria, Lysanias: from Thessaly, Diaktoridas, a Skopad from Krannon: from the Molossoi in north-west Greece, Alkon. There was no Spartan or Corinthian suitor. Most were from the north-west and the Western colonies, and many names are not otherwise known; perhaps Kleisthenes had a court poet who worked the names and styles of the wooers into a local epic on the Wooing of Agariste, and the chances of time preserved it. Among the unsuccessful was Lakedas, who may have been a great-grandson of the famous Pheidon, that is of an ex-royal family which by this time had been exiled from Argos. This theory could explain why Kleisthenes, while hating the Argive government of his day, yet allowed an Argive into his court as a suitor. Both the Athenians were well-favoured candidates, especially Hippokleides the Philaid, who was 'both outstanding in manliness and related ancestrally to the Kypselidai'; but he wrecked his chances in a cheerful but unseemly dance of the kordax type. Kleisthenes chose Megakles the Alkmeonid, whose father Alkmeon had brought troops from Athens in the First Sacred War to fight against Kirrha; and one son of the marriage, named after his maternal grandfather, was the statesman who reorganized Athens after her tyranny (above, pp. 99–104).

Kleisthenes died some time after the wedding, and the hundred-year tyranny ended c. 556 when the Spartans evicted one Aischines, of whom nothing else is known. Presumably Sikyon returned to oligarchy, and before the end of the century – at least sixty years after Kleisthenes' death, according to Herodotos – the people returned to the three old Doric tribe-names, and renamed the fourth tribe Aigialeis. As 'Aigialeus' was supposed to have been a son of Adrastos, we may suspect that Argos had once more exerted her influence on Sikyon. (An undated but disastrous border-raid by the Sikyonians south into the Argolid may have preceded this. They were repulsed from the Argolic town of Orneai. The victorious Orneatai dedicated a sacrificial procession in bronze [statuettes?] at Delphi, as a way of fulfilling their rash vow to offer a daily sacrifice thereafter; its dedicatory inscription is quoted, with others, by a speaker in one of Plutarch's studies of Delphi, who wonders drily why glory should be given to the god because Greeks had killed Greeks.) At all events, about 494 Argos demanded a fine of 500 talents each from Aigina and Sikyon for having supplied ships to carry the Spartan troops to the Argive coast for the Argive defeat at Sepeia. Characteristically, Aigina refused to pay; but Sikyon, vulnerable on her southern border, admitted diplomatically that she had erred, and got her fine reduced to a hundred talents. Had she refused, her best hope for support would presumably have been Corinth, sharing as they did a common border enmity against Argos.[2]

ART

Sikyon had her own artistic tradition, though in painting it was somewhat overshadowed by Corinth. Both places are said to have 'invented' painting; but Sikyon could not hope to compete with the great Corinthian potteries of the seventh and early sixth centuries, though occasionally we find a Corinthian pot inscribed in the Sikyonian alphabet. But if the 'Daedalic' sculptural style did come to the Peloponnese from Crete (below, pp. 193–4), Sikyon may have been one of those places like Corinth which early accepted and cultivated it; for Dipoinos and Skyllis, born in Crete, came to Sikyon in the time of Kleisthenes. According to Pliny they were marble-sculptors, and it is tempting to think that their workshop may have produced the fine 'cattle-raid' metope from the treasury at Delphi, where the herd marches in step, beautifully though improbably, alongside the Dioskouroi and their cousins (Pl. 24). They also trained several Spartan woodcarvers (above, p. 128), and the Quarrel for the Delphic tripod (above, p. 164) may have been in bronze. Certainly Sikyonian bronzework was famous by the late sixth century, though Roman critics later found the style rather hard and archaic. Its great exponent was Kanachos, from whom the Milesians commissioned their cult-statue at Didyma (below, p. 214). This was Apollo Philesios, who was probably the Milesian version of a local Near Eastern deity which held a stag in its hand; for Kanachos portrayed his Apollo thus, with some ingenious mechanism under the stag's hooves which allowed a string to be passed under them without lifting it off the palm of the god.[3]

Elis, Arkadia, Achaia

ELIS AND OLYMPIA

In 471–470 B.C. an official synoecism unified the state of Elis into an enlarged capital city with a wide *perioikis* round it, bounded on the north by Achaia, on the east by Arkadia, and on the south by Triphylia, a narrow strip of land wedged between this state and Messenia which the Eleans had sought continually to bring under their control. The western coast had only one port of any size, Kyllene. The Eleans were never a seafaring people; in summer the prevailing west wind drives the sea hard on the shore in rolling breakers, and inland the flat plains, well watered by the rivers Peneios and Alpheios, encouraged a conservative aristocracy to live a pleasant country life on their estates and to breed horses. Their governmental system received an injection of some democratic principles along with the synoecism, but its earlier character is indicated sufficiently by Aristotle's description of the council (*gerousia*):

an oligarchy within an oligarchy ... the citizen-body itself was small in number, and very few of them ever became councillors, because the latter were only ninety in number, and life-members, and the election was 'dynasteutic' [i.e., confined to a limited circle of families].

The details of the early period here are obscure. The Eleans, as their dialect shows, were a north-western people who crossed from Aitolia into the Peloponnese perhaps *c.* 1000 B.C. as one among the bands of immigrants who filtered in there after the breakdown of the Mycenean civilization. Traditionally led by one Oxylos, they settled 'hollow Elis' in the rich valley of the Peneios. The site which was to become famous as Olympia lay a good way further south beside the river Alpheios, which formed the southern boundary between the whole area and Triphylia. The country around this site was called Pisatis, the 'district of Pisa', though no site of an actual city Pisa there has yet been found. Tradition said that in the Bronze Age it had been ruled by king Oinomaos, a great charioteer; his daughter Hippodameia was married to Pelops son of Tantalos, an adventurer from Asia Minor (Lydia or Phrygia), who murdered his father-in-law and then the latter's driver Myrtilos, thus provoking the terrible curse which hung over Pelops' descendants, the Atreidai, rulers of Mycenae.

The justly famous excavations of the German Institute at Olympia, which have continued with few breaks since 1875, have shown that the site, settled in the angle where the tributary Kladeos flows into the Alpheios, was inhabited as early as *c.* 2000 B.C.; and there are Mycenean remains, notably three beehive tombs, at Miraka to the east. Otherwise there are few traces as yet of the Bronze Age kingdom of Oinomaos and Pelops. If the site of Olympia owned a deity at that time, this may have been some form of the Earth Mother, whose cult would be blended into that of Hera when the worship of Zeus was established. The finds in the area of the sanctuary itself suggest that by the start of the tenth century the cult of a male god, a warrior-type, had been introduced. Since the name 'Olympia' indicates that the Zeus there was the northern warrior-god associated especially with Mount Olympos in Thessaly, it is inferred that the people who started it were not the original inhabitants, the Pisatans, but the northerners settled at Elis in the valley of the Peneios, who had now pushed south as far as the Alpheios. The cult-area proper was a precinct containing a grove of trees called the Altis, and here traces of the older worship seem to emerge again, for in its centre was a small walled enclosure called the 'grave of Pelops', with a pit into which funeral offerings were poured as to a hero or chthonic deity. Black rams were sacrificed, and those taking part, being temporarily polluted by death, could not enter the temple of Zeus. It looks as if the Eleans found here the cult of a hero which perhaps involved funeral games, as such cults often did (above, pp. 79–80), and grafted these games on to their own cult of Zeus Olympios. 776 was the date calculated by the Elean scholar Hippias (fl. *c.* 400; above, pp. 35–6) to mark the first official celebration of the Olympic Games; and, whatever were the means by which he arrived at this date, it fits roughly with that of the majority of the early bronze and clay offerings found in the sanctuary, which belong to the eighth century, though the minority go back to the ninth or even the tenth. They include statuettes of male armed figures, charioteers, chariot-wheels, some female figurines presumably from the Hera-cult, and many fragments of the tall bronze tripods which in early times were one of the standard prizes at games, including funeral ones, elsewhere.[4]

The Games were held quadrennially. The victor-lists established by Hippias, of which a good amount has been reconstructed from scattered references in ancient literature, show only Peloponnesian victors for the first hundred years, except for an Athenian Pantakles, who won the *stadion* in 696 and 692 (Ol. 21–22); indeed, most of these Peloponnesians were from the area of Elis itself and her neighbours Achaia, Triphylia, and Messenia, until a series of Spartan victors starts in the last twenty years of the century, probably signalling the end of the First Messenian War (above, p. 115), and continues intermittently thereafter. By the late seventh century the international character of the Games was starting to become evident with winners from the Western colonies of Syracuse, Sybaris, Kroton, and Kaulonia, and even two from distant Samos and Miletos.

THE PISATAN RESURGENCE

The Games seem to have been under the hereditary control of an Elean family which claimed descent from Oxylos, the alleged first leader (above, p. 167). The tradition said that, the original Games which they founded having lapsed in course of time, Iphitos, one of the family, restarted the festival in 776 with the aid of the Spartan lawgiver Lykourgos and one Kleosthenes of Pisa, and administered the new games as president (*agonothetes*). The visible basis for this tradition was an inscribed disk which still survived in Pausanias' time among the other ancient treasures housed in Hera's temple. It bore an archaic inscription giving the text of the Truce and – evidently – the names Iphitos, Lykourgos, and Kleosthenes; the first two may (as the ancients thought) or may not have been the famous bearers of these names. The Oxylidai continued to provide the presidents till 580 (Ol. 50), when the Eleans began the practice of selecting two presidents by lot from all the Eleans. But twice before this event the Pisatans had apparently won back the control, during the years *c.* 676–576. First, in 676 or 668, Pheidon of Argos came with an army to help the Pisatans to evict the Eleans, and then himself presided, an illegal act (above, p. 136); and secondly, in 644 (Ol. 34) a Pisatan named Pantaleon son of Omphalion seized control of the sanctuary. He held power as a *tyrannos*, and supported the Messenians in their second war against Sparta. But the presidency must have returned to the Eleans at his death if not before, for his son Damophon was accused in 588 (Ol. 48) of plotting to seize the sanctuary again. Damophon managed to allay this suspicion; but after his rule his brother and successor Pyrrhos raised Pisa against Elis once more. Two Triphylian cities, Makistos and Skillous, joined him, as well as a neighbouring town, Dyspontion; but all three were subdued and sacked by the Eleans. Their final reduction may have come much later, after a rising in the fifth century; but by 576 (Ol. 51) the Eleans had won back the sanctuary, and we infer that the removal of hereditary control from the Oxylidai implies some general reorganization of the administration at about this time.

Modern scholars have seen in the Elis-Pisa struggles a reflection of racial

tension, the earlier population rising against the dominance of the later incomers, which may have been among the factors promoting tyranny elsewhere
in the Peloponnese (above, pp. 46–7). Broadly speaking, the policy of Archaic
Elis seems that which prudence would naturally dictate to the possessor of a
great Panhellenic sanctuary: to enforce the holy Truce which forbade any armed
men to enter the sacred ground of Olympia (above, p. 45), filled as its treasuries
were with the riches of the powerful colonies, and to side with Sparta, the rising
power, in any troubles in the Peloponnese, as against Argos or Messenia –
except, of course, during the Pisatan interludes. Her military power was always
very modest. The nature of her authority *vis-à-vis* other states shows more truly
in the inscribed bronze plaques of the sixth century or later which are still
appearing in the excavations, random survivors from the dozens which must
have piled up year after year in the safekeeping of Zeus. Some are ordinances
concerning Elis herself, called (like the rest) by the old name *rhetra*, 'saying'
(above, p. 42). They deal with protection of officials, punishments, and other
matters concerning the precinct. One is a treaty of alliance between Elis and
her boundary neighbour Heraia in western Arkadia (below, p. 170). But other
plaques concern quite different cities. When two Peloponnesian or Western
colonial states made an agreement, each will have kept a copy in its own chief
precinct; but a third copy was deposited at Olympia, where the agreement itself
may have been ratified and sworn to by the ambassadors. Among these stray
survivors is a pact of friendship between Sybaris and the Serdaioi in the second
half of the sixth century, and another between the Anaitoi and Metapioi in the
fifth. Only Sybaris is familiar to us; the others offer a tantalizing glimpse of the
wide area over which the Olympic sanctuary exercised its influence – and, in
the earlier pact, the simplicity of the compact when military aid was not concerned. 'The Sybarites and their allies and the Serdaioi agreed upon friendship,
faithful, guileless, for ever. Guarantors, Zeus and Apollo and the other gods,
and the city Poseidonia'.[5]

ARKADIA

The mannered delights of Arcady are the creation of late and sophisticated town-
dwellers, but Arkadia has always been, as she still is, a pastoral country. Her
stock epithet in poetry was 'of many flocks' (*polymelos*), sheep and goats, and her
fighting men were traditionally acorn-eaters, wild highlanders who went into
battle wearing the skins of wolves and bears. As in other mountainous and
beautiful but poor countries in later times, many Arkadian youths left to go as
mercenaries to other states, especially to settle and serve under the tyrants of
Sicily in the fifth century. It may be only chance that no Arkadian name
shows among the mercenaries of the Pharaoh Psamtik II, mostly east Greeks,
who carved their names in 591 on the statue of Rameses II at Abou Simbel
(below, p. 196).

Some of the settlements stayed small and separate; others grew larger as the
centre of a cluster of villages, though no actual synoecism, i.e., transplanting of
villagers to the main town, is attested in the Archaic period. Tegea was a cluster
of nine villages, Mantineia of five, Heraia of nine. Protected by the remote and

mountainous terrain, the dialect of the Arkadian villages preserved many Bronze Age forms (as did the equally remote villages in Cyprus), and the cults of the Arkadians retained some remarkably primitive conventions (above, p. 23). Their limited art seems to have specialized in realistic bronze dedicatory statuettes of themselves, sturdy in shepherds' cloaks and thick ankle-boots, some grasping a lamb or kid (Pl. 21). For large images they favoured the half-iconic type, as did the conservative Spartans (above, p. 128).[6]

The late tradition alleged that Arkadia had been ruled by a royal dynasty, like Messenia and Sparta. This seems highly unlikely, given the great size and broken terrain of the country; a variety of petty rulers, lasting on like the old dialect and cults, sounds nearer to truth. In the alleged dynasty one Kypselos was reigning during the Return of the Herakleidai, and attached himself to the new rule by marrying his daughter into the Messenian royal line. This symbolizes the later friendship of Arkadia with Messenia, but not until eleven kings later do we meet a certainly historical ruler, Aristokrates of Orchomenos (below, p. 171).

The history of most of the settlements in the Archaic period is virtually unknown. The general picture is of a tough and self-sufficient set of village communities, hedged in by later incomers to the Peloponnese who spoke quite different dialects; only in Triphylia, south of Elis, was there an ethnic link, because this district was pre-Elean by origin. But traces of the local Achaian alphabet and dialect filtered into northern Arkadia along the common border. For example, Pheneos in Arkadia had a famous precinct of Demeter Thesmia under Mount Kyllene, and this is perhaps the most likely provenance for a remarkable sacral law of c. 500, which shows such traces. It decrees that a woman wearing a bright-coloured garment in the precinct of Demeter (instead of a sad colour acceptable to Demeter in her mourning for Persephone) shall be accursed unless she offers it to the goddess. Incidentally, Pheneos could also show her share of (alleged) Bronze Age dedications, like most of the other villages, according to Pausanias. She owned a bronze Poseidon Hippios which had been dedicated by Odysseus, bearing on its pedestal his instructions to the herdsman of his strayed mares which he had recovered there; she also had some statues known as 'the oreichalc ones', which bore an equally suspect dedicatory inscription by Herakles, 'upon capturing Elis'.

The genuine Archaic dedications by Arkadians mostly illustrate their warlike nature. At Olympia Pausanias saw one made by the northern village, Kleitor. It was a bronze Zeus c. 18 feet high on a bronze pedestal, signed by two Lakedaimonian brothers, Ariston and Telestas, and perhaps made in the primitive style (above, p. 128). The Kleitorians had offered it as a tithe 'from the many cities which they had defeated in battle'. A bronze butt surviving from a spear offered in some precinct c. 500 to the Tyndaridai (Castor and Pollux) 'from the Heraieis' (that is, from [the spoils of] the conquered) may also mark one of these victories by Kleitor, though the victor's name is not given. Heraia, as we have seen (above, p. 169), made a pact of military alliance with Elis somewhere about this time.

The states whose histories are best known to us are, predictably, those lying nearest to the borders of Argos and Sparta, namely (from north to south) Orchomenos, Mantineia, and Tegea. Tegea and Mantineia shared uneasily the one good flat plain in Arkadia, which meant among other things that one could damage the other's crops by blocking the water-channels, a fruitful cause for enmity. Both states had military renown; the hoplites of Tegea were famous, while Mantineia was said to have invented the duel (*monomachia*; or, in a variant, the *hoplomachia*, heavy-armed fighting), and 'the old [= pre-hoplite?] panoply of war'. Mantineia had also a tradition of law-giving at least as early as the mid-sixth century, when the Mantinean Demonax was called in to reform the constitution at Kyrene (below, p. 187).

In the eighth century Aigys on the southern border of Arkadia was absorbed into the *perioikis* of Sparta (above, p. 114). When the Spartans went on to attack northern Messenia in the First Messenian War, some of the Arkadians are said to have helped Messenia. They certainly did so in the Second, seventh-century, War, and were led traditionally by Aristokrates, ruler of Orchomenos. During the long struggle Sparta seized and held briefly Phigaleia in southern Arkadia. Towards the end Aristokrates was said to have turned traitor; this might be apocryphal, for the seed of a traitor was usually banished; yet Aristokrates' son succeeded him, we are told, and his granddaughter was married to Periander, tyrant of Corinth (above, p. 149). The power of Orchomenos was spreading across the south-west angle of Arkadia in these generations, for when Spartan forces later penetrated that area in pursuit of refugee Messenians, Orchomenos appears to have defeated them (above, p. 121). But the famous defeat was that administered by Tegea in the first half of the sixth century. The Spartans had been encouraged by a Delphic oracle to attack the Tegeate plain, as 'a dancing-floor' and a new source of *kleroi* for Spartiates. The Tegeates met and defeated them, and used the prisoners as serfs until their ransoms came. The chains in which they laboured were hung as trophies in Tegea's chief precinct, the venerable sanctuary of Athena Alea. A late source adds that a woman called Perimede and nicknamed the Sow ruled Tegea at the time.

But Tegea was always in a difficult position, as a natural corridor between the rival states of Argos and Sparta. Once during the same half-century she and some other Arkadian places under pressure – almost certainly pressure from Sparta – got help from the then king of Argos, but soon found that the Argive people expected the disputed land, once wrested back, to accrue to themselves (above, p. 138); and thus, trapped permanently between two larger powers and ex-acerbated by the one on which she had relied for help, Tegea was probably the more resigned to accepting Spartan leadership in the end. For after the Spartans had stolen a talisman from Tegeate land, the 'bones of Orestes' (above, p. 121), and by new and ingenious propaganda on their 'common Achaian ancestry' had offered her alliance instead of subjection, Tegea did ally herself to Sparta, and thus became one of the earliest members of the Peloponnesian League (*c.* 550).

In all these affrays we hear nothing of Mantineia. She lay uncomfortably be-tween Orchomenos and Tegea, and probably distrusted the one no less than the other. Like Orchomenos, she too joined the League at some time during the sixth century. Common membership of the League did not make Tegea and Mantineia any more friendly, and Sparta was probably resigned to calculating that in any vote put to the League this pair would almost certainly cancel each other out. Nevertheless, in 480 a total of 2,120 Arkadians joined king Leonidas for the march north to Thermopylai, a long journey from their own impregnable mountains: 500 from Tegea, the same number from Mantineia, 120 from Orchomenos, and a thousand from the other village settlements, for once united.[7]

ACHAIA

In the Archaic period Achaia, the 'Shore' of the Gulf beyond Sikyon, was an ethnic but not a political unity. The Achaians spoke a north-west dialect similar to those of the districts on the opposite side of the Gulf, and to that of Elis; but traditionally, says Herodotos, they had come to the Shore from elsewhere in the Peloponnese and had displaced 'Ionians', who thereupon joined the Ionic Migration across the Aegean. Herodotos lists twelve settlements, going westward from Pellene on the Sikyonian border: Pellene, Aigeira, Aigai on the river Krathis, Boura, Helike, Aigion, Rhypes, Patrai (Patras), Pharai, and Olenos – all on or near the coast – and then Dyme and Tritaia inland, above the flat Elean country. Pellene and Aigeira were harassed from early days by Sikyon (above, p. 163). All were villages rather than cities, and their mark on Greek history became definite only in the fifth century, when control of the Gulf as a whole became strategically important to other, larger states. The narrow and irregular strip of territory, backed by the mountains of Arkadia, widened only where the mountain rivers emerged and deposited their silt in small, fertile coastal plains. The best-off were Pellene, Aigai, Helike, and Patrai, which all had access to such plains, and Dyme north of Elis. The settlements were mostly perched for safety on mountain spurs overlooking the coast.

The Achaian settlement of the island of Zakynthos offshore from Elis may well have been early, for the characteristic local script of Achaia appears north of Zakynthos at Ithaca in the early seventh century (though the pottery on Ithaca shows pure Corinthian imports and influences). As far as is known, the Corinthians were ahead of the Achaians in getting to the West (Kerkyra and Sicily), but only a decade or so later the Achaians had begun to settle on the south coast of Italy (Magna Graecia). Sybaris was founded *c.* 720 by men from the central area; Helike provided the *oikistes*, one Fis, while Boura's spring Sybaris and Aigai's river Krathis contributed the names for the two Italian rivers between which the great Western colony was settled. The colonists of Kroton (*c.* 708) were led by Myskellos of Rhypes, whose neighbour Aigion provided Typhon, the *oikistes* for Kroton's own foundation, Kaulonia. The *oikistes* of Metapontion (*c.* 700-680?) remains mysterious, but archaeology and the ancient evidence make it clear that this was an Achaian foundation. All these colonies were agricultural settlements; sent out to lessen the population problem of the cramped homeland, they expanded in their fertile setting, and soon outstripped their small metropoleis in wealth and fame. Most of our knowledge of Achaian cults, dialect, and script comes from the colonies.

Like Arkadia and Sikyon, Achaia had a king-list of startling antiquity, starting with Tisamenos son of Orestes and ending with Ogygos (otherwise unknown). Doubtless the settlements did originally have their leaders, who established local ruling families; but any overall rule seems unlikely. It has been noted that in *Il.* 2. 573–5 (above, p. 135) Agamemnon's five cities west of Sikyon comprise the eastern half only of Achaia, and that the omitted western half includes Patrai, which had an independent tradition; her royal line was not from Agamemnon, but allegedly of pure Spartan ancestry, from 'Lakedaimon' himself down to Patreus son of Preugenes, who founded Patrai. Thus, though the lists may both be bogus, the two areas may really have been separate at first. The tradition goes on to say that 'democracy' came straight after Ogygos; from which we infer that the late authors wrongly ascribed a long ancestry to the democratically arranged Achaian League which appears to have begun during the fifth century.[8]

NOTES

1 The Shore: Paus. 2.5,6–6,8. On the 'Sikyonian records' (*anagraphai*), including the king-list, see Jacoby, Comm. on *FGH* 550–1; the later names may be genuine. Aithe: *Il.* 23. 286 ff. Help to Messenia: Paus. 4. 11,1 and 15,7. Donoussa and Aigeira: Paus. 7. 26,2–3,13 (the Aigeira incident allegedly very early); Steph. Byz. s.v. Aigeira. The tyrants of Sikyon: for the date see Hdt. 6. 126 (stemma); *FGH* 451 (= D. Sic. 8. 24 + *Ox. Pap.* 1365: Menaichmos of Sikyon?); Arist., *Pol.* 1315b; Nic. Damasc., *FGH* 90 F61. Pausanias at Olympia: 6.19,1–4. Dedications by Syracusan tyrants: Meiggs and Lewis nos. 28–9. Kleisthenes' stemma as given by Herodotos (above) is part of the story of the wooing of Agariste, and so may come from some court poem of the time (above, p. 165). Treasury at Delphi: the upper foundation dates from the end of the 6th c., but beneath lies the remains of a round and a rectangular building, to which last are ascribed the metope of the Cattle-raid and its damaged companions (above, p. 166). Sikyonian script from near Thermon: see *LSAG*, 140. Dipoinos and Skyllis: Pliny, *HN* 36.9.

2 Kleisthenes' acts against Argos: Hdt. 5. 67–8; as Will rightly says (*Doriens et Ioniens*, 39 ff.), the belief that they were primarily anti-*Dorian* is merely a modern inference. Szanto, *Sb. Akad. Wien* (1902), 15 ff., argued that the new tribal names were taken from localities which bore names derived from animals; for the latter detail, it seems to me simpler to infer that the animal-meanings were grafted on to like-sounding words by lampooners. Orneai: Hdt. 8. 73,3 and Str. 376 (cf. Andrewes in *HCT* iv, 107 ff.); Hya, Str. 424; Choireai, Hdt. 6. 101,1. Fourth tribe now created: D. M. Lewis, *Historia* 12 (1963), 39 n.145. The wooing: Hdt. 6.126–30. Aischines: Plut., *De Her. mal.* 21. Raid on Orneai and dedication: Paus. 10. 18,5; the speaker, Plut., *De Pyth. Or.* 15 (= *Mor.* 401d). Sikyonian fine paid to Argos: Hdt. 6. 92,1–2.

3 Invention of painting: Overbeck, *SQ* 375, 381. Sikyonian script on pots: see *LSAG*, 143 nn.1 and 4. Dipoinos and Skyllis, see above, n. 1 and Paus. 2. 15,1 and 22,5; Clem. Alex.,*Protrept.* 4. 42. Spartan pupils: Paus. 5. 17; 6. 19. Metope: Richter, *AGA*, 54, fig. 148 (Lynkeus, the last twin, is missing). Roman criticism: Cic., *Brutus*, 18. 70. Kanachos: Apollo, Pliny, *HN* 34. 75 (cf. also Paus, 2. 10,4 and 9. 10,2); cf. also A. W. Lawrence, *Greek and Roman Sculpture* (1972), 94, 334, and B. S. Ridgway, *The Severe Style* (1970), 88, quoting from G. Carettoni in *Enciclopedia dell' arte antica* (1958–66), art. Kanachos. The Near Eastern deity: E. Bielefeld, *Istanb. Mitt.* 12 (1962), 18 ff. It is not known whether Kanachos or another made the cult-statue for the old temple of Apollo at Sikyon, burnt at some time in the Hellenistic period; it contained, incidentally, a staggering collection of alleged antiquities (cf. also the temple of Athena at Lindos, below pp. 197–9), mostly dedications by heroes of the Trojan War or Argonauts, including an unopened box deposited there by Adrastos; see Jacoby, *FGH* 551 Anhang 3, with Commentary.

4 Synoecism of Elis: D. Sic. 11. 59,1. Settlement, and early traditions of Elis, Olympia, and Triphylia: Paus. 5. 1–9. The basic study is still that of Wade-Gery in *CAH* III ch. 22,5. Aristotle on the council: *Pol.* 1306a. Earliest history of precinct: see A. Mallwitz, *Olympia und seine Bauten* (1972), 77ff. Pisa: see Str. 354–6, Buck², 261 no. 63, and Andrewes, *The Greek Tyrants*, 26 f. There are varying versions of the famous story of the wooing of Hippodameia and the chariot-race in which Oinomaos was killed because Pelops had bribed Myrtilos to remove the lynchpins from the king's chariot; see in general Paus. 5, 10; 13,7; 17,7; and 8.14, 10–11. For the story as shown in the east pediment of

the temple of Zeus at Olympia see Paus. 5.10,6–7 and B. Ashmole and N. Yialouris, *Olympia: the Sculptures of the Temple of Zeus* (1967). Date of the earliest offerings: the bronze tripods (Willemsen, *Ol. Forsch.* 3 (1957)) may go back as early as the 11th c. typologically; but we do not know how old they were when dedicated; cf. also P. Amandry, *Gnomon* 32 (1960), 459 ff. and J. Carter, *BSA* 67 (1972), 30 n.27. The dating followed here for the occupation of the site at Olympia is that of Mallwitz. Cult of Pelops in the Altis: Paus. 5.13,1–3; 6. 22,1.

5 Victor-lists: see L. Moretti, *Olympionikai: i vincitori negli antichi agoni olimpici* (1957). Oxylidai and presidency: Paus. 5. 4, 8, and 9,4. Pisatan (Pheidonian) control in 676: Str. 355; in 668, Str., ibid., and Paus. 6. 22,2 (emended); lasting until 576, Jul. Afric. ap. Euseb., *Chron.* 1. 196. The inscribed disk: Paus. 5. 20; cf. Phlegon, *FGH* 257 F 1 (the three names) and Plut., *Lycurg.* 1 (Iphitos and Lykourgos only). Kleosthenes son of Kleonikos of Pisa is otherwise unknown. Lykourgos is a not uncommon name in the Peloponnese (e.g., Paus. 6. 21, 10), and there may have been three Oxylidai of different generations called Iphitos, since three fathers' names are attributed to the original Oxylos (Paus. 5. 4,6). Pantaleon as tyrant and his sons, and the rising of Makistos, Skillous, and Dyspontion: Str. 362, Paus. 6. 21,1 and 22, 2–4. Str. 357 says that Dyspontion was abandoned and her people emigrated to Epidamnos and Apollonia on the Illyrian coast, but gives no date for this event. End of Pisatan rule in 576: Jul. Afric., loc. cit.; creation of two Hellenodikai in 580, Paus. 5. 9,4. The 5th-c. rebellion of Pisa and the Triphylian area: Hdt. 4. 148; Str. 355; Paus. 5. 10,2. The funds for building the 5th-c. temple of Zeus and for Pheidias' cult-statue, Pausanias says, came from the spoils of this war. Relations between Sparta and Elis during the Second Messenian War, see above, p. 131, n. 6. Bronze plaques bearing *rhetrai*: see (e.g.) Buck², 259 ff. no. 61 and 261 f. no. 64; treaty with Heraia, 261 no. 62 (Meiggs and Lewis no. 17). Sybarite pact: Meiggs and Lewis no. 10; pact of the Anaitoi, *DGE* 414.

6 Acorn-eaters and pelt-wearers: Hdt. 1. 66,2 (Paus. 8. 1,6) and Paus. 4. 11,3. Arkadian connections with Sicily: cf. Pindar, Ol. 6 (Stymphalos) and the dedication by Praxiteles of Mantineia, later of 'Syracuse and Kamarina', at Olympia *c.* 475 (*LSAG*, 215 no. 20). Mercenaries at Abou Simbel: Meiggs and Lewis no. 7. Tegea and Heraia: Str. 337; Burn suggests (*Lyric Age*, 184) that Mantineia was already walled round *c.* 550; but (though it is certain that her walls were destroyed *c.* 385) we have no closer TAQ for her *sunoikismos* than 421 (Thuc. 5. 29,1), when she was certainly a democracy and presumably synoecized then if not earlier, 'through the agency of Argos' (Str. 337). For modern views that the *sunoikismos* belongs to the decade *c.* 470–460 see the discussion by Andrewes in *HCT* iv, 59. Dialect: Buck², 144 ff. Statuettes: W. Lamb, *Greek and Roman Bronzes* (1929), 91 ff., pls. 29–33; half-iconic statues, Paus. 8. 48,6.

7 Early kings: Paus. 8. 1–5; on the list in general see Hiller, *Klio* 21 (1927), 1 ff. Achaian elements in Arkadian: cf. for dialect A. Morpurgo-Davies, *PdelP* 98 (1964), 346 ff., esp. 351 f., and for alphabet Jeffery, *JHS* 69 (1949), 30 f. and *LSAG*, 208 f.; for the arguments ascribing some Achaian-influenced inscriptions to Pheneos rather than (e.g.) Kleitor, see *LSAG*, ibid. Sacral law of Demeter: *LSAG*, 214 no. 2. The statues at Pheneos: Paus. 8. 14, 5–7 and [Arist.], *De mirab. ausc.* 58 (59); cf. Antigonos, *Hist. Mirab.* 131 and see *IG* v. 2, p. 81. Zeus from Kleitor: Paus. 5. 23,7; the spear-butt, Richter, *AJA* 43 (1939), 194 ff. (*LSAG*, 215, no. 11). Heraia and Elis, see above, n. 5. The plain and the water-channels, see Gomme in *HCT* iv, 97 f. Tegeate prowess: cf. Hdt. 9. 26–8. Mantineian inventions: Eph. *FGH* 70 F 54 and Hermippos ap. Athen. 154d. Demonax: Hdt. 4. 161,2. Arkadian aid to Messenia in the First Messenian War: Paus. 4. 11,3; in the Second, Str. 362 (= *FGH* 244 F 334). On Aristokrates (whom another tradition alleges to have been of Trapezous) see Paus. 4. 15,7; Huxley, *Early Sparta*, 57; Wade-Gery in *Anc. Soc. and Inst.*, 289 ff. (dating the capture of Phigaleia in the early 6th c.), 296 f. Sparta's war on the refugee Messenians: see esp. Wade-Gery, ibid. Defeat by Orchomenos: Theopomp., *FGH* 115 F 69 and cf. D. M. Leahy, *Phoenix* 12 (1958), 141 ff. (Huxley, *Early Sparta*, 66 f.). Perimede: Deinias of Argos, *FGH* 306 F 4. Thermopylai: Hdt. 7. 202.

8 History of Archaic Achaia: see the valuable survey by J. K. Anderson, *BSA* 49 (1954), 72 ff., differing at many points from the necessarily brief treatment by Larsen in *Studies*

... *D. M. Robinson* II (1953), 797 ff. and *Representative Government* (1966), 26 f. Ethnic unity: cf. Hdt. 8. 73,1; 12 'cities', Hdt. 1. 145; cf. Str. 384, Paus. 7. 6,1. Zakynthos: Thuc. 2. 66,1. Ithaca: cf. Anderson, op. cit., 79 n. 65. Colonies: see Dunbabin, *The Western Greeks*, 24 ff.; Anderson, op. cit., 78. King-lists: Paus. 7. 6,1 and 18.5; Polyb. 2. 41,5; Str. 384. Division of west and east Achaia noted by Anderson, op. cit., 72. League in 5th c., ibid., 80.

IV

The Aegean Islands

12 The Islands

Ionic: Delos, Naxos, Paros and Thasos, Andros and Siphnos

Except for Thasos, the northern Aegean islands contributed little to Archaic Greek history. Many were still inhabited by non-Greeks: Pelasgians in Lemnos, Dolopes in Skyros and probably also in Skiathos, Peparethos (Skopelos), and the smaller fry lying off the tip of Thessaly's Magnesian promontory. Some Chalkidians are said, however, to have settled in Skiathos and the rest, whether before or after the colonization of the Chalkidic peninsula; and this must have been true at least for Peparethos, which produced an Olympic victor named Hagnon in 568 (Ol. 53).

DELOS

The kernel of the Ionic islands in the central Aegean was the islet Delos, which had been a cult-centre since the Bronze Age. Not only the surrounding islands but also the Ionic-speaking cities of both mainlands, Helladic and Asian, sent representatives annually to the great Delian festival of Apollo. Herodotos notes the Delian tradition that certain holy offerings which had been sent there since remote times (allegedly from the Hyperboreans in the far North) reached Greece at Dodona and were passed thence across the country to Malis and over to Euboia, where they went from city to city down to Karystos in the south of the island and then, bypassing Andros, to Tenos and on to Delos. The suggestion here of a link-up between southern Euboia and the tail of islands extending thence is strengthened by Strabo's remark that in the old days Eretria had controlled Andros, Tenos, Keos, and other islands; indeed, they would be essential stepping-stones for her in a trade-route via Naxos and Miletos to the Near East (above, p. 63; and cf. the fine Cycladic pottery, Pls. 25, 27, 29).[1]

Delos itself supported a small population which gained its living from the cults of Apollo, Artemis, Leto, and the many other lesser deities or heroes, of the Bronze Age or later, which occupied most of her territory. As others of the islands waxed in power, they tended at different times to protect or control Delian affairs. About 700 her modest population was increasing in size, and so were the buildings and precincts, an expansion which continued through the seventh century.

In that century (if not before) Naxos seems to have been the chief influence, judging by the impressive relics of Naxian marble offerings compared with those of other states. An over-lifesize 'Daedalic' kore survives (Pl. 26), offered to Artemis by a Naxian lady named Nikandra, whose family is so stressed in the dedication – she was 'daughter of Deinodikes of Naxos, sister of Deinomenes, and wife of Phraxos n[ow]' – that one wonders if she was the priestess of Artemis until her marriage. Fragments survive from an equally large kouros which Euthykartides, a Naxian sculptor, made and dedicated to Apollo some decades later, and the city of Naxos dedicated near the temple a truly colossal Apollo on a vast, separate base, elliptically inscribed: 'of the same marble am I, statue and base'. The city also gave a splendid sphinx on a high column to Delphi in the early sixth century.

At some time in the years *c.* 540–530, in response to an oracle, Peisistratos, tyrant of Athens, having secured Naxos as an ally by supporting a local tyrant there named Lygdamis (below; cf. p. 95), purified all the land of Delos within eyeshot of the temple, which was rebuilt in Attic (Peiraic) limestone. Attic influence seems then to have been superseded by Samian; Polykrates the tyrant seized the adjoining island, Rheneia, during his period of thalassocracy, and attached it to Delos as an offering to Apollo by a chain across the narrow strait between. After his death we hear next of the approach of Datis and the Persian fleet in 490, when the Delians sought refuge on Tenos; but their fears were groundless, for Darius had shown respect to Apollo at other times, and Datis now burnt 300 talents' worth of frankincense on the altar. The island replied ambiguously with an earthquake, to presage dire events to some party, which Herodotos takes to be the Greeks in the next two generations; though to the Greeks and Persians after Marathon the party must obviously have been the Persians. But Datis continued to show respect to Apollo in his retreat back across the Aegean; he asked the Delians to forward to the Theban coastal precinct of Apollo Delios a gilded statue of the god which, prompted by a dream, he himself had rescued from loot taken before the battle of Marathon by one of his Phoenician crews.[2]

NAXOS

Naxos, the largest and most fertile of the Cyclades, sent emigrants *c.* 735 (or earlier) to join men from Chalkis in founding the first Greek colony in Sicily. Chalkis had made her mark in Italy decades earlier (above, pp. 63–4). Now her settlers with their *oikistes*, Thoukles, were the pioneers in Sicily; but the colony was called Naxos, and Thoukles with the Chalkidians left six years later to found Leontinoi and Katane in the good corn-growing area further inland. The colony continued modestly for many centuries. Land shortage at home had presumably sent it out in the first place; but in the seventh century, as we have seen, Naxos increased in power and may have controlled Delos for a time. Her long and bitter troubles with her neighbour Paros (below, pp. 182–3) were apparently inveterate. Both had to get their fish mainly from the same waters; both had fine marble, and produced sculptors competing for work, with Naxos leading in the seventh century, but Paros overtaking her in the sixth. A fragment from the lost Aristotelian *Politeia* of Naxos shows her as a typical island oligarchy, some of her richest families living in the city, but many others up and down the countryside. Some time before the mid-sixth century one of the hospitable country aristocrats named Telestagoras was attacked by young rioters. This spark ignited some more serious smouldering trouble and stasis arose, ending when Lygdamis, leader of Telestagoras' party, defeated the other side and became temporarily tyrant. By the years *c.* 550–546 he was out, an exile living in Eretria, where he offered his money, men, and services to the exiled Peisistratos of Athens. Consequently Peisistratos, after his restoration *c.* 546, ejected the oligarchy from Naxos and reinstated Lygdamis.

Like other tyrants, Lygdamis in power showed great resource in raising revenues by the time-honoured method of confiscating his exiled opponents' property – in this case, land and half-finished statues ordered for dedications – and then reselling it to them. He also helped Polykrates to seize power in Samos *c.* 532 (below, p. 216). But in 517 the Spartans unseated him. This was doubtless a typical pro-oligarchic demonstration by the Lakedaimonian League, for he had been holding as hostages some Athenian oligarchic (anti-Peisistratid) families, who would now be one step nearer their return; also, as the Peisistratidai were on good terms with Persia, Sparta *may* have wished to remove a supporter of Persian 'friends' from this central island, which would be strategically important if the Persian fleet should ever try to advance into the Aegean.

Naxos flourished under her restored oligarchy. Paros, Andros, and others of the Cyclades, says Herodotos, were attached to her; but not for very long. Near the end of the century the people rose once more and exiled a number of the oligarchs; these fled to friendly Miletos, requesting a fleet to reinstate them, and Aristagoras of Miletos started the events which developed into the Ionic Revolt (below, pp. 219–21). Ten years later the Persian fleet, dispatched across the Aegean under Datis to attack Eretria and Athens, was ordered to take vengeance on Naxos *en route*. The Persians enslaved all Naxians whom they caught, and burnt the town and temples.[3]

PAROS AND THASOS

Paros and Thasos have earned their place in history by their art and their poet Archilochos. The natives of Thasos were Thracians from the adjacent mainland, where the Greek Thasians finally established a *peraia*, with a colony named Neapolis (near the modern Kavalla) and a firm grasp on the rich agricultural and mining area inland. The island was well wooded and fairly fertile, with good fishing and marble-quarries; but its chief lure must have been the gold-mines which, according to Herodotos, existed there and had been originally worked by Phoenicians. There was certainly abundant gold and silver on the mainland, the revenues from which made Thasos later one of the richest members of the Athenian empire.

Thasos was colonized at the start of the seventh century by Greeks from Paros, about a generation at least after Paros' neighbour Naxos had disposed of her surplus population in Sicily. The *oikistes* was Telesikles, and his son was Archilochos, who seems to have retained his Parian citizenship while spending much of his life in the colony. Possibly one could hold double citizenship, for a Thasian dedication made to Herakles *c.* 500 says that the donor, a man named Akeratos son of Phrasierides, was once sole archon over both places and also undertook many missions abroad 'for the city' (Thasos). The remains of a stone lighthouse survive at the north end of the bay of Potamia, with an inscription saying that it is his memorial (*mnema*) and adding:

> Here stand I at the edge of the haven
> to save the ships and sailors. Fare you well.

If Akeratos was really archon for Paros and Thasos together, the political connection at that time must have been unusually close. Certainly the Thasian constitution seems to have been derived mainly from the Parian. Both places had archons as their heads of state and also, more unusual, a high-ranking college of annual officers called *theoroi* (observers, envoys), who were responsible for law and order, including confiscations of property; their resemblance in name and duties to the Spartan ephorate has been noted.

Tradition, derived from one of his lost poems, said that Archilochos was driving his father's cow to market when the Muses appeared to him and claimed him, whisking away the cow in exchange for a lyre. As son of an *oikistes* he must have been of good family, but tradition also said that he was a bastard, born of a Thracian slave called Enipo. Much of his life was spent in fighting in the North against Thracians and in Paros against Naxos; he was killed in the end by a Naxian. Most of his poems were not commissioned works: neither choral lyrics like Alkman's to be sung by the children of high families, nor exhortatory marching-songs like the verses by Kallinos or Tyrtaios, whose lifetimes overlapped with his own. Like Tyrtaios he was a soldier-poet, 'a servant of Enyalios and Apollo' (F 1), but not in some old and well-founded mainland city under threat from its border foe. In his verses one can see rather the outlook and temperament of a colonial character, used to fierce forays from Thracians and stormy sea-crossings between Thasos and Paros. His expressed thoughts are realistic and uncompromising, though sometimes put in the mouth of a *persona*, for example 'Charon the builder' (*tekton*; 'carpenter' is perhaps too humble, since the word could be used for an architect in the Archaic period): '*I* don't care about golden Gyges' (F 19). We cannot be sure that all the events which he describes really happened, since the poetic convention of attaching to the 'I' of a poem persons and events which are exaggerated or even unreal may be very early. He can hardly have been the first Greek personal poet, for gnomic and personal poems are part of a widespread primitive genre which probably underlay Archilochos' poems as folk-song lay behind some of the polished poetry from Lesbos (below, p. 238); but he was the first poet to express an individual's reactions to some particular situation with such directness, sensitive or harsh, and such brilliant quotability that his poetry survived, despite its often ephemeral subject-matter, for Hellenistic editors to collect and publish several centuries later. As a fighting citizen he ranked somewhere between Agamemnon and Thersites. He would have appalled a Homeric prince by his frankly phrased preference for a small bow-legged brave leader above a tall striding foppish one (F 114), and even more by his unabashed belief that it is better to return from battle without one's shield than upon it (F 5). On the other hand, he was no Thersites temperamentally or socially, but a citizen-hoplite, a gentleman ranker, a close friend of the commander Glaukos son of Leptines, who led many of the forays against the Thracians. Many of his poems were addressed to Glaukos, whose death was commemorated at Thasos by a cenotaph in the agora as honourably as if he and not Telesikles had been the *oikistes*.

The wide range of this free-running, highly articulate mind shows well even in the few poems and many mutilated fragments which survive: campaigning jokes (Frr. 2, 5–6), consolation to the bereaved (F 13), the physical ache of thwarted love (Frr. 193, 196), the powers of abuse which were alleged by later tradition to have driven Lykambes and his daughters to hang themselves (Frr. 173, 223), or amiable lines like the fragmentary description of a happy girl at some festival:

> . . . she held a myrtle-spray
> and a rose,
> she was gay
> and her hair hung close,
> shadowing her arms and back . . . (Frr. 30–1)

Perhaps the most memorable parts of Thasos today are her city gates and the long lines of her walls as they leave the lower harbour area and climb the precipitous hill behind. The city was under the protection of Herakles and Dionysos; this is attested by the distich inscribed on a long stone block which once adorned a niche in the wall, probably for an altar:

> The sons of Zeus from Semele and long-robed Alkmene
> stand guard here to protect this city.

The main gate was originally flanked by two large reliefs of *c.* 525–500. One survives, showing Herakles as he appears on Thasian coins, in his Archaic type as an archer, kneeling to take aim. The other relief, now lost, depicted Dionysos waving a vine-branch and leading three girls, perhaps the Graces. (Many of the other city gates had reliefs, the best-preserved (fifth century) being a fine satyr holding a kantharos in token of the wine for which the island was noted.)[4]

ANDROS AND SIPHNOS

Paros, Thasos' mother-city, one of the loveliest of the Cyclades, had no source of wealth beyond her famous marble. The Parians who settled in Thasos may well have left home through poverty. Parion on the Propontis, traditionally settled in 710 or 708, was said by Strabo to be a joint colony from Paros, Miletos, and Erythrai; but the latter pair were normally unfriendly, so, *if* Strabo is right (the Parians' presence has also been strongly doubted), the Erythraians were probably political exiles. Paros and Miletos seem to have been friendly; the tale of Koiranos (below, p. 212) may not be strong evidence, but in the sixth century Miletos chose Parians to settle her own internal crisis (below, p. 219). Naxos was the traditional 'border' enemy; with Andros further north the Parians had the close tie of *epigamia* (above, p. 45) until the mid-seventh century, when Paros, Samos, and Erythrai provided a board of arbitrators in a dispute. Andros, another poor island, had sent settlers to join men of Chalkis in founding Sane in the Chalkidike (on the Athos peninsula) *c.* 654. The two parties in Sane evidently soon split, for when Akanthos nearby became vacant, each separately rushed out a scout to claim it. Being the slower runner, the Andrian hurled his spear into

Akanthos' gate in token of its capture. In the subsequent arbitration the Andrians won Akanthos because Samos and Erythrai voted for them; but Paros had supported Chalkis, and Andros broke off all relations with her. The Andrians expanded further along the Chalkidic coast with their colonies Stagiros and Argilos, but stopped before the river Strymon; beyond it lay Mount Pangaion, in the mining area where Thasos made her *peraia*. Thus Andros, nearest of the Cyclades to Euboia and in early days, indeed, controlled by Eretria (above, p. 63), followed the Euboians up to the Chalkidike and firmly staked her claim on its eastern prong. The fact that the Hyperborean route bypassed her (above, p. 179) implies that she was unpopular with one of her neighbours, whether Karystos or Tenos; but for the Archaic history of most of these Cyclades we must depend mainly on archaeology. The present excavations at Zagora on the west coast of Andros are revealing a small hilltop settlement of close-set cottages neatly built of schist slabs. Its floruit, judged by the pottery, was *c.* 750-700, and much of this pottery shows early links with Euboia. It was abandoned probably early in the seventh century, but sixth-century pottery was found alongside the little temple nearby; so – unless the temple itself was later – the cult was not abandoned after the move.

The remains of a Geometric settlement of similar type were excavated before 1939 in Siphnos on the west slope of the ancient acropolis (modern Kastro), and, with Zagora, probably typify the Archaic villages on these windy islands. Best preserved were two or three little dwellings braced back against the steep rock. One was about 9 m. square, with an alcove-cupboard about 50 cm. square in the neat schist slabs of its north wall. A stone ledge built up against the back wall was where the family presumably slept and sat. The house was near a circuit-wall which protected the village, and what appeared to be the community's rubbish-dump on both sides of this wall yielded some of the finest Geometric sherds of the excavation. Somewhere on or near the top of the acropolis (and thus beneath the modern town) there must lie a temple, for two of its votive deposits were found, containing Cycladic and other (e.g., Protocorinthian) pottery of the seventh and sixth centuries, and other trinkets such as bronze, ivory, and bone fibulae, paste beads, ivory and bone sealstones, some faience pieces, all suggesting a female deity. Her clay gifts included miniature helmet-crests and the lower parts of two female 'Daedalic' figures, wheelmade like vases, with painted figure-strips on their cylindrical skirts; one stands some 40 cm. high from hem to waist. The excavator suggested Athena or Artemis, pointing out that Siphnos worshipped an 'Artemis Ekbateria'.

We do not know when the Siphnians first discovered and worked their gold- and silver-mines. In the sixth century the citizens were the richest in the Cyclades, for they ran a co-operative system: after a tithe had been set aside for Apollo from the annual profit, they divided the rest among themselves. During the third quarter of the century they adorned their Prytaneion and agora with carved work in Parian marble, and then used the tithes to build a superb marble treasury at Delphi. The porch was upheld by two richly-dressed Parian caryatid-korai, softer-featured than their Attic and Ionic sisters, and a Parian marble relief-frieze in the Ionic manner, only 64 cm. high, ran round the top of the cella-wall and porch outside. It is shown now at eye-level in Delphi Museum. Two masters apparently shared the work. The north side, justly the most famous, depicts the Gigantomachy in an extraordinary blend of formality and naturalism. Apollo and Artemis advance in step, shooting with stylized precision, but Kybele's chariot-lions rear up to munch their giant with gusto, while other giants lie dying with lax hands and sagging muscles among the feet of the fighters. The artist has cut his signature around the shield of a giant and then 'foxed' the letters to resemble decorative signs: '?D[---]?O[---] made these, and also those behind' (= the east side). Nearly all his name is lost in a break; but expert analysis has interpreted the sculptural style as a mixture of Ionic with Attic and, though other names have been suggested, it has long seemed likely to me that we should read A [risti] O [n Parios] here, as a Parian born who had been working in Athens some ten years before (Pl. 28).

While the building was in progress the Siphnians asked the Pythia how long their run of luck would last. She replied warning them of 'a wooden ambush and red herald'. It was not hard to foresee that some roving fleet would threaten so rich an island sooner or later, and c. 525 some Samian oligarchs exiled by Polykrates landed and demanded 10 talents. The Siphnians resisted vainly, and had to pay a hundred. In the end, we are told, they dropped the payment of Apollo's tithe, and then the mines were flooded out by the sea.[5]

Doric: Thera, Crete, Rhodes, Knidos

THERA

After Thera's great Bronze Age and a succeeding period which is still archaeologically blank, the first Greek pottery found in graves on the island is Middle Geometric, which implies that these settlers arrived in the early eighth century (though its Late Geometric lasted into the next century). Herodotos attests that they were from Lakedaimon, and this fits the fact that they certainly spoke Doric, like the Greeks of Melos and Crete who also claimed some Spartan ancestry, and that like the Spartans they had the ephorate, a magistracy unknown except in cities descended from Sparta. Herodotos further insists that Thera's settlers had left Sparta in the reign of the first royal twins, Eurysthenes and Prokles, and that they consisted of (a) a non-Doric oikistes, Theras, of high 'Kadmeian' lineage (i.e., Theban-Phoenician in Herodotos' view), brother-in-law of the twins' dead father, Aristodamos; and (b) some discontented 'Minyai' (see below), long domiciled in Sparta and now suspected of subversive desires to share in the kingship. Possibly the real oikistes of the eighth century, whatever his name, has been confused with some faintly recalled tradition in Sparta which belonged to a much earlier period. We approach greater clarity in the later seventh century c. 630, with the foundation of Thera's colony, Kyrene. The ruler then was Grinnos son of Aisanios, traditionally descended from Theras; and the oikistes was Aristoteles son of one Polymnestos, a leading citizen of the Euphemidai clan, who claimed descent from the 'Minyai'; for Euphemos had been one of the Argonauts when in one prodigious night among the welcoming women of Lemnos they had begotten the whole next generation there, who were called the

Minyai. Euphemos himself, when the *Argo* docked at Lake Tritonis in Libya, had been given – but had lost – a clod of Libyan earth as seisin by the Triton; so his descendants had an ancestral interest, at least, in owning land in Libya. The *lost* seisin should refer to Dorieus' failure (above, pp. 123–4); but some ancestral details of royal 'Kadmeians' (Theras) and Euphemid rights to Libyan territory may have been invented at this time, *c.* 630, when Thera faced a serious economic crisis. In Herodotos' detailed account both the Theraian and Kyrenaian versions insist piously that the Delphic oracle inspired the whole project—neither Grinnos nor Aristoteles, consulting it, had *enquired* about a colony. Both versions agree, however, that Thera did have a long and serious drought ('for seven years, because she ignored Apollo's instructions'), a thing hinted at by the Hellenistic rainwater cisterns still visible on the ancient site, though the grapes and tomatoes flourish in the volcanic soil; and a political crisis was added to (or produced by?) their distress: Aristoteles, the non-Dorian, led a faction, was worsted, and had to emigrate (above, pp. 52–3). The original suggestion of Libya may have come from the Delphic priesthood, with its Cretan contacts (below, pp. 191–2), and the story of Euphemos and *some* Libyan seisin could have been first evolved then.

Herodotos calls Grinnos 'basileus', but Aristotle says that government in Thera was confined to the descendants of the original founding families, that is, to a close, hereditary aristocracy, in which the offices rested in the hands of those claiming descent from Theras. Perhaps Grinnos' *basileia* was a life magistracy rather than a true monarchy. A big flattish tombstone of black volcanic rock (*c.* 600?) from one of the city's cemeteries has been thought to commemorate a king. It is apparently from a common burial-place, for it bears three names, Rhexanor/Archagetas/Prokles, in the centre, and seven more squeezed in on the stone as space allowed. Is Archagetas here a proper name, or can it be a title, 'First Leader', i.e. king? The best interpretation, I think, sees this as title for the founder of some cult whose members alone could be buried there (Pl. 30).

After the colony had departed, we hear little more of Thera in Archaic history. In the pact which was sworn between the city and Aristoteles' company before its departure (above, pp. 52–3), she had prudently insisted that any Theraian who came to Kyrene later should have the right of Kyrenaian citizenship; so she was cushioned against any further economic disaster through over-population. The city lies on a mountain spur (bleak, but safe from pirates) overlooking the south-eastern, softer side of the island, away from the sheer west coast, the towering rim of the submerged crater. In its south-eastern quarter was the old temple and precinct of Apollo Karneios, and on the rocks of the plateau round about, near the later gymnasium, are carefully cut graffiti, sometimes quite long, written in very archaic letters. The scripts of Thera, Crete, and Melos are basically alike, and these inscriptions may be less old than they look, for, isolated as Thera was, her script was probably just as slow to change its style as her pottery was (above, p. 185); they date perhaps from the middle of the seventh century into the sixth. Some of them are affably obscene, some praise a boy's dancing; one name could suggest Libyan influences from Kyrene: Barbax, the Libyan word for a falcon according to Hesychios, as also (from a gravestone perhaps fifth-century) Bakalos, derived from the Libyan Bakal.

Kyrene became a famous city rich in horses, sheep, grain, and the medicinal plant silphion. Her history does not concern us here, except for a remarkable change in her constitution *c.* 570. At that time, under Battos II the Fortunate (Eudaimon), the colony was evidently in straits for more able-bodied men, for at her request Delphic propaganda recruited a new influx from 'all Greece'. The new *kleroi* were carved out of the surrounding Libyan land, which apparently caused a rebellion by the native *perioikoi*. They were defeated, but when Arkesilas II succeeded Battos, fraternal quarrelling caused the king's brothers to hive off and found Barke west of Kyrene, and also to raise the Libyans again. This time they heavily defeated the Greeks of Kyrene and broke from their control. Arkesilas was murdered by his brother Learchos, who was killed in his turn by the queen, Eryxo, to secure the throne for her lame son Battos III. But the unrest increased, and then the state called in an arbitrator from Greece, Demonax of Mantineia in Arkadia. His actions indicate where the trouble lay. He removed the king's secular power, leaving him only his royal estates (?; $\tau\epsilon\mu\acute{\epsilon}\nu\eta$) and priesthoods; and he gave the government, says Herodotos, 'fairly and squarely to the citizens' ($\acute{\epsilon}s$ $\mu\acute{\epsilon}\sigma\sigma\nu$ $\tauο\hat{\upsilon}$ $\delta\acute{\eta}\mu\sigma\upsilon$), just as Maiandrios, regent in Samos over forty years later, offered it to the Samians (below, p. 218). It was not, surely, that either of these statesmen created a democracy thereby, or indeed intended to, for the citizens in both places were oligarchs; the aim of both men was *isonomia*, i.e., justice for all citizens and an end to arbitrary rule – the king's at Kyrene, the tyranny at Samos. But Demonax also recast the existing tribal structure of Kyrene, an action which suggests that by now the oldest families, the 'Founders' Kin', had too much influence within the tribes. In both Doric and Ionic states the tribes were kinship-based, which meant the perpetuation of social hierarchies within them; perhaps here the 'Founder's Kin' were excluding the recent settlers from the magistracies. At all events, Herodotos says, 'he made them three-tribed by the following distribution: he made one part [*moira*] of *Theraioi* and *perioikoi*, a second of Peloponnesians and Cretans, and a third of All Islanders'. If each 'part' was now a tribe, the three tribes seem to be in a descending social scale: (1) the original families from Thera city and her *perioikis*, *or* these original families plus the local *perioikis*, Libyan or Greek; (2) pure Dorians from elsewhere, such as the family of the Spartan Olympic victor Chionis and those from Sparta's Cretan 'daughter-cities'; and (3) the other islanders, some presumably Ionic, others eastern Doric, like the Rhodian Pankis and his sons (below, p. 198). Modern scholarship disputes over the components of these ethnic 'parts'; but whatever they were exactly, and in whatever way Herodotos thought that the new tribes were formed, I find it easiest to believe that this redistribution of the citizen-body was on the lines used later by Kleisthenes at Athens (above, pp. 100–2) and, perhaps, at Corinth earlier (above, p. 153), in which the new tribe was formed of three different parts – socially different in this case, geographically (i.e., indirectly socially) in the other two. The political and social hierarchy would be weakened if 'Founder's Kin' were now distributed among three tribes, and no one tribe was now regarded as inferior to the others.[6]

CRETE

Crete is multilingual; in it are Achaians,
proud Pure-Cretans, and Kydonians,
three-tribed Dorians and godlike Pelasgians.
(*Od.* 19. 175-7)

The explanation current in the fifth century said that when Minos and his host
had been slain at Kamikos in Sicily, the avenging Minoan forces settled in south
Italy after many adventures and became the Messapioi. A lot of incomers, mostly
Greeks, then repopulated Crete; among these were the Achaians, whose children
under Idomeneus fought at Troy. After their return plague and famine deci-
mated Crete, and so in due time a third settlement joined the survivors. These
last settlers were, we suppose, those Doric-speakers who came in from Lakedaimon and elsewhere. In the Archaic period they formed the main population of
Crete and the belt of islands to her north, from Melos via Thera (with Sikinos
and Anaphe) to Rhodes, Kos, and the Asian peninsula of Knidos. Reaching
about 150 miles across the south Aegean, Crete itself is linked on the west to
Doric Kythera and Lakedaimon – Cretan Lyttos, for example, was traditionally
a Spartan colony – on the south to the Libyan coast and the Nile Delta, and on
the east to Rhodes and Miletos. Thus before and after the Dorians other
foreigners may well have come by sea and settled there, temporarily or
permanently.

By modern agricultural methods the island can have three harvests a year,
from sea-level, inland, and the high plateaux; but in the Archaic period food-
supplies must have been unequally divided, if one contrasts those settlements
which controlled the fertile Mesara plain with the greater number which perched
in the mountains. Classical Crete was known for her long-distance runners (the
Olympic victor Ergoteles of Himera was a Cretan by origin) and for her archers,
much in demand as mercenaries: both being the skills naturally developed by
people who range the heights for their living. She was also noted for the perpetual bickering between her cities, which prevented the island from being a
powerful factor in Archaic history; but the laws, customs, cults, and strange
Minoan traditions of the Cretans were rich soil for later writers to turn over.
Undoubtedly Doric Crete inherited a legacy of Minoan culture, carried into the
Iron Age by the Eteocretans. Relics of law codes, in lettering dated from the
seventh to the fourth centuries, have been found in nine cities. These were
originally written up on the stone walls of some public building, usually a temple.
Apart from the famous fifth-century Code of Gortyn, only stray blocks have
survived; but no amount comparable with this has yet been found elsewhere in
Greece. It looks as if every Cretan city had got some sort of civil code published
before the end of the sixth century at latest; and since the earliest parts of the

Dreros code (below, pp. 189–90) look to be of the seventh, probably the larger cities like Gortyn or Knossos published them equally early, though their earliest surviving inscribed blocks belong to the sixth century. Crete indeed may claim primacy for written law codes rather than Lokroi Epizephyrioi in Italy; for though Ephoros said that Zaleukos in that colony compiled the first written code c. 663, according to Aristotle Xenokritos of Lokroi, teacher of Zaleukos, had learnt his law in Crete, where the poet-lawgiver Thaletas was his contemporary. It has also been pointed out that the strong probability of actual settlements of Semitic craftsmen in Crete between the late ninth and seventh centuries (below, p. 193) could well mean that the Near East helped to familiarize the Archaic Cretans with the concept of a written code.[7]

Monarchy may have survived in Crete after the Minoan period. Aristotle says briefly that 'formerly there was kingship, then the Cretans abolished it', and Herodotos calls Etearchos, a seventh-century leader of Axos, 'basileus'; but Aristotle's source could be referring to Minoan Crete, and Herodotos uses 'basileus' for tyrants as well. Certainly by the late seventh century the constitution of a Cretan city was strictly oligarchic; a warrior society had fashioned it, and the fierce independence of the scattered cities encouraged its continuance.

A board of x men – the maximum known is ten, but the number may have been smaller in the Archaic period – was elected annually to rule the city. Apparently they were all from the same clan (for which the Cretan word was 'startos', metathesized from stratos), and certain clans only were eligible for this honour. The board was called kosmoi (marshals) and led the city's men in war, like the Atreidai κοσμήτορε λαῶν. Between them they also supervised the city's religious, constitutional, and judicial affairs; there were kosmoi subtitled xenios (for dealing with non-citizens), gnomon (recorder), hiarorgos (in charge of sacred matters), and one of the board was the kosmos, something like the eponymos among the nine archons at Athens. He has been plausibly identified with the startagetas, 'clan-leader', a title also found. The kosmoi had for advisers a Council of Elders, elected for life from the ex-kosmoi. We do not know the size of these councils, but their decisions were arbitrary, their authority above that of the laws which bound the other citizens.

The earliest of the surviving laws records the organs of government in Dreros in eastern Crete in the late seventh century (according to its letter-forms). The law was passed by the polis, i.e., by the citizen-body, but this was less democratic than it sounds, for even in Aristotle's day the Cretan assembly had no real power of decision, but merely ratified the decisions laid before it by the magistrates. The select clans seem to have regarded the office of kosmos as a matter for private competition rather than a public service. A kosmos could be forcibly ejected from office by his colleagues or others; he could also resign in mid-office, and so indeed could the whole board if they anticipated trouble, thus creating a state of akosmia (anarchy in its technical sense) for the city. The Dreros law seeks to check a worse danger, illegal extension of office which would produce de facto a tyrant.

When one has been kosmos, the same shall not be kosmos again for ten years. If he does hold the office again, whatsoever penalties he exacted in judgement, he shall himself be liable for double the amount, and he shall be deprived of civic rights as long as he lives, and whatsoever he did as *kosmos* is to be invalid [i.e., this year of office shall be declared invalid, *anarchia*, as happened at least once at Athens in the restless years after Solon's new law on the archonship]. The oath-takers are to be the *kosmos* [probably meaning the whole board] and the *damioi* and the Twenty of the polis.

This is perhaps to be taken as a descending scale of importance: first the *kosmoi*, then a body possibly equivalent to the high officials called *damiorgoi* in some areas (or else to the council?), and then twenty citizens representing the polis, i.e., assembly.

We have then in Crete a near-Homeric picture of a citizens' assembly composed of her fighting men (for, says Aristotle, Crete like Egypt still retained in the fourth century a caste-system of (1) the warriors and (2) the farmers) which met in the agora to stamp their approval upon the decisions of their betters; and within this society an élite of certain clans monopolizing the magistracies. Constitutional parallels for much of this may be seen behind the Eupatrid rule in pre-Solonic Athens, the Bacchiadai at Corinth, and doubtless others. The Cretan social system may also suggest some parallels, though here much caution is needed. A full citizen was called a *dromeus* (runner), i.e., one who had been through the training of the *agelai*. He belonged to a tribe (*phyle*), within this to a clan (*startos*), within this to a company (*hetaireia*); in the men's hall (*andreion*) of the company the citizens had their common messes (*syssitia*), whose similarity to the Spartan system has often been stressed. The food for this came from levies of produce raised from the *perioikoi* (below). The educational system of the youth was in droves (*agelai*), as at Sparta. Endogamy was the rule; unless her tribe rejected her (above, p. 148), a woman must marry within it, and according to fixed degrees if she was an heiress. Outside the citizen-class were the *apetairoi*, free but ineligible for a *hetaireia* and so without citizen's rights. Some might never have had full citizenship, and others might have lost it through debt, for example, or 'cowardice in battle'. Outside the *apetairoi* were the *perioikoi*, who are described as a subject-class, non-Dorians who may have been mostly Eteocretans, for they are said to have used the code of law which Minos had established. They were probably taxed and liable to military service, like the Spartan *perioikoi* and the Athenian metics, but they were not serfs. There was undoubtedly a class of serfs (*mnoitai* or ?*oikeis*), and also of privately owned ones (*klarotai*, ?*aphamiotai*). The names are offered in rich variety by ancient writers and the Gortyn Code; but at least it appears that these Cretan serfs retained some basic rights as of free men, except that they could not practise gymnastics (i.e., train for war) or own weapons; in particular, those working on a citizen's estate (*kleros*) could become legally possessed of it on his death, if he had no kindred to inherit it.

The Helots of Sparta and the Penestai of Thessaly were compared with these Cretan serfs. Attica had not this system, of a dominant group of incomers settled in an area and holding down the descendants of its predecessors there; but it is conceivable that two types of unfree person in Crete may have been something like the *hektemoroi* of pre-Solonic Athens (above, p. 92). The Gortyn Code refers to the *katakeimenos*, a free man who pledged his person to his creditor by mutual arrangement, to be a bondservant until the debt was paid; and the *nenikamenos*, a free man condemned by law for bad debts and handed over in bondage to his creditor. In both these cases, apparently, the bondage was ended if the term of years deemed to be the equivalent of the debt had been served out.[8]

Only isolated details about the Cretan cities in the Archaic period are preserved in the ancient authors, and the patterns of conservatism are usually visible. Sometimes men left to try their fortunes elsewhere. Early in the seventh century a band of emigrants from Crete – city unknown – under Entimos joined a similar band from Rhodes under Antiphemos (below, p. 197) and founded Gela on the south coast of Sicily; the energetic element here was the Rhodian, judged by the archaeological evidence. In the 630s the Theraian emigrants who were seeking a site in Libya (above, pp. 185–7) were guided to the coast by a Cretan murex-fisher; if any other Cretans knew of this rich new world, they had felt no drive to colonize it for Crete. We hear also that in the previous generation Etearchos of Axos (above, p. 189), suspecting (wrongly) his daughter Phronime of promiscuity, ordered her to be thrown into the sea, a barbarously primitive form of punishment. (The Theraian trader to whom Etearchos entrusted the task brought her instead to Thera, where a high-ranking citizen took her as a concubine and she bore Aristoteles, the future *oikistes* of the above-mentioned emigrants.) And when we read how, *c.* 525–519, first Samians and then Aiginetans settled in western Crete at Kydonia, which must have been a strategic point for the sea-route to the Nile Delta, we note that apparently this did not disturb the Cretans. Lastly, their conservatism is well illustrated by their coinage. The first cities to issue their own coins – Gortyn, Phaistos, Knossos – did so *c.* 450–425. Before then, silver Aiginetan coins were current in Crete, some perhaps coined in Kydonia; but a Knossian law of the third century B.C. still refers to cauldrons (*lebetes*) as currency, and in the sixth-century law codes deposits and fines are reckoned in cauldrons. Evidently the Cretans used a barter system, with the bronze cauldron as a unit of reckoning. We can hardly interpret literally a sum of '100 cauldrons', which is mentioned more than once in the sixth-century laws of Gortyn.

Of the many and remarkable religious cults in Crete, only one can be noted here. The old Homeric *Hymn to Apollo* says clearly that the cult of Apollo Delphinios (possibly a Lycian-Minoan title) came with its priests by sea to 'rocky Pytho' (Delphi) from Crete (above, pp. 73–4), and this cult certainly existed at Dreros, for example, already in the eighth century; the earliest offerings there are Geometric, and the seventh-century cult-statues found in the temple, standing on a wall-bench in the Minoan manner, represent the Near Eastern tradition of the young male god flanked by two females (Leto and Artemis). Apollo Pythios too was worshipped in Crete, particularly at Gortyn. Unless the two 'Delphinian' cults arose independently, a transference from seafaring Crete to Delphi makes more sense geographically than Delphi to Crete. The strong connection of the Apolline cult with purification gave Cretan experts a great name for this skill: thus Karmanor of Crete traditionally purified Apollo himself for the slaying of the snake Pytho, and the Cretan Epimenides was called to Athens *c*. 600 to purify the city after the Kylonian murders (above, pp. 87–8). In the late seventh and sixth centuries the Cretan bronze-smiths were making a characteristic panoply of helmet, thorax, and *mitra* (bronze apron hung from the thorax-rim to protect the belly), all decorated with delicately chased pictures of antithetic figures – local Cretan winged daimons, horses, sphinxes, etc. Most have been found in Cretan sanctuaries, notably at Arkades (Afrati), but three typical helmets, one decorated with Europa on the bull, were found at Delphi, as well as other Cretan bronzes. Thus some Cretans did come to this inland Greek sanctuary; but, if the rest of the Homeric *Hymn* is rightly interpreted, the Cretan priesthood was dismissed by the mainland Greeks from its position early in the sixth century.[9]

The seafaring skill of the Bronze Age Cretans is still evident in Archaic and Classical Crete. Much of it doubtless was piracy. Contact of some kind with Egypt and the Levant may have persisted spasmodically through the Subminoan period, to resume more steadily as the Cretan cities expanded in the eighth century. If the *Odyssey* partly reflects that century, it looks as if Cretans were apt then to turn up on other people's coasts, for Odysseus poses as a high-born travelled Cretan who loves 'ships and war and polished javelins and arrows'. Phoenician merchants visit his Crete, and his Cretan sails to Egypt, a five days' journey only, settles there and meets Phoenicians who trade as far as Libya.

FIG. 3. Design on bronze helmet from Arkades, Crete: two youths wearing wings harnessed to their backs and winged sandals grasp a pair of crested and bearded serpents twined in 'caduceus' pattern; heraldic panther-motif below. *c*. 625–600

ART

Some such contacts, direct or via Cyprus, had brought Oriental imports and skills in bronze and ivory – doubtless textiles too – to Crete by the eighth century. The best evidence comes from the cave-sanctuary of Zeus on Mount Ida, where were found a long series of bronze shields or cymbals, hammered in bands of relief pictures, with animals' heads as the central bosses. The dates range roughly from the mid-eighth to mid-seventh centuries, and the direct models are bronzes from Assyria, Phoenicia, and Urartu in Armenia. Indeed, it is now thought likely that a settlement of the foreign craftsmen dwelt in Crete for some time, until Cretan smiths too had learnt the new techniques of hammering bronze sheets over wooden cores to form low reliefs, and of incising the outlines of the figures for greater clarity.

It is possible that Crete was one of the first areas to feel the impact of the Greek Orientalizing style; but it seems that other Aegean islands such as Rhodes and mainland centres such as Corinth and Athens outstripped her in developing it. By c. 700 the Corinthian potters had produced their version of Orientalizing, the Protocorinthian style, and c. 650 they were drawing the human figure with style and often brilliance. Crete also produced potters and bronzeworkers who showed equal ability, with a technique close to the Protocorinthian in many details. But whereas Protocorinthian pot-painting shows an overall unity whose continuous development can be traced chronologically thanks to the mass of this pottery still surviving in many Greek cities, the Cretan material is much scantier and is split among the different regions of Crete itself, and has not much imported material with it to provide help towards an absolute dating (Pl. 31). On such evidence as is available, however, expert analysis of the Cretan puts it as later, and thus as borrowing from the Protocorinthian and island work.

The Cretan contribution to sculpture is rather clearer. Although Athens made a strong bid to claim him, the famous early craftsman Daidalos surely belongs to Crete. To regard him as a myth seems perverse, if Eastern experts in metalwork were already active in Crete in the eighth century (above). Traditionally he was a master-worker in several skills, like the family of Rhoikos and Theodoros at Samos later (below, pp. 215–16). This presumably lies behind the tales of his varied works: the Knossian labyrinth or dancing-floor and, more realistically, statues with legs apart, bent arms, and open (= inlaid?) eyes, well illustrated by the male figure in the bronze Drerian trinity. He even made wings for humans – traditionally for his unlucky son Ikaros, but perhaps in reality for youths to wear strapped to their backs, in ritual dances at sacred festivals, probably representing young deities (e.g., Talos, the legendary 'self-propelling bronze man', shown young and winged on fourth-century coins of Phaistos). Later Greek writers claimed for Daidalos many cult-statues and reliefs elsewhere in Greece and Sicily, but probably this means only that these were unsigned and 'Daedalic' in style, if by that we mean the distinctive early Greek block-like type, male or female, squarely frontal with large eyes and heavy wiglike hair, often with a short curled fringe and thick shoulder-length locks (plaits?) tagged at the ends. The statues were in limestone, the statuettes and reliefs in terracotta and bronze: a widespread type whose final stage lasted into the early sixth century in the Peloponnese (as for the Argive statues of Kleobis and Biton; above, p. 141) and perhaps in Crete too. Certainly the first known examples of the type, the terracottas, appear *c.* 700 in Crete, but evidently it was introduced early to the central and south Aegean islands as well. The prototype for this monumental style may have been simply the Oriental mould-made (and thus rather monotonously frontal) clay figurines of deities, usually Astarte-types, imported among the Greeks. At all events, Crete has yielded enough 'Daedalic' limestone statues and small bronzes of the seventh century to justify the long reputation for early sculpture (*xoana*) which Pausanias says that she had 'after Daidalos' residence at the court of Minos'. But – as with her vases – there is very little material of the sixth century and later. This fits the literary tradition that the sculptors Dipoinos and Skyllis were Cretans by birth (allegedly, indeed, pupils or even sons of Daidalos), but migrated to Sikyon on the mainland, probably at the invitation of the tyrant Kleisthenes (above, p. 166). The 'Daedalic' sculptures in the Peloponnese may conceivably be the results of similar emigrations earlier, but the style is usually held to have come independently by the trade-routes which tied Corinth and Argos also to the East (Pl. 26).[10]

Archaic Crete may have one great claim to the gratitude of the later world. She has long been recognized as one of the earliest Greek receivers of the north Semitic alphabet (above, pp. 25–6), because of the significant likeness of many of her odd letter-forms and her punctuation-mark to the Semitic forms. Her claim to be the first (made by the Hellenistic Cretan Dosiadas, against heavy competition from elsewhere at the time) has now been strengthened by two factors: a Cretan inscription of *c.* 500 which shows indirectly the earliest use yet of the word *phoinikeia* ('the Phoenician things') for the alphabet, and the strong likelihood (above, p. 193) that Semitic craftsmen settled in Crete during the ninth and eighth centuries.

That said, we have to admit that the Cretans themselves contributed little to Greek literature. The stolid formulae of the law codes can hardly be so described, and the classical Cretan's reaction to the poetry of Homer is shown up by Plato in the *Laws*, where the aristocratic Cretan Kleinias, on hearing a quotation from the *Odyssey*, observes: 'That sounds like a very elegant poet. We have perused some other charming pieces of his, but not many, for we Cretans don't have much use for foreign poetry'. There was the old *Hymn of the Kouretes* and the lawgiver Thaletas, who is said to have composed lyrics exhorting the Gortynians to obedience; but the only Cretan song surviving is that by an unknown man named Hybrias. This lyric, it has been noted, would suit well an armed song-and-dance (*hyporchema*) of the kind for which the island was (and still is) famous, and the song itself exemplifies the carefree type of the warrior whose carapace is his fortune, whether guarding his farm borders or roving as a soldier:[11]

> My riches are a spear and sword
> and a fine shield for protection.
> With this I reap
> and tread the grape,
> with this get serf-subjection.

Those who reject a spear and sword
and a fine shield through inertia,
they clasp my knee,
salaam to me,
and call me Shah of Persia.

RHODES

The Doric immigrants to Rhodes were traditionally from Argos and the eastern Argolid. They had succeeded to a rich Mycenean culture in the island; the coast of Asia Minor was very near, and Cyprus, Phoenicia, and Egypt were not far away when the winds were favourable. It is not surprising, therefore, that a marked substratum of the Near East underlay much of the tradition, cults, and general outlook of Archaic Rhodes. Our knowledge of her history before the Persian Wars is minimal, and very patchy still for the fifth century, attaining some solidity only after 408, the year when the island attained political unity and symbolized it by the creation of a capital city, Rhodes, on the north coast.

Until then the three biggest settlements on the large island had been independent polities, the numerous smaller villages presumably siding with their larger neighbour as and when necessary. All three cities were coastal, and the wind blows hard over Rhodes. Lindos on the east side was the most protected, facing towards Cyprus; Kameiros, on the west, looked to the Aegean. Ialysos was on the north-west end, nearest to Asia Minor and the later city of Rhodes. They formed the original 'Doric Hexapolis' jointly with Knidos, the peninsular city jutting from the mainland north-west of Rhodes: Kos, the island beyond Knidos: and Halikarnassos on the mainland just north of Kos. A joint cult of Apollo was maintained on a Knidian promontory called Triopion, but Halikarnassos left the Hexapolis early, allegedly after an athlete of hers had refused to offer to Apollo the tripod-prize which he had won in the Triopian Games. Halikarnassos in fact was essentially a Carian-ruled place with only a thin Greek overlay, and her dialect, as we meet it in Herodotos and her fifth-century inscriptions, was Ionic like that of her mainland Greek neighbours, and her Greek script likewise. Kos may have used the Ionic script from the beginning, though this is uncertain; Knidos' alphabet has a few variants resembling some used in the Cyclades. Rhodes used basically the same script as that in part of her 'metropolis', the eastern Argolid around Epidauros, but employed the letter (h)eta for both aspirate and long e. (For the painted and incised sherds from Kalymnos beyond Kos, showing Argive letters, see above, pp. 140–1.)

There is no surviving record of any early trouble between the three Rhodian cities, nor of common enterprises. Strabo, however, says that long before Ol. 1 (776) 'the Rhodians' had sailed to Spain and founded there Rhodos (he throws in also Parthenope (Naples), Elpiai in Apulia, and the Balearic islands). This is a route more clearly taken by the Phokaians towards the end of the seventh century (below, pp. 227–8), and the east Greek ware found along it is equally likely to be Phokaian; Rhodian pioneering in these parts still seems uncertain, and the high date given to her 'thalassocracy' (see Appendix III) does not improve its credibility. As for the other end of our period, a recent suggestion claimed Rhodes as a dependency in the thalassocracy of Polykrates of Samos (*c.* 532–521), but this too seems unlikely (below, p. 217).[12]

At least it can be said that, like other Doric states, Lindos probably and Ialysos certainly had Heraklid rulers in the Archaic period. Ialysos had the Eratidai; the first known to us is Damagetos in the late seventh century. Though far from the Peloponnese, apparently he sympathized with the Messenians in their Second War, for Aristomenes, their defeated leader, fled in exile to Rhodes and married Damagetos' young daughter. From this union came a famous line of Olympic athletes, the last of whom won his prizes late in the fifth century. The duration of Eratid control in Ialysos is not known; the next Ialysians in our sources are two mercenaries of the Pharaoh Psamtik II, among the Carians, Kolophonians, and others who in 591 under their Egyptian captain 'Potasimto' (Pedasimtawi) went on the expedition up the Nile which reached the temples at Abou Simbel. Like the rest, they cut their names and comments on the colossal statues: 'Telephos wrote me, the Ialysian' and 'Anaxanor [? wrote me], the Ialysian, when the King marched the army for the first time [......] Psam(m) atichos'. Ialysian graves are rich in Egyptian and Egyptianizing material.

Even less of Kameiros' history survives, but the rich grave-goods in her cemeteries from the end of the eighth century onwards and in the temple on her

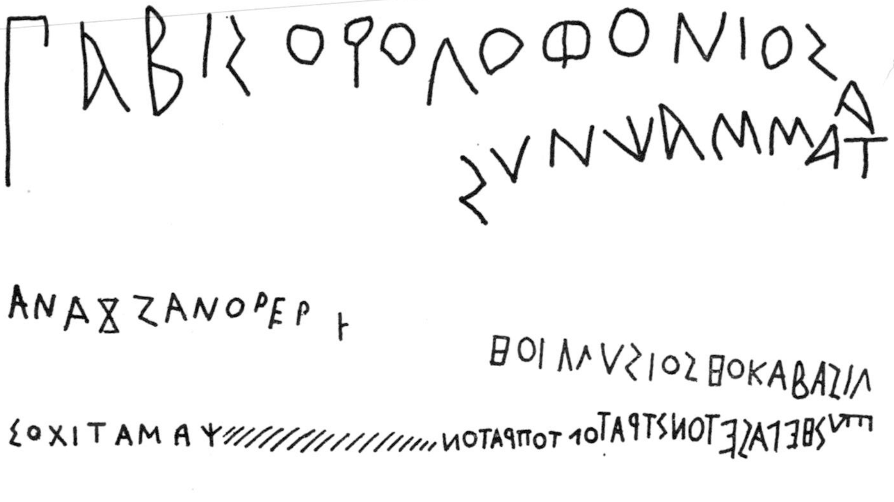

FIG. 4. Graffiti on the colossal statue of Rameses II at Abou Simbel (Nubia), written in 591 B.C. by Greek mercenaries serving under Psamtik II. Some of the names may be misspelt. *Top*: PABIS (sic) THE KOLOPHONIAN, WITH PSAMMATA (sic). *Centre*: ANAXANOR . . . (see above). *Below*: ELESIBIOS (sic) THE TEIAN

acropolis show that she too profited from the gold and other goods that came along the many trade-routes to the island. Behind her on Mount Atabyros (or Atabyrion; a non-Greek word thought to be from the same root as the Semitic Tabor) was a famous cult of an Eastern male god hellenized as Zeus Atabyrios. Among the offerings are many bronze statuettes of bulls. The bull was an essential part of the cult, and Timaios refers to large bronze statues of them which were believed to bellow when any danger threatened the city. This mountain-Zeus with his bulls was also worshipped in Akragas (where the terrible tradition of the bronze bull of the tyrant Phalaris is thought to be a remembrance of the cult); Akragas was a colony of Lindian-Cretan Gela (below), which might well mean that Rhodians from Kameiros had accompanied the Lindians to one or both of these colonies. Kameiros also produced an epic poet named Peisandros, traditionally c. Ol. 33 (648–645), who composed a poem in two books on the Labours of Herakles.[13] (Pls. 32, 34)

Lindos is one of the finest sites in the Aegean islands, with her sheltered harbour at the foot of a sheer acropolis crowned by the ancient precinct of Athena Lindia. The early pottery (c. 750–650) from a cemetery at Exochi not far away offers stylistic links via the Cyclades with the Attic-Eretrian area, while from c. 700 onwards both she and Ialysos were importing large numbers of Cypriot vases and figurines. About 690 she planted a colony, Phaselis, in Lycia on a coast rich in timber and leading on further east to Soloi, also traditionally a Lindian settlement, not far from Tarsos in Cilicia. To the south she had links with Crete, for in 688 Crete and Lindos joined in sending out a colony to Sicily, where emigrants from Chalkis, Corinth, and Megara had already occupied the east coast. The colony settled at Gela on the south coast. Gela itself planted the colony Akragas in 580 further west along the coast, and a few years later more Rhodians (city unspecified) accompanied a venture by Knidos, their colleague in the Pentapolis. Led by Pentathlos, a Knidian, they seized Lilybaion, the strategic height on the western tip of Sicily. This was a direct threat to the Carthaginian interests in these southern parts which faced Libya, and Phoenicians joined the native Elymians to expel the inhabitants. If this was indeed an attempt by the Rhodian element to get control of southern and western Sicily, it failed completely.

More light on Lindian ventures comes from the Lindian Record (*anagraphe*), inscribed in the first century B.C. on a tall stone stele in the precinct of Athena. The heading says that it was decided to publish thus the inscriptions on the objects of historic interest dedicated there which, now destroyed, had been described in local records and the reports of the successive priests made to the *mastroi* (councillors). The first fourteen entries are obvious forgeries, offerings by, for example, the eponymous founder Lindos, heroes of the Trojan War, and so on.

But the next series illustrates well the links overseas: for example with Crete, Gela, and Akragas: a krater-stand with a bogus inscription on its rim (Adrastos gave it as a prize for the funeral games of Aigialeus), and the real dedication added by the givers, a trading family, as 'a tithe of the ship from Crete' (15); a big cauldron sent from the Geloans (25); and another offered by Phalaris of Akragas, an 'antique' labelled suitably as a guest-gift from Daidalos to Kokalos (27). The colony Phaselis under its *oikistes* Lakios sent war-spoils, helmets and curved knives taken from the Solymoi in Lycia (24). From 17 we learn that the second-ary, sixth-century settlement at Kyrene included Lindians (above, p. 187): 'The Lindians who with Pankis' children founded Kyrene with Battos, to Athena and Herakles a title from war-spoils' (a lotus-wood group of Pallas Athene watching Herakles strangle a lion). The gifts from the Pharaoh Amasis are listed (29): the famous linen breastplate, ten sacrificial bowls (*phialai*) and two gold statues bearing inscriptions in Greek and hieroglyphic. Herodotos had also des-cribed the breastplate and statues ('stone'). More important, he tells us also what the connection was – the Rhodian share in the great Greek *emporion* of Naukratis which Amasis had granted to twelve Greek states (above, pp. 53–4). Lindos, Ialysos, and Kameiros had a joint stake there as members of the Hellenion; Phaselis too was a member. Lindos was the nearest to Egypt, for not far from her on the southern tip of Rhodes lay the small port now called Vroulia, town and cemetery, clearly a point of departure for ships, where the north winds (upon whose strength and persistence day and night the excavation report comments with feeling) drive ships down towards the Delta. Indeed by the seventh century there were workshops in Rhodes itself producing faience ware.

One man may well be associated with Lindian prosperity. Kleoboulos son of Euagoras, claiming to be of Heraklid descent, ruled her during the first half of the sixth century, and was included by tradition among the Seven Sages. The earliest silver coinage of Lindos, bearing a lion's head in profile and dated on style to the mid-sixth century at latest, is tentatively ascribed to him. He is said to have renewed the temple to Athena, and the modern excavators found the old pot-tery and other small offerings not just thrown out, but carefully buried to form a terrace in front of the temple. An epitaph in hexameters is quoted as his work:

> A bronze girl am I, on the tomb of Midas offered.
> While water goes on running and tall trees leafing,
> the brilliant sun and the bright moon rising,
> ιivers flowing and the deep sea pounding,
> so long will I stay on his sad grave-mound
> and tell the passer-by that here lies Midas.

A bronze kore, even if a grave-siren, sounds unusual at a date so early, but many years later the poet Simonides attested that Kleoboulos had at least backed the survival of a gravestone:

> What man of sense could praise Kleoboulos
> who dwelt in Lindos?
> Streams that never fail, flowers each spring,
> the fire of the sun and the golden moon,
> and the swirling seas – he backed against them all
> the strength of a gravestone.
> Nothing is as strong as the gods; and a gravestone
> even mortal hands can break. He spoke folly.

Simonides was not quite right, however, on the durability of stelai. The 'kore' and any grave-memorial of Kleoboulos himself have disappeared, but the Lin-dian stele preserves a contemporary tribute to his leadership (23): a dedication to Athena Lindia of eight shields and a gold crown for the statue, by 'the men who went on a campaign to Lycia with Kleoboulos'.[14]

KNIDOS

The long, rugged peninsula of Knidos is joined to the Asian mainland by a very narrow isthmus, only one kilometre across at its thinnest point. The Archaic and Classical city (modern Burgaz) lay in the only fertile area, about halfway along the south coast. The name Triopion (three-way-facing) belonged to the whole west half of the peninsula, but specifically, it seems, to the area of modern Kumyer some distance west of Burgaz, where the old precinct of Apollo is most probably to be located. This precinct presumably commemorated the place where the Doric settlers landed, and the cult of Triopian Apollo was extended to those in Halikarnassos, Kos, and the three Rhodian cities – a hexapolis from which Halikarnassos was ejected later, allegedly through an incident (above, p. 195), but basically, we suspect, because she remained essentially a Carian city. Kos, her neighbour offshore, remained in the band, but Koan history proper begins with the Classical period.

Knidos was said to be a colony of Sparta, like Thera. Two recorded actions show her as a friendly, non-aggressive city, willing to help any other Spartan offshoots. In the 520s some ships carrying citizens of Kyrene as prisoners to Cyprus, where their king, Arkesilas III, had arranged for their execution, put in for shelter at Knidos, where they were rescued and sent safely off to Kyrene's metropolis, Thera. About a generation later king Darius asked the Knidians to restore an exile, Gillos, to his city, Taras, also a Spartan settlement. The Knidians, who had a *philia* with Taras, agreed and did their best, but the Tarentines refused, and the Knidians, says Herodotos, were not strong enough to use force. The friendship with Taras was perhaps connected with commerce, for Knidos was certainly a trading city, like her colleagues in Rhodes. About 580–576 she sent out emigrants to Sicily; it was the Eldorado for hopeful Doric mother-cities, and her Rhodian friends had already shared with Crete in founding Gela, and were now joining Geloans to found Akragas. Pentathlos led the Knidians, and some Rhodians joined them also. The colony, planted on the strategic west point of Sicily at Lilybaion, was soon evicted by the local Elymoi and Phoenicians. The survivors, returning along the north coast, stopped at the Aiolian islands and settled in Lipara among the local people, whence they subsequently farmed the smaller islands in a kind of commune; some manned the fleet, others grew the food, and the spoils captured from Etruscan privateers provided some remarkably rich offerings from the Liparaians to Apollo at Delphi.

So Knidian hopes of trade with a rich Sicilian colony were dashed; but shortly afterward we find her and her Rhodian colleagues as members of the Hellenion at Naukratis (where Halikarnassos was also a member, but not Kos). There we note a probable *philia* with Miletos also; Didymaian Apollo must have approved of his Triopian aspect, for the Knidians were allowed to make their offerings to 'Apollo Milasios' in the separate Milesian precinct. It may well have been the profits from her south-eastern trade which enabled Knidos (*c.* 550–540?) to build a costly treasury at Delphi. Part of the dedication survives, inscribed on the architrave, but the crucial piece has gone; it must have been uninformative, for though Pausanias identified the building, the dedication, he says, gave no clue as between war-spoils (which sounds to us un-Knidian) or some other source. Little remains of the sculpture, except for the bodies of two caryatid-korai, rather earlier in style than the surviving Siphnian one.

The Knidian reaction to the Persian threat *c.* 540 was typical. She neither raised her militia nor gave in, but started energetically to turn herself into an island by digging across the narrowest part of the isthmus. When the rock splintered and wounded the workers, she appealed to the Pythia, who answered her as she answered all such questions at this time, with a strong implication that Apollo counselled non-resistance; so Knidos submitted.

Something is known of her early government: it was of the ancient, rigidly oligarchic type which is attested elsewhere (at Massalia, for example, and perhaps Bacchiad Corinth; above, p. 145). Only the head of a house could hold office, and only his eldest son could succeed him in this. Control rested with sixty officers called *amnemones* who, like the Athenian Areiopagites, had life-tenure and were overseers of law and order; as a probouleutic body they also controlled the agenda, and were not accountable – hence, it was said by later writers, this name Unmindful – 'unless, by Zeus, they remembered only too much'.[15]

NOTES

1 Delian festival: *Hymn to Apollo* 146–64; Thuc. 3. 104,3–6; Wade-Gery, *Essays*, 17 ff. Hdt. on the Hyperborean offerings: 4. 32. For this tradition and the variant Paus. 1. 31,2 see R. Tréheux in *Studies ... D. M. Robinson* II (1953), 758 ff.; G. Bolton, *Aristeas of Prokonnesos* (1962), 196; Burn, *Lyric Age*, 348. Delian lists of the 4th c. B.C. still record the offerings (Tréheux). Eretrian control: Str. 448; cf. also Hdt. 5. 31,1–3: Aristagoras persuaded the Persians *c.* 500 that if they won Naxos, they would mop in with her Paros, Andros, and 'other islands', and proceed thence straight to Euboia. Eretrian influence on the pottery of Andros and Tenos in the 9th c. is noted by Desborough, *The Greek Dark Ages*, 186.
2 Early Delos and the cults: see esp. F. Gallet de Santerre, *Délos primitive et archaïque* (1958), esp. 276 ff. Naxian dedications: Richter, *Korai*, 26 no. 1 (Nikandra); *Kouroi*, 53 no. 16 and esp. G. Bakalakis, *BCH* 88 (1964), 539 ff. (Euthykartides); *Kouroi*, 51 f. no. 15 (colossus; its ambiguous inscription, Guarducci, *Ann.* 21-2 (1959–60), 243 ff.); *AGA*, 28, fig. 46 and *Korai*, pl. x*if-h* (sphinx). Tyrants and Delos: Hdt. 1. 64,2; Thuc. 3. 104,1–3. Limestone temple: Gallet de Santerre, op. cit., 302 f. Rheneia: Thuc., loc. cit. Datis at Delos: Hdt. 6. 96–7. Apollo respected by Darius: Huxley, *The Early Ionians* (1966), 118; Meiggs and Lewis no. 12. Earthquake: Hdt. 6. 98. Thuc. (2. 8) says that Delos had her first earthquake before the Peloponnesian War; Gomme in *HCT* ii, 9 implies that there were two, in 490 and 431. The statue: Hdt. 6. 118; the Thebans collected it from Delos twenty years later.
3 Naxos in Sicily: Thuc. 6. 3; Hellan., *FGH* 4 F 82. Oligarchy and stasis: Athen. 348b-c. Lygdamis' exile in Eretria: Hdt. 1. 61. Revenues: [Arist.], *Oeconom.* 2. 3. Help to Polykrates: Polyaen., *Strat.* 1. 23. Spartan action: Plut., *De Her. mal.* 21. Oligarchy between 517 and 500: Hdt. 5. 28,1 and 31.2. Sack of Naxos: Hdt. 6. 95–6.
4 Mines on Thasos: Hdt. 6. 46–7. The Greek settlement: Thuc. 4. 104. Akeratos' dedication: *IG* xii. 8, suppl. 1939, 412; cf. J. Pouilloux, *Histoire et cultes de Thasos* I (1954), 269 f., no. 31. Lighthouse: *IG* xii. 8, loc. cit. and addenda, 683. For the general problem of double citizenship, see the thorough discussion by Graham, *Colony and Mother-city*, 71 ff. (deciding finally against the likelihood); for a different view, P. A. Brunt in *Anc. Soc. and Inst.*, 71 ff., esp. 75 f. Thasian and Parian governmental systems: see Fredrich in *IG* xii. 8, p. 76, M. Launey, *Études thasiennes* I (1944), 210 ff., and Pouilloux, op. cit., 238 ff. References to Frr. of Archilochos are from West, *Iamb. et Eleg. Graec.* I. Inscribed wall-block: *IG* xii. 8, 356. Early association of the Graces with Dionysos: see E. R. Dodds's edition of Euripides, *Bacchae*, ad v. 414. S. Reinach (*Rev. Arch.* 1 (1885), 69 ff.) recorded the loss of both reliefs after they had fortunately been sketched by M. Christides of Thasos; but Herakles was rediscovered later: *BCH* 18 (1894), 64 ff., pl. 16; cf. also Launey, op. cit., 126 and Picard, *Les Murailles* I (1962), 43 ff. (I have not accepted his view, 43 ff., that Dionysos' followers here are maenads.)
5 Parion: Str. 588; Parians doubted, cf. Forrest, *Historia* 6 (1957), 169 f. and n.1 (p. 170); Huxley, *Early Ionians*, 178 n. 25; Paus. (9. 27,1) omits Paros from the founders. Dispute over Akanthos: Plut., *QG* 30. Stagiros and Argilos: Thuc. 4. 88,2 and 103,3. Zagora: N. Zapheiropoulos, *ADelt* 16 (1960), *Chron.* 248 f., and esp. A. Cambitoglou, *Zagora* I (1971); cf. also J.P. Descoeudres, *Ant. Kunst* 16 (1973), 87 f. Siphnos: J. K. Brock, *BSA* 44 (1949), 1 ff. Artemis Ekbateria: Hesych. ed. Latte (ekbakterias MSS). The Siphnians and Delphi: Hdt. 3. 57–8; Flooding of mines: Paus. 10. 11,12. The Treasury: see P. de la Coste-Messelière, *Au Musée de Delphes* (1943), 322 ff.; Richter, *AGA*, 101 and *Korai* nos. 104–5; only one caryatid survives.
6 Pottery: Coldstream, *GGP*, 165 ff., 185 ff. Ephorate: cf. *IG* xii. 3, nos. 322,

18; 326, 55; 336,1. History: Hdt. 4. 145-9; 'Kadmeians', 5. 57; Thera and Kyrene, 4. 150-8. Euphemos: Pind., *Pyth.* 4,1-57; cf. Bowra, *Pindar* (1964), 140. The *loss* of the clod was probably inserted in the story later, to explain why Dorieus of Sparta failed with his colony on the Kinyps river (above, pp. 123-4). Political background, see further above, pp. 52-3. Theraian government: Arist., *Pol.* 1290b. Tombstone: *IG* xii. 3, 762 (*LSAG*, 317 f.); cult burial-ground, Vollgraff, *L'Inhumation en terre sacrée* (1941), 18 f. Graffiti near temple: cf. *IG* xii. 3. 536-7, 540, 543, 573, 767. Barbax as a Greek name taken *by* the Libyans: L. Robert, *Noms indigènes dans l'Asie Mineure gr.-rom.* I (1963), 192 n.3 and O. Masson, *Rev. de philologie* 41 (1967), 231; but could the borrowing not be the other way round? Bakal: see Masson, ibid., 229 f. Demonax: Hdt. 4. 161 and cf. above, p. 171; Chionis, Paus. 3. 14,3. Interpretation of the *moirai*: see Jeffery, *Historia* 10 (1961), 142 ff. D. M. Lewis (*Historia* 12 (1963), 39 n.146) finds this interpretation of the text impossible. He may well be right, but both views have their problems: on the above view, why is Herodotos elliptic? and on the standard view, why does he say 'moirai' if he is speaking here of *phylai*?

7 Historical background: Hdt. 7. 170-1. Lyttos: Arist., *Pol.* 1271b; Ephoros, *FGH* 70 F 149 (17); Polyb. 4. 54.6. Ergoteles: see W. S. Barrett, *JHS* 93 (1973), 23 ff. Cretan customs: see *FGH* 457-68. Gortyn 5th-c. code: Guarducci, *IC* iv. 72 and Willetts, *The Gortyn Code* (1967); cf. also Buck, 314 ff. no. 117 and Meiggs and Lewis no. 41; on the Cretan codes in general, *LSAG*, 310 ff. Xenokritos: Arist., *Pol.* 1274a ('Onomakritos', but cf. Huxley, *Early Sparta*, 43 f. and n.282, who emends this name and also 'Thales' to Thaletas from Plut., *De musica* 9 = *Mor.* 1134b-c). Immigrant craftsmen and the first codification of the law in Crete, see Boardman, 58 ff. The prominence of the great lawgivers Minos, Rhadamanthys, and Aiakos in the old Cretan tradition may also imply that the inhabitants of Archaic Crete had a ready-made foundation of oral tradition here on which to build: cf. *LSAG*, 310.

8 Monarchy: Arist., *Pol.* 1272a; Hdt. 4. 154. *Startos* of the Aithaleis: Gortyn code col. 5, lines 4-6. *Kosmoi* and Council: *Pol.* 1272a-b. Dreros law: Meiggs and Lewis no. 2, with the differing modern interpretations of the oath-takers (for the view here given cf. Morpurgo-Davies and Jeffery, *Kadmos* 9 (1970), 129). At Gortyn the interval between two tenures of office for the chief *kosmos* was 3 years (*IC* iv. 14, *g-p*). Two castes in Crete: *Pol.* 1329b. Training: see the full discussion in Willetts, *Aristocratic Society in Ancient Crete* (1955), pts. I, III-IV, and on the social classes free and unfree, Pt. II. *Perioikoi*: *Pol.* 1271b. I take the view here that *perioikoi* and *apetairoi* were different types; but cf. Willetts, op. cit., 37 ff., for the view that 'apetairoi' can include *perioikoi*. Serfs inheriting the *kleros*: G. code col. 5, lines 25-8; Willetts, op.cit., 10, 50 f. Gymnastics and weapons forbidden to serfs: *Pol.* 1264a. *Katakeimenos* and *nenikamenos*: Willetts, op.cit., 35, 54 ff.

9 Gela: Thuc. 6. 4,3; Rhodians preponderant, Dunbabin, *Western Greeks*, 311. Phronime: Hdt. 4. 154. Cretan coinage: Le Rider, *Les Monnaies crétoises du Ve - Ier siècle* (1966), 163 ff. 3rd-c. law: *IC* i. vii, 5; 100 cauldrons, *IC* iv. 1,6; cf. *LSAG*, 313. Cretan cults: see esp. Willetts, *Cretan Cults and Festivals* (1962). On the dates of the composite *Hymn to Apollo* see Wade-Gery, *Essays*, 17 ff.; he argues that the part referring to the Cretan priests was written 'long before 504 B.C.; probably before the Sacred War *c.* 600-590 B.C.' (ibid., 22). Dreros temple: P. Demargne and H. Van Effenterre, *BCH* 61 (1937), 27 ff., 333 ff.; cult-statues, cf. Richter, *Kouroi*, 26, figs. 12-13 and *Korai*, nos. 16-17, figs 73-5. Cretan origin of the Pythian-Delphic cult: Willetts, *Cretan Cults*, 262 ff., 267 f., 271 (Karmanor); Parke, *Greek Oracles* (1967), 34. Decorated armour: see the definitive publication by H. Hoffmann (with A. E. Raubitschek), *Early Cretan Armorers* (1972); earlier discussions, Snodgrass, *Early Greek Armour* (1962), 28 ff., 74 ff., 87 ff., and *Arms and Armour of the Greeks* (1967), 63 f. Cretan material at Delphi: see Hoffmann, 22 and n.4 (helmets); Rolley, *FD* v (1969), 172, pl. 1 (kouros-statuette); Boardman, *The Greeks Overseas*, 59 (shields); archaic Cretan wooden statue at Delphi, *Pyth.* 5. 40-2.

10 Odysseus' Cretan: *Od.* 13. 256-7; 14. 245-97. Semitic craftsmen: above n.1. Relative dating of early Cretan and PC pottery: Dunbabin, *The Western Greeks*, 461 ff., J. Brock, *Fortetsa* (1957), 213 ff.; Boardman, *The Cretan Collection in Oxford* (1961), 144 ff.

Sculpture: the Athenian claim to Daidalos and the confused tradition that the Attic sculptor Endoios (fl. *c.* 530–500) was his pupil, D. Sic. 4. 76; Paus. 1. 26,4 and 27.1. His works: Paus. 9. 40,3; D. Sic., loc. cit. Wings strapped on young deities: see the helmet and plaque, Hoffmann, *Early Cretan Armorers*, 2 ff., 35, pls. 1–7 and fig. 6. Talos on Phaistian coins: Le Rider, *Les Monnaies crétoises*, 195. Works attributed to Daidalos: Paus. 2. 4,5; 8. 35,2; 9. 40,4; Apollod. 2. 6,5; Ps-Skylax p. 39,4 Fabr. 'Daedalic' style: see the basic work by R. Jenkins, *Dedalica* (1937); a recent, thorough discussion arising from the early Cretan examples at Gortyn, G. Rizza and V. St. M. Scrinari, *Il santuario sull' acropoli di Gortina* I (1968). Origin of the style related to adoption of the relief-mould: see Boardman, *Preclassical* (1967), 87 f.

11 Early Cretan script: cf. *LSAG*, 309 ff. Dosiadas: *FGH* 458 F 6; cf. Jeffery in *Europa* (Festschrift E. Grumach, 1967) 159 f. Inscription *c.* 500 B.C.: Morpurgo-Davies and Jeffery, *Kadmos* 9 (1970), 118 ff., *BMQ* 36 (1972), 24 ff. (Spensithios). *Poinikastas* is used here apparently for some high office such as Recorder. Our view (stated above) is that the noun does not concern penalties (*poine*), and that *phoinikeia* (letters) do not mean the 'red' but the 'Phoenician' things. Some archaic inscriptions on stone, and doubtless those on wood too, had their letters filled in with red paint, but black may also have been used, for all we know; and for graffiti, and inscriptions on bronze and papyrus, the use of red is very unlikely. Kleinias' remark: *Laws* 680c. Hymn of the Kouretes: Willetts, *Cretan Cults*, 210 ff.; its style suggests a date *c.* 300 B.C., its lettering is probably 3rd c. A.D., but its substance is clearly much older, an invocation to Zeus the great Kouros of Dikte, born of Rhea, praying him to leap into all their households, flocks, herds, fields, cities, ships, and '*law*' (*themis*). Thaletas' lyrics: Plut., *Lycurg.* 4,5. Song of Hybrias: Bowra, *GLP*², 299 ff.; cf. also Willetts, *Glotta* 51 (1973), 64 ff.

12 Excavations in Rhodes: cf. *Clara Rhodes* (G. Jacopi ed.) I–X (1928–41); C. Blinkenberg and others, *Lindos* I–II (1931–60). Hexapolis: Hdt. 1. 144, 174. Local scripts: *LSAG*, 351 ff.; Kos (Ionic in late 5th c.), Konstantinopoulos, *AAA* 3 (1970), 249 ff. (epigram restored by W. Peek, *AAA* 4 (1971), 412 f.). Western exploration: Str. 654; identification of east Greek ware in these areas, Boardman, 210; on the high dating of the thalassocracy, Burn, *Lyric Age*, 64.

13 Cemeteries of Ialysos: *Cl. Rhod.* III (1929), VIII (1939); 8th c. B.C. onwards. Family of Eratidai: Paus. 5. 24,1–3 and 6.7. For the career of Dorieus II, the last winner (victories 432, 428, 424) see the summary by Gomme in *HCT* ii, 260 f. Inscriptions at Abou Simbel: Meiggs and Lewis no. 7. Kameiros, cemeteries: *Cl. Rhod.* IV (1931); VI–VII (1933); and C. Roebuck, *Ionian Trade and Colonization* (1959), 87 ff.; acropolis and Cypro-Phoenician-Egyptian objects dedicated there, *Cl. Rhod.* VI–VII Pt. B. Zeus Atabyrios: *Cl. Rhod.* I, 88 ff. (bronzes, p. 90, fig. 71). Bulls: Timaios *FGH* 566 F 39b and cf. Dunbabin, *The Western Greeks*, 320 n.6; cult at Akragas, ibid., 211. Peisandros: see Gow, *Theocritus* 2 (1950), 546 ad Epigr. xxii, and Huxley, *Greek Epic Poetry* (1969), 100 ff.

14 Lindos: K. F. Johansen, *Exochi* (1958); he inferred an Attic connection, but Boardman, *AJA* 63 (1959), 398 f. (review), argued strongly for an Eretrian. Near Eastern imports: Roebuck, *Ionian Trade and Colonization*, 65 f.; cf. (e.g.) *Lindos* I, 23 ff., 41 ff. Phaselis: see G. Bean, *Turkey's Southern Shore* (1968), 151 ff. Gela and Akragas: Thuc. 6. 4,3–4. Pentathlos' settlement: D. Sic. 5. 9; Paus. 10. 11,3. Rhodian attempt at control: see Dunbabin, *The Western Greeks*, 328 f. Lindian Record: *FGH* 532. Amasis' gifts: Hdt. 2. 182,1 and 3. 47,3. Naukratis: 2.178. For Egyptian and Egyptian-type articles found in Rhodes see M. Austin, *Greece and Egypt in the Archaic Age* (1970), notes to 13 ff. Vroulia: F. Kinch, *Vroulia* (1914; etesian winds, 5); the town and its cemetery yielded a great quantity of early Greek pottery and Cypro-Phoenician objects. Local faience workshops: Boardman, 110. Kleoboulos: D. Laert. 1. 6 (89–93; renewing of temple, 89); Plut., *Mor.* 385e, refers to him in passing, as *tyrannos*; cf. in general Blinkenberg, *Lindos* II, 13 ff. Coinage attributed and dated by Cahn, in *Charites*, 18 ff. The two verses: D. Laert., loc. cit., and see Bowra, *GLP*², 370 f. In v. 1 of the epitaph the verb (*epitithenai*) is the standard one used for setting a memorial

over the dead. But is this poem, with its 'bronze maiden' and elegant conceits, a later production? Was Simonides elaborating on a much simpler original?

15 Knidian peninsula: see Cook and Bean, *BSA* 47 (1952), 171 ff.; their new and illuminating interpretation of its topography superseded all earlier studies, and cast much light on the development of the early and later city sites. Triopion: Hdt. 1. 144; Knidos a Spartan colony, 174,2; aid to Kyrene and Gillos, 4. 164,2 and 3. 138,1. Akragas: see Dunbabin, *The Western Greeks*, 310. Lilybaion and Lipara: D. Sic. 5. 9; Paus. 10. 11,3–5; Dunbabin, *The Western Greeks*, 328 f., 331. Liparaian offerings at Delphi: Paus. 10. 11,3 and 16,7. Hellenion: Hdt. 2. 178; Knidian graffiti on kylikes to Apollo Milesios, *LSAG*, 352. Treasury at Delphi: Paus. 10. 11,5; cf. Pouilloux and Roux, *Enigmes à Delphes* (1963), 67 f. (inscription), and Richter, *AGA*, 310 and *Korai* nos. 87–8 (statues); on the head once thought to belong to one of the latter see *Korai* no. 86. The canal: Hdt. 1. 174,2–6; government, Arist., *Pol.* 1305b and Plut., *QC* 4 (*amnemones*). It is doubtful what Plutarch's last remark means; I take it here as a joke (cf. W. R. Halliday, *Plutarch: Greek Questions* (1928), 48). A(na)mnemones (recorders) is possible.

V

The Eastern Greeks

13 The Ionic Greeks

The Background

The river-valleys of Hermos and Maeander, piercing from east to west through the rugged inland parts of Asia Minor, divide the living-space on the west coast, where the Greeks settled, into three horizontal bands. The southernmost was Caria, south of the Maeander. The Carians spoke a language still virtually unknown to us, though their use of a script apparently taken in part from the Greek has enabled scholars to go a little way towards decipherment. A Greek tradition said that the Carians had once spread north as far as Ephesos, and had controlled many of the Aegean islands; and their concentration in this mountainous district does indeed suggest that, like the Arkadians, they were the survivors of a people once more widely spread, which was driven into the hills by the pressure of later arrivals. The Greeks knew the Carians as a mountain breed of hard fighters who made their mark as mercenaries in Egypt in the seventh and sixth centuries, and resisted the Persians to the last ditch in the Ionic Revolt.

In the central part north of the Maeander were the Lydians, whose empire under their Mermnad dynasty (c. 675–546) spread north beyond the Hermos valley as far as the Propontis. This topmost zone north of the Hermos was originally Phrygian territory, but the greatness of Phrygia under Midas I had been broken by the first Kimmerian invasions towards the end of the eighth century, and the Lydian power gradually took over as that of the Phrygians faded.

The Greek settlements followed this natural pattern of zones. Each of the three Migrations in the Late Bronze and Dark Ages filtered through the Aegean islands to the opposite shoreline, and there fanned out as the geographic barriers allowed. In the southern zone, as we have seen, were the Doric-speakers, the dialect going from the Peloponnese through Melos, Thera, and Crete to the Doric Hexapolis. Above them lay the Ionic zone, the dialect going from Attica and Euboia through the Cyclades to the Dodekapolis. This was the shortest sea-route of the three. From the Saronic Gulf to Samos a ship was never out of sight of land, a fact which obviously helped to foster the close relations between Athens and Samos in the fifth century. The Ionic emigrants, settling first around the bay at the mouth of the Maeander, in time spread south from Miletos for some way down the Carian coast. In the north, Ionic Phokaia actually lay inside the zone of Aiolis beyond the Hermos, while Aiolic Smyrna, on the other hand, lay south of the river. But she became Ionic soon, though never one of the Twelve Cities. The topmost zone, again, was the eastern end of a dialect-bridge. Aiolic was spoken alike in mainland Thessaly and across the Aegean in Lesbos and most of the Asian coastal area behind her, which became known as Aiolis.

The Ionic Dodekapolis

Though scattered down a long and deeply indented coastline between Hermos and Maeander, the twelve Ionic cities had elements in common which tended to guide their respective histories along similar lines at a similar pace. They all spoke the same dialect, though varied by local nuances. Their wives came often from the local non-Greek families; hence many Ionic men had a Carian or Lydian name. Examyes, father of the philosopher Thales, may have been a Greek with a Carian ancestress whose father's name was perpetuated in the family, or a Greek whose father called him after his own Carian guest-friend, or a Carian who had won Milesian citizenship for some service. Each Ionic settlement had much more room for expansion than the average Greek mainland city could command, and thus the Ionic estates were often large, but manageable, because the owners had a supply of serfs and slaves available from supplanted native populations. The settlements began as petty kingdoms, for an *oikistes* had (actually or tiaditionally) led out each one, and his family became the *genos basilikon*; so kingship was at first the usual Ionic form of government. But oligarchy, when it came, throve long in this atmosphere of large estates, rich possibilities for trade along the old-established routes to the East, and the intellectual stimulus of the knowledge stored in the older civilizations that they met. The tyrannies which cropped up in many of these states during the seventh and sixth centuries may not have been real breaks in the system of government (below, pp. 229–31), and democracy did not easily take root, even in the fifth century with the aid of the Athenians. The Ionians lived in a benign climate which Herodotos thought was the fairest in the world; but all had a common problem, the threat of war from the Lydians.

The Panionia and Panionion

The core of Ionia lay in the south, around the gulf of the Maeander. Here between the two powerful states Samos and Miletos lay the out-thrust coastal spur Mykale. This promontory became the focal point of the Dodekapolis; for here representatives from all twelve cities held the Panionia, a common Ionic festival to Poseidon Helikonios; here, traditionally, the first settlers had landed. When was the start of this festival, significant in that the name implies a consciousness of common unity among the scattered cities of Ionia? And, more important, when was the crucial stage at which it became also the secular federation known as the Panionion?

A good fertile plain, with a place called Anaia at its northern end, lay immediately north of Mykale and was overlooked by a fortified acropolis (modern Kaletepe) on Mykale which also, like a pirates' stronghold, overlooked the narrow strait between Mykale and Samos. This acropolis stronghold was apparently abandoned, after several generations, about the end of the eighth century. It is thought to have been Melia (Ionic Melie), a Greek or – perhaps more likely – Carian settlement which, according to the Roman architectural writer Vitruvius, was destroyed by the Ionic cities 'through the aìrogance of its people'. When

Lygdamis, the Kimmerian leader, attacked Ionia *c*. 650 Samos and Priene were already holding parts of the Anaian plain, and we hear that 'after the war with Melia' her land was divided up and Priene got two places on Mykale, Miletos and Samos exchanged some districts, and Kolophon (though well north of this area) was also concerned in some way. How many cities joined in this, one of the earliest allied Greek wars of which we know? Was it fought because Melia had been endangering an existing Panionic cult of Poseidon on Mykale? Or did Melia's Ionic neighbours destroy her simply to stop piratical raids and to take over the good plain? If so, did they take over also an existing local cult (Greek or Carian), or did they create then a new, common cult of Poseidon, in which the other Ionic cities later joined? The start of the cult cannot yet be dated by archaeology; there are traces of a great altar and a council chamber on the Otomatik Tepe (now definitely identified as the site of the precinct); but they are not earlier than the sixth century, although on the Ilica Tepe nearby are traces of habitation which go back apparently to the Mycenean period.

Action by the Panionion is not attested before the attacks by Persia in the 540s (below, pp. 214, 228), when the representatives met and agreed to send an appeal to Sparta for military aid. There is no evidence that the previous attacks on some cities by the Lydian tyrants Gyges and Alyattes had produced any such reaction; the mutual aid then afforded was based on individual treaties. But an attempt had been made in the first half of the sixth century: Thales of Miletos had tried vainly to get the Ionians to form a common government based on Teos (an unpretentious city, and the geographic centre of Ionia) on the analogy of Athens city and the Attic demes. This suggests that the Panionion did already exist then – that the unique opportunity offered by the Panionia for pooling information and discussion among all the cities had already been taken, and that the usual meetings which were held after any big festival before the various delegations dispersed were already recognized at Mykale as representing essentially a federation, however loose, however rarely summoned for emergencies. Thales evidently believed that the Ionians could never become powerful against the *barbaroi*, despite the impressive total sum of Ionic wealth and sea-power, unless they formed a permanent political and military combination. But this was asking too much of twelve cities which had the usual common-border problems.[1]

The Southern Cities: Miletos, Samos, Priene, and Myous; the Ionic Revolt

MILETOS

Miletos was the greatest mainlander of the Dodekapolis. She claimed to be the first Ionic settlement, from Nestor's Pylos via Attica, and to have founded 'a hundred colonies'; and indeed, though 'trading settlement' (*emporion*) is a juster term than colony for many of her daughters, their number far surpassed that of any other metropolis, even if by that term a matriarch is meant rather than a mother. The site of Archaic Miletos has not yet been fully excavated, and a brief survey of her Archaic history is inevitably superficial – as is indeed the case with all these cities, since nothing like a connected record survives in the litera-

ture. It was said that kingship ended there after a struggle between two of the
Neleidai, her royal family. The loser, Amphitres, later murdered the winner,
Leodamas, and ruled despotically. But the exiled sons of Leodamas returned
with Phrygian help and killed Amphitres. On this the citizens turned against
the Neleid rule and elected a temporary dictator (*aisymnetes*), one Epimenes,
who put a price on the heads of the sons of Amphitres; but the Neleidai
long survived as a powerful clan in Miletos. All this must have happened
before the end of the seventh century, and may have begun at its start, for
we are told of Leodamas that he had once won a war against the Karystians
of southern Euboia – perhaps he was leading the Milesian forces which
supported Eretria *c.* 700 in the Lelantine War, for Eretria and her neighbour
Karystos were not always friends. After Epimenes there was apparently a period
of oligarchy in which control of the city rested with the *prytanis* and Aristotle
says that one reason why oligarchies were apt to generate tyrants in the old days
was because they gave one official supreme authority over all the other offices: 'as
happened specifically at Miletos with her *prytanis*'. She did indeed have a
powerful tyrant, Thrasyboulos, later on (below, p. 213).

The largest cluster of Milesian colonies was in the north-east from the Hellespont to the Euxine. The late tradition asserted that some of them were founded in
the eighth century, but this is not yet established by archaeology. In the Hellespont and Propontis the Milesian settlers tended naturally to keep to the
Asian side: their best-known colonies were Abydos (settled by permission of
Gyges of Lydia, for some reason unknown to us); Kyzikos (allegedly eighth-
century) on the neck of a peninsula in the Propontis near Prokonnesos, an island
rich in marble; and in the Euxine, Sinope on her peninsula, also allegedly
eighth-century, but more probably established in the late seventh, after the
Kimmerians had occupied the area and then left it. She was one of Miletos'
richest daughters, particularly as purveyor of the famous Sinopian ruddle
(*miltos*); beyond her were Amisos and Trapezous (also said to be eighth-century),
a port for the metals, especially iron, mined by the Chalybes inland; and finally
Phasis in Kolchian territory, the eastern limit for Greek seafarers. On the north
shore among the Scythians were later settlements mostly of the sixth century, for
example Pantikapaion on the Tauric Chersonese, Olbia, Istros, Tomis, Apollonia
Pontica. In all these places there had probably been Milesian traders prospecting
for markets before the settlers went out; no names of *oikistai* there are known,
which is one reason for inferring that many of the settlements were made by
private enterprise, and only later produced a tradition of an orthodox foundation
with Apolline blessings and so on. After the mild airs of Ionia the icy winters in
parts of Thrace and Scythia must have been a trial. We hear of donkeys which
could not be reared in this climate, and of imported bronze hydriae splintering as
the water froze inside them. The settlers sensibly adopted the local dress, a
woollen or leather tunic and trousers, ear-protecting bonnet, and brightly striped
cloak. The cold was bearable when balanced against the huge profits: slaves
(Thracian and Scythian), cattle, and hides formed a staple trinity, but there
were also the great grain harvests of the steppes, and honey, wax, and dried
fish, especially the big tunnies which bred in the Sea of Azov by the Crimea. In
exchange the Greeks offered mostly luxury goods: bronze vessels of all types,

painted pottery, gold and silver jewellery and fine-woven patterned chitons for chiefs' wives and daughters, scented oil in pretty little aryballoi, and so on. Milesian wool became famous, spun perhaps from northern as well as from Ionic fleeces. In the sixth century Miletos was trading with Sybaris, the wealthy Achaian colony in southern Italy (above, p. 172). The Sybarite women were famous for their skill in fancy weaving, so the finespun Milesian wool may have been one of the imports. When Kroton destroyed Sybaris in 510, tradition said that all Miletos donned mourning.

The stages of Milesian economic prosperity from the seventh century onwards can be traced in the sanctuary of the great Apolline oracle at Didyma, about 12 miles south of Miletos. The name Didyma seems to be analogous to other known Carian place-names such as Idyma, and the cult, centred on a spring and a tree (traditionally a laurel), with a legend that here Leto conceived her son Apollo, has suggested to scholars that the original deity there was female; certainly Artemis and Hekate also shared the precinct in the Archaic period. The Branchidai, a family allegedly descended from one Branchos – again, probably a Carian name – administered the cult. In the eighth and seventh centuries it was a simple, mud-walled precinct, but about the end of the century a long hall was built of mud-brick on a stone socle, clearly for housing more important offerings. At about this time Milesian traders had got a footing in the rich Egyptian Delta, at 'Fort Miletos' (Milesionteichos), and the first Greek pottery appears on the site of Naukratis (above, pp. 53-4). The Pharaoh Necho II (c. 609-593) dedicated in the Didymaion the garment which he wore when defeating king Josiah at Megiddo; and by the first half of the sixth century rich Milesians had begun to dedicate colossal marble statues, clearly inspired by Egyptian models. The finest of these Greek adaptations is the couching lion, the commonest the heavy seated figure in chiton and cloak. They were clustered along one stretch of the Sacred Way leading to the precinct; several figures might form a single dedication made by a family or similar group, as the dedications indicate: 'The sons of Orion (?) dedicated these statues' (two huge lions in antithesis, one, sadly battered, now in the British Museum, the other still at Miletos); 'Hermesianax dedicated us' (on a seated statue surviving from a group); and so on. Samian families did the same in their Heraion (below, p. 215; Pls. 35, 37).

Meanwhile c. 675 the old 'Heraklid' royalty of Lydia had been overthrown by Gyges, a vigorous military usurper and founder of the Mermnad dynasty, whose reign first brought the Eastern word 'tyrannos' into the general Greek vocabulary. He opened up a series of assaults on Miletos and others of the prominent Ionic cities, which his successors were to continue. Miletos stood up stoutly to these attacks. Like the other east Greek cities she had strong walls against which the Lydians' chief weapon, their famous cavalry, was useless; she had also brave though ill-disciplined citizen-soldiers, and skilled archers sent down from her northern colonies. Above all she had her fleet, so that the Lydians, not being seafarers, could never make a siege full-circle; in the seventh century their attacks were probably commando-raids rather than sustained offensives. Miletos' chief link with the Greek mainland at this time was Megara, whose colonies around the entrance to the Euxine met no opposition from the Milesian settlements. Diplomatic relations with Paros in the Cyclades emerge from fragments of a poem by Archilochos which mentioned a Milesian embassy to Paros wrecked in the straits between Paros and Naxos with only one survivor, named Koiranos, who was saved (tradition said) by a worthy dolphin. In Ionia itself at some date before the sixth century the Milesians sent a force to help Chios against her perennial boundary-rival Erythrai in an anonymous early campaign which may have been some part of the widespread Lelantine War (below, p. 231), in the sense that the antagonism between Chalkis and Eretria must have fired the latent hostilities existing between their respective trading partners too. Chios and Miletos were naturally friends, having a common enemy in the trade rival which lay between them, Samos, the island for which Miletos reserved her sharpest enmity. They shared a common 'boundary', the entry to the Gulf of Latmos; and Samos had the advantage, since her ships could swoop down on homing Milesian traders more easily than the Milesians could retaliate, for the prevailing coastal wind was against them.[2]

SAMOS

Samos, like the other Ionic cities, was originally ruled by kings. The royal line traced its descent from one Prokles of Epidauros (above, p. 151), who was said to have led his people across the sea to colonize the island when the Dorians came into the Argolid. In the reign of his son Leogoros the Ephesians expelled the people on the pretext that they were pro-Carian; but after ten years of exile at Anaia by Mykale (above, p. 208) Leogoros and his followers recovered the island. By the end of the eighth century or some decades later, possibly, Samos was laying the foundations for her reputation as a bold sea-ranger, for some tie with the trade of Corinth at the Isthmus presumably underlies the contract given to Ameinokles the Corinthian to build four warships for Samos (cf. p. 159, n. 2). Predictably, she sided with Chalkis in the Lelantine War (which suggests that Chalkis may have received from her some at least of the luxury goods from the East which finally reached the Chalkidic colony Pithekoussai and the Etruscan market).

The Eastern contacts of Samos from at least the early seventh century onwards are abundantly attested in the German excavations at the great precinct of Hera, patron deity of Samos, near the main city (modern Pythagoreion) which lies on the south-east side of the island, with a fine harbour and a good arable plain. The Heraion contained luxury goods from Assyria, Syria, Egypt, as well as from nearer home (Cyprus, the Cyclades, Euboia). Her merchants were certainly trading with Egypt by the 630s, for the Samian Kolaios (above, p. 53) was allegedly making for the Nile Delta when he was swept on westwards along the Libyan coast to the island of Platea. Here his crew gave food-supplies to the Cretan guide Koroibos whom a band of Theraians had left there to mark their claim while they returned to drum up the numbers for the colony which was to become the wealthy city of Kyrene. According to Herodotos, it was this generous Samian act which first caused the subsequent close friendship between Kyrene and Samos, a connection which was obviously of great economic profit to both sides. Meanwhile Kolaios sailed on westwards right through the straits of Gibraltar and up to the district in Iberia which was called after its river, the 'silver-rooted' Tartessos (Guadalquivir). He brought back so much silver bullion to Samos that his enormous thank-offering to Hera (a bronze cauldron with griffin-protomes, supported by kneeling statues) was still proudly exhibited in Herodotos' day. Herodotos believed that the last leg of the journey was due to a miracle, a 'divine escort'; but probably by this pious claim the Samians meant to discourage anyone else from trying to tap the riches of Iberia. The Samian ships, like those of other nations skilled in Eldorado-tapping, were great privateers. Hera's precinct contained more than one choice offering originally destined for other owners. The Spartans complained about a great bronze Lakonian mixing-bowl which never got to their *xenos* king Kroisos of Lydia, and also about a show-piece of Egyptian skill, a padded linen corslet marvellously woven, a present from the Pharaoh Amasis, which never got to Sparta. (Pls. 38, 39)

Aigina, another island of vigorous traders, was an enemy of Samos from the days before the Samian monarchy ended; a king named Amphikrates attacked Aigina itself and did great damage there, and the Aiginetans retaliated with inveterate hostility. The chief cause was evidently their rivalry for the southern markets of Egypt and Libya; Aigina was the only non-Eastern Greek state in the *emporion* of Naukratis. There may even have been a hereditary antipathy; Aigina had early defied and rejected her metropolis Epidauros, which was the traditional home of Samos' *oikistes*.

MILETOS AND LYDIA

By the start of the sixth century the tyrant Thrasyboulos was in power at Miletos, and Samos also was under the despotic rule (*monarchia*) of one Demoteles – whether he was the last king or a tyrant is not clear. Samos, being an island, had as yet no cause to worry over threats from Lydia; but Miletos was enduring an annual invasion, siege, and destruction of her crops by the troops of Alyattes, great-grandson of Gyges. Thrasyboulos had a *xenia* with Periander, tyrant of Corinth (above, p. 149); so Miletos' old friendship with Megara must have lapsed for the time. This tie with Corinth saved her in the siege; for Periander sent a private message to Thrasyboulos telling him to bluff and hold out, because the Delphic oracle had replied to a Lydian embassy sent by Alyattes that the Lydian monarch would never be cured of an illness until he rebuilt the temple of Athena at Assesos (a satellite of Miletos which the Lydians had burnt). So the Milesians concealed their food shortage and held out; the Lydians drew off, and Alyattes transformed the Lydian-Milesian relationship. He signed a pact of *xenia* with Miletos, which was maintained by his son and successor Kroisos. Periander, diplomatically friendly with Lydia also, must have worked hard for Miletos if (as we suspect) he had advised Delphi's priests what the oracle should reply. Thrasyboulos in his turn apparently did a service to Periander, though the exact date is unknown; he is said to have seized the harbour of Sikyon in the Corinthian Gulf (above, pp. 149, 163), an action hard to explain unless Corinth and Sikyon were border-fighting at the time and Milesians were serving along-side the Corinthians.

At Didyma meanwhile a small temple had been erected during the first half of the sixth century to house a cult-statue of Apollo; then, about the middle of the century, a large temple was begun (cf. Pl. 36) – probably, like the Artemision at Ephesos (below, p. 222), with benevolent aid from king Kroisos, whose mother had been a Carian; certainly he dedicated many golden offerings at Didyma, as he had done at Delphi. Meanwhile the death of Thrasyboulos, even if he were a younger man than Periander (d. 585), must have occurred before the middle of the century; and it will have been then that Miletos experienced the unsettled period described by late sources; first, 'the tyrants centred round Thoas and Damasenor', whatever is meant by this phrase (see below, pp. 229–31); and then a stretch of continuous brawling between two aristocratic clubs (*hetaireiai*) called Ploutis (Wealth) and Cheiromacha (?Close-fighting; but also interpreted as the equivalent of 'Labour'), whose leaders in their alternate bouts of power wrought atrocities on the defeated party. This was probably the stasis which, according to Herodotos, occupied two generations before Miletos became prosperous again near the end of the century.

Her troubles must have been heightened economically by the fall of Lydia to king Cyrus of Persia in 546. The oracle at Didyma had failed previously to make the grade (with several others) when Kroisos had tested its poweis of divination before deciding upon his disastrous expedition against Cyrus in 547. Only the Delphic Pythia and Amphiaraos at Thebes had passed the test. Kroisos chose Delphi for his next enquiry – should he attack Persia or not? – and interpreted its deliberately ambiguous reply as favourable. With the defeat and capture of Kroisos the Asiatic Greeks lost a generous benefactor, and the Persian troops, having mopped up Lydia, advanced to the west coast and reduced the Greek cities to dependency, except for some defiant resistance groups which left their cities and started life again elsewhere (below, pp. 227–8). Miletos, however, was saved from disaster by the pact of *xenia* guaranteed to her by the Lydian rulers. It was accepted and maintained by Cyrus, who naturally preferred the prospect of a grateful and busy seaport in his new dependency, rather than a fiercely resisting one.[3]

SAMOS: THE TYRANNY OF POLYKRATES AND ITS PERSIAN SEQUEL

Meanwhile in Samos the ruler, Demoteles, had been assassinated many years back, and an oligarchic government had come to power, called collectively the Geomoroi (land-sharers), a title used also in oligarchic Syracuse. Disaster befell this government in due course, from a colonial campaign. Byzantion, Megara's great northern colony, had herself set a colony, Selymbria, on the coast only 20 miles or so to her west: and Samos had settled a colony, Perinthos (*c.* 602), west again from Selymbria, and nicely placed to intercept the Megarian trade-route; Megara, it will be recalled, was normally the friend of Miletos. Both these settlements must have been dependencies, for when trouble boiled up between them it was the two mother-cities which undertook the campaign. A Megarian force was sent up to attack Perinthos, bringing fetters for the anticipated captives. The Geomoroi at once sent up nine generals, whose loyalty to them was suspect, and thirty ships to help the Perinthians – hoping, presumably, that after victory the disaffected element would settle there permanently. Two of the ships were struck by lightning outside Samos harbour, but the expedition

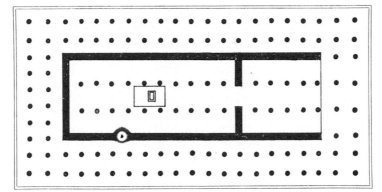

FIG. 5. Samos, Heraion: ground-plan of the great temple of Rhoikos and Theodoros. Date, about 570–560

pressed on, and 600 Megarian troops were captured. The Samian generals returned home in triumph and suborned the captive Megarians, with the fetters draped unlocked round their legs, to massacre the unsuspecting Council of the Geomoroi in their own council chamber. The government collapsed, and those of the Megarians who desired it were given Samian citizenship.

The government which succeeded is not described. Some scholars hold that a tyrant arose, Aiakes, the father of the famous Polykrates; but Herodotos, who knew Samos well, mentions him only as Polykrates' father. Certainly Samos flourished materially in the years after 570. In the precinct of Hera about 4 miles outside the city a great dipteral temple was built *c*. 570–560 (Fig, 5, above) on the foundations of much smaller predecessors which go back to the eighth century. It seems to have been the model for the Artemision at Ephesos, indeed for all Ionic temples thereafter. The naos was enclosed by a double colonnade of towering Ionic columns, their round marble bases channelled in curves and arrises, all smooth-turned on a lathe. The offerings are still rich in this period, and include much Lakonian pottery. A (priestly?) family dedicated six life-size marble statues of its members, old and young, labelled with their names, on a long base edging the Sacred Way; the group is signed 'Geneleos made us'. The temple was burnt down *c*. 540, and another temple in the same style, but with a triple row of columns east and west, was built on its foundations. Parts of the colonnade and roofing remained in a makeshift state; but clearly from the surviving column-bases and capitals it was a fine and costly building. Herodotos says of the temple that it was one of the three great building feats of sixth-century Samos, and Rhoikos son of Phileas was its first architect. This means presumably that more than one architect was involved in the various stages of building, but that the glory for the project should go to Rhoikos, who perhaps executed the first temple and got some way with its replacement. Later writers couple his name with that of Theodoros son of Telekles (a famous Samian artist in metalwork and gem-cutting, who made a signet-ring for Polykrates); they offer us family trees which combine them and their sons in divers ways, and state that Rhoikos and Theodoros built this great temple jointly. (It was probably the same as the ruin with 150 columns to which Pliny refers as 'the labyrinth of Theodoros', and the remains which the emperor Caligula knew as 'Polykrates' palace'.) Since Archaic Greek craftsmen were versatile, it could well be that Theodoros the graver was also concerned with the temple.[4]

About 532 Polykrates son of Aiakes rose with his brothers Pantagnotos and Syloson against the current government, and seized power. It is an axiom that tyranny breeds only in an area which is politically and economically depressed and smouldering; Samos may have suffered badly in the late 540s when, according to Herodotos, 'the islands' gave in, like the Asian coastline, to Cyrus and his general Harpagos. Unlike Miletos, she had no pact of *xenia* to soften the severity of barbarian control; Harpagos, who had already burnt the temple of Athena at Phokaia, may have been responsible for the destruction of the first Heraion (above). Polykrates began by sharing the power with his brothers, but he soon executed Pantagnotos, the elder, and exiled Syloson. In his ten years or so of rule he left so many memorials of one kind and another in Samos that two generations later Herodotos, who had lived for some time on the island, can give us a lively account which is free from the horror-tales such as he recounts of the early tyrants in Corinth and Sikyon – places where he had not lived himself and where, by the mid-fifth century, the sieve of popular memory would retain more colourful scandal than any substantial record of events some five generations back.

Polykrates, says Herodotos, was said to be fortunate in all that he did, and rapidly achieved power and fame. He had a thousand archers and a hundred pentekonters which, known generally as the 'Samian types' (Samainai), were broad in the beam with a snub ram shaped like a boar's snout. This fleet raided friend and foe alike on the sea and enabled him to 'seize many of the islands and of the mainland cities'. He defeated a Lesbian flotilla which came to help defend Miletos, and used the Lesbian captives to dig a ditch round his city wall. His relations with Persia were more complicated. Although the islands had given in to Cyrus, Polykrates seems to have acted as a ruler with no obligations to Persia; indeed, Mitrobates, satrap of northern Asia Minor (centred on Daskyleion), was said to have stung Oroites, satrap of the southern district centred on Sardis, by saying that Oroites had never acquired Samos, though it lay adjoining his district. Perhaps Persia officially had rights over Samos, but prudently left Polykrates alone, since she had not yet the naval power available to alter the situation. Polykrates too showed prudence when necessary. He had a *xenia* with the Pharaoh Amasis, doubtless arranged to benefit Samian trade at Naukratis; but *c.* 525 the *xenia* was dissolved (according to the Samian tradition, by Amasis, on most unlikely grounds). This was just before Cambyses, successor of Cyrus, attacked and mastered Egypt. Polykrates, on demand, supplied forty ships for Cambyses' fleet, manned by his own political enemies, the Samian oligarchs. Evidently he hoped at one blow to rid himself of trouble and to keep well in with Persia. In fact he nearly met the fate of the earlier Geomoroi. The forty returned to Samos and forced a landing; they were repulsed, but then sailed to Sparta and asked her to honour the old Samos–Sparta alliance made in the Messenian War (above, p. 120). The Spartans agreed to send help, alleging that the piratical

Polykrates had twice stolen their property (above, p. 213). The same type of motive was ascribed to the Corinthians, who now joined the Spartans on this ambitious overseas campaign to dethrone the tyrant: Samos had once insulted Periander and sympathized with the hated Kerkyra (above, p. 149). Obviously, if made at all, these were pretexts for deeper motives. Samos may well have been one (if not the only) channel whereby the luxuries of the east Aegean and Lydia had come to Lakedaimon. Theodoros of Samos had built the assembly-place called Sunshade in Sparta; Lakonian pottery and bronzes (Pl. 14) have been found in Samos, and indeed the Spartans of the seventh century may conceivably have learnt the technique of hollow-casting from the Samians, whose contact with Egypt will have made them early starters in this skill. Thus both Sparta and Corinth may have lost good Samian trade-contacts when Polykrates overthrew the oligarchic régime. But the united assault failed before the courageous Samian defence, and so did a forty-day siege. The Peloponnesians departed home, and Sparta's next ruler, Kleomenes, warily rejected all further pleas for help from Greeks across the Aegean.

The Samian exiles, true to their blood, turned to privateering in the Aegean. They lifted a hundred talents from Siphnos (above, p. 185), bought the island of Hydra from Hermion and entrusted it to Troizen, perhaps to tap the Aiginetan trade-route, and finally landed at Kydonia on the north-west coast of Crete, allegedly to help the Cretans to expel some intruders from the western island Zakynthos. Here the Samians dug themselves in, built their own temples and one to the local goddess Diktyna, and throve for five years before Nemesis finally caught up with them. About 519 an Aiginetan fleet attacked and defeated their Samainai, shore off the boar-snouts as a gift to the goddess Aphaia in Aigina, enslaved the Samians, and took over Kydonia. Allegedly this was revenge for the ravages done long ago by Amphikrates of Samos (above p. 213), but – on a more realistic view – a privateering fleet based on Kydonia could menace the southern trade-route from the Peloponnesian coast down past north-west Crete to Libya and Egypt. Much of the Aiginetan middlemen's trade must have depended on this rich source; they were founder members of Naukratis, and the forced entrance of Egypt into the Persian Empire after the defeat of Amasis did not necessarily harm the trade of Aigina, independent as ever but prepared to show respect to the Great King when necessary. As for Crete, the large quantity of Aiginetan coins found there indicates that after the settlement, if not before, the Aiginetans had a strong trading contact with the island.

In ten years' rule Polykrates enriched Samos materially and culturally. He is said to have collected the scattered songs of Homer and had a definitive written copy made; his court gave hospitality to many poets, among them Ibykos from Rhegion in Italy and Anakreon from Teos; and according to a late tradition he annexed the island Rheneia to Delos as a dedication, by a chain across the channel between. He seems even to have proposed to institute a new festival on Delos; we are not told in what way it differed from the existing old Ionic panegyris, but it was in any case short-lived. (That he or his son ever controlled Rhodes, as a modern theory once suggested, has been shown to be most unlikely.) Two great engineering feats are accredited to his rule. A Megarian named Eupalinos drove a tunnel over a thousand yards long and over 6 feet in height through a mountain outside the city, to pipe water in from an abundant source beyond the mountain; and the city's harbour was protected from the southern gales by a mole over a quarter of a mile long and 20 fathoms in depth. Much of the tunnel and traces of the mole may still be seen today.

About 522 he was duped and murdered by Oroites of Sardis. The satrap apparently played on some megalomaniac instincts, for Herodotos says that Polykrates had it in mind to rule the sea (*thalassokratein*) with all Ionia and the islands as subjects; and Oroites, pretending that king Cambyses was planning his own assassination, asked Polykrates secretly to come and rescue him, offering as bait half his treasure. True or not, the story says that chests filled with stones and a gold top-dressing were accepted as genuine by the confidential secretary whom Polykrates sent to check on the offer. This man was Maiandrios son of Maiandrios, 'one of the *astoi*'. Despite some sinister omens Polykrates kept the rendezvous with Oroites, and was brutally murdered; 'all his run of good fortune ended in this'. Oroites then contrived the murder of Mitrobates, the gibing colleague at Daskyleion, and Mitrobates' son; but Darius, succeeding Cambyses in 521, had Oroites executed by his own Persian guards.

Meanwhile Samos continued under a ruler; for Polykrates had appointed Maiandrios to be his deputy before departing himself to see Oroites. It was clearly improbable that the aristocrats of Samos, who were presumably not sorry to hear the end of Polykrates, should tolerate for long the rule of the despot's paid servant. Scenting this, possibly – or else, as Herodotos says, he *was* a very just man – Maiandrios dedicated an altar and precinct to Zeus of Freedom, a new cult, and offered to resign his power and bestow *isonomia* on Samos in return for 6 talents of silver from the tyrant's property and the perpetual priesthood of the new cult. This would achieve for his descendants wealth and the status of aristocratic rank, implied by the ownership of a family cult; and Samos would have *isonomia*, which here meant the rule of equity claimed by any just and lawful constitution, oligarchy or democracy – the offices which replaced the tyranny being opened to all those eligible. But the leading aristocrats merely rebuffed Maiandrios as a criminal upstart and demanded his accounts. So he withdrew to the acropolis, where, under pretext of rendering them to these leaders, he seized and chained each individual on arrival; and shortly afterwards his brother Lykaretos murdered them. But Nemesis, invited in by all these ill deeds, now came in terrible form to Samos. Polykrates' brother Syloson (above, p. 216) had spent part of his exile in Egypt and then in Persia, as a benefactor to Darius the king (traditionally, he had given Darius on request his own fine red cloak, when Darius was only one of the royal guardsmen); and now, hearing of his brother's death, he asked the king to give him Samos to govern, 'but with no bloodshed or enslavement'. When he arrived (*c.* 517) with a Persian force under the general Otanes, Maiandrios and his supporters, unresisting, obtained a truce for themselves to leave the island; but, says Herodotos, Maiandrios arranged for his other brother, a poor halfwit named Charilaos, to lead the ex-tyrannic guard of mercenaries suddenly against the unsuspecting Persian noblemen, simply to ensure a ruined heritage for Syloson, since Otanes would certainly avenge the massacre. This Charilaos did, while Maiandrios, with all the treasure he could seize, made off to Sparta and vainly tried to bribe the shrewd king Kleomenes to give him aid to recover Samos, presumably to hold as a Persian dependency. After his banishment from Sparta we do not hear of him again; but the Persian troops on Samos massacred all the males, old and young, whom they could catch, even in temple precincts, and then 'netted' the island, that is, fanned out and worked across it in long lines, flushing out the fugitives like game. Syloson, Herodotos says, received in effect a desert island; but later Otanes, afflicted by a venereal disease, was told in a dream to resettle Samos. Certainly by 494 the island was powerful enough to provide sixty ships at the battle of Lade in the Ionic Revolt (below, pp. 220–1).

Mention of the great revolt brings us back to Miletos, for she was its main-spring. When Cyrus' generals conquered the western seaboard of Asia, the non-aggression pact granted to the city by Kroisos was reaffirmed by Cyrus, but this protection did not save her from a long period of internal strife. This was finally settled by the arbitration of a panel of three high-ranking citizens of Paros, who made a list of all estates in Milesian territory which looked well-kept and prosperous – a very small list, Herodotos says – and entrusted the government to their owners. This emergency cabinet pulled the city together again. We are not told whether or not one of its members was Histiaios, soon to become famous. About 512 he was the ruler of Miletos, for we meet him as leader of the pro-Persian Greek *tyrannoi* whom Darius had picked out in every Greek city from the Hellespont southwards to govern that city. Histiaios was chief among these rulers in averting disaster from Darius' rash expedition against the Scythians (c. 514–512), when the king's main forces were north of the Istros (Danube) and the other Greek *tyrannoi*, to whom had fallen the duty of guarding the east bank of the river where the bridge of boats began, were dissuaded by the Milesian from breaking the cables and marooning the Persians in Scythia – the course advocated by Miltiades, the Athenian ruler of the Greek settlements in the Chersonese. The tale may be coloured by Athenian propaganda; but subsequently Histiaios received from Darius the valuable site of Myrkinos on the river Strymon in Thrace, in the area called the Nine Routes (*Ennea Hodoi*) where the great trading city Amphipolis was founded in 437; here were silver-mines, great forests for ship timber and oars, and a local population of Greeks and Thracians ready to work for the new Milesian settlement. Warned by his able general Megabazos, Darius soon removed the Ionic tyrant to Susa as a compulsory guest; and Histiaios' desire to get back to Miletos or Myrkinos was one of the causes of the east ('Ionic') Greek Revolt which flared up in 500/499.

The man who first proclaimed the revolt was Aristagoras, nephew and son-in-law of Histiaios, who was regent of Miletos in his uncle's absence. Herodotos says that he did this for two reasons. First, the oligarchic ex-government of Naxos in the Cyclades had asked for his aid against their democratic successors; he had borrowed a fleet and troops from Artaphernes, satrap of Sardis, 'to win Naxos and the other Cyclades for Persia', but the project failed utterly, chiefly because of a quarrel between him and the Persian commander Megabates, and he was left with unpaid troops and a broken pledge to Persia. Secondly, Histiaios, chafing at Susa, then sent him the famous secret message to revolt, in words tattooed on the scalp of a faithful slave. According to Herodotos, Aristagoras had really hoped to rule Naxos himself, and only turned against his Persian over-lords in panic after the quarrel and the failure. A modern theory suggests that his motives were higher: he had already planned the rising, and he entered on the Naxos project simply because only thus could the Ionic fleet, being part of the Persian navy, be mustered separately, and start the revolt. Herodotos was fond of Samos, where he had spent many years after his own exile from Hali-karnassos, and possibly his Samian sources gave him no very good account of this revolt engineered by Milesians. He has to make the best case that he can for the behaviour of the majority of Samian ships at Lade (see below,). But whatever were the true motives of the leaders, it is likely that deeper reasons underlay the rising. The economy of the whole coastal area may have suffered now that the riches of Lydia were diverted to Persian satraps and the *emporion* of Naukratis was now in the Persian empire along with the rest of Egypt. More-over, the fierceness with which the cities threw out their Greek tyrants at the very start of the revolt suggests that they resented bitterly the rule of quislings.

The account in Herodotos forms an epic of heroes and traitors, brilliance and confusion, persistence and apathy, division and defeat; little need therefore be said here. The cities flared up one after the other from Byzantion to Cyprus. On the mainland Athens, as traditional metropolis of Miletos, sent twenty ships which she withdrew upon the first defeat (understandably, since this was nearly a half of her total fleet and Aigina was menacing her own coasts); Sparta under king Kleomenes sent no aid at all; Eretria sent five ships to honour the old Lelantine alliance. The first Greek successes were startling, but the terrain was not on the Greek side: the natural communication lines run east–west along the river valleys (above, p. 207), and whereas the Persian levies, once raised and set on their way, poured steadily along these routes and out onto the coast, intercommunication for the Greeks up and down the ragged, indented coastline was difficult by land, and in bad weather hardly easier by sea. Aristagoras abandoned his leadership when the tide began to turn against the Greeks, fled to Myrkinos, and was killed there later by the Thracians. Histiaios, who had escaped from Susa on the pretext that he would bring the Greeks under Persia once more – indeed, he promised to add Sardinia to the spoils – arrived at a late stage, was – perhaps rightly – mistrusted by the Milesians, and took to privateer-ing in the Hellespont (below, p. 232). In 494, at the last stage, the Panionion resolved to concentrate the combined fleet of 353 ships on the islet of Lade off Miletos, the city which had been under siege throughout the war; and there the final battle was lost. Forty-nine of the Samian squadron, which formed the west wing, broke away just before the engagement and departed, by agreement with their exiled quisling, Syloson's son, Aiakes; the remaining eleven ships defied orders and fought. In the centre the hundred ships of Chios, the biggest single contingent, battered the Persian fleet until over half their own number had been lost and the Greek line had broken into fragments. So the defeated Greeks came once more under Persia, except for such cases as Dionysios, the captain of the Phokaian ships. Before the battle he had managed to make the crews of the ships off Lade train hard together for a week, but no longer; now, sooner than serve the Persian satrap, he left his city, as most of the Phokaians had elected to do when in this situation fifty years before, and took to privateering off the coast of Sicily. Miletos, after six years' siege by land and sea, was taken and sacked, with Didyma, by the Persians. The losses on both sides must have been great. The inevitable full-scale attack by Persia on the mainland Greeks was nearly fifteen years later (in the Marathon campaign of 490 the Persian fleet under Datis was a probing arm, sent 'to punish Athens and Eretria' and to see how far it could penetrate); and for that interval the mainlanders surely had to thank the cities of the revolt. Meanwhile the young Persian general Mardonios showed a wise tolerance at least in the settlement of mainland Ionia. He abolished the system of quisling rule, substituting some kind of acceptable government in each city. Herodotos describes it as 'democracy', adding that his readers may be incredulous at this; at any rate, it must have been a workable system. But the tyrants were restored in the islands of Samos (Aiakes), Chios (Strattis), and Kos (Skythes, then Kadmos), and at the battle of Salamis in 480 Halikarnassos was still under her sagacious but fierce queen Artemisia.[5]

The ruins of Priene visible today belong to the fourth century B.C. and later. The original town lay at the mouth of the Maeander by Mount Mykale, and the slow silt has blotted out the site and undoubtedly much history with it. The surviving literary evidence, however, suggests that the history was modest. The royal line was called Aipytidai, being traditionally descended from Neleus, presumably the same who was the Bronze Age *oikistes* of Miletos. A local story said that some Thebans led by one Philotas later joined the settlement and perhaps founded the settlement called Thebes-on-Mykale; Bias son of Teutames, one of the Seven Sages and Priene's chief cause for fame, was said to be of Theban descent. Late authority asserts that Priene was among the Greek cities attacked by Alyattes of Lydia early in the sixth century, but that by the traditional ruses used to conceal your straits from the besieging enemy (in this case, two stout mules and some sand-heaps topped with grain) Bias startled good peace terms out of the Lydian. In the 550s the city evidently yielded to Kroisos, like the rest; in fact a late tradition said that Kroisos in some campaign was helped by funds from a Prienean exile named Pamphaes. According to Herodotos Kroisos was dissuaded by Bias from attacking the Greek islands after he had won Ionia; the Lydians, inlanders and horsemen, had no idea of seamanship, and Bias suggested that Lydians assaulting these Greeks in ships was as absurd a picture as Ionic sailors on horseback. This left Chios and Samos free for another generation at least, which makes the sage's remark admirably disinterested, for Samos was Priene's chief enemy. The two had quarrelled since early times over the area of Mykale; for Samos claimed a *peraia* there which encroached on Prienean territory and may have affected the control of the Panionia (above, p. 209). We hear of a great battle in which Samos lost a thousand men, and then – strange bedfellows – Samos and Miletos apparently joined to defeat Priene 'at the oak-tree'. Again, Bias negotiated the peace-terms. In the late 540s, when the Persians had defeated Lydia and were assaulting the Greek cities, he evidently felt that it was useless for the Ionians to try to hold out for ever against successive waves of barbarians, and accordingly he advised them (vainly) at the Panionion to emigrate and settle Sardinia as a common Ionic island with one capital city. So Priene became a Persian subject with the rest. In the Ionic Revolt she contributed twelve ships at Lade, no mean effort for a little country town.

Hardly anything is known in Archaic history of her eastern neighbour Myous on the gulf of the Maeander, except that she was noted for her fisheries. Kydrelos, a bastard son of the Attic king Kodros, was said to have founded her; his parentage could be merely a piece of imperial Athenian propaganda in the fifth century. She lay near enough to Miletos for their relations to be uneasy. Indeed, it is said that in their early wars truces were made only for the festival of Artemis at Miletos; and in Hellenistic times she was a Milesian dependency. The bay of Myous was large enough for the Ionic fleet of 200 ships to moor there in 499, but she could furnish only three ships at Lade. The lower temple-area has produced some fine relief-friezes and other sculpture (Pl. 45).[6]

The Central Cities: Ephesos; Kolophon and Smyrna (with Klazomenai); Teos and Phokaia

EPHESOS

Ephesos at the mouth of the Kaystros made no great mark in Archaic Greek history, perhaps because she absorbed more of the non-Greek element (Lydians and Leleges) around her. The terrain encouraged this; a direct route ran inland from Ephesos to Sardis, which was to become the first stage of the Persian 'Royal Road'. The chief cult was of an Anatolian goddess of fertility and wild creatures, whom the Ephesians interpreted as Artemis; the visible change was not great, for even late copies of the famous cult-statue show her still in the xoanon-stance, with multiple egg-shaped breasts, and clusters of animals modelled or painted on her dress. The precinct itself outside the city may go back to early times; the first stone temple was built during the first half of the sixth century, with a huge dipteral plan based probably on that of the Samian Heraion. Kroisos of Lydia contributed generously to the building costs, and dedicated some golden heifers there; his name may survive from the donors' inscriptions which once were written under the relief sculptures of the lowest column-drums. The temple's foundation deposit yielded some of the earliest Greek gold and silver 'dumps' and coins (c. 600), an invention copied from the Lydians. Indeed, a very early electrum stater and trite ($\frac{1}{3}$-stater) which show a dappled deer grazing and the name of the man who had the series struck ('of Phanes', Φάνεος) have now been identified as Ephesian or Halikarnassian (Pl. 40).

The royal line of Ephesos, the Basilidai, claimed descent from Androklos son of king Kodros of Athens, and in the Roman period it still provided the *basileus* for a vestigial office called 'the kingship of the Ionians', which carried certain traditional honours – front seats at all Games, the scarlet device of the royal clan, a tall staff, and the priesthood of Eleusinian Demeter. He is mentioned in a fourth-century inscription found on the site of the Panionion, along with other 'sceptre-bearing kings', and so it is tempting to ascribe to Ephesos some kind of leadership in the establishment of the Panionia, though Priene, which provided a 'priest', might also claim this. Androklos allegedly drove the Samians under their first king, Leogoros, into exile at Anaia, though they returned to Samos ten years later (above, p. 212).

About 640, when Gyges, the bulwark of Lydia against the marauding Kim-merioi, was killed by them, Lygdamis, their leader, attacked Ephesos as well as Magnesia inland, and burnt the Artemision. As Tyrtaios in Sparta exhorted the youth of the citizen-army to stand fast against the Messenian enemy, so in Ephesos Kallinos, another elegiac poet, exhorted the Ephesians against 'the host of terror-dealing Kimmerians'. A longer fragment may refer also to these foes, or (perhaps more likely) to the Greeks of Magnesia, north of Ephesos, who fought the Ephesians intermittently until Lygdamis wiped out Magnesia for a time. In words reminiscent of Hector's to Andromache, Kallinos offers the code of the aristocrat:

> Go headlong forward . . .
> since it is fated that no man miss death,
> not even with immortals for his forbears

and later:

> . . . as a tower the people look to him,
> for he does the work of many, alone.

The last line implies, among other things, that battles in Ionia did not as yet know the phalanx, but still worked in the Homeric way with duels of champions (*monomachiai*).

Following the standard pattern of early Greek governments, the royal clan had apparently taken over control of the city from their last king, for they were overthrown by one Pythagoras about the end of the seventh century. He proved a very harsh tyrant to the rich. After him came Melas (his son?), then Pindaros, then Melas son of Pindaros, who married the daughter of Alyattes. This will have staved off the threat of Lydian attacks for a time; but Alyattes' successor, Kroisos, exiled the next tyrant, Pindaros son of Melas, and renewed the war. He nearly reduced Ephesos, but the city resourcefully tied itself by a very long rope to the precinct of Artemis outside the walls; Kroisos respected the rights of this multiple suppliant – prudently, for the Kimmerians had been struck by a plague after burning that sanctuary, and the same punishment had befallen Alyattes after his army had burnt the temple of Athena at Assesos (above, p. 213).

Ephesos still had tyrants in the second half of the sixth century, of whom a pair named Komas and Athenagoras exiled their satiric fellow-citizen Hipponax to Klazomenai. Apart from railing and complaints, his poetry often refers to Lydian objects or phrases. The romantic tradition that because of a love-quarrel he hounded to suicide Boupalos and Athenis, the sons of the sculptor Archermos of Chios (below, p. 233), is probably false, the standard inferences of a later age, as is the anachronistic detail that they in their turn had made cruel 'portrait-statues' of him; probably they just sketched him in insulting detail on walls. The Greek portrait-statue proper does not antedate the fifth century (cf. Appendix II).

It is presumed that, as Ephesos had settled down under the rule of Lydia, so she accepted that of Persia when it came *c.* 545–540. In 499 the rebel Ionians mustered there, to take the road to Sardis. Koressos, a village in the area, provided guides, but Ephesos itself stayed neutral; and when the cause was lost at Lade in 494, the Ephesians massacred some of the men from damaged Chian ships who were making their way home by night through her territory, mistaking them, they alleged, for marauders because the Ephesian women happened to be celebrating the Thesmophoria at the time.[7]

KOLOPHON AND SMYRNA (WITH KLAZOMENAI)

Andraimon from Neleid Pylos was said to have founded Kolophon, with a later addition, apparently, of Attic Ionians led by two quarrelling sons of king Kodros. The Archaic city was not maritime; it lay about 8 miles inland on rising ground crowned by a steep citadel, and controlled a large, fertile plain which spread out on its east and south-east sides, in the bend of the river Kaystros. Hence most Kolophonians owned large farming estates and bred horses, and this oligarchic government, says Aristotle, was one of the few in which the rich governing class really did outnumber the poorer element. The horsebreeding and big estates suggest an aristocracy like that of the Thessalians but without their stolidity. The Kolophonians stand out in the fragments of their Archaic history as a spirited people, enterprising and resourceful, quite different in type from their neighbours in Ephesos. Before the end of the eighth century some Kolophonian political exiles, having settled down in Aiolic Smyrna, had taken over the city by a ruse, and had somehow persuaded the Smyrniotes to depart quietly with all their movable property and settle in with the other Aiolic cities who were their allies. Gyges of Lydia (*c.* 687–650) attacked Kolophon in his series of assaults on Greek cities, and captured the lower town; the reaction to this by some at least of these inlanders was to band together, sail off to the West, and settle by the river Siris in the new world of Great Hellas (Magna Graecia) between the Achaian colonies Sybaris and Metapontion. The poet Archilochos on Thasos noted this enviously, but did not join them (above, p. 51). Gyges' offensive against the Ionians slackened as the Kimmerian raids began to press him hard; and the remaining Kolophonians had resisted him fiercely, if we may judge by the unnamed man in a poem by Mimnermos (p. 225), who harassed the ranks of the Lydian horsemen with his long ashen spear.

About 600 Alyattes of Lydia renewed the attack on these cities. Once more, evidently, some Kolophonians left their country, to serve in Egypt as mercenaries to the Pharaoh; there is a signature by Pabis (*sic*) of Kolophon among the Greek soldiers who got 'beyond Kerkis as far as the river allowed' in the Ethiopian expedition of Psamtik II in 591 (p. 196). To the same Lydian offensive, presumably, belongs the great blow suffered by the Kolophonian cavalry when Alyattes proposed an alliance, with a tempting pay-offer for military service; when the horsemen came to the meeting, his Lydians assassinated them, and impounded the horses tethered outside the walls. But later authors preserved for us the proverb commemorating their reputation: 'to put the Kolophon on it', as the decisive factor in any battle.

Meanwhile Smyrna, the city of ex-Kolophonians, had undergone a long siege by Alyattes' troops. Her Archaic history has been ably reconstructed and presented since the detailed excavation of the site at Bayraklı outside modern İzmir. According to this, the type of monochrome pottery in the lowest strata confirms the tradition that the city was originally an Aiolic settlement on a peninsula; by the start of the eighth century the predominance of Geometric painted ware implies strongly that by then she was 'a thoroughly Ionic city', so that we should not be surprised at the Kolophonian takeover. If indeed she was rejected later on application to the Panionion, as Herodotos says, we can only guess at reasons: perhaps some assenting Aiolians had remained there, or perhaps Kolophon blocked the proposal because she herself had exiled these Ionians in the first place. Be that as it may, by the late eighth century Smyrna's import of luxuries had begun, attested to us by the presence of Chian wine-jars, Attic oil-amphorae and Dipylon-style vases, and soon by early Protocorinthian tableware; and during the seventh century the houses had spread outside the city walls on to the surrounding coastline. A precinct was made for a Hellenized native goddess, probably Artemis, as at Ephesos; and during the late seventh century a stone temple was started, with fine white tufa columns and capitals carved in a lotus-and-leaf pattern. But about 600 Alyattes' troops threw up a great earthen siege-mound to overlook the city walls, and Smyrna was at last taken and sacked. By the mid-sixth century she had recovered to some extent and was partly rebuilt, perhaps by the encouragement of Kroisos, since there is distinct evidence of Lydian inhabitants in the city at the time. She evidently submitted peacefully to Persia, and there is no evidence that she took any part in the Ionic Revolt, except for the puzzling fact that the whole site, though apparently flourishing, was abandoned in the early fifth century (on the archaeological evidence) – possibly, it is suggested, in the last stages of the revolt, when Klazomenai, her neighbour, was seized by Otanes, and that site too was abandoned. Of Archaic Klazomenai it may be said that otherwise we know hardly anything, except that her foundation story is interesting, because the people were said to be exiles from Kleonai and Phleious after the arrival there of the Dorians (above, p. 135). They settled first in Kolophon, and then, after two abortive moves (up to Mount Ida in the Troad, and down again to Kolophonian territory), moved up finally to the coast of the gulf of Smyrna not very far west of Smyrna itself. Their moment of glory came in Alyattes' general onslaught, when they beat back his troops from their walls. The site of the city has been identified with the island offshore to which the people migrated when the Persians were threatening them – not in the 540s, for the finds there continue into the early fifth century, but probably upon the failure of the Ionic Revolt. The most impressive sight there now is the stone causeway built over a hundred years later to link the coast and island. (Pls. 41, 43)

Thus Smyrna and Kolophon came under Lydia; and the Kolophonians then, if not indeed earlier, adopted the luxurious ways of the Lydians. Mimnermos, the Kolophonian poet of Smyrna in the seventh century, had recorded (perhaps himself typified) their two aspects, the brave one which fought the Lydians and the light one which enjoyed present pleasures; and Polymnestos, another Kolophonian poet, had also enjoyed this dual aspect as he found it in

Alkman's Sparta. But Xenophanes, the Kolophonian sage and poet (c. 565–470), scolded his people for their habits: they go to the assembly in scarlet cloaks, he says, with elegant hair-styles and scents, as they had learnt from the Lydians. He says also that they were 'in all a thousand, no less', which suggests that Kolophon had a type of oligarchy encountered elsewhere in Archaic Greece, in which the voting body was supposedly confined to this traditional number (as at eastern Lokris; see pp. 75, 238). Lydian rule cannot have seemed really alien to them, and they remained equally quiet under Persia.[8]

TEOS AND PHOKAIA

Teos and Klazomenai lay not far apart, on opposite sides of the big coastal spur which ended in Erythraian territory and the island of Chios offshore. Teos, on its southern side, might have become a new Panionion, if Thales' advice had been taken (above, p. 209); she was roughly central, and – who knows? – the ancient Teians may have had the same geniality to strangers as is attested for the people today. Traditionally their origin was mixed: Boiotians, Attic Ionians, Carians are all reported. The story of how she got the name Teos (τέως = 'while') goes back at least to the fifth century:

> Athamas [the Boiotian founder], returning from inland, found Area his daughter frisking round piling up stones (the ones now in Teos); he asked her: 'What are you doing?', and she said: '*While* you were hunting for where to build a city, I've found one'. This startled him, and he called the place Teos.

Little is known of her early history from the literary sources, but two inscriptions give valuable glimpses of a small, probably typical, Ionic oligarchy settled on its ancestral estates. One seems to be a list of landowners, and the estates are called *pyrgoi* (towers, or 'manors'), a term also used by ancient authors to describe the property of local landowners in Asia Minor in Classical times. Typical entries are: 'Seuches, of the *pyrgos* of Mystes; son [or descendant] of Eurymestor. Two ownerless [properties?]. Tharsunon, from the *pyrgos* of Hierys; son [or descendant] of Zorios'. The other inscription deals with all cases of persons unknown who have committed (or may commit) any crime against state or individual which carries the death penalty; it is called *The Cursing*, but is halfway to a law code, though it might have sounded rather antiquated to an Athenian archon at that date:

> Whoever works baneful spells upon the Teians, on state or individual, death to him and his seed. Whoever hinders the import of grain to Teian territory by any means or device, by sea or land, or re-exports any imported grain, death to him and his seed ... Whoever [disobeys?] or rises against a *euthunos* or *aisymnetes* of the Teians, death to him and his seed. Whoever in future as *aisymnetes* in Teos or Teian territory (?)wrongfully kills any man [– – –] or wittingly betrays the city or land of the Teians [– – –]. Whoever in future betrays [– – –], or counterfeits or receives counterfeits, or plunders or receives plunderers wittingly carrying [goods] from Teian land or waters, or

plots any ill for the Teian commonwealth wittingly in relation to either Greeks or natives, death to him and his seed. Any magistrates who do not do the cursing at the statue of Power [at three city festivals] are to be included in the curse.

A final curse follows on anyone damaging the stelai carrying these instructions.

Teos, with Phokaia and Klazomenai (above, p. 54), was among the nine cities which founded the Hellenion at Naukratis as the focal precinct for their deities. At Abou Simbel also, in 591 (above, p. 196), at least one Teian mercenary, called Hegesibios(?), was present who signed his name, rather badly, with the rest. He may have left Teos when Klazomenai and Kolophon were under attack by Alyattes, though we do not hear of an attack on Teos. But the Persian advance in the 540s inevitably came her way, and the Teians responded as the Phokaians, their kindred, had done, by leaving their city and making a new home on the site of Abdera in Thrace, a city once colonized by Klazomenai but snuffed out by the Thracians. In Teian hands the settlement survived, though some of them returned later to live in their old city again under the Persians. Anakreon, the lyric poet, one of this number, found a living at the court ot Polykrates in Samos. In the Ionic Revolt the city rose with the rest, and sent seventeen ships to Lade.

Phokaia, the northernmost of the Ionic cities, had ties with Teos. She lay just north of the Hermos in Aiolic territory. The first settlers chose this spot presumably because it has a fine double harbour, the approach protected by a flock of islets resembling seals sufficiently to suggest how the city may have got her name and put a seal (phokos) as a canting device on her coinage. Certainly the traditional view, that the settlers came from Phokis in mainland Greece, led by Athenians (the inevitable Kodridai), sounds unlikely. On the other hand, they were not allowed to join the Panionion until Teos and Erythrai sent rulers to the city. Perhaps in any case Phokaia could not be accepted until Smyrna to her south had become Ionic. Could it be, in fact, that Teos and Erythrai 'ionicized' the hybrid settlers at Phokaia in the same manner as Kolophon had 'ionicized' Smyrna?

The Phokaians in their pentekonters were the most daring pioneers at sea of all the mainland Ionians. They founded Lampsakos on the Hellespont c. 615. By the end of the seventh century they were on the track of the Spanish silver-mines which Kolaios of Samos had discovered a generation earlier. Apparently they did not go by the southern route along the Libyan coast, but used the Sicilian straits through the friendship of the Rhegines (who helped them further after Alalia; below, p. 228), and then proceeded up the Italic coast and across to Corsica (Kyrnos), where they founded a settlement, Alalia, c. 565. Here the etesian winds blowing westwards would take ships across the western Mediterranean to the Balearic islands off the coast of Spain. Thence the Phokaians worked round Spain to the silver-rooted Tartessos, where the local king, Arganthonios, traded them silver, probably tin also from the north-west of the peninsula, and perhaps ingots of ready-made Tartessian bronze. Returning across the western Mediterranean against the wind, presumably they hugged its northern coastline, and thus c. 600 Massalia was founded on a site at the Rhône delta where traces of Greek trading activity go back to the eighth century. Massalia grew into a prosperous city governed for centuries on rigid oligarchic principles under Ionic laws which probably reflected those of her metropolis in the sixth century (above, pp. 43–4). Both cities colonized jointly in north-east Spain about the part called Emporion (modern Ampurias), and it is not clear to us always to which metropolis a place belonged. Nor does the tale of Phokaian business enterprise cease there. Along with their Ionic colleagues Teos, Klazomenai, and Chios they were among the Greek cities which founded the great *emporion* at Naukratis.

Herodotos records no Lydian aggression against Phokaia. But she built strong walls (traditionally with gifts from Arganthonios) when the Persians had conquered Lydia and were directly threatening the Greeks. The Ionic cities, except Miletos, sent a deputation to Sparta, the strongest mainland power, for military aid, and its spokesman was Pythermos, a Phokaian, whose eloquence had some effect; for though Sparta gave no troops, she sent a pentekonter back to Phokaia with an ambassador named Lakrinas, who went to Cyrus at Sardis and told him that Sparta would not allow him to harm any Greek city. According to Herodotos, Cyrus' reply was that this Sparta, whatever it was, would have troubles of its own soon enough – a threat against Greece, but a vain boast at the time, for the Persians had as yet no subject-fleet. Phokaia was the first city to be besieged by Cyrus' general Harpagos, who used a siege-mound. Harpagos offered her 24 hours to accept the equivalent of peace with honours and dependency; she should give only tokens of surrender, one tower in the wall and one building in the city. But the Phokaians used the hours to load their pentekonters with their families and possessions, and sailed over to neighbouring Chios, still free, where they hoped to buy some offshore islands, the Oinoussai, for a new settlement. The Chians refused; Herodotos says that they feared Phokaian trading competition. So the Phokaians made a lightning return, caught the Persian garrison off guard, and cut it down. Then they sank an iron weight in the sea and made a pledge never to return until the iron floated (apparently an Ionic form of naval pledge, since the Delian League repeated it in 478). Less than half of them, however, sailed thence, for the rest, having seen their city again, could not bring themselves to leave it. The exiles settled with their compatriots at Alalia, but were forced to leave Corsica after five years under the attacks of the allied Carthaginian and Etruscan fleet; finally, after a sojourn in friendly Rhegion, they made a permanent home at Velia (Elea) on the west coast of Italy in Oinotrian territory north of Poseidonia. We hear no more of Phokaia as an Ionic sea-power, and it may be that Persia retaliated severely after the massacre of the garrison, for though Phokaia evidently joined in the Ionic Revolt, she could only send three ships to Lade.[9]

The Northern Cities: Erythrai and Chios

ERYTHRAI

The foundation legends admitted that Erythrai was of mixed population. After a mysterious Cretan settlement under an *oikistes* 'Erythros', one Knopos, allegedly of the Attic Kodridai, collected settlers there from other parts of Ionia. It was even believed that he had imported a Thessalian priestess, who helped to win the site from the existing occupants by doping the sacrificial bull, with startling results.

Since the island of Chios blocked Erythrai's exit to the Aegean, one might infer a mutual hostility. Certainly they disputed over the administration of an ancient cult of Herakles, and Erythrai won; and again, when Hippoklos, king of Chios and so presumably of early date, was killed in a drunken fight by the bridegroom's party at a wedding, the party was exiled for blood-guilt and went to a place called Leukonia, which 'the Koroneis [unidentified] had formerly taken from [the Chians?] and held, with Erythraians'. Erythrai, further described as the most powerful state in Ionia at the time, fought the Chian settlers over this place and finally forced them to leave on honourable terms. If Leukonia was itself on the island of Chios and the Koroneis and Erythraians had got a foothold there at this early time, the enmity is not surprising. But a change of government brought temporary friendship. At some time probably in the seventh century Erythrai was under the rule of three men, Ortyges, Iros, and Echaros, who had killed a certain Knopos and seized power, aided by two men who then ruled Chios, Amphiklos and Polyteknos. All five men are described as 'tyrants', which must be technically incorrect, since a tyrant rules alone; perhaps one may infer here the wording of contemporary lampoons (below, pp. 230–1). At all events, the trio with their party ruled Erythrai tyrannically. They allowed no citizen within the walls, holding all law-courts outside the city gates. Their luxurious habits – wearing scarlet, jewellery, false curls, and travelling in litters – suggest that, like the Kolophonians, they copied the Lydian fashions; but not for long, because, like Athens's tyrannicides later, Hippotas, brother of Knopos, killed them at a festival, and so freed Erythrai. This Knopos, we assume, was not the alleged founder but the last ruler of the royal family. Hippotas could hardly have hoped to put the clock back to monarchy, so perhaps it was he who established the ex-royal clan, the Basilidai, in a narrow but able oligarchy which, Aristotle says, ruled Erythrai until 'the demos' forced a change of constitution. When oligarchy thus took over, the Chians evidently reverted to antagonism; they were foes again before the early sixth century, for Chios helped Miletos then (against Alyattes of Lydia) because previously Miletos had helped Chios 'to bring to an end the war against [i.e., to defeat?] Erythrai'. Clearly, any political change in either city affected its relations with the other. Indeed it has been suggested that the Lelantine War (above, pp. 64–7) was at the bottom of it all: Erythrai under Knopos *may* have been pro-Chalkis, which would make the later 'tyrants' turn her pro-Eretria, i.e., pro-Miletos and Miletos' friend Chios; hence Erythrai and Miletos jointly colonize Parion, Erythrai helps Miletos in an aristocratic war with Naxos, and votes *against* Chalkis in settling a Chalkis-Andros dispute (above, pp. 183–4).

Nothing is recorded of her relations to either the Lydian or the Persian aggressors in the sixth century, so presumably she offered no notorious resistance or support; but she joined the Ionic Revolt, sending eight ships to Lade which were drawn up to fight alongside the Chian squadron.

Perhaps the most enduring non-Greek element in Erythrai's origins was her famous Sibyl. The noun has no obvious Greek derivation. Erythrai's Herophile is the first sibyl recorded in extant Greek literature, and it is thought that both the word and the type, the prophetess speaking riddles in ecstasy from a cavern, may have originated in Asia Minor and arrived at Cumae in Italy with the Aiolic immigrants in the eighth century B.C. According to some utterances which were found inscribed in a spring-house of the second century A.D., Erythrai's line of sibyls still existed at that date.[10]

CHIOS

The island of Chios is over half the size of Attica, and only a few of her settlements have yet been excavated. The ancient capital underlies the modern one, facing the Asian coast. The Chian poet and gossip-writer Ion (*c.* 480–422) wrote a prose *Foundation of Chios*, admitting its Hellenization to be comparatively late: after the rule of Agelas(?) and Melas, grandsons of Poseidon and a local nymph, he says, Oinopion of Crete settled there with his five sons, along with some Carians and Abantes from Euboia. Then a Greek influx led by one Amphiklos from Histiaia in northern Euboia seized the kingship from this family and held it, and the fourth king after Amphiklos was Hektor, who expelled the Abantes and Carians and got Chios accepted as a member of the Panionion, presumably because Euboia was Ionic.

That the Chian Greeks should have come from Euboia sounds, geographically, quite likely and the date of their arrival has been inferred from a Chian tombstone dated *c.* 450 on its lettering, which records one Heropythos and his direct forebears for fourteen generations back. On an average of thirty years to a generation the first ancestor, Kyprios, would have been born *c.* 900; if we visualize him joining the exodus with Amphiklos *c.* 875, this would fit roughly with the archaeologists' reports that as yet no Protogeometric pottery is recorded on Chios, though there is both Mycenean and Geometric.

One of the kings, whether earlier or later than Hektor, was Hippoklos (above, p. 229), who was killed at a wedding-party, after which the exiled murderers and their kindred settled in a place called Leukonia, whence they were driven finally by the Erythraians who had previously lived there. This raises an interesting point. The natural inference is that Leukonia was on the Asian coast and that Chios was establishing a *peraia* at Erythrai's expense; but later evidence implies a place of that name on Chios, which would mean that in Hippoklos' time parts of the island were still independent of the capital city and that Erythrai had actually managed to get a foot on the island. The next rulers of whom we hear were the two 'tyrants' Amphiklos and Polyteknos, who helped to install three 'tyrants' at Erythrai (above, p. 229). The name Amphiklos recurring here suggests that after kingship had ended, the royal clan took over the offices of government; if this were so, then any individual member who held the chief office for a long period and behaved intemperately (like the *prytanis* at Miletos; above, p. 210) could, with his brothers in office, be labelled *tyrannoi* by contemporaries, as was Hipparchos, brother of the tyrant Hippias at Athens – though Thucydides demonstrated that Hipparchos was wrongly so called – and Pittakos at Mytilene. Thus, when late authors writing on early Ionic history describe one man, or a group, as *tyrannos* or *tyrannoi*, perhaps they were relying on surviving verses which, like the lampoons of Alkaios or the Attic *skolia,* had labelled thus a hated figure or members of his family, whatever his actual title might have been. At all events, Chios and Erythrai were friendly during this 'tyrannic' phase; but early in the sixth century Chios helped Miletos against Alyattes because previously Miletos had helped Chios to end a war against Erythrai. This last war has been interpreted as remote, part of the old Lelantine War (above, pp. 64–7); but there is also a ready place for it here, in the gap between the 'tyrannic' friendship and the reign of Alyattes.

Until the famous 'Chian Laws' of *c.* 575–550 the constitutional history of Chios is little known to us. Her social and economic life is slightly better documented. Her wine had early gained a reputation (hence, it is thought, the name, true, or not, of her first king, Oinopion), for by the end of the eighth century the tall white Chian amphorae had arrived at Smyrna (above, p. 225); and at some time in the seventh century Chians sailed north to the Thracian coast and founded Maroneia in the area of Ismaros, already known for its wine and possessing good arable soil inland behind its hills. To set off their city's wine the Chian potters of the seventh and sixth centuries made chalices as delicate as Chinese porcelain, flared like the lotus flower, with red lotuses painted inside on a black ground and a white ground outside decorated with a single motif sketched in black (Pl. 44). The mass of this ware found in the precinct of Aphaia at Aigina suggests that these two islands had a trade-link in the Archaic period. Both were members of Naukratis, where much Chian ware has also been found. More links with the foreign nations east and south were revealed when the excavations at modern Emporio, a harbour in the south-east of the island, brought to light a small but flourishing town, settled at first on a hill (*c.* 700–600), with a walled acropolis containing a *megaron* (seventh-century or possibly even earlier) and a temple to Athena, where the offerings included Eastern wares – faience, scarabs, Cypriot figurines, and wide Phrygian bronze belts, offered probably by girls on marriage. Perhaps slaves were shipped in there too. In this large island there must have been many big estates. The Chians were known in Classical times for the number of slaves used in their economy. Most came probably from the Asian mainland; Chian slave-traffickers co-operated with the Lydians in this, with a central mart at Sardis.

The 'Chian Laws', a broken stele found south of the town, provide a glimpse of an east Greek constitution in the first half of the sixth century, showing that the winds of change blowing in Athens in Solon's time were blowing in at least one other Ionic city. The best-preserved section says:

> [. . .] verdict appealed against [. . .]; and if he has been wronged in the *demarchos*' court, let him [deposit *x*] staters, and appeal to the council of the *demos.* On the ninth day of every month the council of the *demos* is to assemble, with power to exact penalties; elected, fifty from each tribe. It is to transact the other affairs of the *demos,* and to [pass?] final [judgement on?] all verdicts which have been appealed against during the past month . . .

As in Athens after Solon's laws, so the high magistrates here are no longer supreme in their courts. The rights of appeal against their verdicts have been granted to the *demos,* the whole citizen-body. Chios must already have had the

traditional council of elders common to Archaic Greek oligarchies. Was this
council of the *demos* first created now, its duties specified only vaguely (at least, in
the surviving lines), except for the most important one? Or did this council
already exist to 'transact the affairs of the *demos*', duties known and thus not
specified here, but did it only now acquire this additional, powerful right? And
did it transfer the actual decision-making mostly to the assembly? Or (as the language would seem to imply, though the last, crucial main verb is partly missing)
was the assembly's power of decision in its day-to-day business vested effectively
in these its representatives? Yet some comparison with Solon's new Council of
Four Hundred seems inevitable: perhaps that council too 'transacted the affairs
of the *demos*', and even, possibly, acted as the new court of appeal, although the
Ath. Pol. gives this newly won power to 'the jury-courts' ($\tau\grave{\alpha}$ $\delta\iota\kappa\alpha\sigma\tau\acute{\eta}\rho\iota\alpha$, here an
anachronistic term usually interpreted to mean in fact the *ekklesia*). Indeed, our
speculation may range further and ask whether, as in Athens, in Chios too the
high magistracies were now being opened to rich men hitherto barred from the
closed ruling circle of families. Some of these magistracies are indeed mentioned
in the other fragments of text: somebody is 'guarding the *rhetrai* [enactments]
of the *demos*'. (*Nomophylakia* was a traditional duty of the Areiopagites at Athens.)
Also, 'if while *demarchos* or *basileus* a man (?)accepts bribes, he is to pay over
[*x* staters, sacred] to Hestia', duly exacted by a financial officer. But whether this
caution is spelt out here because the pool of candidates is indeed now widened,
or simply because some Chian Hesiod has at last had his point taken concerning
gift-swallowing *basileis*, is quite uncertain.

In the early sixth century Chios with her navy had defied the landlocked power
of Lydia by helping Miletos (above, p. 231); but in the 540s she evidently submitted with the other islands to the Persians, for twice she supported them. When
Cyrus had left the conquered Lydia and Ionia, a Lydian named Paktyes started
a revolt, which failed, and consequently he was smuggled as a suppliant to
Kyme in Aiolis, thence to Mytilene, and thence to the Chians, who were persuaded to hand him over to the Persians in exchange for a *peraia*, the district
Atarneus in Mysia. They recognized it as bought with blood-money, for they
never used the grain from its fields for any religious purpose. Again, when exiled
Phokaians who had killed a Persian garrison sought to buy the Oinoussai islands,
Chios refused. Undoubtedly, as Herodotos says, she suspected that a nest of
these bold traders so near her would damage her own trading; but perhaps she
feared also to antagonize the Persians. In the Ionic Revolt, however, the next
generation of Chians showed no such caution. At the start they ejected their
tyrant, Strattis, and sheltered some Paionian clans from Macedon who, exiled
by Megabazos in 512 to the Phrygian hinterland, now made a dash for freedom
and, helped also by the Lesbians, got back to Paionia. When the tide of the revolt
was turning *c.* 495, after the ringleader, Aristagoras, had fled, Chios received his
uncle, Histiaios, in the belief that he intended to carry on the offensive. Even
when his own Milesians had rejected him, the Chians took him in again, but
refused to let him take any of their ships; so he moved on to Lesbos and, with
eight Lesbian triremes, made for the Hellespont and held up all Ionic shipping
there. Because of his actions later, it does not look as if this was a genuine attempt
to raise an anti-Persian fleet. At Lade a hundred Chian triremes formed the

largest squadron in the fleet, each carrying forty picked hoplites as marines. They fought as long as any other ships stayed by them, cutting through the Phoenician line to ram the enemy vessels broadside on; in the end those which stayed afloat got home to Chios, but the crews of the crippled ships, landing at Mykale, were cut down by the Ephesians (above, p. 224). It was, says Herodotos, a year of death for Chios. Earlier, all but two of a hundred boys sent to compete as a choir at Delphi had died there of some infectious disease, and shortly afterwards a defective school building collapsed and killed all but one of 120 children. Then came the defeat at Lade, and immediately after it Histiaios and his eight Lesbian ships returned to Chios, massacred those who resisted him, and seized the weakened island. Thasos and Lesbos itself, faced by the same threat, were saved because the Persian general Harpagos caught Histiaios on a foraging expedition to the adjacent mainland, and summarily executed him as a leader of the revolt. Herodotos tells us without comment that he had been about to harvest the corn of Atarneus.

In the next year the Persians netted Chios as they had done once in Samos (above, p. 218), before proceeding northwards to do the same to Lesbos and Tenedos. Evidently they replaced the quisling Strattis as *tyrannos*, for late in 480, after the Greek victory at Salamis, six Chians, refugees after an abortive attempt to assassinate him, sought out the Greek fleet off Aigina and urged it to sail at once and lead the Ionians against the Persians. This could not be done at once, but a year later, after the victory at Mykale, Chios was one of the first Ionic states to join the Greek alliance.[11]

Chios produced a famous technician and an equally renowned family of marble-sculptors. The technician was Glaukos (fl. *c.* 600?), traditionally the first Greek to discover how to weld or solder iron plates and rods together, instead of the more primitive nailing or rivetting. A masterpiece long survived at Delphi, dedicated there by Alyattes: a tall openwork stand to hold a silver cauldron, with 'little human figures wrought in it, and animals and plants'. The marble-sculptors were the great Archermos (fl. *c.* 560–550?) and his sons Boupalos and Athenis. Archermos made a famous flying Nike; according to one tradition he was the first sculptor to attempt this difficult theme. It was dedicated on Delos by one Mikkiades (whose name also occurs on the fragmentary base of a lost work on Paros), presumably for some victory there in the Panionian festival. The statue itself was discovered there in 1877, with part of its rectangular plinth carrying the verse dedication; details are uncertain, but Archermos' signature is clear: 'by the skill of Archermos' (statue, Pl. 42). Winged both fore and aft, the Nike races through the air; in fact she must have been attached to the plinth by the long central fold of her skirt, but foreshortening helped to hide this, for the plinth was originally mounted on a pillar. 'Archermos of Chios' also signed a column on the Athenian Acropolis which once carried a marble statue; but the lettering is of the late sixth century, so possibly this was a grandson, child of Boupalos or Athenis. No sculptures by this pair survive, but Hipponax of Ephesos ensured that they should live in his savage lampoons, particularly Boupalos:[12]

> Hold my wraps while I black his eye
> – I never miss, I'm ambidextrous,

NOTES

The following books, basic for the study of the eastern Greeks, are referred to by their authors' names only: C. Roebuck, *Ionian Trade and Colonization* (1959); J. M. Cook, *The Greeks in Ionia and the East* (1962); G. L. Huxley, *The Early Ionians* (1966); G. E. Bean, *Aegean Turkey: an Archaeological Guide* (1966); J. Boardman, *The Greeks Overseas*[2] (1973).

1 Greek notes on Carians: Pherekydes *FGH* 3 F 155, Thuc. 1. 8,1; mercenaries, Archil. F 216 West, Hdt. 2. 152–4 (Egypt). Script and language: See O. Masson, *Bull. de la Soc. de Linguistique de Paris* 68 (1973), 187 ff. Ionic climate, sub-dialects, Carian wives: Hdt. 1. 142 and 142,2. The Panionia: H. T. Wade-Gery, *The Poet of the Iliad* (1952), 2ff. War with Melia: Vitruv., *De architectura* 4. 1,3–5; inscriptions, C. B. Welles, *Royal Correspondence in the Hellenistic Period* (1934), no. 7; *FGH* 491 and 535 F1; archaeology, Bean, 216 ff.; cf. Huxley, 47 f. and for a detailed discussion G. Kleiner, P. Hommel, and W. Müller-Wiener, *Panionion und Melie* (1967). Appeal to Sparta: Hdt. 1. 141, 152–3,1; Thales 170,3. The Panionion: Roebuck, 24 ff. and *CP* 50 (1955), 24 ff.

2 Early Miletos: Conon *FGH* 26 F 1, xliv, Nic. Damasc. *FGH* 90 Frr. 52–3; Huxley, 50 f. *Prytanis*: Arist., *Pol.* 1305a, 1310b. Colonies: Huxley, 64 ff. Gyges and Abydos: see for recent views Graham, *JHS* 91 (1971), 41 f. Cold winters: Str. 307. Dress à la Thrace: K. F. Johansen, *The Attic Grave-reliefs* (1951), 97. Sybaris and Miletos: Hdt. 6. 21,1. Early history of Didyma and statues: K. Tuchelt, *Die archaischen Skulpturen v. Didyma* (1970). Fort Miletos: Str. 801. Necho: Hdt. 2. 159,3; inscriptions, Rehm, *Didyma* II (1958). Lydian attacks: Hdt. 1. 7–27. Paros: Archil. F 192 West and p. 183 (arbitration). Chios: Hdt. 1. 18,3. Miletos, excavations: see now *Istanb. Mitt.*, 1968 onwards.

3 Early Samos: Paus. 7.4,2–3. Date of Ameinokles: see above, p. 159, n. 2. Imports to Heraion: see B. Freyer-Schauenberg, *Elfenbein aus der sam. Heraion* (1966); Walter, *Samos* 5 (1968; Cypriot pottery among the 7th-c. Samian); G. Schmidt, *Samos* 7 (1968), statues from Cyprus; U. Jantzen, *Samos* 8 (1971), bronzes from Egypt, Assyria, Syria, and elsewhere. Kolaios: Hdt. 4. 151–2. Spartan complaints: Hdt. 3. 47. Amphikrates: Hdt. 3. 59,4. Aigina and Epidauros: Hdt. 5. 83. Alyattes and Miletos: Hdt. 1. 17–22. Thrasyboulos and Sikyon: Frontinus, *Strat.* 3. 9,7 – an event not recorded elsewhere. Kroisos' gifts to Greek oracular sites: Hdt. 1. 50–52, 92. Stasis in Miletos: Hdt. 5. 28–9; Plut., *QG* 32; at this early date a *hetaireia* called 'Labour' seems to me unlikely. Kroisos and the oracles: Hdt. 1. 46–9.

4 Demoteles, the Geomoroi, and Perinthos: Plut., *QG* 57. Theory of Aiakes as tyrant, see M. White, *JHS* 74 (1954), 36 ff. and cf. Meiggs and Lewis no. 16 (the dedication by one Aeakes (*sic*) of a seated statue to Hera at Samos. The inscription appears to say that as an *epistates* (some kind of overseer?) he 'exacted the booty' for Hera (from the spoils of privateering); but this is uncertain). Successive temples: see Boardman, *AntJ*. 39 (1959), 175 ff., 199 ff.; G. Grube in Berve and Gruben, *Greek Temples, Theatres and Shrines* (1963), 447 ff. Geneleos' group: see most recently Richter, *Korai*, nos. 67–9, with photographs and references to E. Buschor's basic publications in *Altsam. Standbilder* II and V (1934, 1961); she rejects no. 69 from the group. Rhoikos and Theodoros: Hdt. 1. 51, 2; 3. 41,1 and 60,4; all refs. of later writers, Overbeck, *SQ* nn. 262, 273–93. Early tyranny: latest discussion, Schmidt, *AM* 87 (1972), 181 ff.

5 Islands submit to Persia: Hdt. 1. 169,2 (qualified in Thuc. 1. 13,6). Polykrates' career: Hdt. 3. 39–46, 54–7, 60, 120–6. Samainai: Plut., *Per.* 26,3; description, Hesych. s.v. *Samiakos tropos*. Skias: Paus. 3. 12, 10. Samian exiles: Hdt. 3. 57–9. Delos: cf. Parke, *CQ* 40 (1946), 106 ff. (Thuc. 3. 104,2); Huxley, 126. Theory of Rhodes as a dependency: see Bowra, *GLP*[2], 249 ff.; but cf. J. Labarbe, *Ant. Class.* 31 (1962), 186

n.125 and esp. J. Barron, *CQ* 58 (1964), 219 f. Tunnel and mole: Hdt. 3. 60. Maiandrios' career: Hdt. 3. 142–9. Hdt. calls him an *astos*, which *may* have here the meaning 'commoner' as opposed to aristocrat (cf. Pindar, *Pyth.* 3. 71); his enemies called him ill-born (Hdt. 3. 142), but in the same chapter all the Samians whom he addresses, including his denigrator Telesarchos, are called *astoi* by Hdt. I would think that Hdt. here uses the term broadly for 'citizens', which in 6th-c. Samos presumably meant oligarchs. Maiandrios was not offering democracy, but fair play to all *citizens*. On *isonomia* in this passage see however Ostwald, *Nomos and the Beginnings of Athenian Democracy* (1969), 107 ff. The red cloak: Hdt. 3. 139–40. Parian arbitration: Hdt. 5. 28–9. Histiaios' services and reward: Hdt. 4. 137–41 and 5. 23. The Revolt: Hdt. 5. 30–8, 49–55, 97–126. Modern theory of Aristagoras' high motives: G. B. Grundy, *The Great Persian War* (1901). Settlement by Mardonios: Hdt. 6. 43; Ostwald argues that it was true democracy (op. cit., 109 f., 167, 179).

6 Priene: foundation, Str. 633, Paus. 7. 2,10; cf. Cook, 90; Huxley, 27; Bean, 197 f. Bias' Theban ancestry: Phanodikos *FGH* 397 F 4b. Alyattes' siege: D. Laert. 1. 5,2(83). Pamphaes: N. Dam., *FGH* 90 F 65.4 and Ael., *VH* 4. 27. Bias and Kroisos: Hdt. 1. 27. The Oak battle: Plut., *QG* 20. Sardinia: Hdt. 1. 170. 'Little country town': see the excellent description of Priene in Cook, loc. cit. Myous: Str. 633; Paus. 7. 2, 10–11; H. Weber, *Istanb. Mitt.* 15 (1965), 43 ff., 17 (1967), 128 ff. Truces with Miletos: Huxley, 49.

7 Artemision: H. Berve and G. Gruben, *Greek Temples, Theatres and Shrines* (1963), 456 ff; cf. Bean, 162 and pl. 36 (statue). Kroisos' offerings: Hdt. 1. 92,1; fragments of sculptured column-drums and inscriptions, A. W. Lawrence, *Greek and Roman Sculpture* (1972), 93, 333. Foundation deposit: P. Jacobsthal, *JHS* 71 (1951), 85 ff. (small objects) and E. S. G. Robinson, ibid., 156 ff. (coins and dumps). Coins of Phanes: see now Kraay, *Arch. and Class. Greek Coins* (1976), 23: Ephesos or Halikarnassos? Ephesos–Sardis road: Hdt. 5. 54; 6. 84; 8. 103. Basilidai and *Basileus*: Pherekydes, *FGH* 3 F 155; 4th-c. inscription, Kleiner *et al.*, *Panionion und Melie*, 45 ff.; it regulates the money-dues and fines to be administered by the 'kings', and perquisites for the priest; cf. for the general problems Momigliano, *Atti del III Congresso Nazionale di Studi Romani* (1934), 429 ff. and Roebuck, 31 and *CP* 50 (1955), 26 ff. Priene's priest: Str. 384, 639. Lygdamis' attacks: Callim., *Hymn.* 3. 251–8; Kallinos Frr. 5 and 1 West. Hector's speech: *Il.* 6. 486–9. Pythagoras: Baton, *FGH* 268 F 3; stemma of the tyrants, see *CAH* III, 518 f. Kroisos' attack: Hdt. 1. 26. Boupalos and Athenis: see above, p. 233; exile of Hipponax, Suda (s.v.). Ephesos and the Revolt: Hdt. 5. 100–1, 6. 16.

8 Foundation of Kolophon: Mimnerm. F 9 West; Paus. 7. 3,3. Geographic position: Roebuck, 11. Horses: Str. 643 (Strabo also mentions naval power, but this is otherwise unattested). Oligarchy: Arist., *Pol.* 1290b. Takeover of Smyrna, Mimnerm., loc. cit., Hdt. 1. 150; date, cf. Paus. 5. 8, 7 (Smyrna already Ionic in 688) and Cook (below). Gyges' attack: Hdt. 1. 14. Siris: Str. 264; Dunbabin, *The Western Greeks*, 34. Unnamed man: Mimnerm. F 14. Kolophonian mercenaries: Meiggs and Lewis no. 7; Hdt. 2. 161. Murder of the horsemen: Polyaen., *Strat.* 7. 2,1–2. Proverb: Str. 643. History of Archaic Smyrna: see J. M. Cook, *BSA* 53–4 (1958–59), 11 ff., on which the above account is based. Rejection by Panionion: Hdt. 1. 143,3. Artemis at Smyrna: Cook, *BSA* 53–4, 12 n.4 and Jeffery, *BSA* 59 (1964), 39. Klazomenai seized by Otanes: Hdt. 5. 123; her foundation, Paus. 7. 3, 9; repulse of Alyattes, Hdt. 1. 16. For the site see Bean, 129 ff. Polymnestos: see Huxley, 53. Xenophanes' comments: F3 West. Mimnermos a Smyrniote: see Cook, *BSA* 53–4, 28.

9 Teian origins: Paus. 7. 3,6; foundation-story: Pherekydes *FGH* 3 F102; friendliness, Cook, 90, and Bean, 136. Landowners' list: see D. Hunt, *JHS* 67 (1947), 68 ff. *The Cursing*: Meiggs and Lewis no. 30. Naukratis: Hdt. 2. 178. Abdera: Hdt. 1. 168. A Hyperborean creature, the griffin, appears on the coins of both Teos and Abdera, which are believed to have started *c.* 540: see J. Balcer, *Schweiz. num. Rundschau* 47 (1968), 5 ff. Site and name of Phokaia: see Bean, 119. Alleged Phokaian origin: N. Damasc., *FGH* 90 F 51; Paus. 7. 3,10. Lampsakos: Charon *FGH* 262 F 7; Roebuck, 113. Phokaians in Spain: Hdt. 1. 163; the trade-winds, Poseidonios ap. Str. 143; see Carpenter, *The Greeks in Spain*, 12 ff. A Phokaian silver coin was among those in

the foundation deposit of the Artemision at Ephesos (Roebuck, 55); thanks to her Tartessian market, she may well have been among the first cities to coin money. Tin and bronze cargoes: Roebuck, 97. On Massalia, see most recently Boardman, 210 ff. Pythermos and Lakrinas: Hdt. 1. 152. Phokaians and Persians: Hdt. 1. 162–4, 3. Settlements at Alalia and Velia: Hdt. 1. 167.

10 Foundation: Str. 633; Paus. 7. 3,7; the priestess, Polyaen., *Strat.* 8. 43. Cult of Herakles: Paus. 7. 5,5–8; for the type as on coins of Erythrai see Bean, 154 and pl. 60, no. 5. Story of Hippoklos: Plut., *De mul. virt.* 3 (= *Mor.* 244e–245a) and Polyaen. 8. 66; cf. P. Stadter, *Plutarch's Historical Method* (1965), 41 ff. Leukonia would be interpreted most naturally as in Erythraian territory (so Huxley, 49), but Thuc. 8. 24,3 records a Leukonion on Chios, and cf. M. Sakellariou, *La Migration grecque en Ionie* (1958), 197; Chios is a large island, and the city may have had no control over some parts of it at this time. In Plutarch's account the people from whom Leukonia was taken by the Koroneis and Erythraians can only be Chians; but admittedly that would not preclude its being a mainland site near Erythrai, seized at an early date by Chios as her *peraia*, retaken by the Koroneis and Erythrai, and finally seized once more by the Chian exiles. Story of Knopos' murder and the tyranny: Hippias of Erythrai (*FGH* 421 F 1). Oligarchy of Basilidai: Arist., *Pol.* 1305b. Chios helps Miletos against Alyattes: Hdt. 1. 18,3. Connection with Lelantine War: see W. G. Forrest, *Historia* 6 (1957), 168 f., n.9. Parion (708 B.C.?): Str. 588 and see Forrest, op. cit., 170 n.1. The Naxos war: Andriskos (*FGH* 500 F 1); Plut., *De mul. virt.* 17 (= *Mor.* 254b–f). Chalkis–Andros dispute: Plut., *QG* 30. Erythraian sibyl: see Huxley, *GRBS* 2 (1959), 95; J. Pollard, *BSA* 55 (1960), 198 f.; H. Parke, *Greek Oracles* (1967), 49 ff.; and Bean, 156 f.

11 Ion of Chios: *FGH* 392 F 1. Cf. Wilamowitz, *Sb. Ak. Berlin* (1906), 38 ff. and 59 ff., who put Amphiklos *c.* ?800–750, and Wade-Gery, *The Poet of the Iliad* (1952), 6 ff. (Amphiklos *c.* 900 or a little earlier?). On the occurrence of the name Hektor in both the *Iliad* and the Chian king-list see ibid., 7. The gravestone of Heropythos: ibid., 8 ff., fig. 1 (correcting the misprinted texts in *SGDI* 5656 and *DGE* 690). The Protogeometric gap: Desborough, *The Last Myceneans and Their Successors* (1964), 159, and *The Greek Dark Ages* (1972), 366; Boardman, 27 ff. The tyrants: above, p. 236, n. 10. Hipparchos: Thuc. 6.52. Chian wine at Smyrna: Cook, above, n. 8. Maroneia (Ismaros): cf. *Il.* 9. 71–2, *Od.* 9. 196–8; Archil. F 2D; cf. Roebuck, 106 and Boardman, 237. Chian chalices: Boardman, 120 f.; in Aigina, Boardman, *BSA* 51 (1956), 55 ff.; Roebuck, 83 f.; at Naukratis, Boardman, 120 f. Emporio: Boardman, *Greek Emporion* (1967); *The Greeks Overseas²*, 72 f., 80, 87 f. Slave-traffic: Hdt. 8. 105; Thuc. 8. 40,2; cf. Roebuck, 108 n. 19. The 'Chian Laws': see Meiggs and Lewis no. 8. In the first section here quoted, 'in the demarchos' court' may apply either to the wronging, or to the depositing of staters; I see no way of deciding. In the discussion here I have followed my own belief that this council itself judged the appeal cases; but for the view that it acted only probouleutically, that is, sieving cases to send to the *ekklesia* for judgement, see Wade-Gery, *Essays*, 198 f. and Forrest, *Emergence*, 166. Chios and Paktyes: Hdt. 1. 160; and the Phokaians, 1. 164–5; and the Paionians, 5. 98; and Histiaios, 6. 2,5; at Lade, 6. 15–16. The disasters to Chios and the death of Histiaios: Hdt. 6. 26–30; netting of Chios, 6. 31. The six conspirators: Hdt. 8. 132. Chios joins the Greek alliance: 9. 106,4.

12 Glaukos: Hdt. 1.25; cf. in general Overbeck, *SQ* 263–72, Stuart Jones 29–31. Detail on the figures: Athen. 210b–c. Archermos and his sons: Overbeck, *SQ* 314–19, Stuart Jones 25 (= Pliny, *NH* 36. 11)–28. The first winged Nike: Schol. Ar., *Av.* 573. Base-fragment on Paros: Rubensohn, *DM* 1 (1948), 38 f., n. 1. Pliny, loc. cit., jumbles into the sculptors' ancestry the names of Mikkiades and also of Melas, a Chian founding hero (above, p. 230), both mentioned in the Delian dedication, from which Pliny's source clearly derives. See in general Richter, *Archaic Greek Art*, 116 f. with n.143 (M. J. Milne), and for the reconstruction of Nike A. Gotsmich, *Probleme d. fruhgriech. Plastik* (1935), 87 ff., Rubensohn, op. cit., 38 ff., Raubitschek, *DAA* 484 ff.; Gotsmich's research showed that the connection of statue and base is highly probable. The acropolis dedication: *DAA* 3. Hipponax: Frr. 120–1West; cf. above, p. 223.

14 The Aiolic Greeks

Kyme and Mytilene

The Greek settlers on Lesbos, Tenedos, and the Asian mainland behind them came traditionally from eastern Thessaly and Boiotia, and certainly the dialects were similar. The settlement in Asia seems to have started at the southern end of the Aiolic zone with two early foundations, Kyme and Smyrna, on either side of the river Hermos. Smyrna on the southern side was captured and repopulated by Ionians from Kolophon before the end of the eighth century, leaving Kyme as the focus of southern Aiolis. The most northerly city was Pitana beyond the river Kaikos. Then came the territory of the Mysians, a local Anatolian people, where no Greek settlements appear, and thence the coast juts out westwards, forming the long bastion of the Troad, with the island Lesbos in the nook of the great bay thus formed. The two main cities of Lesbos lay on her protected sides, Methymna on the northern, Mytilene on the eastern; the settlements on the windy west side never grew prosperous. The Troad was the common *peraia* of these two and its south coast, facing Methymna, was naturally her preserve. The Mysians being already settled on the coast facing Mytilene, surplus Mytilenaians had to go further afield. They moved right out of the bay and had settled on the long coastline beyond during the eighth century, as far as the site of Ilion (Old Troy) at the entry to the Hellespont. Beyond this the Milesian emigrants were settling, lining the south sides of the Hellespont and Propontis from Abydos onwards. So the Mytilenaians crossed to the north side, the Thracian Chersonese, and founded Sestos (*c.* 670), Madytos, and Alopekonnesos on its further shore.

The nearness of the Troad, scene of the Greek ancestral epic, may have been the main reason why the Penthilidai, the royal clan of Mytilene, alleged that their ancestor Penthilos (who traditionally led most of the Aiolic migration over the Aegean) was a son of Orestes – though he makes no appearance in early epic, and the family name may have come from a place in Lesbos called Penthile. Kyme too claimed that her founders Kleuas and Malaos were descendants of Agamemnon and had set out from Greece at the same time as Penthilos, but arrived later, having delayed in eastern Lokris before the crossing (from Aulis, presumably); so they made for the Asian mainland, built a fort, Neonteichos, evicted the local Pelasgians from Larisa nearby, and called their settlement 'Phrikonian Kyme' after Mount Phrikion in Lokris. These, says Herodotos, were the first three of the twelve cities of Aiolis. Of the rest, Smyrna became Ionic, and the Archaic histories of Temnos, Killa, Notion, Aigiroessa, Pitana, Aigaiai, Myrrhina, and Gryneia – humble places all, when compared with the

Ionians – are hardly known to us. But snatches of Kyme's history survive (assuming that they all belong to Aiolic, not Italic, Kyme), possibly because the fourth-century historian Ephoros, whose works were widely known, was himself a Kymaian. We hear that the founders of Phokaia, when they arrived in Aiolic territory (above, p. 227), won their land by helping Ouatias, brother of Mennes, tyrant of Kyme, to foment a rising, stone Mennes to death, and set up Ouatias in his place; and again, that when one Agamemnon was king of Kyme, his daughter Demodike (or Hermodike) married 'Midas the Phrygian' (not necessarily the great ruler, for the name was still borne by later Phrygians after the power had passed to Lydia), and was said by some authors to have first introduced coinage to the Greeks. We do not know what lies behind this claim, but if it has any validity, her generation should be roughly that of the foundation deposit in the Artemision at Ephesos, i.e., *c.* 600–575 (above, p. 222); the name Agamemnon could well be traditional in this royal family. At all events, the agricultural wealth of Phrygia makes a trade connection between her and Kyme quite likely. Kingship was duly succeeded by oligarchy; the highest official was called *aisymnetes* as at Mytilene, and it seems that, as in Chios and elsewhere, the title *basileus* was retained for another high magistracy; for we are told that if 'the kings' were suspected of any crime, the council debated the case at night, and a Guardian of the Prison removed the suspects and held them while a secret ballot was taken. The oligarchy altered when one Pheidon extended the franchise to all *hippeis*, and again when one Prometheus fixed the citizen-body at the oligarchic number of a thousand, as in Lokris and Kolophon. The law on homicide was still fairly primitive in Aristotle's day: the defendant was adjudged guilty if the accuser could produce 'a certain number' of his own kin as witnesses; so too at Gortyn in the fifth century an alleged adulterer was adjudged guilty if his captor could produce four witnesses (or two if the defendant was only an *apetairos*, or one if he was a slave). Many jokes were current about the slowness of the citizens of Kyme; but they did their best, *c.* 540, to uphold the rights of a suppliant against the power of Persia and took their share in the Ionic Revolt.[1]

Mytilene was the greatest of the Aiolic cities, thanks to the dynamism, mental and physical, of her people. They bred fighters and poets, which meant that their deeds, good and bad, were recorded at a time when, prose literature being still in its infancy, the deeds in other cities less poetically gifted are lost to us. Popular song, the chant with a beat dictated by the rhythm of the job – sea-songs, mill-songs, loom-songs – may have helped to create the famous Lesbian lyric tradition of monody rather than choral song; its greatest exponents were Alkaios and Sappho in the early sixth century. The poetry of Sappho does not concern us here; it lies outside politics, and even if that were not so, its qualities are like those of glass, molten or prismatic, easier to observe than to formulate. But Alkaios was in the thick of things. Abroad the Mytilenaians fought fiercely to retain their *peraia* in the Troad, at home the ship of state rocked perilously in wild party-quarrels; and enough of Alkaios' poetry survives to give direct patches of light, and also to indicate that much in the prose accounts of local writers later may be derived from his lost work. First there was the war with Athens over Sigeion, apparently lasting for two generations, *c.* 610–540 (above, pp. 89–90). This was a strategic site at the entry to the Hellespont, which one Archaianax had fortified for Mytilene, using the stones from Old Troy. About 620–610 emigrants from Attica, led by Phrynon, an Olympic victor, got a footing in Sigeion. Mytilene sent up a force under Pittakos, the man who was to become *aisymnetes* later, and in 607–606 Phrynon and Pittakos fought a duel to settle the matter, a Homeric practice still resorted to by some states even in the fifth century. Phrynon was slain by 'a net, trident, and knife'; perhaps a contemporary song had compared Pittakos to a fisherman who nets and spears his prey – unless indeed the technique of the *retiarius* had, like Romulus, a Trojan ancestry. But the war dragged on, for a fragment by Alkaios says to his friend Melanippos that he is safe, but the Attic men have got his armour and hung it up in the temple of Athena Glaukopis in Sigeion. Eventually Periander of Corinth (died 585) was appointed arbitrator and pronounced the formula 'Each side to keep what it holds', that is, Athens was to retain Sigeion. The Mytilenaians evidently rejected the arbitration, for later Peisistratos of Athens (*c.* 600–527) seized Sigeion by force from Mytilene and installed his son Hegesistratos (Thessalos) to rule it as a family estate. The Mytilenaians fortified the Achilleion (Achilles' Tomb) as their base, and counter-attacked. Herodotos reports all the above, but apparently conflates the tenures of Phrynon and Peisistratos, omitting Phrynon and making it one war, fought by Alkaios and the Mytilenaians against Peisistratos and settled by Periander's arbitration. No attempt to clear him of error here has been satisfactory. Nevertheless, the Peisistratidai held Sigeion and submitted quietly to Persian rule when it came, until the Asian Greeks became free after the victories of 480–479. Athens had already encroached on Mytilene's interests in the Hellespont, for she had established a settlement at Elaious (above, p. 89). But Mytilene had interests in the south too by the sixth century: she was the sole Aiolic member of the Greek *emporion* at Naukratis. The chief tangible evidence there is only the plain grey bucchero ware of Lesbos; but Sappho's poems speak of her brother's connections there and of the foreign luxuries in the homes of the girls of Mytilene.[2]

Meanwhile feuding among the families had been running high since the seventh century. The Penthilidai, the ex-royal family, held the powers of government and misused them; they, or their bodyguards, are said to have clubbed unoffending citizens in the streets until their rule was forcibly ended by one Megakles and his companions. The family's influence and habits persisted, however, for later another Penthilos was killed by one Smerdes for similar lawless acts. Then Melanchros, 'a tyrant', was overthrown *c.* 612–608 by a coalition including Pittakos and the elder brothers of Alkaios. But Myrsilos, the next claimant to power, won and controlled the city for some time, and this was in great part owing to Pittakos, who forsook the coalition to support him. Alkaios and his brothers had already been exiled to Pyrrha in central Lesbos after a failed rising. Now they and others, Sappho among them, were exiled from Lesbos. Antimenidas, one of the brothers, spent some time in the Far East as a mercenary with the king of Babylon. The Lydians – either the wily Alyattes or the philhellene young prince Kroisos – gave 2,000 staters to the party funds to help them to get back. From that time Alkaios' poems scourge Pittakos incessantly as a traitor to the party, redoubling the attack when Myrsilos died and the city, doubtless to avoid yet another renewal of the feuding years, elected Pittakos as *aisymnetes* for a decade. It was a far cry now from the time when Alkaios gaily listed the stores of armour hung up in the *andron* of some house, all ready for action 'since first this work was undertaken': the bronze helmets with their nodding horsehair plumes, the greaves, shields, swords from Chalkis, tunics, belts, and new linen corslets. But despite Alkaios' slanders on his nature, figure, and drinking habits Pittakos gave Mytilene stable government. His early association with Alkaios' brothers and his later marriage to a Penthilid indicate that by birth he qualified as upper-class. His father's name was Thracian (Hyrras), a fact of which his enemies made full use; but there were Thracians too of high birth, and it could even be that Hyrras' mother was the Thracian (above, p. 57). Pittakos was included among the Seven Sages, and one of his sayings was that the 'painted wood' (that is, the Law, perhaps inscribed on axons like those in Athens?) was the best protector of a city; but only a few of his sumptuary laws survive. The tradition adds that he pardoned and recalled Alkaios, duly gave up his office *c.* 580, and died ten years later.

How near, one wonders, did the political and economic situation in Mytilene before his rule approach that in Athens before Solon's reforms? In each case we have the testimony of a well-born citizen on the crises harassing a large, potentially rich agricultural and seafaring state during the start of the sixth century. The great difference lies in their characters as reporters. Alkaios is a party leader, Solon a painstaking judge. Alkaios does not speak, like Solon, of desperate citizens labouring as serfs or slaves; admittedly the existence of cheap barbarian slave-labour would give this problem a different aspect in Lesbos, but the same basic trouble must have been there, or why did the people demand an *aisymnetes*, and one who attacked the extravagance of the rich? Alkaios' '*demos* which must be rescued' (F 127) is the mass of voting citizens, who *will* insist insanely on electing Pittakos. Solon attacks the corrupt administration of a whole ruling class; Alkaios, by name, his political opponents. Once (F 117) he approaches Solon's viewpoint, and appeals for an end to stasis which leads the *demos* to ruin; but the fact that the stasis also 'gives splendid glory to Pittakos' seems to upset him even more. Yet it is easy to be over-critical here. His verses show also the desperate misery of the active mind in long political exile:

> How wretchedly I drag this cloddish life,
> longing to hear the summons to the assembly,
> Agesilaidas, and to the council –
> offices which my father and his father
> held to old age in this self-spiting city –
> I have been forced from these to farthest exile. (F 128)

A hereditary seat in the council and a lively audience in the assembly – one the traditional privilege of the aristocrat, the other the common right of all citizens – have both been denied to him.

The city continued an oligarchy through the sixth century; we hear of officers called the *prytanis* and *basileis*. The Lydians seem to have continued friendly. Like Chios, Mytilene did not defy the Persians when they came; she was prepared, *c.* 540, to give up the rebel Paktyes to avoid trouble (above, p. 232), and Mytilenaian ships were serving in the fleet which accompanied Cambyses to Egypt in

525. At some time in the 520s her fleet was sent to help Miletos against Polykrates of Samos, who soundly defeated it and used the prisoners-of-war to dig a ditch round the city wall of Samos. About 514 a Mytilenaian named Koes was one of Darius' advisers on the Scythian expedition, and, having given good advice at the Danube bridge (above, p. 219), was made tyrant of Mytilene as his reward – to the fury of his fellow-citizens, who did not merely depose him at the start of the Ionic Revolt in 499, but stoned him. Like Chios, the island was one of the pillars of the revolt, giving eight ships to Histiaios in 495 and sending seventy to Lade. After that defeat Histiaios and his ships returned briefly in what looks more like a private raid than a final defiance of Persia (above, pp. 232–3). The Persians punished the Lesbians severely, by 'netting' the island, as they had done in Chios and once before in Samos.[3]

East Greek Art

Contact with the non-Greek nations to east and south naturally affected the sculpture of the eastern Greeks. Certain types were taken from Egypt: the couching lion came direct into Ionic art; so did the seated, clothed official, and – except in one detail – the kouros (above, pp. 30–1, 211). The kore, however, emerged from the cocoon of the general 'xoanon' type and developed in a manner fundamentally Greek – east Greek, if Herodotos was right in saying that the loose, trailing, pleated shift (chiton) was originally Asiatic ('Carian'): the girl in her best festal attire – hair-band, earrings, necklace, bracelets – who steps forward like the kouros, one hand holding up her skirt to clear her feet, the other bearing her gift to the god. Attic sculptors (p. 98) took this over via the Cyclades, as perhaps they took over also, late in the sixth century, the characteristic east Greek funeral stele depicting a man with his hunting-dog. The korai are not portraits, but they have in essence the facial type which the sculptor saw around him in his part of the Greek world. The Ionic korai on the Didyma capital-bases have small, plump faces, slit eyes, and wide catlike smiles; the Attic faces are longer, squarer, and rounder-eyed, and between the two the Cycladic-Attic korai half-smile and duck their heads down slightly towards the viewer from their high pedestal-bases (Pls. 11, 36).

In their vase-painting the east Greeks had not got a long and assured Geometric tradition behind them. They were close to the sources of the 'Orientalizing' style, but in the early seventh century, unlike Athens, Corinth, Crete, and the islands, they did not concentrate on the human figure. The motifs which they took from the eastern metals, ivories, and textiles brought the sights of the countryside onto their 'Rhodian' vases: stylized trees and flowers, butting goats, racing hounds, stumping bulls, waddling geese, prim quails, dappled fawns and antlered deer, as well as the stately sphinxes, lions, and horses on which the mainland vase-painters dwelt rather more often (Pls. 32, 43–4, 46). They liked polychrome effects, sometimes using a pale ground to show up the figures. Though making use of floral and linear filling-motifs, they had no such *horror vacui* as sometimes beset the Corinthian painters; in the sixth century the Chian white-ground chalices and the 'Fikellura' amphorae (Rhodian?) exploit the single figure with great effect. When they drew narrative-scenes, quite often they drew comic ones, as on the 'Caeretan' hydriae, which appear to have been produced about the mid-sixth century for the Etruscan market by one Ionic workshop. (The sole inscribed fragment shows good Ionic script.) We are not in the epic world of the Corinthian and Attic painters, but in something nearer to our own size. After all, it was the Ionians who first made prose respectable in Greek literature. Its public use for dedications, epitaphs, didactic works, was early accepted by Ionia, again, presumably, from the usage of the Near East, where the mass of prose documents of all kinds, from royal rock-inscriptions to private correspondence, encouraged the Ionians to take early to papyrus and the *diphthera* (a primitive parchment), which may in turn have encouraged the rather hasty, informal look of many sixth-century Ionic inscriptions on stone. The dedications at Milesian Didyma, for example, are all in prose, and so are such early Ionic epitaphs as have been found. But the mainland Greeks kept to the verse tradition for their dedications and epitaphs. To have the sentiment cast in verse offered both dignity and remoteness: the poet claimed that a Muse outside himself dictated what he said, and he could use 'I' as a *persona* without always meaning himself and his personal life (above, p. 37); whereas prose, the equivalent of daily speech, was apt to reveal the individual more directly. 'I am [the memorial] of Phanodikos son of Hermokrates of Prokonnesos; he gave a winebowl with its stand and strainer to the Sigeians for their town hall' (Sigeion, an epitaph of about the mid-sixth century). 'I write the following as the truth appears to me' (Hekataios F 1).[4]

NOTES

1 For a detailed study of the Troad see J. M. Cook, *The Troad* (1972). Aiolic settlement of Troy: cf. Boardman, 81; Graham, *JHS* 91 (1971), 42. Kyme's founders: Str. 582, 621; cf. Wade-Gery, *The Poet of the Iliad*, 57, 65 f. n.22. The twelve cities: Hdt. 1. 149; cf. Boardman, 30 f., 82. Foundation of Phokaia: N. Damasc., *FGH* 90 F 51; of Kyme, Pollux 9. 83; Arist. F 611,37 R; Heracl. Lemb., *Exc. Polit.* ed. Dilts (1971), 26.37. Wade-Gery (op. cit., 7 and n.21) held that it was the great Midas, and that king Agamemnon's date was *c.* 700. Trade between Kyme and Phrygia: Huxley, *Early Ionians*, 52. Suspected 'kings': Plut., *QG* 2. Pheidon and Prometheus: Heracl. Lemb., op. cit., 26. 42. Homicide law: Arist., *Pol.* 1269a; adulterers at Gortyn, Code II. 35–44. Jokes against Kymaians: see Halliday, *Plutarch: Greek Questions*, 42. The suppliant: Hdt. 1. 157–60 (above, p. 232). The Revolt: Hdt. 5. 123.

2 Popular songs: see esp. Bowra, *GLP²*, 131 ff. Archaianax: Str. 599; the duel and Alkaios, ibid.; see the full references in Page, *Sappho and Alkaios* (1955), 153 ff., an indispensable work for the history of this period. Peisistratos and Alkaios: Hdt. 5. 94–5, 1–2. There is no convincing way out of our problem: Peisistratos and Hegesistratos cannot have fought in a war which had been settled by Periander before 585; there must have been two separate campaigns. Page demonstrates most attractively (loc. cit.) from Herodotos' own wording that he *was* aware of the two; but if so, Herodotos must be convicted of equal carelessness – of omitting the crucial point that after Periander's death the Lesbians rejected the arbitration. Elaious: Str. 599. Naukratis: Hdt. 2. 178; Boardman, 122.

3 Penthilidai, Megakles, and Smerdes: Arist., *Pol.* 1311b. Melanchros: Str. 617; D Laert. 1. 4,74. Armour: Page, *LGS* F 167, *Sappho and Alkaios*, 209 ff.: Snodgrass, *Arms and Armour*, 64 f. Both authors note the absence of a spear and the Eastern associations of the linen thorax and belt. (Did the east Greek horsemen perhaps find this less constricting than the bronze?) Myrsilos and Pittakos: see Page, *Sappho and Alkaios*, 161 ff.; Antimenidas, F 163; Lydian money, F 116. Pittakos: *aisymnetes*, Arist., *Pol.* 1285a; marriage, see Page, *Sappho and Alkaios*, 235 ff.; the laws, Arist., *Pol.* 1274b; D. Laert. 1. 4,75–7; Cic., *De Leg.* 2. 26. Cf. in general the estimate of Mytilene in this period, Andrewes, *The Greek Tyrants*, ch. 8. *Prytaneis* and *basileis*: Theophr. ap. Stob., *Floril.* 44.22. Paktyes: Hdt. 1. 160; ships with Cambyses, 3. 13–15; against Polykrates, 3. 39,4; Koes, 4. 97,2–6; 5. 11,1 and 37–8,1; in Ionic Revolt, 6. 5,2–3 and 27,3–28; the netting, 6. 31.

4 'Carian' chiton: Hdt. 5. 88,1. 'Cycladic-Attic' here describes loosely the typical Acropolis korai, the style developed by sculptors during the Peisistratid tyranny. Man-and-dog stelai as an Ionic invention: Ridgway, *JdI* 86 (1971), 60 ff. 'Rhodian' vases: Chr. Kardara, 'Ροδιακὴ ἀγγειογραφία (1963); R. M. Cook, *Greek Painted Pottery²* (1972), ch. IV.9, 116 ff. – an outstanding study of east Greek pottery as a whole; Arias-Hirmer-Shefton, 279 ff. Chian: Cook, op. cit., 126 ff. and 'Fikellura', 132 ff. 'Caeretan' (Phokaia? Ephesos?): Cook, 160 f., Arias-Hirmer-Shefton, 311 ff. Influence of 'bookhand' on Ionic inscriptions: *LSAG*, 57 f., 327. Early prose: cf. E. Rudberg, *Eranos* 40 (1942), 128 ff.; Friedländer and Hoffleit, *Epigrammata* (1948), 8 f. Sigeion inscription: *LSAG*, 366 f.; Guarducci in Richter, *Archaic Gravestones of Attica* (1961), 165 ff.

Appendices

The Date of the Law on Ostracism

Androtion (*FGH* 324 F 6): Ἵππαρχος ὁ Χάρμου . . . ὅτι συγγένης μὲν ἦν Πεισιστράτου τοῦ τυράννου καὶ πρῶτος ἐξωστρακίσθη, τοῦ περὶ τὸν ὀστρακισμὸν νόμου τότε πρῶτον (var. lect. πρώτου) τεθέντος διὰ τὴν ὑποψίαν τῶν περὶ Πεισίστρατον, ὅτι δημαγωγὸς ὢν καὶ στρατηγὸς ἐτυράννησεν. (= A)

Ath. Pol. 22.3–4: . . . τότε πρῶτον ἐχρήσαντο τῷ νόμῳ τῷ περὶ τὸν ὀστρακισμόν, ὃς ἐτέθη διὰ τὴν ὑποψίαν τῶν ἐν ταῖς δυνάμεσιν, ὅτι Πεισίστρατος δημαγωγὸς καὶ στρατηγὸς ὢν τύραννος κατέστη. Καὶ πρῶτος ὠστρακίσθη τῶν ἐκείνου συγγενῶν Ἵππαρχος Χάρμου Κολλυτεύς . . . (= AP)

In the long modern dispute between 508–507 (the date indicated by *Ath. Pol.* 22.1–4, which ascribes this law to Kleisthenes among his others aimed at alluring the common people) and 488–487 (apparently stated in a quotation in Harpokration's *Lexicon* s.v. Ἵππαρχος which is taken from Androtion's *Atthis* Bk 2, above), the first date appears now to be well in the lead – surely rightly, since two drawbacks have always harassed the second: (1) that the AP passage, while echoing A's phraseology at times, makes logical sense, while A itself will not read throughout as sense without either emendation or at least some reading between the lines; and (2) that later authors never mention a clash between these two authorities as to the date of the law, nor even A's (alleged) date for it. They ascribe the law to Kleisthenes (i.e., to *c.* 508–507, since nothing implies that he was still alive and drafting laws in 488–487). See the arguments for the first date as advanced most recently (with full lists of the earlier writers on both sides, of which the most influential for the later date was perhaps Jacoby in 1954, commenting on A in *FGH*): H. Bloch, *Gnomon* 32 (1959), 492 f., reviewing Jacoby; K. J. Dover, *CR* 77 (1963), 257 f.; G. Sumner, *BICS* 11 (1964), 79 ff.; and especially J. J. Keaney, *Historia* 19 (1970), 1 ff., a thorough and far-reaching examination of all aspects of the problem, based initially on a fresh study of the recensions of Harpokration's text, at the crucial passage. The most rational conclusion seems to be that in A, the earlier of the two works, the text originally read similarly to that in AP, i.e., the latter is following Androtion here; and that the suggested date of 488–487 for the law's creation rests on some disturbance of Androtion's text in Harpokration – whether τότε πρῶτον (as Keaney holds) is an unfortunate ancient emendation made to cure an earlier corruption τότε πρώτου (for the priority of which see Keaney, loc. cit.) from an original πρὸ τούτου in Harpokration, *or* a confusion made by Harpokration, or an intermediary, in excerpting from a text which originally read something like that in AP (cf. Bloch,

Dover, Sumner). Evidence for further confusion in A may exist in its remarks about Peisistratos (cf. Sumner). Hipparchos, born only shortly before Peisistratos died of old age in 528–527 (see Davies, *APF*, 451 f.), could correctly be termed συγγένης, a word which need not imply contemporaneity; but to class him among 'the circle of Peisistratos' sounds unnatural for 508–507, when the obvious circle to speak of would be that of the tyrant Hippias. It could be replied that anyone setting out to *seize* tyranny would be compared more aptly with the Peisistratos-type; but there is the further point that the clause δημαγωγὸς ὢν καὶ στρατηγός, perfectly apt in AP because it explains τῶν ἐν ταῖς δυνάμεσιν, has no proper relevance to A's text as it stands. Keaney does not accept the theory of careless excerpting here. He argues that τῶν περὶ Πεισίστρατον in A is not anachronistic for 508–507, if it refers to a Peisistratid 'party', a specific group of his relations and supporters: and that AP, because there was a further tradition which maintained that a wider group was aimed at, has added here the phrase on 'those in high positions' to include this wider field. But I still find the explanation δημαγωγὸς ὢν καὶ στράτηγός puzzling and unnecessary in A here, since there is no suggestion in the text that Hipparchos was in either of these positions, a comparison which seems required if the explanation is to be relevant.

APPENDIX II

The Lykourgan rhetra; *Polydoros and the* kleroi

The *rhetra* (Plutarch, *Lycurg.* 6)

The disputed clauses (2)–(4) are (with Plutarch's comments added):

(2) οὕτως [?τούτως W-G] εἰσφέρειν τε καὶ ἀφίστασθαι . . . (Plut.: τοῦ δὲ πλήθους ἀθροισθέντος εἰπεῖν μὲν οὐδένι γνώμην τῶν ἄλλων ἐφεῖτο . . .)

(3) ...⁺γαμω[=δάμω?]δαναγοριανημην[=εἶμεν?]κα[=καὶ?]κράτος⁺. (Plut.:... τὴν δ' ὑπὸ τῶν γερόντων καὶ τῶν βασιλέων προτεθεῖσαν [γνώμην] ἐπικρίναι κύριος ἦν ὁ δᾶμος.)

(4) αἰ δὲ σκολίαν ὁ δᾶμος ἕροιτο, τοὺς πρεσβυγενέας καὶ ἀρχαγέτας ἀποστατῆρας εἶμεν. (Plut.: τοῦτ' ἐστι μὴ κυροῦν, ἀλλ' ὅλως ἀφίστασθαι καὶ διαλύειν τὸν δῆμον, ὡς ἐκτρέποντα καὶ μεταποιοῦντὰ τὴν γνώμην παρὰ τὸ βέλτιστον.)

Allegedly the *rhetra* had been brought back to the city from Delphi by Lykourgos, the great reformer (dated variously in the ninth or eighth centuries by ancient authorities; seventh century, by Huxley, *Early Sparta*, and Forrest, *Hist. Sparta*), as an oracle concerning the *gerousia*. The text is partly in Attic Greek, partly still in its original Doric. The classic exposition of the problems is still that of Wade-Gery, *Essays*, 37 ff.; cf. more recently Huxley, op. cit.; J. H. Oliver, *Demokratia, the Gods, and the Free World* (1960), ch. 1 (with full bibliography); D. Butler, *Historia* 11 (1962), 385 ff.; Forrest, *Phoenix* 21 (1967), 11 ff., and *Hist. Sparta*, 40 ff. (Excursus I) and bibliography, 60. As for the interpretation suggested above, pp. 117 f., on clauses (2)–(4), cl. (2a) at least seems straightforward: the *rhetra* states, and Plutarch (= Aristotle in his lost *Lak. Pol.*?) explains, that only the *gerousia* could propose a motion. For (2b), that the *gerousia* can 'stand aloof', i.e., quash a proposal made by one of its members: ἀφίστασθαι, the verb used both here and again by Plutarch in his gloss on the noun ἀποστατήρ in cl. (4), has been variously interpreted. In the active it means to remove, 'to make *x* stand away from'; in the middle (as here), 'to make oneself stand away from', most commonly in the sense 'aloof from', i.e., to decline, baulk at; in prose it does not often bear the literal, neutral meaning 'depart from the scene' (as ἀποχωρεῖν), for which cf. Forrest, *Hist. Sparta*, 47. The noun of agent ἀποστατήρ (a *hapax legomenon*), from the active voice, should mean 'a remover', and Plutarch explains the phrase 'to be removers' as meaning 'wholly to stand away [i.e., baulk], and dismiss the assembly'. I infer that he adds here the technical verb διαλύειν (to break up) because it is stronger than ἀφιστάναι (to remove), and ὅλως because to deal with this illegality (argument from the floor of the House) and its punishment (summary dismissal) the *gerousia* must show a united front. In cl. (2b) a majority among the *gerontes* would suffice either to introduce a proposal to the *damos* for decision, or to block it – cf. the story in Plut., *Agis* 11.1: for the *gerontes* at Sparta, 'because their power lay in *probouleusis*', a bare-majority decision barred a proposal from the agenda. The *gerontes* at Carthage (Arist., *Pol.* 1272b–1273a) could only bar a proposal if they were unanimous; otherwise, the Carthaginian assembly had the right to decide whether or no a proposal should come before it for discussion. But the *damos* at Sparta had not this right, nor, surely, the right of discussion. *Pol.* 1273a specifies that the latter is *not* allowed in 'the other two states' (Sparta and Crete); and in cl. (3) of the *rhetra* the (now mangled) word there, which is presumably a noun coupled with the following noun 'power' ($\kappa\rho\acute{a}\tau os$), must have squared with the explanatory paraphrase: 'the people had the power to pass the final judgement on the proposal laid before them'. If the mangled word did mean 'discussion', Plutarch's paraphrase would be wholly inadequate. The conviction that this word *must* have meant 'discussion', despite the evidence of *Pol.* 1273a, seems to have haunted many of the attempts to explain cl. (4). But, as I see it, whenever the assembly (illegally) broke out into discussion, inevitably this involved addition, subtraction, or alteration to the proposed formulation (how else could one discuss it?); and Plutarch correctly describes such a proceeding, from the legal viewpoint, as perversion, 'crooked' speaking (cl. 4) because it is not the legal, 'straight' decision made by acclamation or refusal.

Polydoros and the *kleroi*

The evidence for 'the good Polydoros' is difficult to assess. As co-king with Theopompos he was associated with at least cl. (4) of the *rhetra* (Plut., *Lycurg.* 6.4), more doubtfully with the rest (cf. the suggestions of Huxley, op. cit., 40 ff. and Forrest, *Phoenix* 17 (1963), 171 f. and *Hist. Sparta*, 65 f.). Apart from this, we hear also that in the second century A.D. a portrait-statue ($\epsilon\grave{\iota}\kappa\acute{\omega}\nu$) of him still stood in the Spartan agora by the tomb of Orestes, and that his – or, equally possibly, its – likeness was carved on the public seal used by the Spartan authorities (Paus. 3. 11,10). No date is given for either object, but honorific portrait-statues and likenesses on sealstones hardly antedate the fifth century (cf. Richter, *The Portraits of the Greeks* I (1965), 3 ff.); which implies that then, or later, Agid propaganda was publicizing him for political reasons, truly or not, as a great benefactor to Sparta. Thus the picture given elsewhere in Pausanias and Plutarch may rest on late propaganda, or genuine tradition, or a mixture of both. Pausanias speaks of a ruler kind to the *demos*, a humane and honest judge, his murder, and how the place now called $\tau\grave{a}$ $\beta o\omega\nu\eta\tau\acute{a}$ (the 'ox-bought' property) was once his home, sold to the city by his widow for oxen in those pre-coinage days (3.3,2–3 and 12,3; 8. 52,1). Plutarch says (*Lycurg.* 8 (hinted at also in ps.-Plut. *Apophtheg. Lac. = Mor.* 231d–e); cf. Jacoby, *FGH* 596. 15, Comm.) that, although some said that it was Lykourgos alone who had first redivided the Spartiate land into 9,000 lots ($\kappa\lambda\hat{\eta}\rho o\iota$) for fair distribution to the citizens, according to others he had distributed only 6,000, or even 4,500, lots; the rest of the 9,000 were added later by Polydoros, from military victories. The substance of this tradition, again, may be true; but it must be questioned whether the actual number of citizens at the time was *c*. 9,000. All good 'three-tribed' Dorian states seem to have had standard conventions based on the number 9 (3 × 3) and maintained especially in their religious festivals: cf. *Sparta* itself in the Karneia (D. Skeps. ap. Athen. 141e–f: the citizen-army represented by 9 'tents' each holding 9 men who represented 3 phratries); *Rhodes* (9 ships to Troy, 9 panoplies dedicated on their return (*Il.* 2. 654, *Lind. Chron.*, *FGH* 532 B 9): 9 runners in each of 3 tribes at the old festival to Athena Lindia, in the same *Chron.* B 15: 9 new tribes, 3 in each city, after the synoecism of 408); possibly *Kyrene* (above, p. 187, and cf. Meiggs and Lewis no. 5 vv. 15–16, '9 *hetaireiai*'); *Kos*, with her 9 'ἀγρέται' (Hesychios s.v.) and – more relevant to our Spartan problem – her tribal units called χιλιάστυες ('1,000-units': Buck no. 108) which, if taken literally, would mean that she too had *c*. 9,000 citizens (cf. p. 131, n.5).

APPENDIX III

The Thalassocracy-List

The *Chronographia* of Eusebius (I, 225, ed. Schoene) preserves this list as 'epitomized out of the writings of Diodoros from the periods of the thalassocrats who ruled the seas'.[1] (In Eusebius' *Canon* it reappears as separate items entered each under its date, with some variations in the year-numbers from those given in the list; typical examples are shown bracketed below.) It is a list of 17 peoples who successively 'ruled the sea from the Fall of Troy to the crossing of [Xerxes]', with the years of duration attached:

Lydians and Maionians, 92; Pelasgians, 85; Thracians, 79; Rhodians, 23; Phrygians, 25; Cypriots, 32 (23); Phoenicians, 45; Egyptians, ?45; Milesians, 18; Carians [*sic*], 61; Lesbians, 68; Phokaians, 44; Samians, 17; Lakedaimonians, 2 (12); Naxians, 10; Eretrians, 15 (7); Aiginetans, 10 (20).

A basic authenticity for this list (that is, a fifth-century authority, independent of Herodotos and Thucydides but later worked over) has been advocated by J. L. Myres and A. R. Burn, and recently by W. G. Forrest, who sees the working-over as perhaps by Sosibios (*FGH* 595)[2]. I have not made use of the list in my text because I follow the other view,[3] regarding it as post-fifth-century, scissors-and-paste work, erudite but uncritical, originally based on some annalistic writer or writers, in whose narrative each of these peoples was mentioned as notable in the year *x* for some sea-victory, or colonization, or defeat. The sceptic holds that the excerptor (x) inferred the number of years between such separate events to have been a 'thalassocracy' enjoyed by that people. (x may well have been the chronographer Kastor of Rhodes, who is said to have compiled a (lost) Thalassocracy-List (*FGH* 250 T 1); Diodoros may have repeated this list, *or* made separate references to the ruling peoples (as apparently in the case of the Carians, below), in which case our list represents a shortened version taken from him; cf. the quotations in n.1 below.) The interesting section from Miletos down to Aigina sounds convincing precisely because it rests ultimately on the narrative of Herodotos. The list might seem designed to fill the space in time between the two old thalassocracies of Minos and, in a sense, the Greek fleet that sailed to Troy, and the great Athenian thalassocracy which arose after the 'crossing' (and defeat) of Xerxes. It confines itself to 'rulers' in the Aegean ambit, north up to Thrace and Phrygia, south to Egypt and the Near East; it ignores the Western sea-powers of Carthage, Etruria, Kerkyra, and, odder still, the Hellenic cities Corinth and Megara (see below) and Chalkis, all of whose well-known colonial (i.e., naval) achievements were first and foremost in the West. Oddest of all, it excludes Athens while including Aigina, her rival. All this could suggest a compilation intended to bridge the chronological gap and show who had ruled before Athens took over and created her thalassocracy in this area, ruling, or at least ranging, the seas from Scythia down to Egypt; hence the list would exclude Athens, and include only those 'sea-powers' concerned with the area later controlled or affected by the Athenian fleet. A compilation of this kind seems well suited to the later period when scholars were interested in specialist productions of 'Lists of First Inventors' and the like; less well suited to a pre-Thucydidean date. Ephoros' work, for example, might have provided an impetus by stressing how Athens under Themistocles set out to take the hegemony of the sea (*FGH* 70, T 20 and F 97; cf. D. Sic. 11.41).[4]

Corinth and Megara. The tenth name in the list is missing in the *Chronographia* but survives in Jerome's Latin version of the *Canon*, where we read 'Cares' (Carians). A Carian rule at this time is agreed to be incredible by believers as well as sceptics. Burn has suggested a corruption from *ΜΕΓΑΡΕΙΣ*, perhaps made by Eusebius himself from a damaged text of Diodoros; Forrest would argue for an original reference to *Κορίνθιοι*. Myres had proposed an inference drawn by x from the 'Ionians and Carians' who went to serve in Egypt under Psamtik I (Hdt. 2. 152–4). Diodoros certainly stressed an *early* Carian thalassocracy in the Aegean (Bk. 5. 53 and 84), so, if the list is indeed taken from his work, it should start with the Carians. Myres saw this, and transferred them to the top of the list, but did not shift the Lydians into their place. R. Ball has suggested to me that the error might have occurred if Eusebius' series of names came from an original double-column list, in which the series did begin with the Carians, at the top of the left-hand column (names 1–9); while the next column (10–17) was headed by the Lydians, placed between the Milesians and Lesbians (possibly through vague recollections of the power of Alyattes); then 'Carians' and 'Lydians and Maionians' (whenever the latter were attached), being adjacent on the same line, might be carelessly transposed by a copyist.

NOTES

1 For the Armenian text, our sole source here, the German translation (Karst, 106) has: 'Aus denselben Diodor-Schriften auszugsweise von der Zeiten Meeresbeherrscher, die die Seeherrschaft haben'; the Latin translation by Petermann in Schoene's edition (cf. D. Sic. 5 F 11 ed. Vogel) has: 'Ex Diodori scriptis breviter de temporibus Thalassocratorum, qui maria tenebant'.

2 Myres, *JHS* 26 (1906), 84 ff. and 27 (1907), 84 ff.; Burn, *JHS* 47 (1927), 165 ff. and *Lyric Age*, 58; Forrest, *CQ* 19 (1969), 95 ff.

3 Cf. Fotheringham, *JHS* 27 (1907), 75 ff.; Aly, *RhM* 66 (1911), 585 ff.; Kubitschek in *RE* s.v. Kastor (1919), 2355 f.; Helm, *Hermes* 61 (1926), 241 ff. (to whom Jacoby, while refusing to consider Kastor as source here for Diodoros in the absence of positive evidence, briefly refers his reader, *FGH* 250 Comm., 816); Sakellariou, *La Migration grecque en Ionie* (1958), 473 ff.

4 Thucydides (7. 48; 8. 63) and later writers used *thalassokratein* alike for persons and peoples, Herodotos, our earliest-attested user (3. 122; 5. 83), for persons only; but these scanty examples are little help towards a TPQ for the conception of such a list of sea-peoples.

Glossary

agathoergoi ('workers of good'): a board of five Special Agents in the Spartan state

agon: contest

aisymnetes: judge, ruler; dictator (elected)

amphiktiony: band of states ('dwellers around') administering a common cult-centre

apoikia: settlement abroad, colony

archegetes (Doric *archagetas*): 'first leader', founder

archon: annual board of high officials (nine in Athens); see also *eponymos*

aristinden: elected according to rank

astos: citizen; for possible social nuances, see p. 235, note 5 (Samos)

Atthis: annalistic history of Attica

axiomachos: 'able to fight', able-bodied

axon: 'roller', axle; wooden shafts at Athens on which the laws of Solon were inscribed

demarchos: head official of a deme (q.v.)

deme: local unit, perhaps averaging about the size of a modern parish; characteristic of Attica, but also found elsewhere

demiourgos (Doric *damiorgos*): 'public worker'; high official, usually one of a board, in some cities (Argos, Chios, for example); see also *epidemiourgos*

demos: citizen-body, usually as opposed to an élite aristocracy

diallaxia: arbitration

diaulos: race twice the length of the stadion (q.v.)

dunatoi ('powerful'): unofficial title for the leading aristocrats in a city

dynasteia: rule by a small and self-perpetuating number of families or individuals

emporion: trading-settlement abroad

ephor ('overseer'?): annual board usually of five officials, peculiar to Sparta and her offshoots

epidemiourgos: demiourgos in charge of a particular duty; see reference on pp. 58–9, note 4 (Corinth)

epigamia: mutual arrangement between two cities whereby intermarriage could carry with it the citizenship of the other city

epimachia: military alliance, defensive only

eponymos: the head of a board of officials, whose name dated the year of that board

eunomia, see *nomos*

genos: race; clan; ancestry

hektemoros ('sixth-parter'), see p. 92 (Athens)

hetaireia: company; political and social club, usually aristocratic

255

hieromnemon, see *mnemon*

horoi: local annals (usually Ionic)

isonomia: equality for all citizens before the law, a claim made by oligarchies as well as democracies

katakeimenos (Cretan legal term); see pp. 92, 190–1

kleros: lot (general); citizen's allotment of land

kordax: revellers' dance

kore: maiden

kosmos ('marshal'): Cretan high official, political and military

kouros: young male

lebes: large cauldron, usually of a tripod

leitourgos ('public worker'): at Athens, occasionally elsewhere, wealthy citizen who financed some public event or possession (play, warship, etc.)

logos: account, either narrative or calculation

megaron: great hall; often the original 'palace' of a city's early ruler

mnemon: remembrancer of profane or (*hieromnemon*) of sacred decisions, laws, etc., made by his city

nenikamenos (Cretan legal term); see p. 191

nomima: institutions or customs of a city

nomos: law, cf. *eunomia*, law and order ('the condition of good habits'), and see p. 42

nomothetes: lawgiver

oikistes: official leader of a colony

panegyris: united religious festival of several villages

peraia: the continental area acquired by an island city-state lying offshore

philia: friendship, including official non-aggression pacts

ploutinden: elected according to wealth

rhapsode ('song-stitcher'): singer or reciter of traditional songs

stadion: (a) race-track *c.* 600 feet long; (b) race (sprint)

stasis: civil strife often ending in attempted revolution

stater: standard coin; in some places the equivalent of two drachmas (didrachm)

stele: rectangular stone pillar bearing an inscription or relief

stratos: band, army; cf. *startos* (Crete), p. 189

symmachia: military alliance (general), or, specifically, an offensive and defensive alliance; see also *epimachia*

synoecism: official amalgamation of a large district of scattered villages into a united state with a capital city, usually involving the transfer of the villagers to the capital

temenos: portion of land, usually sacred, hence precinct

theoros ('observer'): religious envoy

Thesmophoria: religious festival to Demeter

thesmothetes (pl. *–ai*): 'law-stablishers'; a board of six judges at Athens (not lawgivers)

xenia: guest-friendship; of states, official friendship, cf. *philia*

xenos: stranger; guest-friend

Maps

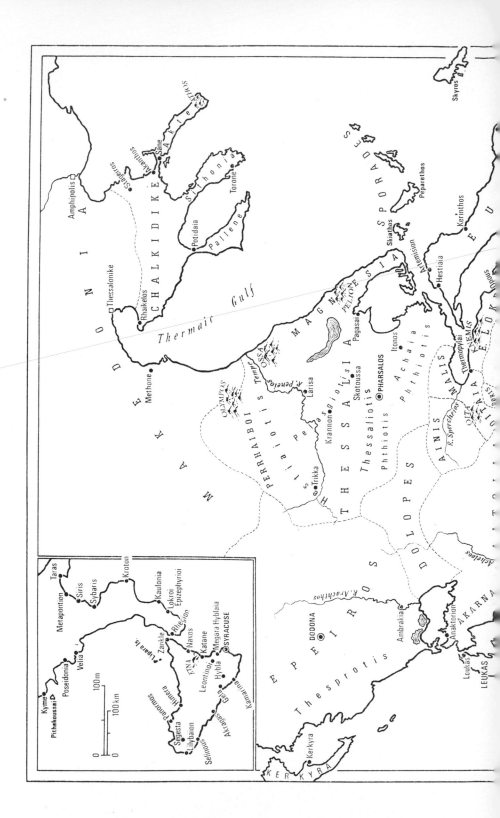

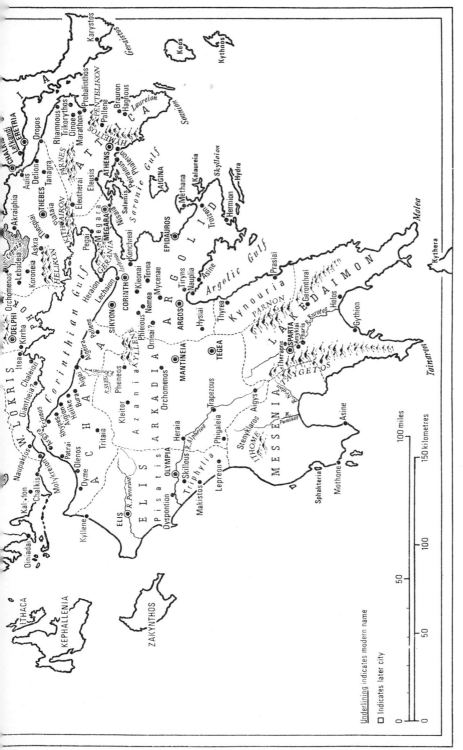

Mainland Greece; inset, Sicilian and south Italian colonies ('Magna Graecia')

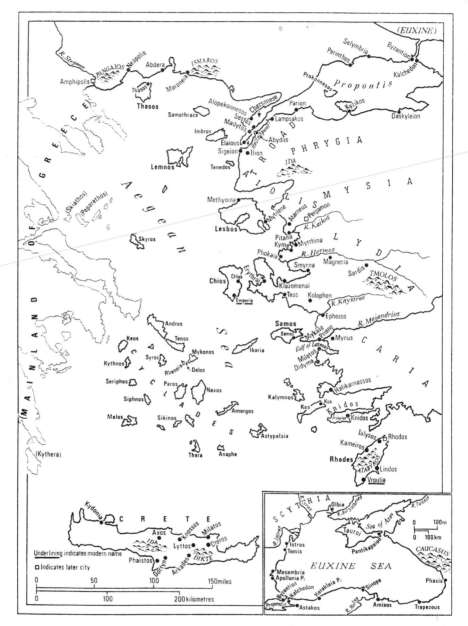

The Aegean and east Greek cities; inset, Euxine colonies

Index